On A Wing And A Prayer

Terry Reilly

Dedication

To the memory of Monsignor James Horan who instilled in his people in the dark days of the 1980s the confidence to stand up and demand a fair deal for their region, and to all the marvellous people who responded.

"It is not the critic who counts; not the man who points out how the strong man stumbles, or where the doer of deeds could have done them better. The credit belongs to the man who is actually in the arena, whose face is marred by dust and sweat and blood, who strives valiantly; who errs and comes short again and again; because there is not effort without error and shortcomings; but who does actually strive to do the deed; who knows the great enthusiasm, the great devotion, who spends himself in a worthy cause, who at the best knows in the end the triumph of high achievement and who at the worst, if he fails, at least he fails while daring greatly. So that his place shall never be with those cold and timid souls who know neither victory nor defeat."

Theodore Roosevelt (26th US President, 1858 - 1919)

On A Wing And A Prayer

The story of Knock Airport, now known as
Ireland West Airport Knock

By Terry Reilly

Published by Yew Plain Publishing

First published in 2006 by
Yew Plain Publishing
Ballina, County Mayo, Ireland.

Email: info@historyofknockairport.com
Website: www.historyofknockairport.com

© Terry Reilly, 2006

ISBN 978-0-9553699-0-2
0-9553699-0-8

Cover Design by Handeye Studios, Newport, Co. Mayo.

Contents

Acknowledgements

I wish to acknowledge the help and courtesy I received from so many people in the preparation of this book: many of those who assisted in putting the story together are quoted.

Many thanks to those who so willingly made time for interviews, those who contacted me from home and overseas with helpful information which may not be individually acknowledged, and all those who encouraged this undertaking in any way.

Thanks also to the staffs of the National Library of Ireland and Mayo County Library Services at Ballina and Castlebar, and to Mayo County Librarian Austin Vaughan for his support and valued assistance.

Christy Moore and Terry Eagleton for permission to quote from their songs on Monsignor Horan and Knock Airport, and Joe Byrne of Mid West Radio for his help in identifying other songs associated with the Airport.

Seán Balfe and Frank Harrington who worked to design and build the airport, and Dr Ken Holden who did the original feasibility study in 1980 for making themselves available for interview.

The Chairman, Joe Kennedy, management and staff of Ireland West Airport Knock and former directors, including the great Monsignor Dominick Grealy who died shortly after being interviewed.

Special thanks to photographers Henry Wills of the *Western People*, and Michael McCormack of Mixpix, Ballaghaderreen, Frank Dolan of Westport and Tom Campbell of Castlebar for making photographs available, and to other photographers whose work may have been used but not identified: this was because identification could not be established. Thanks also to all who helped put names on people in photographs.

Fr. Paddy Kilcoyne, parish priest of Kiltimagh, for access to his comprehensive newspaper clippings and photographs, and Eithne Leydon, Ballina, for background information.

Jim Fahy of RTÉ and the many commentators/journalists who covered the story and whose contributions are used in chronological order to give what turned out to be a real roller-coaster story a sense of time and place.

Thanks also to Pat Tracey of Handeye Studios, Newport, Co. Mayo, for his front cover caricature, and to Padraig Corcoran, Knockmore, Ballina, for design and make-up.

And to anyone else who feels their contribution to this book was not acknowledged: please be assured this was not intentional: you also have my thanks.

Please enjoy, and thank you for reading and accepting the book in the spirit in which it is written. Your indulgence for any unintentional oversights or errors would be appreciated: corrections/omissions, where appropriate, will be carried in future editions if brought to the notice of the author; an email address is included for that purpose.

Finally, to my wife Mary for her help and enormous support and patience over the protracted period of time it took to produce this book.

Terry Reilly
September 2006

Foreword

THIS is the story of what folk-singer Christy Moore called the miracle airport up in Knock. Unbelievably, the airport sprouted wings amid the bracken and heather on top of a mountain called Barnacuige in County Mayo, from the top of which you can see parts of all the provinces in Ireland if you squint hard enough and it's not raining. Half the country were saying it could never happen and when it did it was indeed something like a miracle of the kind the faithful pray for at the Marian shrine in Knock village a few miles away. As much as anything it came about through an act of faith by one man, Canon James Horan, who years before had built a ballroom in remote countryside and saw no reason why he couldn't build an airport too on mountainy bogland.

The Knock Airport idea had been floating around Canon James's mind for some time before he scaled the heights of Barnacuige to turn it into reality. Some years before there had been any talk of an airport in such an unlikely place, I interviewed Horan on another matter. Out of the blue he started talking about an airport for the west of Ireland that, among other things, would bring multitudes of pilgrims into Knock. I thought it was a passing and improbable fancy not worth mentioning in the story I wrote from the interview. But matters took a more concrete turn after Charlie Haughey was anointed leader of Fianna Fáil and later became Taoiseach.

Haughey, born in Castlebar, was of course a Mayoman (among myriad other personae) and always felt a warm kinship for his native county, even though he had spent only a brief period of his infancy there. (Haughey was delivered into the world by the same Mayo midwife who assisted at the birth of Henry Kenny, Enda's father, and Joe Leneghan, the famous Belmullet TD. About this interesting juncture of political births, Leneghan later remarked: "Any woman who did that has a lot to answer for!")

The Mayo connection of course was greatly fostered by Haughey's *simpatico* relationship with John Healy, one of Ireland's most influential journalists who started his career on the *Western People* and wrote a celebrated political column for *The Irish Times*. Healy was from Charlestown, just a few miles from the airport site, and a staunch champion of the west in general and Mayo in particular. Probably more than any other journalist, Healy had the ear of Haughey at a time when he was the most powerful politician in the land. And when the possibility of an airport at or near Knock took shape, Healy became one of its strongest advocates and he made sure Haughey knew how he felt about it.

Of course, early on Canon Horan himself unabashedly made a direct pitch to Haughey about his dream. In the summer of 1980, Haughey attended the funeral in Knock of Gardai John Morley and Henry Byrne who had been gunned down during a bank raid. After the burial, Horan approached Haughey to sound him out on the chances of Government backing for an airport at Knock. From the outset he became a cheerleader for the Knock project. Horan may not have known it but he may well have been preaching to the converted: Haughey already had been thoroughly briefed on the exciting possibilities of an international airport for the west of Ireland by John Healy, local Fianna Fáil Minister Padraig Flynn and P.J. Morley, a TD living in Knock. With Haughey voicing support for the airport from an early stage, the project took on a political hue and became known as something of a Fianna Fáil project.

During the gestation period and from the time the first earth-movers rolled onto Barnacuige, the Irish political scene was unstable and there were a number of government changes in quick succession. When Garret FitzGerald came to power, his government expressed doubts about the possibility of an airport being built at Knock. Even Jim Higgins from Ballyhaunis, a senator during the FitzGerald regime, showed conspicuous courage under fire you might say, when he attended a public meeting in Charlestown meant to whip up enthusiasm for the idea, and expressed the view that building an airport on a mountainy bog might be problematic. But whatever scepticism was engendered by the proposal was quickly swept away by the tsunami of approval that swept across Mayo.

Other parts of the west were less enthusiastic, notably Galway city which had its own airport that it was eager to promote and maybe enlarge. One businessman in Galway referred scathingly to the waste of money on an airport that would 'never be used short of some fantastic miracle,' and others were equally dismissive of the idea. I must confess that as a journalist covering the west for *The Irish Times* I was dubious about the entire enterprise and wrote articles questioning its merits. One such piece was taken up by RTÉ Radio's John Bowman, who was hosting a current affairs morning programme at the time, and I found myself in a no-holds-barred debate on the radio with a Charlestown man who challenged what I had written.

In any event, regardless of what people thought, James Horan, sporting a Russian astrakhan hat, was suddenly up on the foggy, boggy plateau of Barnacuige building an airport. RTÉ's Jim Fahy soon arrived with a camera crew to film Horan among the bulldozers, JCBs and muck-shifters, presiding over his aviation dream. The word spread across the world, and I was contacted by Morley Safer of the CBS's *Sixty Minutes* show to find out what was going on. I had worked with Safer on television news in Canada and knew that he had covered a number of stories in Ireland, including, indeed, a *Sixty Minutes* item on the Knock Shrine marriage service which he found utterly fascinating.

In pursuit of the airport story, Safer came to Knock and went up on the mountain with Canon James to film the miracles that were coming to pass there. When the final approval for the airport came through and the Government loosened its purse strings, I sent the word to Safer that everything was in place and the show went out on the CBS Network to be viewed by millions. At that stage, there was no stopping Knock Airport: it had sprouted wings, and the sceptics could only look to the skies in awestruck wonderment. There was some irony in the fact that the first money for the enterprise came not from a Fianna Fáil government but from Garret FitzGerald's Rainbow regime despite its misgivings about the whole thing. In the political musical chairs of the time, Garret's crowd happened to be in power, and they were the dispensers of the first funding.

But Fianna Fáil still managed to steal the thunder of its political opponents, and was in power when the sod was turned for the airport and, eventually, for its official opening. Albert Reynolds led a clutch of Fianna Fáil Ministers to preside over the sod-turning ceremony, to which a frisson of excitement was added when word came through that a plane had been hijacked in Shannon and the ministers had to rush off to deal with the incident. Charlie Haughey, along with Brian Lenihan and P.J. Mara, was of course on hand to conduct the official opening of the completed airport. Fittingly, Haughey was also accompanied by another Mayoman, the poet Paul Durcan, whom he commissioned to write a poem about the great event. It rained unmercifully from the heavens on the opening day, drenching the huge crowd, but even a deluge of Biblical magnitude could never wash away the marvels spread out across the mountain with open arms to welcome in the world.

Sadly, only a few months later, James Horan, by then Monsignor, died while on a visit to another Marian shrine, Lourdes. Some of the people gathered in Knock to await his remains threw money into his open grave, perhaps making a wish in the belief that here was one man who could make it come true. A woman, looking down at the grave and the money being thrown in, said: "They wouldn't be long filling that grave with a fortune, but sure where he's gone to, he'll have no need of it." In this book, with loving care and meticulous research, Terry Reilly has put together the uplifting story of how a man with unblinkered faith in a dream can indeed move mountains – even foggy boggy ones!

Michael Finlan
Galway
2006

Fighting for the crumbs

FROM behind he looked an old man dressed in black, his shoulders hunched, that trademark Russian astrakhan hat – favoured by such communist Soviet General Secretaries as Leonid Brezhnev and Mikhail Gorbachev – on his head, as he peered up at a bank of monitors in an airport near Rome.

But from the front he took on another persona. His eyes twinkled. His face bore a wide beam of delight.

"Look at that," he pointed proudly. "Here we are in Ciampino Airport in Italy, and the monitors show three flights listed for Knock. Connaught Airport has entered the international aviation league." The dateline was 1 November 1985.

To get here had taken an awful lot out of the man who had brought Pope John Paul 11 to Ireland only six years earlier. The Pope had come to Knock, the goal of his pilgrimage to Ireland. And now Monsignor Horan and his faithful handmaids and stewards had flown direct to Rome from Knock to celebrate their Golden Jubilee with the Polish Pope, and to invite him back again.

What had been accomplished in those six short years was nothing short of amazing. An airport capable of taking the biggest aircraft in the world had been built, and along the way had not only lost the financial support of a government but had been derided by the national press and a cackle of politicians who needed a handy cockshot on a volatile political landscape.

Not long after work began on the project atop a hill with a commanding view of the neglected province of Connaught in the first week of July 1981, it was labelled a 'white elephant' and was destined to be kicked around as the political football of the 1980s.

An unsuspecting nation got its first real inkling of the scale of what was afoot in 1981 when RTÉ's Western Correspondent Jim Fahy called to a scarred hilltop site with a camera crew. He found frantic bulldozers and heavy lorries, manoeuvred by skilled men who had returned home from the building sites of England. Some had worked on building a runway at Heathrow Airport in the 1950s, and had played Gaelic football thereon during their lunch breaks. Others had worked on some of the biggest construction sites in Britain.

"What is going on here?" asked an incredulous Fahy of the Monsignor.

"I think they're building an airport, Jim," he replied with a smile as wide as the runway he was dreaming about.

"But have you planning permission?" pressed the RTÉ man.

"Do you know, I'm not sure whether or not we have," retorted the Monsignor with his characteristic hearty laugh.

It was vintage, typically 'hamming', Horan. Locals knew the style well. But more than a few having their tea that night in front of their television sets around the nation must have thought him mad. And some said so. So it was little wonder that on his helter-skelter way to realising his latest, most outlandish and last dream, the parish priest of Knock was to suffer many political setbacks. December 1983 was to prove perhaps the most difficult time of all. Less than two weeks before Christmas the axe fell: Fine Gael/Labour government funding was withdrawn at the completion of Contract 2 stage.

A gaping hole in the ground seemed destined to be filled with West of Ireland tears of yet another 'might have been'.

"When you would expect Santa Claus, we got the Scrooge treatment," said the Monsignor. He was used to seeing the West scramble for the crumbs from the national cake, and now his great smash-and-grab bid for just a few of those crumbs to sustain his flock had been thwarted. The rebuttal had a familiar ring to it.

By then £9.2 million of State funds had been pledged for the airport. Others less resilient might have gone away and licked their wounds. But not Horan. For him it was time to get going in earnest.

He had seen it all before. He remembered many days like these: whenever a Government happened to be in some financial difficulty it never failed to make a symbolic gesture by closing down something in the West of Ireland, whether it be a railway or a seaport, or even the Tuam beet factory, he wryly observed.

He was about £3m shy of finishing his airport, a lot of money in the pre-Celtic Tiger days when the country was on the verge of bankruptcy, but it didn't faze him. Not so many years earlier he had raised £1.8m to build a magnificent Basilica at Knock, and in 1979 Pope John Paul 11 had come to the Shrine at his behest to celebrate the centenary of the Apparition at the gable of the old church.

Miracles had been performed at Knock before. The national media chided it would take another miracle to dig this stubborn old cleric out of a boghole he had insisted on digging himself into, despite the advice of some politicians and learned economists. And yes, even men of the same cloth doubted him, but held their reservations under their breath when he was about.

But an old man in a hurry had his mind firmly made up and had gone too far to turn back, even if he had the slightest notion of so doing.

To understand the economic and social factors that drove Monsignor Horan in pursuit of an airport as an essential piece of infrastructure for the region – and equally to, in some way, understand the counter arguments of those who opposed the project – a brief overview of the state of the country's economy, particularly in the 1970s/1980s, provides a useful backdrop.

The Organisation for Economic Co-operation and Development (OECD) predicted that Ireland's balance-of-payments performance in 1982 would be by far the worst in the Western industrialised world. Inflation was projected to rampage ahead, with prices expected to rise by an average of almost 19%. In 1982 nett foreign debt hit £5,114m, up from £3,451m in 1981.

Earlier, in the 1940s Mayo had lost 40,000 of its brightest and youngest to emigration, the highest in the country apart from Dublin. In fact, Mayo's population dropped by 33% between 1922 and 1986.[1] Other western counties suffered somewhat similarly. Census returns show that between 1921 and 1991 Connaught's decline in population was 24%, while the population of Leinster had grown by a massive 62%. Much more recently, the Western province lost 2% of its population in the five years between 1986 and 1991, with Mayo's loss being twice that figure.

Net emigration from Ireland in the 1940s hit 250,000, rising to 409,000 in the 1950s, before dropping back to 135,000 in the 1960s. A net inflow of 104,000 was recorded in the 1970s, before the outflow recommenced in the 1980s when 208,000 emigrated.

While the 1961 Census showed that the population was again starting to rise, Leinster and Munster were the main beneficiaries. Connaught and Ulster (part of) continued to decline. Connaught plummeted from 419,500 people in 1961, to 402,000 in 1966, to 390,900 in 1971, and started to rise only in 1979 when the Census showed an increase to 418,500. It rose to 424,4000 in 1981, and 431,400 in 1986. However, Connaught's percentage share of the national population continued to decline. The province fared badly under every key economic indicator.

In 1975 Mayo had 24,500 full-time farmers; by 1991, the number was down to 11,000.[2] And of the county's population of 114,000 in 1981, only 5,879 worked in industry.[3]

In 1981 the Economic and Social Research Institute (ESRI) reported that the average income of a family in the West of Ireland was 25% lower than that of a family in any other part of the country. It also stated that the unemployment percentage in Mayo was twice the national average.

Nationally, unemployment figures rocketed from 141,000 in 1981 to 226,000 by 1987.

Inflation rose from 8.7% in 1972 to 11.4% in 1973 to 17% in

---

1   Tony Varley, Thomas A Boylan, Michael D. Cuddy. *Perspectives on Irish rural development.* John J Smyth and Thomas A Boylan *Industrialisation and the Contribution of Multinational Companies to Economic Development in County Mayo* (Galway: Centre for development studies 1991) p.158

2   Rosa Meehan, *The Story of Mayo* (Mayo County Council 2003), p.152

3   Bernard O'Hara *Mayo/Galway* (The Archaeological, Historical and Folklore Society 1982) p.6

1974, to 20.9% in 1975, before descending to 7.6% in 1978. However, by May 1980 the inflation figure zoomed to 20%.[4] It worsened to 20.4% in 1981 before steadily declining to 8.6% in 1984 and 2.1% 1988, according to the Central Statistics Office.

In 1979 taxes rose from 33% of GNP to 42% in 1982 as foreign debt mounted. The country was now gaining half its income from taxes.[5] Public dissatisfaction in the years 1979/80 saw up to 700,000 PAYE workers take to the streets across the country in protest at the inequity of the tax system, with the pay-as-you-earn sector carrying most of the burden. The top marginal tax rate in 1975/77 was a whopping 77%, dropping to 60% in 1979, rising to 65% in 1984/85, before easing to 56% by 1990.

Figures from the Central Bank show that the Associated Banks were charging up to 16.5% on house purchase loans in 1980, rising to 17.25% in 1982 as against 3.75% to 4.03% in March 2006.

In the early 1980s a trade unionist claimed the unemployment rate in the area known as the Black Triangle – in the middle of which was sited the airport – was running at 49%. And government statistics showed that over 50% of farmers in the West had an income of £50 per week or less from their 1989 farm enterprises.

Garret FitzGerald's Coalition Government, which pulled the plug on the unfinished airport in 1983, did succeed in bringing down the balance of payments deficit from 14.7% of GNP in 1981 to 3.6% in 1985.[6]

Overall though, it was not a pretty picture, Ireland of the 1980s.

*   *   *

People took up opposing positions on the building of the airport. Views were strongly held for and against, based on the uncertain political climate of the time, the perilous state of the economy and perceived priorities and needs. Some were brave, others saw them as foolhardy. Some dreamed, some feared. One man dared. Some were envious. That is life. Readers will make up their own minds.

From the battle for survival came good. Enough people stood up and were counted. A marvellous piece of infrastructure emerged for the West, jobs have been created, a great service has been provided, and the State has got back its initial investment many times over through various forms of taxation.

Now fasten your seat belts and read on.

---

4   Dermot Keogh *Twentieth Century Ireland: Nation and State* (Dublin: Gill and Macmillan 1994) p.348

5   Keogh *Twentieth Century Ireland* p.348

6   J.J. Lee *Ireland 1912-1985 Politics and Society* (Cambridge: Cambridge University Press 1989) p.500

CHAPTER ONE

1879/1930s: Michael Davitt and Land League - Railways -
Apparition - Ecclesiastical Commission - The Coynes' role at Shrine

It all started in 1879

IT all began in Knock just over one hundred years before Monsignor James Horan gathered a small team around him and set out to build an international airport that was to cause so much controversy in an uncertain political period.

Up to 1879 Knock was an inauspicious place, a small unremarkable village in east Mayo, struggling to find its feet. Recollections of the Great Famine were still fresh in the villagers' memories. And though not a lot appeared to be happening around the place, the country was in the midst of radical change.

The railway network was being pushed into the West and the tracks had already reached nearby Ballyhaunis (1861), Claremorris, Castlebar and Sligo (1862), Westport (1866), Ballina (1873). Kiltimagh and Charlestown were to follow in 1895. With this transport revolution came both opportunities and challenges to small and hitherto isolated communities.

The 1870s also witnessed the stirrings of land reform that would effect enormous changes in Irish rural life. And Mayo played a key role in that transformation. Native son Michael Davitt of Straide, near Foxford, led the Land League movement as Charles Stewart Parnell strode the countryside like a colossus providing the radical political leadership required in the fight against the excesses of landlordism.

And the wind was well and truly tested in Ballinrobe in south Mayo where the infamous Land Agent Captain Boycott was ostracised because of his treatment of local tenantry in the late 1870s: the campaign became a worldwide *cause célèbre* and gave the English language the verb to boycott, meaning 'to ostracise completely'.

On April 20, 1879, the first tenants' rights meeting was held in Irishtown and had the full support and backing of Davitt who was one of its chief organisers and who wrote the resolutions for the meeting, the results of which were to have far-reaching consequences for the future of land ownership. On August 16 1879 the National Land League of Mayo was established in Castlebar and land agitation in the county was to grow into the Land War.

However, the focus of attention was about to shift to the quiet backwater village of Knock, and in the most extraordinary and enduring fashion. The portents were unremarkable: it rained cats and dogs on that Thursday evening of 21 August, 1879, and most people stayed indoors.

But Miss Mary McLoughlin (45), housekeeper to Archdeacon Kavanagh, scurried along to visit at the nearby cottage of Mrs Margaret Byrne at about 8 pm. On the way she passed by the south gable of the parish church. "On passing by the chapel, and at a little distance from it, I saw a wonderful number of strange figures or appearances at the gable; one like the Blessed Virgin Mary, and one like St. Joseph; another a bishop; I saw an altar," she later recalled.

Miss McLoughlin thought that possibly the Archdeacon had been supplied with the figures from Dublin or elsewhere, and passed on to the home of the widow Margaret Byrne and her children, where she said nothing initially of what she had witnessed at the church.

After half an hour, when Mary McLoughlin returned to the church with Miss Mary Byrne (29) to lock up the building, they saw the vision. Mary Byrne went to fetch her brother, Dominick Byrne (20). He was resting at the time after working in the fields. Shortly after she sent a little girl, her niece, Catherine Murray (8), who was staying with them, running back to fetch her mother, Mrs Margaret Byrne, and her sister, Miss Margaret Byrne (21).

In all, fifteen people, whose ages ranged from six years to seventy-five and included men, women, teenagers and children, gathered and witnessed Our Lady, St. Joseph, and St. John the Evangelist in a blaze of heavenly light at the south gable of the Church of St. John the Baptist. Behind them and a little to the left of St. John was a plain altar. On the altar was a cross and a lamb with adoring angels.

The poor humble witnesses watched in awe the Blessed Virgin Mary clothed in white robes with a brilliant crown on her head. Over the forehead where the crown fitted the brow, she wore a beautiful full-bloom golden rose. She was in an attitude of prayer with her eyes and hands raised towards heaven. St. Joseph stood on Our Lady's right. He was turned towards her in an attitude of respect. His robes were also white. St. John was on Our Lady's left. He was dressed in white vestments and resembled a bishop, with a small mitre. He appeared to be preaching and he held an open book in his left hand.

The witnesses watched the Apparition in pouring rain for two hours, reciting the Rosary, spellbound. Although the witnesses standing before the gable were drenched, no rain fell in the direction of the gable. They felt the ground carefully with their hands and it was perfectly dry as was the gable itself.

Tom Neary, Head Steward at Knock Shrine and right-hand man of Monsignor Horan, was encouraged by the Monsignor to research newspaper reports of the time and write a book on his findings. *I Saw Our Lady* was the result.

In this book are references from 14 newspaper articles, written in 1880. In the first account, published on January 23, 1880, the reporter wrote: "The Catholic world has heard of the name and fame of Lourdes, once a wild spot but now frequented by all the world, far away in the mountainous region to the south of France. A second Lourdes is rising at Knock, a small village surrounded by little hills which, as expressive of the natural character of the locality, is known to the natives as the 'village of the hill'."

An ecclesiastical Commission of Inquiry was established by the Archbishop of Tuam, Most Rev. Dr. John MacHale. The Commission's final verdict was that the testimony of all the witnesses taken as a whole was trustworthy and satisfactory. At a second Commission of Inquiry in 1936, the surviving witnesses confirmed the evidence they gave to the first Commission.

Sociologists, while neither accepting nor disputing what had occurred, but seeking to understand its cultural context, found in the timing of apparitions a common theme: at Lourdes and Fatima for instance the 'visitations' occurred at a time of immense cultural, social and economic change, and occurred to people whose traditional society was under threat from dramatic change.

Sociologists have written that in a time of change, symbols like the Virgin Mary and St. Joseph (known together within Catholicism as the Holy Family) marked a reminder of stability and tradition in a society whose change many people found bewildering. Depending on whether one accepted the validity of the apparition or the religious beliefs underpinning it, it could, the theory goes, be seen either as a delusion by a marginalised traditional society clinging to old certainties, or, in a Catholic religious context, as the appearance of the 'Mother of God' to people marginalised by society to show her support and offer her comfort.

Countless numbers of people have accepted the latter version: a deep and abiding devotion to the Shrine and Our Lady has endured over the years. The Shrine now attracts over 1.5 million visitors annually and is indisputably Ireland's major visitor attraction. Many cures have been attributed to the Shrine.

As part of his many improvement works at Knock Shrine, Monsignor James Horan built a chapel off the apparition gable. Large marble statues representing the figures in the apparition, Mary, St. Joseph, St. John, and the table with the Lamb and Cross surrounded by angels are in front of the original wall. The statues were commissioned in Italy in 1960 by an extraordinary woman, Judy Coyne who died in 2002. She resided with her husband, Judge Liam Coyne, at Bridgemount, near Belcarra, Castlebar, and the couple are credited with reviving an interest in the shrine which, after the initial enthusiasm following the Apparition, had slipped out of the public eye and was in danger of being forgotten.

The Coynes' story of devotion to the Shrine is an inspiring one recounted in a book, *Providence My Guide* (Mercier Press 2004), edited by Ethna Kennedy. In 1997, Judy Coyne was conferred by Dr Michael Neary, Archbishop of Tuam, with the title 'Dame Commander of the Order of St. Sylvester,' an honour never before bestowed on any woman in Ireland. What she and her husband achieved against enormous odds and Church torpor was truly astonishing.

And most significantly, between them the Coynes were to write the script many years in advance for a number of Monsignor Horan's most extraordinary undertakings.

CHAPTER TWO

1930s/1963: Dame Judy Coyne - Publicising Knock Shrine - Fr James Horan - The Devil Story and Christy Moore - Albert Reynolds Accused - Eye for a Bargain - Impact on Parishes

The woman who set the agenda

MONSIGNOR James Horan was not the first to think about building an airport in the vicinity of Knock – he never claimed to be. Nor was he the first to consider inviting a Pope to the Mayo Marian Shrine – again he never said he was. In fact, Judy and Liam Coyne and their small band of Knock Shrine Society devotees first had the idea of building an airport – a grass strip for light aircraft which would convey invalid pilgrims to the holy place – way back in 1935.

But in the mid '30s Knock did not even have running water. The facilities for pilgrims were almost non-existent. Determined to have Knock and the Apparition of 1879 recognised and promoted, the Coynes and a few friends formed the Knock Shrine Society. A long uphill battle got underway. Publicity was generated for Knock. Pilgrimages were planned. People walked, some barefoot, or cycled or came by donkey and cart or horse-drawn cars to the devotions. Long-distance pilgrims came by train to Claremorris and were transported by bus along narrow twisty roads to the Shrine, disabled pilgrims by improvised ambulance. In inclement weather conditions, cover for invalid pilgrims was non-existent. The Coynes and their Society established the stewards and handmaids as helpers, and worked over many years to improve facilities there.

Arising out of discussions with interested parties, as Mrs Coyne recalled in her book, *Providence, My Guide,* proposals were worked out for improving the village and its accessibility and were put before Mayo County Council in the mid '30s.

"Apart from the predictable issues like roads and water, they included plans for improvements in the rail system, and an airfield. With air travel then in its infancy – a dream of the future for most people – that suggestion caused as much derision within its context as Knock Airport did in the 1980s," she wrote.

Fifty years after the original quest, in 1985, I interviewed Mrs Coyne at Ciampino Military Airport in Rome as the highly successful Knock Shrine Society Golden Jubilee pilgrimage prepared to return to Connaught Regional Airport. She never sought publicity for herself and had turned down the BBC for a televised interview a short time before, despite the pleadings of Monsignor Horan. To put it mildly, she shunned personal publicity. At the airport as we milled around waiting for our return flight, I asked this formidable private woman her thoughts at that time. I did so with a certain amount of trepidation for here was a woman who had marshalled all her forces, with her husband, over the years to place Knock at the centre of Marian Shrine adoration – and she had a reputation for being direct!

However, she expressed delight, in that serene but direct manner of hers, that the airport had at last come to pass. She said the idea for such a facility originated fifty years earlier when they were looking at transport to the shrine in the light of their evolving plans. "Yes, it was one of the many needs highlighted then, and it was included in plans for the area and placed before Mayo County Council, but it dragged on and on over the years. I believe the airport will now open up the way for Knock to become a major international shrine within a short time," she said.

She had also campaigned for the advancement of the Shrine and for those who used it through the national media, and in the pages of the widely circulating *Knock Annual* magazine which was founded and largely edited by herself. A rest-home had been opened, facilities provided and land and property either secured or earmarked for future development as she encouraged the Church to plan ahead for busier times.

And all the time she sought to validate Knock as an international Marian Shrine centre. The breakthrough came in 1953 when the Shrine banner was amongst 20 singled out of 400 from around the world for a special blessing at pre-Marian Year ceremonies in the Vatican. That was vindication for all the work that had been put in. Knock was on the official church map, and rose to even greater heights the following year as a centre for the Marian Year devotions.

Of course, it would help the cause if a Pope were to visit Knock Shrine: she determined to encourage church authorities to bring this about after reading of Pope Paul's visit to the Holy Land in 1964. If a Pope could visit one Marian Shrine what was to stop him visiting another? she mused. The centenary of the apparition was still fifteen years away and much remained to be done to prepare the way.

Father James Horan was by then ensconced in Knock parish as the new curate and four years later, in 1968, he was made Administrator. He was the catalyst Judy Coyne had been waiting for even if their relationship was to prove to be a stormy, tempestuous one. It was inevitable that two strong creative wills wanting to get things done would lead to discussions that ended in disharmony. But with James Horan a row was not an end to a relationship: he quickly put differences aside, as Mrs Coyne confirmed. She had by then been labouring in the cause of the Shrine for 33 years. Like him, once her mind was made up, she focused on her goal. And she saw the big picture, too.

But while she had to go through frustrating official Church channels, he had a businessman's approach: he took short cuts, he always went to the boss man, and working with committees did not always suit his temperament. They just slowed him down.

However, he had an undoubted pedigree for getting things done: he was perfect for Knock and its need to shift up through the gears. He was a great motivator. And, as one of his subsequent curates, Fr. Colm Kilcoyne, pointed out when this book was being researched, "James respected his church superiors but I suspect he felt they had their jobs to do and he had his and there wasn't much point in bothering them."

So who was James Horan? Born on the 5 May 1911 in the townland area of Tooreen, in the parish of Partry, in west Mayo, the son of a small farmer and tradesman, he was the eldest of seven children – four girls and three boys. By the time he had finished primary school in Partry he had begun to look to the priesthood as a vocation. It wasn't surprising, therefore, when he entered for a scholarship to St. Jarlath's Diocesan College in Tuam, Co. Galway, which he was successful in winning. In September 1929, he and six other fellow students from St. Jarlath's went to Maynooth College to train for the priesthood. He was ordained seven years later, in 1936, with 71 other students.

As there were no vacancies at home, he took up his first duty in Glasgow, in a parish called Dumbarton, in August 1936. During his third and final year there, his parish priest asked him to act as chaplain on the Anchor liner, *California*. He was delighted to get the opportunity to go to America and meet all his friends and relations.

When he returned to Dumbarton after the trip, he received a letter from the Archbishop of Tuam, Dr Thomas Gilmartin, asking him to return to Ireland. At the end of August 1939, he took up the position as Chaplain to the Franciscan monastery in Ballyglunin. After only two months he was transferred to Tiernea in the parish of Carraroe, in Co. Galway, where he became fluent in the Irish language.

In July 1944 he got word that he was to take up a new appointment back in Mayo, in Tooreen in the parish of Aghamore as curate. One of the first things he noted about this area was the poor postal facilities, and without delay he was presenting himself before post-office officials in Dublin's GPO. No doubt he asked to see the boss man that day too!

It could be said that he also 'lit up' the parish of Aghamore, because it was he who was responsible for the introduction of electricity to the area, cajoling the ESB to come in after he had canvassed and balloted households to make the switch from oil lamps to the electric. He also introduced projects such as group water schemes, afforestation, and even road works and drainage schemes.

He was probably best known at that time as promoter of Tooreen Hall. And it was there that he first experienced the smell of sulphur and national publicity. Tooreen Hall was a mecca for dance-goers: Fr. Horan had raised £8,000 in the US to build it, and once built, in the early 1950s, he ran it like the entrepreneur he was. Supervision was strict and personally overseen by Horan, and no drink was allowed into the hall. He booked all the best acts and promoted them widely in local press advertisements. But competition was intense from rival ballroom promoters and created, in his own words 'some jealousy' in the surrounding areas.

A pamphlet by a Limerick-based Redemptorist priest, 'The Devil at Dances', told a fictitious story of a girl who went to a dance one night and was asked to dance by a debonair young man. They danced together, but when they had finished she noticed that he had cloven feet. With that he vanished in the midst of a cloud of sulphur smoke. The story worked its way from the south of the country and eventually washed across the floor of Tooreen Ballroom in the 1950s.

Songwriter and singer Christy Moore admits to being present the night the 'devil' appeared in Tooreen Ballroom. He will not be drawn on the circumstances! But he recalls he got severe cramp in his right hand on occasions 'counting the Monsignor's shagging silver lodgements in the National Bank in Ballyhaunis' after gigs at the hall. The Monsignor, it appeared, like paying in small change: it saved him time banking!

However, British literary critic and philosopher Terry Eagleton wrote a dance-hall song about the devilish incident, and says he believes the devil-in-the-dance-hall-prank was perpetrated by an exuberant local youth, with an old goat and a couple of flashlights!

He penned his song for the weekly Oxford Irish music session that Tooreen native Mick Henry used to run in the 1970s/1980s. Courtesy of the composer, Terry Eagleton, here is a sample of how the song goes:

> You remember our dance hall on Tureen's fair soil?
> 'Twas a stately affair, twice the size of the Dail,
> Where young Father H would be packing them in
> Each Sunday night just to keep us from sin.

There I danced and I jived in my best Sunday suit
While that handsome young curate sat counting his loot,
But my knees turn to water, my heart leaps in fright
When I think of that one diabolical night!

A young maiden was dancing called Brigid McGinn
Sure I swear her lips ne'er knew the taste of gin,
When there came a dark stranger or so I've heard tell,
Who said, 'Dance with me, Mary. Come on. What the hell!'

Her eyes were a-burning, her heart was a smile,
And all the while Horam sat counting his pile,
But when the dark stranger arrived with her coat
Sure she looked down and saw the cleft foot of a goat.

With a thunderous crack did your man disappear
Leaving sulphurous smoke spreading all through the air,
And the grass where he stood sure it withered and died.
It won't grow again to this day, boys, for all that they've tried.

And young Father H he sat down feeling sick,
To think he'd been diddled and done by Old Nick,
"Would you credit it now, boys," was all he would say,
"That I never did get that old devil to pay".
(to the tune of 'Where the Mountains of Mourne Sweep Down
to the Sea').

But former Taoiseach and ballroom impresario Albert Reynolds
got the blame for the 'old-Nick-in-Tooreen story'.

"He accused me," recalls Reynolds, "though I don't think he was
serious, of spreading the rumour that the devil had been seen in
Tooreen. He'd always accuse me of that. I used to take the ballroom in
Ballyhaunis and that was opposition to him. I was booking for all the
ballrooms at the same time and I'd be booking The Royal Showband,
the biggest draw at the time, or the Clipper Carlton and I'd move one
occasionally into Ballyhaunis and it used to drive him mad. And next
thing the story came out and he always blamed me. He'd tell you to
your face. He'd tell you what he thought."

So was it a rumour or did it really happen? Depends on who you
talk to. Christy Moore says he was there; Terry Eagleton believes it was
a prank. Monsignor Horan variously called it 'lies', 'a joke and a skit'
and 'a crude joke'. Whatever the circumstances of the prank, it did no
harm to business at Tooreen Hall!

Another memory Reynolds has of Monsignor Horan as a
ballroom promoter relates back to the time when the future Taoiseach
was booking up a tour for a British act, Kenny Ball and the Jazzmen.

9

"I needed a particular Wednesday to be filled and it was not a good night for dance-halls anywhere, but I wanted a connection between North and South dates, and I asked him if he'd take them, and he said he'd consider it. A short time later he came back and said, 'No, no one here knows anything about Kenny Ball and the Jazzmen' and he wouldn't take them.

"So I gave the band the night off on my calendar because there was no point in trying to push them in anywhere else. In between anyway, they released a record and it went into the Top 20 and about five or six weeks before they arrived in Ireland Monsignor Horan got on to me. 'That band you were talking about?' – he wanted them now, so I said they are not available. But he wasn't put off and hit back, 'Wherever they are, take them out. If they are half as good as you think they are you will get more money in Tooreen, I will give you 60/40 of the door.'

"I replied, 'OK, fair enough, I will try and get them for you.' So I rang him back in a few days and told him, 'OK, you have them.'

"It ended up rather than him giving me what I had offered them for the night, I think it was 60 quid, he paid me £275," recalls Reynolds with a chuckle. One up for the future Taoiseach, but Horan was to come calling again – and for much higher stakes in the 1980s!

Legendary Band Manager Nelius O'Connell has fond memories of Horan. His bands, Jim Farrelly and the Kerry Blues, each played Tooreen up to three times a year. "Horan was a good businessman, he had a way of approaching you. When it came to booking bands he did not take 'no' for an answer . . . and when it suited he'd beat about the bush, break you down, tell you a tale of woe, cry on your shoulder if he had a bad night – you'd think butter would not melt in his mouth.

"Yet, he was universally acclaimed, well liked, a kind, decent man. He'd say, 'You'll have to do better for me,' and you'd have to compromise for he was a great negotiator," he remembers fondly.

His friend and successor at both Knock Shrine and the Airport, Monsignor Dominick Grealy, was a native of Tooreen and when Horan arrived there the younger Grealy was a student. He recalled Horan stayed in digs for the first year and busied himself running socials in the school, dances and quizzes.

"Sometimes he had to have two bands, one in each section of the school, to cater for the crowds that used attend. It was from that really that this idea of building the hall came. He'd put on a question time before the dance, and he'd make up the questions and local characters would take part. It would be the greatest of fun; the laugh he had, it was infectious. He'd be on stage and he'd start laughing and everyone laughed with him. He had that extraordinary gift, he could diffuse anything; he could say things no one else could say and then he'd roar laughing," said Grealy.

"He went to America to raise money to build Tooreen Hall and, as always happened with him, he collected in excess of what he needed, so when he started to build the hall the other half of the parish wanted a community centre. He handed over some of the money and, of course, that left a debt on Tooreen Hall which he quickly wiped out through dances which attracted up to 3,000 on Sunday nights," he added.

In fact, the building of a ballroom in Tooreen 'twice the size of the Dáil' as the song goes, had led to a split in the parish over its location. There were slogan daubing and protests, and Horan was even accused (shades of a later era) of building a 'monumental white elephant'.

Horan could make a pound go a long way when it came to doing jobs like refurbishing or providing facilities around the parish. Tom Beisty, who now lives in London and is a past Chairman of the Mayo Association in that city, recalls that when he worked at Kilkelly Concrete Products the Monsignor used to come for broken concrete blocks. "The boss, Paiki Gibbons, used to be amused with him because no matter whether he said he could or could not have the blocks Horan would say, 'When can you run them up to me?' He did not understand 'no' even then."

After 14 years in Tooreen Fr. Horan left in July 1959 to go to his next parish, Cloonfad. Not long after arriving, he formed an afforestation committee. He also organised drainage schemes which were badly needed in the area due to its low-lying boggy state. This experience with boggy terrain was to stand to him in the much bigger tests ahead.

Senator Jim Higgins' uncle and Monsignor Horan were ordained together in the same class, so he knew Horan going back to the time he was a curate in Tooreen. "I remember him going to Cloonfad as a curate – he was the man responsible for removing the sheer hill on the road which a bus with a full load couldn't negotiate. When we'd be coming home from school, St. Jarlath's in Tuam, we had to get off the bus to enable it to get up the hill. He succeeded in getting Roscommon County Council to remove the hill completely and grade it properly. He was responsible for all the afforestation around Cloonfad, and all of the land around there was planted and has now reached maturity."

On 12 September 1963, Fr. Horan was transferred to Knock Parish as curate, and from 1967 as Parish Priest. He now had a challenge that was equal to his organisational abilities and that great well of energy that fired him. One of his first engagements was with the Knock Development Association which had been pressing for an airstrip for years and sought his help. He journeyed to Dublin, met Aer Lingus and government officials but hit a brick wall: he found there was no interest in internal transport, and weren't there plenty of

CIE trains available anyhow to get people to Knock? he was told. Though disappointed, a valuable lesson had been learned. He now set that objective to one side and got on with the work of improving Knock Shrine and Knock village. Catching the ear of a Pope was a much more manageable objective . . . and a great deal less controversial!

CHAPTER THREE

1963/79: Stalls Go - Basilica 'shelter' - Airport team formation - County Council meetings - Pope count-down - Visit to Harlem - Pope arrives - Bishop Marcinkus - Disappointment

Knock Shrine gets ready...

THE very day before 52-years-old Father Horan arrived in Knock as the new curate in September 1963, a consignment of magnificent statues, which Judy Coyne of the Knock Shrine Society had commissioned in Rome in 1960, was delivered to the Shrine. They were intended as an accurate representation of the Apparition and the work was carried out by famed Italian sculptor Professor Lorenzo Ferri.

But things moved slowly at Knock then, and the works of art sculpted from snow-white Carrara marble, so chosen because all the figures in the apparition were dressed in white, were to remain incarcerated in their wooden boxes for sixteen long years.

Fr. Horan came quietly too and did not make an immediate impact. He was seen by Judy Coyne and the Knock Shrine Society as just another curate: priests came and went at Knock, and he did not cross the paths of those working as volunteers at the Shrine for several years. His time was in the future, recalled Mrs Coyne, who was still swimming against the tide to get her many plans implemented. In the shadow of the Second Vatican Council in 1964, even statues were being looked at in a new light, and in some cases were being taken away. Would the same fate befall the precious consignment in those wooden boxes?

One pilgrimage season followed another, and another four years elapsed before St. Joseph's Rest and Care Centre was opened in 1968. And that was the year that a clerical whirlwind was unleashed, Archbishop Joseph Cunnane elevating his old friend Fr Horan to the post of Administrator. The response was immediate; the tightly rolled spring-coil was released. Fr. James had closely observed and learned over the previous four years and was well aware of the demands for a transformation of the Shrine. An almost blank canvas lay before him and he couldn't wait to get on with the job.

And, of course, behind him Judy Coyne was turning up the pressure on the church with her 'count-down' in the *Knock Annual* magazine to the centenary year: 'eleven, ten, nine, eight years' she reeled off in her challenging reminders. No doubt these rankled with Fr. James and led to some of the disagreements they had: she had envisaged, when few else had, the potential interest in the shrine and wanted things done. He also wanted things done but he would do them in his own way and in his own time. And, more importantly, he had the ear of the Archbishop. For him the time for talking was over.

Bit by bit, the whole face of Knock began to change, change utterly. With upwards of 75 tatty stalls selling religious artefacts, lack of amenities for growing numbers of pilgrims, poor roads, an inadequate water supply and insufficient car-parking space, Knock was a far cry from the Marian Shrines at Lourdes and Fatima of which Fr. Horan was very much enamoured.

Former Government Minister and EU Commissioner Padraig Flynn – who was to become closely involved with the Monsignor's plans to build Knock Airport some years later – was then a member of Mayo County Council, and recalls that Horan's interest in Knock and the Blessed Virgin would have made him extraordinarily pleased when he was appointed to Knock.

"He set about developing Knock into something special. I recall, as a member of the County Council, all the preparations and permissions he actively pursued to change the infrastructure in the village. He told me he had been in Fatima and Lourdes, and other places, to see how things were done there. Of course, it was from that he got the idea of building up the pilgrimage traffic, and it was from those visits that a better way of getting to Knock came into his head," he said.

As the son of a small builder, Horan moved from plan to foundation to construction in a very systematic fashion. As a boy he had helped his father mix mortar. Now he had the power of the church behind him; in those days not too many people were going to cross an Administrator or parish priest when it came to developing a church or shrine that needed mending or modernising. Stallholders did, of course, object to the removal of their canvas-covered pitches and the case went to court but all ended well when alternative display space was provided.

Former Mayo County Council Planning Officer Seán Dunleavy has vivid recollections of Horan's single-mindedness. "He was a man of action. He didn't suffer fools gladly. He went straight for his objective. I remember meeting him on a frosty evening in 1968 in Knock village with local Councillor P J Morley and walking up the street past all the unsightly stalls. He had plans to tidy up the whole place, and when people who he felt should share his dream got in his way he could be abrupt."

Dunleavy instanced the case where the nuns owned a field behind the convent and Horan wanted to acquire it for a car park. The mother superior pointed out that if they disposed of the field they would not be able to keep a few cows and so would be without milk.

"Are you trying to hold up the development of Knock Shrine for the sake of a cow?" the Monsignor demanded of her. He got his field. The Shrine got its badly needed car park.

P J Morley, who later went on to serve as Fianna Fáil TD for Mayo East, was a national teacher in the parish when Horan arrived in Knock and became his school manager. "He was very progressive. He came with a reputation for getting things done. He did good work wherever he went. He was all for helping people, getting improvements carried out, and he got people involved in many Local Improvements Schemes.

"He would not take no for an answer if he got involved in something he believed in, and he was constantly checking that the County Council was keeping its side of the village renewal pact," he said.

Local Improvement Schemes were one thing, but the Monsignor now had bigger things on his mind. Having acquired the land, he set about building the biggest church in the country, the Basilica of Our Lady, Queen of Ireland.

Distinguished architect and town-planner, Daithi Hanly, was invited to Knock early in 1970. The Church authorities wanted to build a church/shelter, and some preliminary work had been going on; indeed, a fund had been opened.

The 'shelter' part of the brief was central to what Horan set out to accomplish. He had seen sick and elderly pilgrims gather in awful weather conditions, and he wanted to ease their stay.

Fr. Colm Kilcoyne, who was his curate in Knock at the time of his death, explained that was the real reason for building the Basilica. "He built it to give shelter from the rain. No other reason. Until his dying day he saw it as a place where the sick and the old would avoid getting colds. Others might see its liturgical possibilities. Not he. It was just one big umbrella for the guests who came to visit Knock.

"There was something very characteristic of the man in that. He had a great sense of what people needed, and he would satisfy their needs and then there was this frightening energy to get out there and do it. He never took his eye off what prompted any project in the first place. That, I believe, gave him the tenacity that wore down all opposition and a skill in dealing with bureaucracy."

That skill was to be severely tested in the years that lay ahead.

The impression the Monsignor made on award-winning architect Daithi Hanly was immediate: "Here was a man in a hurry, charming, coaxing, teasing, humorous, but in work, efficient, decisive and he always answered letters! Above all he was serious in the purpose of his mission – to develop Knock into a major international Marian Shrine."

After Hanly and his two colleagues, Louis Brennan and Brian Brennan, had been briefed, the Monsignor gave them a coloured leaflet about the Martyrs Shrine in Auriesville in New York, which was what he had in mind.

"It was a huge circular building, called the Coliseum, which accommodates 6,500 pilgrims. Both he and Archbishop Joseph Cunnane stressed the importance of speech acoustics and of absolute economy in building cost," said Hanly.

And so in April/May of 1970 Hanly set out to plan this 'challenging building'. By February 25 of the following year, the final plans were accepted, and the main contractor, with the 'somewhat prophetic' name of John Paul and Company, was appointed. Archbishop Cunnane cut the first sod in November 1973, it was completed in 1976 and was solemnly dedicated in March 1979.

Building such a huge structure in Knock capable of accommodating up to 10,000 people attracted some criticism, of which local newspaper editors were aware at the time. Its detractors said it was too big, too grandiose for Knock; indeed it was even classed as a white elephant (the forerunner of a much bigger one still gestating in the wings a few miles way!). And it was rumoured that Church authorities were alarmed at the cost, £1.8m.

At the time Archbishop Cunnane refuted such suggestions. He pointed out that there was almost twice as much money spent in one week in Ireland on drink than it cost to build the Basilica. "This building," he said, in reply to a journalist's question, "will be here to serve the people for hundreds of years to come," adding that it had cost no more than a recent gambling spree at a three-day Galway race meeting!

Monsignor Dominick Grealy, who succeeded Horan at Knock in 1986, recalled there was a lot of criticism of Horan putting advertisements in the papers looking for individuals to sponsor blocks to build the basilica. Some of that criticism came from priests. "But that criticism ran off him like water off a duck's back: he was convinced that what he was doing was right, and he got on with it."

Horan himself was to acknowledge that he had expected the usual criticism, "As is inevitable with every building. It is a great tribute to all concerned that I have heard nothing but the highest praise from priests and pilgrims." Clearly any criticism had been brushed aside.

As for the cost, the money was paid off before the building was officially dedicated: benefactors and generous pilgrims had made sure of that. "We had no trouble in meeting the cost; we were never in debt," the Monsignor proudly recalled some years later.

It was during the transformation of Knock that the team to eventually plan and build the airport was being put together and tested by Horan. He had the full backing of Archbishop Cunnane, devout pilgrims were delighted that the whole place was being pulled up by the bootlaces and developed to its true significance and they loved Horan for that. And two men who were to play a central role seven or eight years later in the Monsignor's airport plans were on board, John X Balfe of nearby Claremorris, and road builder and contractor Frank Harrington of Kilkelly.

Balfe was appointed as site engineer for the Basilica project, and his role gradually grew to take charge of general development at the Shrine. And it was he who was to do much of the physical planning for the airport in 1980.

"Archbishop Joseph Cunnane asked me in 1972 to look after the Knock developments, and little did I realise where that would lead me," he recalls.

A year later Frank Harrington was busily making his hay in the quiet fields of nearby Kilkelly when Fr. Horan came a-calling with John Cunnane, the Archbishop's brother, who was Clerk of Works for the Basilica project.

"The Monsignor said he had some work to be done at the Shrine, making roadways, etc., to make ready for the building of the Basilica. I was delighted to be asked. We did about a mile of roadway through the land bought from the Byrnes. We had to fill in the lake, pipe away the water, build a bridge and in fact we spent six years working there on various projects in the lead-up to the Pope's arrival."

Harrington met the hands-on Monsignor every morning after 10 a.m. mass. The dynamic cleric would have his wellingtons on and would inspect the work on hand. "I recall one day, in July 1975, we were finishing up a particular contract for him and preparing to move on to another job. We were tidying up really, and taking it easy. As fate would have it, wasn't the Monsignor saying 3 p.m. Mass on the altar which looked down over the field where we were working. We were going through the motions as it was too late in the day to move on to another job. He saw we were not doing too much and when Mass was over he came down the field in a hurry, his robes flying in the breeze. I fled the site for I knew it was not a time for confrontation, but I also knew I'd have to call up to him the next day, which I did. I explained we had completed the job and were finishing off the previous afternoon. He had cooled down by then, and said he had more work for us to do around the Shrine."

Though he did not realise it then, little more than five years later Frank Harrington, like John Balfe, was to undertake the biggest challenge of his life. And that challenge was to be shored up by the relationship built with Monsignor Horan in the intervening years. "It was a relationship based on trust and respect," said Balfe.

Another firm relationship built up then was to also stand the future airport project in good stead: Michael O'Malley, who was baptised in the same church as Monsignor Horan, was by now Mayo County Manager. A former county footballer, he too was a doer, much admired in his native county. And he recognised in Horan a man on a mission.

Charlestown-born reporter John Healy of *No One Shouted Stop* and *Nineteen Acres* fame, recounted a story that summed up their relationship. Coming out of the Parish House in Knock one day with O'Malley, the Monsignor said: "Michael, you will take all of the left and I'll take the right and we will make a village of it yet." They did, and O'Malley went on to become a staunch supporter in the building of the airport.

Paddy O'Toole quickly got to recognise the wiles of Horan when he was elected to Mayo County Council on the Fine Gael ticket in 1974. He saw at first-hand just how streetwise politically was the parish priest. "On more than one occasion he arranged for Council meetings to be held in Knock. He was very shrewd in that he arranged for an enormous dinner for councillors and then came in to address the Council on the items on the agenda concerning Knock. He invariably got what he wanted," he recalls.

Horan was now in overdrive. The momentum was with him as projects fell into place and the beckoning spire on the new basilica, which could be seen from miles away, heralded a new confident Knock. He could see the possibilities for opening up the Shrine to pilgrims from outside the country: the potential would be enormous, especially if, one day, the Pope were to visit. And that long-fingered but not forgotten airport would be of enormous help in putting the jigsaw together.

In 1977 he went to his local county councillor PJ Morley and advocated one decent airport for Mayo. At that time the privately-owned airport at Castlebar, which had the first tarmacadam surface in the West, was rumoured to be closing and efforts were being made to find a new location outside the county town. A small airport was also mooted for Ballina by a group of North Mayo businessmen.

The *Western People* recorded Morley raising the issue at a meeting of the County Council in April of 1977. He urged that all interests should get together and build a properly equipped central airport for the region rather than a number of small facilities which would not meet requirements, as Horan had discovered from his overtures to the Department of Transport in the 60s.

A marker had been put down but before that particular challenge could be fully taken on board Monsignor Horan was endeavouring to do something that had not been done before, bring a Pope to Ireland and more especially to Knock!

Judy Coyne and her Knock Shrine Society had not lost sight of their campaign to have the Holy Father invited for the centenary year of the Apparition in 1979. She placed the matter on the agenda at a meeting attended by Horan early in 1976, but he ignored it. Towards the end of the year she again put the item on the agenda, and this time the parish priest pointed out that Archbishop Cunnane would have to be present. Within a matter of weeks the Archbishop was invited to attend another meeting in Knock which he accepted. But when he saw a motion to have the Holy Father invited to Knock he reminded those in the room that that was a matter for the bishops and the bishops alone! There the discussion ended. Away from the meeting, however, Cunnane and Horan were wondering how they might pull it off.

In cases like these the Monsignor's nature was to get stuck in. Tom Neary, who saw him operate at close quarters for many years, said he'd go through fire and water to achieve his goals, and he was also a man of great courage and charity, traits he again saw underlined when he accompanied Horan on a promotional trip to America before news of the Pope's decision to visit Ireland was announced.

Neary recalled that Bord Fáilte was keen to do some promotional work to attract US visitors to these shores. "Remember, there was a big postal strike and an awful petrol crisis as well. Bord Fáilte realised they needed to do something to convince American tourists the country had not shut down, so they asked the Monsignor to help out by going to America and talking to people.

"They gave us support and a PR company in New York set up media appointments," he said.

While they were there, one night after a busy day of engagements the phone rang in their hotel bedroom and Horan answered the call. It was from an Irish woman who had heard the Irish priest on the radio and knew he was in town. She told him she had a daughter who was an invalid and they'd love if he could come and visit.

"The Monsignor asked her what part of NY she lived in and she replied, 'Harlem.'

'Oh, I see,' said the Monsignor. 'I'll do the best I can. I'll see if we can make it tomorrow.'

"When he put down the phone he said, 'Those people live in Harlem.' I replied I didn't think many Irish lived in Harlem any more. At that time Harlem was a very dodgy place, but he decided he was going to go out the next day.

"Next morning he went out to hail a taxi but found it very difficult to get any taxi driver to take us there. One of the guys said, 'I'll take a chance. I'll bring you out, but we don't go in there at night, so you know what you are letting yourself in for. It's not safe.'

"It just happened to be the 4 July, Independence Day, and we set off in the taxi. Harlem did not look that bad but they had these piles of black plastic litter bags all over the place. We found the house and the taxi dropped us and sped off. All the windows were open in the adjoining apartments and these coloured faces were looking out.

"We climbed up the steps and knocked, and this lady (the mother) opened the door. The first thing I noticed was that she had seven locks on the door with three iron bars to further secure it. I said to her, 'What's all this about?' and she replied matter-of-factly they had to have that level of security. They were afraid of being broken into.

The visitors had lunch with the two women over a long chat. Their host explained that most of the Irish, when they improved their lot, moved out of the area, but that she and her daughter were not in a position to move and buy a house.

"Before we left the Monsignor asked, 'Would ye like to come to Ireland someday?' and they replied, 'We'd love to.' 'Well,' he said, 'I'll bring you over, pay your way, and I'll put ye up in Knock,' which he did, and they enjoyed it very much.

"He was that sort of man, nothing put him off. It was still daylight when we came out of the apartment and we walked down the street in the rain, and eventually got a taxi back to our hotel. Just nothing daunted him," said Neary.

While all this was happening, behind the scenes in the Vatican Pope Paul VI was considering an invitation to visit Knock. Earlier Monsignor Horan had accompanied the Irish Bishops to Rome on their quinquennial visit. The Pope was told of the plans for Knock and asked would he like to come and take part. His reply was, "Why not?" and he told his secretary to write it down just in case it might be useful to his successor if God called him. God did call him, and when Pope John Paul II took over, Monsignor Horan and Archbishop Cunnane wasted no time in asking the Episcopal Conference in Maynooth to invite the Polish-born Holy Father. Hopes rose and fell, and rose again. There had been rumblings in the local and national press that an historic visit was on the cards, and on Saturday, July 21, 1979, the announcement was made: the Pope was coming to Knock on Sunday, September 30.

Monsignor Horan was ecstatic. "I am absolutely flabbergasted. It is the biggest thing in Irish history. The news is so big that I really cannot find words to express my delight," he told *The Connaught Telegraph*.

He admitted he had been losing heart just a few days before he was tipped off in advance of the official announcement. Later, in an interview with Fr. Colm Kilcoyne in the *Western Journal* of January 11, 1980, he said on his return from Poland, Pope John Paul II had turned to his Irish-born secretary John Magee and asked: "What kind of a reception do you think we will get in Knock?" That was the first inkling that the visit was a runner.

Now, under the supportive wing of Archbishop Cunnane, the dynamic James Horan had less than ten weeks to plan for the Pope's arrival at Knock and an expected 450,000 pilgrims, security, media, communication links, and the thousands of things that had to be done. As the clock ran down, more than a few, amongst them bishops, doubted that Knock would be ready: in places it resembled a building site with rubble and sand and cement mixers and steel girders strewn all over the place.

Building operations came easy to him. Much more testing was that now he had to interface with innumerable committees planning the visit. "I suspect he saw the committees as a nuisance – he was brilliant at motivating people when he had direct access to them and was hampered by layers of decisions-makers," says Fr. Kilcoyne.

But the builder of Knock was up to the task. Everything was in readiness. John Healy and fellow Mayoman Michael Foy of the Irish Sugar Company advised the Monsignor on the media arrangements, and especially those for photographers. Phone lines and darkrooms were installed in abundance and banks of teleprinters were laid out in the crypt.

Horan wanted everything to run smoothly, Healy recalled. "If we had said we needed a satellite over Knock James's reply would be, 'All right.' And if we further suggested the press corps would want to relax once the job was done and two dozen girls from the *Folies-Bergère* should be flown in, he wouldn't have batted an eyelid, except to enquire if they should be accommodated en masse or privately.

"The system James had installed worked like a dream, and the man from Reuters, a veteran of many European summits, was so impressed by what he saw at Knock that he filed a glowing piece separately. That was James Horan the organiser. Never mind the cost: if we are to do a job, we will do it right," Healy recorded.

The day dawned full of expectation. An estimated 450,00 people filed into their places from the night before. Those who were there have their own memories of the day. Monsignor Horan had a special one: "The single greatest thrill for me was the sight of the Pope's helicopter circling over Knock. At that moment it all became a reality for me."

He had a few well chosen words ready for the Pope as he got from the helicopter, in Irish, English and one word in Polish. "He smiled at that little effort and said I was very nice," recalled Horan.

Fr. Kilcoyne, who was attached to the Shrine at the time and handled media affairs, recalls one significant newspaper photograph when the Pope landed. "It shows the Pope and James looking at each other with mutual admiration. Archbishop Cunnane is to one side, out of it, like a little boy looking at two celebrities talking to each other."

Unfortunately, the visit to Knock, 'the goal of the Pontiff's journey to Ireland', was cut short. He had been delayed two hours in Galway when the youth celebrations there, hosted by Bishop Eamon Casey, badly overran schedule, and after the ceremonies in Knock, when the Pope was expected to tour through the lanes between the massive crowd in his Popemobile, it was announced that he had to return to Dublin by helicopter as the light was rapidly fading.

Monsignor Horan was told afterwards that one of the Pope's regrets was that he didn't spend a night in Knock. And Horan was very disappointed that the Pope hadn't time to go around among the pilgrims. He also revealed that Bishop Paul Marcinkus, the Pope's personal bodyguard, had expressed fears that the Popemobile was too small and very vulnerable and he was unhappy with it from a security point of view.

However, Horan flatly rejected comments alleged to have been made by Bishop Marcinkus that the people in Knock broke ranks and made it unsafe for the Holy Father to go around. "I don't accept that because we have TV pictures to show that the roads and passageways were clear," he said. Marcinkus, who died in early 2006, went on to become Chairman of the Vatican Bank and later became embroiled in a series of scandals that led to the death of a banker named Calvi in what was rumoured to be an Italian Mafia job.

But back to the Pope's visit to Knock. The really important thing about it, Horan observed, was that the Pope said Mass at Knock. He blessed the sick. He prayed at the shrine. And he raised the new church to the status of Basilica.

Monsignor Horan was, however, sorely disappointed that the Pope's visit was cut short. Monsignor Grealy, who died in late December 2005, said his friend was very down over the way the day had ended. "We holidayed together for over 40 years and when we went away to relax and play some golf after the papal visit he was not his usual self. I felt he was very disappointed that the Pope's visit had to be so curtailed and he had been unable to get to the people in the corrals, some of whom had been there all night and had remained there patiently, and yet didn't get close enough to see him," said Grealy.

But the redoubtable Monsignor Horan was never down for long. He just happened to have another project up the sleeve of his commodious soutane!

CHAPTER FOUR

1979/80: Airport Monsignor's new goal – Castlebar background and hijack claim – Steering committee formed – Feasibility study gets underway– Galway refuses invitation – Ministerial appointment – Haughey in frame – 500 acres purchased

Watching an old man go!

THE Polish Pope had come. He had seen. He had conquered the hearts of the near half-million people who had flocked to Knock. And he had bestowed on the Marian Shrine the official seal of recognition.

The man who had brought him there, the 'simple country parish priest' of Knock, must have felt he could now take on anything and succeed. He had transformed the Shrine and the village, built a magnificent Basilica and, quite literally, brought the Pontiff to Ireland through his sheer persistence and hard work. Where others had asked why, he had again asked why not? And again he had exceeded expectations.

But where others might have relaxed after their momentous exertions and a particularly busy decade of activity at Knock, Horan was not a man to let the grass grow under his feet.

Indeed, it was said around Knock that as he watched the Pope's helicopter rise into the darkening sky, the Monsignor made a mental note: it was time to tackle that long-fingered airport project again.

He had just seen devoted people flock into the village to greet the Pope – it was the stuff of legends. He believed Knock, properly promoted, could now become a major international Marian Shrine. And that meant many thousands of pilgrims coming from all over the world. He would have calculated what that influx would have meant to the region: as a believer in the philosophy of Seán Lemass, he realised that the rising tide at Knock could lift many boats in a depressed region.

"My only fear now is that we won't be ready for the millions of pilgrims who will come," he admitted in an interview.

Good-class accommodation was scarce in the area but he was elated to hear that five hotels were now being planned for the village. He also knew, however, that a major shortcoming was accessibility. Connecting roads were poor and the nearest railhead at Claremorris was inadequate.

The chances of CIE upgrading facilities or pushing a railhead to Knock were non-existent. Cutbacks and retrenchment had been the order of the day on the western lines, and creaking tracks and antiquated rolling stock were stark reminders of the ongoing neglect. In fact it was going to take most of the next two decades before the rail links were eventaually brought up to scratch.

The Pope departed from Shannon Airport on Monday, October 1 and on that very day, recalled Monsignor Horan's close friend Tom Neary, the Chief of Staff of the Army and an engineer were having lunch with him. Everyone was happy with the way things had gone organisationally at Knock the day before. However, the topic quickly turned to the need for a decent airport to open up the region. It was brought up by the Monsignor who frequently spoke about accessibility as one of the keys to developing the West. The topic dominated the conversation that afternoon and the Monsignor was very keen on the idea of an airport for Connaught. He had been down this road before, though on a much less ambitious scale, and wanted to know if he could stir the thing again now that the need and potential seemed so obvious. The Army brass listened as General Horan mused.

Horan was not a complete novice to planes and airports. He had, in fact, an abiding fascination with aviation. Tom Neary recalls that as long as he knew him he had a great interest in flying and airports and any opportunity he got when he came to Knock he took school kids on a trip, usually to Shannon Airport, looking at the runway and watching the planes. "Indeed, I remember him telling me that in the late forties and early fifties when Shannon Airport opened he would drive down and sit for hours on the balcony overlooking the runway, watching the planes taking off and landing."

He had crossed the Atlantic twice in the thirties and forties, first as chaplain on a liner and later to raise funds for Tooreen Ballroom, and in the mid and late fifties he had taken to the air, travelling with Aer Lingus to Rome and to Lourdes and other parts of Europe. In more recent times he had flown to and around the United States in a Bord Fáilte effort to attract more tourists to this country.

Neary said the Monsignor was very interested in Lourdes Airport and had examined the benefits it had bestowed on the Marian Shrine there. When it opened in 1947 only 1,300 pilgrims used it that first year but by 1979 the number had grown to 359,000. So having studied how Lourdes Airport had flourished he felt an airport in Connaught, servicing pilgrim traffic as well as business and linking with Irish centres of population in England and, ultimately the United States of America, was worth examining. He told friends such an airport would start small but would grow in its own time.

Now, with the papal visit done and dusted, the Monsignor did not rest on his laurels. Not indeed that he could afford to, for business interests in Castlebar had also recognised the potential at Knock and were making the case at the highest level for the expansion of the 2,000 ft runway on the Breaffy Road on the outskirts of the town. A fully-fledged airport fitted in perfectly with the expansionist ambitions of the county town which had secured some major industry.

Castlebar had had a long history in aviation. William Munnelly of that town and James Mee of Mullingar, who later settled in Castlebar, were among the members of the Royal Flying Corps, forerunners of the Royal Air Corps, who landed regularly in Castlebar during the First World War. After the war, pleasure flights came into vogue and this interest eventually developed.

A transatlantic flight from Castlebar had first been attempted on 28 August 1927, with tragic results. Undertaken by Terry Tully from Carracastle, an experienced pilot of the Royal Flying Corps, he flew a sponsored flight from London – Ontario – London in the John Carling airplane. Unfortunately, the flight never made its destination and the crew and craft disappeared without trace.

In August 1966, a private airport at Castlebar had been opened with the financial backing of two Mayo brothers, Peter and Hugh Ryan of Westport. Peter Ryan maintains Castlebar had the first tarmac runway in the country outside of Dublin, Shannon and Cork. Roadstone Managing Director Tom Roche was looking for the use of a strip to land his plane when he visited his quarry in Castlebar en route to the company's other sites around the country.

"I had the land and he approached me to see if we could create a grass strip runway, and I agreed. Later on, due to bad weather at times, I decided to do an upgrade to a tarmacadam surface," said Ryan.

"Actually," added Peter Ryan, "Charlie Haughey gave me a bit of a grant to put down the tarmac!" Surely a happy portent of things to come!

A four-seater plane, chartered by Bobby Smith and Frank Gill of the Royal Blues Showband from Claremorris, was the first to land on the new airstrip. And the multi-millionaire head of the transatlantic aerospace and defence company, Denis Ferranti, used the airport regularly en route to his holiday home at nearby Massbrook, overlooking Lough Conn. It's now the home of Ireland's first woman President, Mary Robinson, a native of Ballina.

Early in December 1979 a copy of *The Connaught Telegraph* newspaper landed on the Monsignor's desk with a front page story by Tom Courell telling of plans to extend the runway in Castlebar to 4,000ft. The additional footage would accommodate 50-seater planes, said the report, adding that discussions were taking place at the highest level. There was, however, one problem: to extend the runway it would be necessary for the tarmac to stretch right across the busy main Dublin road into lands owned by the IDA on the opposite side. To complicate matters further, the other end of the runway was hemmed in by railway tracks.

On the same page and in the same edition of the Castlebar-based newspaper, a headline proclaimed "Castlebar man is voted Taoiseach", referring to Charles J Haughey taking over the reins of the Fianna Fáil party and the country in succession to Jack Lynch. In a reshuffle of his Cabinet, Denis Gallagher of Achill was dropped as Minister for the Gaeltacht, and East Mayo Deputy Seán Calleary of Ballina was promoted as Minister of State.

In relation to the Castlebar airport plans, Hugh Ryan revealed in an interview for this book that he had purchased 30 acres of land on the Pontoon side of Castlebar to construct a new and longer runway. His brother, Jim, a former Fleet Air Arm pilot, who was to play a key role in Monsignor Horan's airport creation, did a lot of preparatory work on the runway planning and in seeking out more land. He had also made contact with contractors in Cork to do estimates for carrying out work on the runway.

East Mayo Fianna Fáil TD and civil engineer Seán Calleary recalls being approached by an earthmoving contractor to do a quantities survey at the new Castlebar site. "I did not have the time nor the personnel to do it at that time," he says.

Peter Ryan remembers Horan coming down to meet with Jim Ryan at one stage to see the site. "The Monsignor was delighted with it, so it was all fine and I thought it was going ahead. However, it appeared certain interests wanted the airport to be built in the east of the county, so we got a bit tired and said OK. We let it go. It was costing us money."

Over the previous two years, Jim Ryan had tried to get a helicopter base established at the airport to service offshore oil rigs. A company called Gael West Limited – a consortium representing Aer Arann Teo, Ireland West Airways and Schriner Airways of Holland – had sought a licence to operate the service out of Castlebar. The Schriner firm was described as the second largest helicopter operator in Europe and the third largest in the world.

Initial applications to Transport Minister Padraig Faulkner had been turned down on the grounds that the demand in the foreseeable future could be handled by a company already authorised to provide a helicopter service.

Brian Trench, writing in the *Sunday Tribune* in May 1986, interviewed Jim Ryan who told the reporter he had met Monsignor Horan in Knock on 10 October 1979, ten days after the Pope's visit, and put a proposal to him to develop an airport. No doubt Ryan still had in mind Castlebar/Pontoon as the location.

The Ryans had been looking at their Castlebar asset and would likely have had discussions with people like the Mayo County Manager, Michael O'Malley, and County Development Officer, Seán Smyth, who were also very much aware of the Monsignor's ambition to secure a fully-fledged airport. In fact, Horan and Ryan were brought together by Smyth to discuss their mutual interests. Smyth was very pro-active in attracting jobs to the county and he would have appreciated more than most that the provision of a proper airport would help the drive to attract inward investment.

But back to the *Sunday Tribune* article by Trench: "Ryan started briefing the Monsignor on the operations and economics of airports. Very quickly, as Ryan recalls, the energetic priest had made the idea his own, assimilating easily large amounts of technical information."

That is not strictly correct, for Horan's efforts to provide an airport were well-known and well-chronicled years before that, and, as we have seen, the idea had originally come from Dame Judy Coyne in 1935, though she was not thinking on the same grand scale as was the Monsignor 45 years later.

However, Frank Durcan, a Castlebar businessman and a former colourful and controversial member of both the local Urban Council and Mayo County Council, to this day believes the airport project was 'hijacked' out of Castlebar by the wily Monsignor.

"People from Castlebar," he recalls, "went off to Knock when the Monsignor had a vision. The new site in Castlebar was a much better site than Knock and would have done a lot more for industry in Mayo than the present location. In Castlebar there would have been no problem in getting support; the business people of the town were there and would have been prepared to invest. And I'd say the Government of the time would have been prepared to back it because the small airport had proved successful and the industry was here and in Westport."

With potential sites being discussed, Jim Ryan recommended that Horan call a meeting of key players to advance the proposal. Horan did not hang about. The meeting was held on January 2 1980, in Knock and those present included Mayo County Manager, Michael O'Malley, the County Development Officer, Seán Smyth, Jim Ryan, engineer Seán Balfe, and Ireland West Tourism official, Dan O'Neill who was based in Galway.

Mayo-born O'Neill, a former Louth All-Ireland football winner who also wore his native county colours, had built up a good rapport with the Monsignor in the lead-up to the Pope's visit when they had worked side by side. He recalls: "When this small group met with the Monsignor it was a workmanlike discussion, and it was quickly agreed that a study would need to be carried out to check the viability of building an airport. Some preliminary investigation had been carried out and it was known that such a study would cost £18,000, and that the Department of Transport had recommended either Aer Rianta or Transportation Analysis International (TAI)."

TAI were chosen because they were international consultants and had carried out work for the government. O'Neill was asked to contact Bord Fáilte for one third of the study cost, the County Council was to pay a third, and the Monsignor was to fund the remainder.

As it happened, Joe Malone, a Breaffy, Castlebar man, was Director General of Bord Fáilte at the time and he immediately agreed there was merit in having a study done. He had just seen what the Papal visit had done for the country, and he was anxious to tap in on the potential tourism benefits. He was the most honoured man in the Irish tourist industry, being the first Irishman to be elected World President of Skal and now, in 1980, being honoured as the World Travel Awards' Committee 'Man of the Year in Europe'.

He was a good man to have in Knock's corner. "So I got my cheque from Bord Fáilte and it was the first money on the table when we next met on February 12 1980," says O'Neill.

February was a good month for the Monsignor and Tuam's Archbishop Joseph Cunnane, for they were presented with the Mayo Meitheal Award in Dublin at the annual bash of the Mayo Association in recognition of their role in improving facilities at Knock Shrine and bringing the Pope there.

Meanwhile, the Monsignor had sought representation from Galway to join his Steering Committee and later admitted that he had considered Tuam a possible location for the airport. In fact, he had suggested that his committee could hold its next meeting in Galway to facilitate the attendance of the Galway Port authority, public representatives and other interests. The invitation fell on deaf ears.

Observed Tom Neary: "The sad thing was that Galway ignored the moves that were being made; they saw it as a threat, so they never became involved which was a pity really."

With Galway refusing to play ball and the cat now well and truly out of the bag, experience told the Mayo rump that it had to move quickly. In fact, it soon became clear that Galway, which, from a Mayo perspective, usually grabbed the plums in any Galway-Mayo amalgamation of interests, was looking to provide its own airport. So there was very real pressure on Mayo to press on: in the ensuing battle there would only be one winner between historic rivals whose combats on Gaelic football fields were – and are – legendary.

Belfast-born Dr Ken Holden of TAI, who was within the year to become head of the Central Remedial Clinic in Dublin in succession to Lady Valerie Goulding, undertook the study on the understanding that he would give an independent finding.

He recalls: "A friend at Shannon Free Airport Development Company Ltd (SFADCO) rang me and set up a meeting with Monsignor Horan in the Old Grounds in Ennis. He didn't tell me who we were meeting or what it was about. The Monsignor set it out very simply – he said he'd like to see direct access to the Knock region from outside the country and he'd like to see if he could get the money together to build an airport capable of taking 737s. He said he was not interested in small airports, not interested in services to Dublin, the only thing that interested him was an airport close enough to Knock, maybe 5, 10 or 15 miles away, and it had to be capable of taking 737s."

The Monsignor told him he fully realised it was not worth building it for Knock alone but it was worth it for Connaught. "His words were: 'Take that commission and come back and tell me if there are enough people around to use it – that it makes economic sense.' He did not dictate any detailed terms whatsoever," revealed Holden.

Horan made it clear he did not want to embark on the project if it did not make economic sense. TAI met with the Monsignor and his group monthly. "We talked to all the business and tourism interests, and the one thing they were all adamant on was that the airport would have to be able to cater for direct flights to London," says Dr Holden.

Meanwhile, on the political front the pieces were also falling into place. John Healy's prediction in December of 1979 in the *Western Journal* that Castlebar's Padraig Flynn would get a State car as Minister of State at the Department of Transport and Power was finally fulfilled in March.

Castlebar, and West Mayo, had been used to State cars over the years, with Joe Blowick (Clann na Talmhain), Miceal O'Morain (FF), Henry Kenny, father of current Fine Gael Leader Enda, and Denis Gallagher (FF) all getting their Mercs, so party activists in that constituency felt a bit miffed when Seán Calleary was given the nod in East Mayo by Haughey and elevated to Minister of State. It re-ignited the old rivalry between the party in the two Mayo constituencies.

Strong representations were made to Haughey by the Castlebar Fianna Fáil wing, and subsequently John Healy, who had the Taoiseach's ear, was confident enough to predict some months in advance that Flynn would be promoted.

With an undisguised whiff of nepotism, Healy wrote in the *Western Journal* of April 4: "There was never a countryman yet who didn't want where he could, to do a stroke for his birthplace: it's ingrained in all of us and in the case of the Mayos it's a national anthem in the rallying song: 'County Mayo'." Haughey had been born in Castlebar; better still, he had been fully reminded of that when he was fêted by the Mayos when they chose him as their Mayoman of the Year in early 1978!

But if teacher man Padraig Flynn was in any danger of getting a swelled head, Healy planted his feet firmly on the ground with an admonition: "It's no secret that, as far as I am concerned, he has been in my book a bit of a political gedgeemeen (or a gillygooly), but I've seen bigger gedgeemeens settle down and turn out to be good politicians once given a bit of responsibility and office."

Healy predicted that if the Castlebar man had the talent a full ministry lay ahead of him; but he warned that if he hadn't it was back to the back benches, and he had ten months to prove himself. It was putting it up to Flynn.

A few weeks later, again in his own paper, the *Western Journal*, Healy was elated with the performance of Flynn, whom he had by now christened the 'Sunflower Kid' (Flynn at that time owned a pub in the county town called the Sunflower Lounge). Drawing attention to a sparkling performance on a BBC television programme on Irish Republicanism, Healy said Flynn performed as 'a coming man in Irish politics'.

But somewhat prophetically, he observed: "There is always the danger that Flynn would say something 'eejity' if you'll pardon the word, but there was nothing 'eejity' about him last week; he spoke slowly, confidently, very levelly and relaxed as if he were Minister for Foreign Affairs and in the seat for years."

The Junior Minister, observed the Charlestown scribe, had come a long way since the day he entered the Dáil, 'dressed in a white suit designed to make him stick out like a sore thumb'.

Added Healy, warming to his theme: "I suppose the desire to be instantly recognised is a natural one but he grated on most people in that opening day and came close to putting most people's teeth on edge." That was precisely the impression the ambitious Flynn had sought to create on his first day in national parliament.

Now that Flynn had redeemed himself, Healy was showing that he was keeping a mentor's eye on the Castlebar man's progress. Healy was also being kept very much in the picture as to what was happening in relation to the airport project. But as so often happens when one is so close to the scene, he felt obliged to sit on confidential information. It must have come as something of a shock therefore when the rival *Western People*, where he had started out as a cub reporter in the late 1940s, splashed a front page lead on March 19 to the effect that TAI had been engaged to carry out a commercial airport feasibility study by the Regional Aerodrome Committee.

The paper's South Mayo correspondent Michael Ronayne was constantly on to Horan as one of his best news contacts. "I was just looking for a story for my paper and rang him. He said he would get back to me. He came back within half an hour and outlined details of the TAI study that was underway," recalls Ronayne who went on to become economics correspondent with RTÉ.

A day later another Mayo newspaper, *The Connaught Telegraph* revealed that the Castlebar Airport ambitions were far from buried as far as the local Chamber of Commerce was concerned. A regular air service was to be introduced between Castlebar and Dublin within the next two months, on two days a week initially.

But with only a five-seater plane envisaged for the service, the news hardly rocked the Monsignor and his tightly-knit team. He had been here before in the '60s when Knock Development Company's humble proposal got nowhere.

The net effect of the two reports, however, forced John Healy to release some of the information he had. In the *Western Journal* of March

21 he detailed the involvement of the Monsignor and County Manager Michael O'Malley in the project, and wrote that a decade earlier such an ambition would have been something of 'a pipe dream' but now, he said, the major influx of multinational companies into the region – Travenol, Abbott, Asahi, Snia, Hollister and Hanson – had altered the whole economic climate of Mayo and the West.

Healy also indicated that sites in the Black Triangle area between Foxford, Knock and Tubbercurry, including Swinford, Pontoon, Charlestown and Kilkelly, offered the most suitable location were the project to proceed.

"The urgency is to capitalise on the Papal visit and the Papal elevation of Knock – which is why Monsignor Horan has moved with commendable speed and with equally commendable help from Joe Malone in Bord Fáilte. I think it only fair to warn Charlie Haughey, the third Mayoman in the link, that he had better be prepared for the Horan whirlwind to hit him within a matter of months," he wrote.

By then Charlie Haughey had been brought into the frame by Healy whose brother, retired Charlestown postman Gerry, remembers the sequence of events.

"John had gone to Charlie and told him about the proposal and said, 'We want a bit of action in the West of Ireland', and Charlie's initial reaction was that he thought John and Monsignor Horan were dreamers but it happened that they weren't.

"John believed in Charlie Haughey and Charlie Haughey believed in the West and between the three 'Hs,' Haughey, Horan and Healy, they brought it about. There is no doubt about it, he (John) had a big influence with Charlie and he knew Charlie was interested. And fair play to Charlie, and I was never a great admirer of him, he was to give us that airport."

Charlestown businessman John Mahon, who was much later to become an airport board director, had reclaimed bogland at Sonnagh, along the main Charlestown/Swinford road and turned it into a huge green tract of pastureland which was much admired by people passing the way. He recalls one day late in 1979 when John Healy was heading for Achill and he pulled up and said, 'John, after reclaiming all of this land – in a short time that might be something else.' I didn't know what he was talking about but he just replied, 'My brother, Gerry, will keep you posted if there are any developments.'

"Six months or so later Gerry came along and said, 'You know, John, we are going to have an airport.' I told my father and he said, 'Oh, that's for the birds!'"

It transpired the reclaimed Mahon land had been considered a potential site for the airport.

Fr. Kieran Waldron vividly remembers the day Horan planted the possibility of an airport in the minds of over one thousand people

31

involved in tourism in the region. It was April 1980 and Waldron happened to be involved in a community tourism scheme of Holiday Cottages in Louisburgh.

At that time, Ireland West, or Western Regional Tourism Organisation Ltd, was very active. Its AGMs were media events and busloads of voters came to support their local would-be directors. The AGM of April 1980 in the Beaten Path Ballroom, Brize, near Claremorris, was the day Horan chose to talk publicly about an heroic enterprise.

The two priests knew each other well. Waldron grew up in Tooreen and had boyhood memories of Horan, his greatness as a spiritual man and a priest, his personal charm and his childlike traits. "For instance his predictable outbursts to mischievous taunts, as he naively rose to a bait delivered by a colleague – and exploded. He would then realise he was being led on, and finish with a chuckle."

At the AGM Horan greeted Waldron and said curtly: 'You sit beside me.' "I don't know was it the black uniform or myself he wanted there but I gathered he was going to make a speech," says Fr. Waldron.

"As always he was well prepared. He knew the event was being covered by RTÉ and at the appropriate time, he stood up and made an impassioned speech on behalf of Connaught. Connaught, he said, was 'entitled to an airport'. He made a great impression and sat down to thunderous applause. When he had regained his composure, he whispered to me in his simple way, 'Wasn't I right?' I told him of course he was, little dreaming, however, that such a thing would happen," avers Fr. Waldron.

Again in the *Western Journal* of May 23, Healy gave fuller details of the study being finalised by Ken Holden and his colleagues at TAI. The site would be in East Mayo close to Charlestown, 500 acres would be required, the traffic figures stacked up, flights to the Shrine would be the cream on the cake, and it would provide for a regular service to Dublin and London. And the promoters visualised a 7,500 ft runway 150 feet wide.

Actually, the TAI study recommended a 6,000 ft runway with scope for extension but even by then Monsignor Horan and his team were pushing for 7,500 ft after examining airports on the Continent.

Two weeks later, having seen the completed report, Healy told his readers the airport would cost between £5m and £6m.

The main conclusions of the TAI study, issued in May, were:
• A Connaught Regional Airport capable of handing 737s on a regular basis could be built at a cost of between £5m and £6m for a 6,000ft runway at 1980 values (no site had been chosen at that time).
• While the airport would be unlikely to produce any monetary return on the original investment, it could be operationally self-

sufficient in terms of both its day-to-day running expenses and its future development costs.

• An airport of the scale envisaged could only be justified in terms of its use for scheduled services and, initially, the only potentially viable scheduled service that could be seen was one linking the area to London.

• The 1983 traffic on the London route was projected to be at least 35,000 passengers, supporting two to three flights per week in winter, increasing to daily service in the summer peak.

• In time the airport would also probably support seasonal scheduled services to one or more UK provincial points such as Glasgow or Manchester; series charters catering to Knock pilgrim traffic from the UK and possibly Europe; scheduled services to Dublin if subsidies were initially provided as part of an overall reappraisal of National Transportation Policy.

• The potential traffic was put at between 40,000 and 50,000 a year with longer-term potential for handling up to 100,000 passengers a year. Total traffic was unlikely to exceed 150,000 passengers a year within twenty years.

• The runway should be no more than 6,000 ft long, 150 ft wide.

• The airport should have easy access to the N5 or N7 main roads, both of which pass through Charlestown.

• With low activity levels the airport must be so managed as to permit the maximum use of local part-time staff.

The benefits to the business community in Connaught and its contribution to the industrial development of the region were stressed, as were the benefits to Knock Shrine, and tourism generally in the region.

And the report showed that an airport in the Charlestown region would have a catchment area of over 4,000 square miles with a population of just under 250,000 and an estimated manufacturing work-force of 18,500 in 1983. In total the catchment area would account for just under 4 per cent of total Ireland to UK/Europe air travel in 1983 – the year the airport was expected to be operational.

The consultants were of the view that the benefits to the business community in the area were alone sufficient to justify its development having regard to the ambitious industrial development targets already set for the region.

That positive recommendation was, however, critically dependent on two factors, namely:

(a) that a London scheduled service was operated from the outset, and

(b) that acceptable full-time/part-time labour practices could be worked out (particularly in relation to the critical areas of Security, Air

Traffic Control, Rescue Services and passenger/aircraft handling) so as to permit operational break-even at a level of not more than 50,000 passengers a year.

The report was to be much derided by detractors of the proposal, but looking back twenty-five years to 1980, Ken Holden says if anything their assessment was too cautious. "We always thought afterwards it was one of the best pieces of work we ever did. The Monsignor gave us a tight schedule but we were very conscious of doing it right. It was a good report but in retrospect it was overly cautious. None of us at that time foresaw the increase in air travel. There were only 2.5m passengers going through Dublin at that time whereas passenger throughput in airports throughout Ireland is now approx. 20m (2005). You would have been thrown into an asylum if you had predicted 20m back in 1980."

Holden and Horan had quickly established a firm working relationship: Holden respected Horan for his pragmatism, Horan knew he could count on Holden to tell him as it was.

Specifically, Holden is mindful of a day when TAI were reporting to the Monsignor and his committee and during the dissemination of facts and figures there was plenty of good-natured banter. One of the committee lobbed the ball at the Monsignor: "Do you know Ken is a Protestant?"

"Of course I do," he replied, "that is one of the reasons I hired him; he is going to give me an objective answer!"

Sitting at the table that day was Mayo County Development Officer, Seán Smyth, an indefatigable worker for industrial progress in the county and a staunch and active supporter of the project. He remembers Monsignor Horan's great facility to crack a joke or make a comment and then laugh for three minutes. "His laugh was infectious, and then it would be down to the serious business at hand again," he says. "Only for his conviction he would not have got anywhere with his idea of an airport in the West of Ireland, with Dublin, Shannon and Cork already there, and to put it into Mayo of all places! But if anyone said it was a silly idea he would have asked why not?"

Men like O'Malley and Smyth loved working with Horan principally because he thought outside the box and, above all, he was not afraid of big projects. And, goodness knows, in Mayo of the early 1980s big projects did not land in their laps every week.

Said Smyth: "He had handled a fair degree of money in his many projects over the years, so he was not scared of big money projects or where the money would come from. But it never occurred to him either that it would not work; he had done it all before in his parishes and at Knock Shrine. He had the track record.

"If every county had a man like him they'd have had major amenities, and the wonderful thing about him was that as a cleric he wanted nothing for himself, he wanted it for his people. He was an extraordinary individual, a man of unshakeable conviction."

East Mayo FG TD Paddy O'Toole remembers attending a meeting in Monsignor Horan's house in Knock in 1980. Present were Archbishop Cunnane, the Monsignor and two laymen, including Jim Ryan. O'Toole was advised that the TAI study had proved positive, that he should bring it to the attention of Garret FitzGerald and the party generally and report back to the Monsignor.

"The mood within the party to the proposal was positive. There was some doubt expressed about the viability of an airport totally dependent on pilgrim traffic. However, the overall view was one of support because it was felt that Fianna Fáil was hijacking the project for their own political ends. By this time Charlie Haughey had become personally involved and statements made by Monsignor Horan indicated that Fine Gael would play a secondary role no matter what it did."

At around the same time that TAI were issuing their findings, Professor A.A. Horner of the Department of Geography, University College, Dublin, was finalising a completely independent study on optimal locations for international airports in Ireland. It was published by the Royal Irish Academy in Dublin at almost precisely the same time as Monsignor Horan was seeking government backing for his project. Horner set out to identify one to five airport solutions based on minimising the aggregate distance travelled for the population as a whole. His study showed that having for historical reasons missed the optimal nationwide three airport solution of Dublin, Mallow and Boyle, the natural (and only) sensible location for a fourth (and probably final) main airport was in the general vicinity of Knock (Boyle to be exact).[7]

"As such it provided the strongest possible academic underpinning of the fact that Knock was the right airport, built in the right location at the right time," said Ken Holden when interviewed for this book.

Days after the TAI feasibility study was completed, Minister of State Padraig Flynn and his party colleague in the East constituency, P J. Morley, were travelling together from Mayo to the Dáil and in friendly banter were doing their best to score points off each other.

"By that time," said Morley, "I had seen the TAI feasibility study and Padraig said to me 'I was over in your parish (Knock) at Mass on Sunday and the Monsignor gave me a copy of the Report and he asked me to lobby Charlie. But I can tell you, P.J., if there's going to be any airport it's going to be in Castlebar!'"

Already knowing the Monsignor's determination and Charlie's disposition towards the Airport plans, Morley replied with a wry smile, "We will see, Padraig, we will see!"

---

7   A. A. Horner *Population Distribution and the Location of Airports in Ireland* (Royal Irish Academy Dublin 1980) p.171

"Coming back home a few days later I could not stop laughing when Padraig said to me, 'I have to go over to Knock to meet Monsignor Horan to tell him he is going to get his airport'. "I knew Padraig had met Charlie in the meantime and had had his cards marked," said Morley. It was to be one rare time when Flynn was to lose out on an opportunity to secure a meaningful piece of infrastructure for his native town!

By then the Monsignor had his core team about him. None of them was really surprised at the decision of the 68-year-old priest to build an airport, but they were nevertheless taken aback at the faith he had in them.

Engineer John Balfe was taken to see the two sites selected from six as most suitable by Captain R. M. Reidy of the Aeronautical Operational section of the Department of Transport. In Reidy's view, the location at Barnalyra, near Charlestown, was the most promising.

"Then the Monsignor told me the scale of the airport envisaged and the engineering plans that would be needed. I had no experience in the aviation field and pointed out that we would need expert help," says Balfe.

'John, you can do it,' he said quietly.

'Hold on,' I replied, 'this is international stuff.'

But he wasn't taking no for an answer, and countered again firmly, 'John, you can do it.'

"I didn't believe it myself really, but thought, well, let's look at it and see how it goes. Pretty quickly I discovered it was not such a difficult operation because airports are so tightly controlled by regulations, and all the guidelines are there to be followed.

"So we got stuck in and then I found we could do it and where I needed additional expertise I brought in Ray Goggin and Jimmy Millar of Maloney and Millar with whom I had worked before in Dublin and whom I trusted implicitly. Vincent Feehan and Paddy White of the Department of Transport, and Patrick Hackett from Aer Rianta guided us along the way," he said.

The net result was a feasibility study of the selected site, and in a matter of weeks John X Balfe and Associates, Claremorris, issued their findings. The site was free of any obstructions, houses, overhead lines or any form of building, and fencing of boundaries was minimal. The land was owned by a number of small farmers and was used for the harvesting of peat.

The site was an elevated one, with a maximum elevation of 214.6 metres (704 ft), and a minimum elevation of 166m (545 ft) above sea level. Initial discussions with the meteorological service centred on fog incidence and elevation, and it was the Met Service's considered opinion that fog incidence in the valleys would be much greater than hill fog on the site. It was also of the opinion that fog incidence should be at a minimum during daylight hours. But, the Balfe study pointed out, 'the incidence of low ceiling due to cloud may be a factor which requires further investigation'. A meteorological officer from Dublin Airport, Mr B. McWilliams, followed up on these issues and reported the conditions were better than Cork Airport and in some respects better than Dublin and Shannon, and any low cloud difficulty could be overcome with an instrument landing system.

The Balfe report addressed the surface of the ground. It found it was covered in cut-away peat and virgin peat, varying in depth from 2.5 metres (8 ft) to 0.200 metres (8 inches). The underlying subsoil was variable glacial drift with varying boulder sizes and sandy clay.

Referring to the proposed runway, Balfe pointed out that while Monsignor Horan had requested that the concept of a 10,000 ft runway in the future should not be lost, the desired objective was a runway length of 2,287 metres (7,500 ft) and a width of 46 metres (150ft).

Working on meagre aerial survey contour data initially available, Balfe did his calculations, and the question of conforming to International Civil Aviation Organisation (ICAO) Standards and Recommended Practices (SARPS) seemed problematical for a long runway.

"So perhaps the Department men felt the longer runway was not going to be an issue," says Balfe. "But when we came away from one such meeting we looked at the aerial survey contours again and found we could meet the required international standards by altering the proposed runway profile. We submitted an addendum saying for an approximate nett sum of £7.5m (at 1980 prices) a 7,500ft Class A-B type runway could be constructed on the proposed site.

"As far as we were concerned we were going for a fully fledged 7,500ft runway from day one, and it was all clearly spelled out in my report, that 7,500 ft was absolutely essential and we never altered that target, based on our study of other airports, the demands of 737s, etc. The length of runway, which later turned out to be a controversial point, was contained in my report and was handed to the Department of Transport the day we went to Dublin on the deputation. From that day on we never decreased our aspiration for a runway of 7,500 ft; we saw it as both necessary and prudent, looking to the future," says Balfe.

The highly efficient PR machine at Knock, well honed during the papal visit, was now cranked up again. Monsignor Horan wasn't hiding his latest project under a bushel and issued a press release, on behalf of the ad hoc committee, on June 26, setting out the main findings of the TAI study. What was planned, he said, was a major airport capable of accommodating 737 jets, with services to Dublin and London. There was no intention, he explained, of interfering with the existing developments mentioned at Castlebar, Galway or Sligo which would, he said, be enhanced by the existence of a proper regional airport.

Horan anticipated future critics when he pointed out that the

West's biggest drawback was poor communications. "We are too far from Dublin and from the main seaports and airports. Our roads badly need modernising but a recent National Economic and Social Council (NESC) report says that it would take £500 million to bring the roads up to date. It would take a similar sum to bring our antiquated railways up to modern standards. Arising from the NESC report, it was suggested that internal air transport should be developed to take the pressure off the roads and the railways."

He informed the public that if a regional airport was to become a reality it must be provided by the Government. "A prosperous Connaught will contribute substantially to a prosperous Ireland. A poor and undeveloped Connaught is a drain on national resources and prevents the whole country rising to its full height. I believe our Government, realising this, will respond positively to the challenge."

Behind the scenes John Healy was also keeping the Minister for Transport, Albert Reynolds, informed of the plans. "Yes, I first heard of the project from John Healy. I knew him well and used to meet him occasionally. He mentioned about a report being done. I said I'd read it with interest. Let's see what the consultants say; the principle is fine. My reaction was if you could build an airport at a reasonable cost and open up accessibility why not do it; we could pay more in a grant to an industry setting up in Mayo, so let's see what the figures say," he recalls.

*   *   *

The selected Barnalyra site overlooking Charlestown now became the immediate concern. News of the proposed development attracted the attention of speculators who were reported to be all over the place like a rash. If they got their hands on plots of land the price of the 500 acres required was likely to rocket.

Affable Jim Ryan, secretary of the committee, had already been sent in to bat on that front. "The committee knew that when news broke there would be awful racketeering for the land," says Tom Neary.

Ryan, with a background in aviation and widespread experience overseas as a representative for Caltex Oil, worked on commissioning refinery plants in such far-flung places as Bahrain, Japan, the Arabian Gulf, India, Turkey, Germany and Australia where he met his wife to be, Marine, a native of Sydney.

Ryan was key to the land acquisition and he went around his task with great zeal and tact. First he went to Dublin and secured Ordnance Survey maps for the whole area, identified the 27 owners and invited them to a meeting in Shammer. Those that did not come he made it his duty to call on personally, even if that meant going to England. The going rate being paid by the Department of Forestry for bog land at that time was £70 per acre; the committee decided to pay £200.

The Monsignor later recalled that there was so much euphoria in the area that an airport was going to be built in the Black Triangle that many wanted to hand over their lots for free. It was an offer the committee believed they could not in all fairness accept, and he later put on record his appreciation of them, saying he hoped that the airport would be so successful that in future years they would be proud of the gesture they made then.

Bachelor farmer John Tiernan of Kilgarriff West, Charlestown, just under the shadow of the airport, was one of the 27 landowners and he remembers well the day Jim Ryan came knocking on the door.

"It was a wet day and he came in and introduced himself. 'I am coming here to get land for the airport,' he explained. My mother was sitting at the table and she was delighted and said, 'Certainly so, sir. We will knock our house if needs be and give all our land,' never thinking it would happen, but it came the way. She looked forward to the day it would open but unfortunately she died around the time the sod was cut by Albert Reynolds in May 1981."

A native of Westport and one of nature's gentlemen, Ryan was the ideal person to interface with the landowners. His widow, Marine, says he had many the cup of tea in small farmers' houses. "He was a people's person and it was a very good experience for him. He had a great way about him. He had an easy charm and that really was his great gift.

"I can just see him in all those houses, in front of a turf fire, talking to the owners. A lot of them would be elderly. He even had to go to England to chase up some owners who had emigrated. It was a huge job and he'd often come home in the small hours of the morning. He worked at it non-stop, day and night," she said.

"There were problems, of course, complex ones. For instance, some farmers had turbary rights and needed their turf. But the Monsignor, as usual, had a solution. He offered to give good bog to those with rights and he bought 20 acres further away from the site, developed roads, drains, etc., so each got one acre, and the potential deal-breaker was quickly resolved," says Tom Neary.

The resolution of the land ownership issue was the most remarkable thing about the whole project, reckons former East Mayo TD and county councillor, P J Morley.

"When the Monsignor told me of the number of landowners whose agreement would have to be secured, I surely felt this was a lost cause having had experience of how difficult it was to get four or five people to agree on Local Improvement Schemes. I felt this is a fierce task altogether, a very long-term prospect. It will take many years! Indeed four or five landowners did come to me to express their reservations.

"But he pushed ahead. He spoke to them and he got around them so quickly. That was the most astounding aspect of the whole project as far as I was concerned. No one really persisted in their opposition or came back to me after he had spoken to them and got over their concerns."

Senator Jim Higgins concurs with that assessment: "All of that land was owned by different individuals and it shows the manipulative negotiating skills of the Monsignor. He was able to get all of the landowners collectively to hand over the huge land bank and convert what was originally, back in the sixties, an airstrip concept into an international airport with a 7,500 ft runway. It was an astonishing feat."

A local farmer was amazed at the manner in which Horan put any fears of landholders to rest. "The few that hesitated initially were met by the Monsignor, usually in his car outside their door, and he'd quickly allay their concerns in that easy-going manner of his. They had great respect for him and what he was trying to accomplish and he for them. It was real patriotism in action."

Another observer of the Monsignor's methods recalled that in a few instances where landowners were hesitant he pointed out to them that they were holding up one of the greatest projects ever to be undertaken in the area. Given the motivational spiel, they too quickly conceded, as the Revd. Mother had conceded over the car park in Knock years earlier.

Extraordinarily, by the summer of 1980, the Airport committee had taken up an option on 520 acres at £200 an acre. Waterford might have been campaigning for 30 years for an airport, but the implications in Mayo were clear: there would be no hanging about!

Now there remained the small matter of convincing the Government, and specifically Taoiseach Charlie Haughey, that a regional airport built in Mayo was an idea worth supporting.

CHAPTER FIVE

1980: Morley / Byrne funerals – Most expensive lunch – Approval in principle – Working Group claims Ministerial interference – Roscommon's bid for airport – Padraig Flynn's crash – Flag raised

Charlie Haughey's most expensive lunch

LIFE in Mayo certainly did not revolve solely around the proposed airport. In fact not everyone was aware of what was planned for the top of a hill at Barnalyra, near Charlestown. Day-to-day existence in a deprived region, scarcity of job opportunity, growing emigration, slow business, the accelerating drift from the land, unstable interest rates, and the hopes of the county teams in the Connaught football championship that summer formed the background against which people got on with their lives.

Then, on the afternoon of Monday, July 7, word broke on the national airwaves – this was before the advent of local radio – of an attempted robbery on the Bank of Ireland Branch at Ballaghaderreen, Co. Roscommon. Worse news was to follow: in pursuing the robbers two young gardai were gunned down and murdered.

Former star Mayo footballer Detective Garda John Morley (37) and Garda Henry Byrne (29), were shot dead at Aghaderry, Co. Roscommon, as they chased the raiders. Both gardaí were married with children and were then stationed at Castlerea, Co. Roscommon. Both were also natives of Knock and their tragic deaths were widely mourned; John Morley was especially well known throughout the land through his football prowess with his native county and with his province.

Three days later, at their funerals in Knock, Monsignor Horan met Taoiseach Charles J. Haughey for the first time, although he had known Haughey's mother, brother Fr Eoghan and other members of the family for many years through their visits to the Shrine. In fact, Mrs Haughey never visited Knock without seeking out the parish priest.

After the Requiem Mass and burials, which were attended by huge crowds, Monsignor Horan hosted lunch for Haughey, former Taoisigh Liam Cosgrave and Jack Lynch, and Dr Garret FitzGerald, the Fine Gael Leader, who stayed only for a cup of tea before moving on to another appointment. By then Haughey and some of his ministers had received copies of the TAI feasibility study and in his few words of welcome Monsignor Horan referred light-heartedly to the plans for the proposed airport.

Tom Neary recalls that, in like jovial fashion, Haughey replied: "Oh, I will give it sympathetic consideration."

To which Jack Lynch warned with a smile: "Now James, don't take too much notice. That's not a commitment that he's going to do it."

Monsignor Dominick Grealy had no problem in visualising the scene: he had seen his lifelong friend in action so many times before in similar circumstances. "He'd have said, 'Of course you will, Charlie. Of course you will. Why wouldn't you?', and roaring laughing at the same time. Nobody else could have done it, anyone else would not have said it so publicly. They'd wait for the occasion, maybe take the person into the other room and say it quietly. But that was James's approach, the direct approach, and he'd do it with this big infectious laugh.

"Himself and Charlie were so alike in ways. They didn't always follow the conventional route; they just got on with it. They were business-like people and if they thought they were right they'd go for it. Without them the Airport would not have happened."

One way or another Horan took the exchange as encouraging. In fact his right-hand man at the Shrine, Tom Neary, in an interview for this book, says he always considered that as 'the beginning of some serious business, almost the confirmation that Charlie was really keen all along to do something for the area'.

That lunch became to be known as the most costly Taoiseach Haughey ever had. The man who coined the memorable lines was John Healy, who, in his colourful *Irish Times* column a year later wrote: "It must have been the most expensive lunch the Taoiseach ever had. He has given the people of Connaught the greatest break that they ever got during the past century." It was a descriptive stick to be taken up time and again and used by politicians opposed to the airport to beat the project around the head.

Monsignor Horan wrote in his Memoirs that though he met Haughey on several occasions while he was Taoiseach, he never met him alone, so, as he put it, there were no opportunities for 'strokes,' 'deals' or 'intrigues'. But he knew Haughey had a sentimental attachment to the West of Ireland, in the same way that Jack Lynch had for Cork or Garret FitzGerald had for Dublin.

On September 23 Monsignor Horan was to bump into Haughey again when he attended the opening of the Central Remedial Clinic in Dublin, which Dr Ken Holden, the author of the TAI report, now headed up. They exchanged pleasantries and Haughey said he was looking forward to attending Mass in Knock the following Sunday. Later in the corridor their paths crossed again when the Taoiseach was passing with his entourage.

"Mr Haughey laid his hand on my shoulder and said, 'I am hopeful that your airport will materialise', to which the Monsignor responded, 'I hope so'," the Monsignor later recalled. The cause had received the official nod, the green light had been given: that was certainly the impression the Monsignor's smile conveyed to those who collected him from the train that evening at Claremorris.

The following days were to prove even more encouraging for the project and its promoters. Indeed Thursday, September 25, was to be a landmark day. It was just over four months since TAI had finished their report, and now the Monsignor was taking his deputation to the Department of Transport in Dublin in search of approval. Monsignor Horan later recalled that they met Minister of State Padraig Flynn in a nearby hotel beforehand, and Flynn turned to him and said: "You shut up and let me do all the talking." A brash and confident Padraig Flynn was obviously emerging.

A high-powered team of civil servants received the deputation. The Monsignor and his delegation had prepared well for the meeting which lasted for over two hours and was, according to the Monsignor, forthright and candid. Two main issues were discussed, the meteorological conditions and the make-up of the soil, issues which the Monsignor felt were comprehensively dealt with there and then.

The deputation had hardly reached the outskirts of Dublin on the way home when Minister of State Flynn issued a press release, headed 'Approval for Co. Mayo Airport'.

This crucial statement read: "Mr Padraig Flynn, T.D., Minister of State at the Department of Transport, has announced approval in principle for the development of an airport in Co. Mayo to cater for current and future Western needs, including particularly pilgrimage traffic for Knock Shrine. Mr Flynn made his announcement after a meeting with a deputation led by Monsignor James P. Horan, Parish Priest of Knock, Co. Mayo, in connection with proposals for the development of airport facilities to serve Knock and the Connaught region generally.

"The deputation was accompanied by Mr K. Holden of Transport Analysis International Ltd., Shannon, whose company had carried out an assessment of the feasibility of developing a Regional Airport to serve Connaught.

"As a result of earlier discussions between the Minister of State, Mr Flynn, and Monsignor Horan, representatives from the Technical Services of the Department of Transport had visited Mayo and carried out preliminary inspections of a number of sites which had been identified locally as being suitable for airport development purposes. The meeting reviewed the outcome of these technical inspections and went on to discuss broader issues affecting the cost and viability of the project. Further detailed examination of these aspects is to be undertaken in order to establish the nature of the facilities to be provided and the scale of operations that would be appropriate. (Author's Note- This last sentence had all the hallmarks of a civil service attempt at damage limitation!).

"Mr Flynn said he was extremely pleased to be in a position to convey this approval in principle and he congratulated Monsignor Horan and the other members of the deputation who had undertaken the preliminary work. He was satisfied that the development of the proposed airport would confer significant benefits on the region in terms of industrial development, the growth of pilgrimage traffic to Knock and the facilitation of tourism in Mayo and the adjoining counties. It would represent a major step in the improvement of accessibility to the West of Ireland which had been handicapped in the past by transport and communications difficulties. He believed that with the continued increase in our population and the resumption and acceleration of economic growth and taking account also of the tremendous potential for mariculture development along the Western Seaboard, there would be an increased role in the future for air services to regional centres, with connections to the three existing international airports at Dublin, Shannon and Cork."

It was an extraordinary press release by any stretch of the imagination in that there had been no Government decision to go ahead with the project, and one can only imagine the chagrin within the key departments of the civil service. However, such approval could only have come with the acquiescence of the Taoiseach.

The very day after the 'approval in principle' announcement, the Minister for Finance, Gene Fitzgerald, informed his department – which was concerned by the cost implications – that what the Taoiseach had in mind for Knock was a grass airstrip and not an airport as announced. This despite all the evidence that Haughey had been furnished with the TAI report and was well aware of what the Monsignor was seeking and had already agreed in principle. Gene Fitzgerald would also have been aware that a precedent had already been set when Waterford and Sligo were given virtually 100% subventions towards the provision of local airports. On the same day that Flynn made his 'in principle' announcement, the Minister for Finance was being advised that the country already had at least one surplus airport of scheduled flight standard . . . and arguably two. He was warned by his key advisers the country did not need a third.

Back in Mayo the euphoria was palpable: within a year of the Pope's visit to Knock, an airport had been conceived, a feasibility study done, a legal option on land secured, money had been spent on engineering surveys and outline planning permission had been sought from Mayo County Council, and now 'approval in principle' had been granted by the Minister of State at the Department of Transport. It was surely all too fast for the mandarins in the civil service, but they were being swept along by the momentum which the project had gathered with Monsignor Horan firmly in the driving seat.

On Sunday, September 28, when Taoiseach Haughey attended Mass at Knock on a tour of the West, accompanied by Fianna Fail politicians, there was no reference made to the airport. But later that evening the Taoiseach attended a function in his native Castlebar where a plaque was being unveiled on the house where he was born at Mountain View. Two years earlier Haughey had been named Mayo Person of the Year by the Mayo Association in Dublin. Horan had been asked to unveil the plaque and say a few words, in the course of which he mentioned the quest for the airport and suggested that Haughey was the man to do it.

In a spontaneous gesture, the Taoiseach stood up and shook the Monsignor's hand firmly and said, 'Cinnte' meaning 'certainly'. Haughey was firmly on board. However, in Castlebar the local paper, *The Connaught Telegraph,* remained highly sceptical. It had seen promises before which quickly fell by the wayside, and in its issue of September 30 it took the approval in principle announcement with a large pinch of salt. "It (announcement) didn't state how much the airport would cost, what traffic it would handle or, even more significantly, where it would be based." And it added: "For what it's worth, on the day following the decision in principle on Mayo, Mr Flynn also gave his conditional blessing to an airport in Letterkenny. And he did so in the teeth of refusals by local landowners to sell the only suitable land available for the airfield."

Some twenty-five years later, looking back at the landmark events of 1980, Padraig Flynn painted the picture of the time as he saw it. "When the Pope came to Knock in 1979 it set Knock up as a major Marian Shrine, like Lourdes and Fatima. And it gave impetus to the Airport simply and solely to improve communications because we really were at a great disadvantage both in transportation infrastructure and communications infrastructure in the West of Ireland – it was always one of the great disabilities the West suffered."

Flynn said he believed when he announced approval in principle for the airport that a key consideration was the commitment given by the Government to small airports to serve the regions under the Investment Programme.

"Charlie Haughey was very high on this commitment to opening up the regions. There was a new era as regards transportation coming along, and isolation and the whole question about our position in Europe became a key element for the development of economic situations in Ireland."

He said Haughey was very keen to eliminate the bottlenecks of bad transportation. Small airports already existed at Farranfore and Castlebar, and under consideration were Sligo and Waterford and the proposed ones for Mayo and Donegal. "It was against that background that the commitment in principle came about. It was always intended and stated by me that the pilgrimage element of it was a key factor."

Flynn continued: "There was enormous goodwill for the airport and the thing was 'get it in place before Galway' who were making noises. But it was also a question of size of runway and this became the key element in the whole development of it, to cater for what was intended by the promoters.

"The Monsignor was a motivator and he had the two visions, the religious and economic vision. The religious one was very much in place, the visit by the Pope and his personal devotion to the Blessed Virgin. He had the economic vision as well and he talked about unemployment – he had a great social conscience. From our perspective, in my mind and the Taoiseach's mind, the airport was going to give the necessary lift to a deprived region and that was part of the Investment Plan 1981," added Flynn.

The civil service interpretation of the Investment Plan was very specific. To them it implied a small airport near Knock, similar to the one that existed at Castlebar. So, positioning themselves for the Interdepartmental Group which Minister of State Flynn had announced to look into the core issues, some civil servants were already homing in on the size of the airport, the cost of the airport, and on whether the promoters would put their money where their mouths were.

And the Department of Finance was particularly agitated, Minister Gene Fitzgerald being advised in the days and weeks following the approval in principle that the financial implications were immense, that the airport could not be operated at a profit, and not only would the State have to finance it, but it could be operated only with a continuing subsidy for the indefinite future.

Over in the Department of Transport, Posts and Telegraphs, Albert Reynolds had been keeping abreast of the quickly unfolding proposal: "After I received a copy of the TAI feasibility study I spoke to the Taoiseach about it and, as I suspected, Healy was in before me. I said I would bring it forward, but I had to study the proposal first, and whether we went any further or not was a matter for the Government. At that time there was little or no outside talk about it."

The Working Group had representatives from the Department of Transport, Department of the Taoiseach, Department of Finance, Department of Industry, Commerce and Tourism, Aer Lingus and Aer Rianta on board. It did not have a representative from the promoters. The Group was charged with undertaking a thorough review of the TAI plan, and, if, in the light of the outcome of the review, some adjustment of the promoters' proposals was suggested, it should formulate alternative proposals which would not be out of keeping with the spirit of the commitment in principle made to Monsignor Horan and his ad hoc committee.

Critics of the airport project were later to make reference to the extremely tight timescale allotted for the task. Usually, a six-month period would have been deemed reasonable for a review of this nature, but the Working Group was instructed to get the job done in weeks rather than months. The implication was clear: there would be no pussy-footing around!

The Group buckled down to the task, assembling for the first time on October 30, and it met on nine occasions, in addition to meetings some members had with the promoters. Assistance was also sought from and given by Bord Fáilte, Coras Trachtala and the IDA.

The national media began to take closer attention to what was happening in East Mayo and, in late September, Eanna Brophy, writing in the *Sunday Press,* found a confident Monsignor Horan proclaiming work would be underway inside a few months and Boeings would be landing at the runway two years thence.

But not before the influential magazine, *Business and Finance,* in its edition of October 16, raised the spectre of a 'White Elephant' for Mayo. It posed the question: does anyone seriously believe that Mayo (and as much hinterland as you care to add) can support an international airport? It also questioned Monsignor Horan's take on the costs.

And it asked Horan who would pick up the tab for building the airport?

"The Government, of course. Didn't they pay for all the others?" he replied. He did concede the airport would not make money, but, run on economical grounds, he hoped it would break even.

The article advanced the opinion that, economically, the airport was a complete white elephant. But, it added, " . . . it is not unknown in our little country for white elephants to breed – helped along by political necessity."

However, *Business and Finance* didn't see any immediate threat of a payout from the Government given the 'detailed evaluation' that had to be carried out, and that could take a long time, it reckoned. It asked Monsignor Horan if he would wait that long? "No," he replied, "if the Department shows signs of dragging its heels then we'll have to help them out of their rut!" Given the battle that lay ahead with the Civil Servants, unwise language perhaps, even if those who knew his style would have heard his laugh and seen the mischievous twinkle in his eye – but also recognised the steel in his resolve.

The last word on this occasion was with the financial magazine which warned: "He believes Mayo has been starved of infrastructural spending and he wants to change this. He is absolutely right of course but what a pity he has chosen so foolish and grandiose a scheme! He runs the risk of turning Mayo into a pressure group all on its own."

During this period a painting of Pope John Paul 11, by the celebrated artist Harold Riley of Manchester (his mother had Sligo connections), was on its way to Knock Shrine Basilica having been donated by the painter to the Irish community in Manchester who in turn presented it to the Shrine. Intermediary was Mayo-born Manchester business magnet Joe Kennedy who had approached Archbishop Joseph Cunnane with the offer which was accepted. Irish Customs and Excise charged £6,500 in duty, later returned on appeal. "It was crazy. Everyone was giving and yet Customs and Excise wanted £6,500 out of it!" Joe Kennedy later recalled. "Amen to that," Monsignor Horan probably said when he heard the story. Kennedy, as it transpired, was to become Chairman of the Airport Board almost twenty years later.

Another rival to Knock appeared in November when Strokestown in Co. Roscommon staked its claim as the most suitable location for a regional airport for the province. The Strokestown project was being backed by Westward Garage, one of the biggest garage groups in the country, and the promoters had stated that whether or not their site was approved as a regional airport centre for Connaught, it intended to press ahead with the construction of a £2.5m landing strip within Strokestown Park. It had taken its steer from the aforementioned Horner report (See Chapter 4.)

Galway, too, was casting envious eyes across the border, and John Healy was warning that there were moles at work trying to swing the Connaught Airport, if not to Galway itself, at least to Tuam. Anywhere in fact but the present Charlestown site in Mayo, he reckoned.

He went on: "Now I've had more than a bellyful of the regionalisation policy concept in which, in the interests of rationalisation, Mayo and Galway are treated as one unit for so-called better administration purposes; I've had a bellyful of it because when Mayo agrees, Mayo is left as the hind-tit, and the action moves into Galway, and once it has gone in there it's like trying to draw blood out of a stone. It isn't on: it doesn't happen. We get waffle – they always keep the action."

This time in Mayo there was action. On December 1 1980 Connaught Airport Development Company Ltd was incorporated as a private company, and on December 2 the promoters were granted outline planning permission, having made application in October.

And on a bitterly cold and wet December 6, Minister of State Padraig Flynn was scheduled to raise the Connaught flag on the site at Barr na Cuige to signify that the project, in the eyes of the promoters, was going ahead. After the approval in principle decision the likelihood of a change of mind in Dublin was unthinkable. Bishops, the Kilkelly national school band under the supervision of Eamonn McAndrew, politicians from all over the region – with the notable exception of Galway, community supporters and a large crowd gathered on an exposed hillside.

However, as the clock ticked down to the appointed time, Flynn was heading not in the direction of Charlestown but for Casualty at the County Hospital! He had been travelling through Breaffy, outside Castlebar, in the State car towards his keenly anticipated appointment when there was a thudding collision with a tractor. The Minister of State's long legs took the brunt. "As a result I lost a knee joint and spent nine months on crutches. The injury put me above in St Vincent's Hospital in Dublin and Castlebar Hospital and left me with one knee joint less . . . Flynn paid a little for Knock," he remembers somewhat painfully.

His Ministerial colleague in East Mayo, Seán Calleary, stepped into the breach and praised Monsignor Horan for his vision and also praised the goodness of the people who gave the land.

In reply Horan gave fulsome praise to Taoiseach Charles J. Haughey, Transport Minister Albert Reynolds, Padraig Flynn, who, he said, had done a wonderful job, and the landowners who had given the necessary lands quickly and at a very moderate price.

Local contractor Frank Harrington, who had built up a very good working relationship with the Monsignor over much of the previous decade, was aware of talk of a small airport. "That was really the basis on which we became involved, for if we had heard mention of a big airport we would probably have backed off, thinking we did not have the expertise. Then we heard more land was being purchased for a bigger airport and we continued on. It happened just like that. I knew the Monsignor was not a man to start something that he could not finish."

His first job was to cut out a road into the site in preparation for the raising of the Connaught flag on December 6. Consulting engineers Maloney and Miller were later employed to do the trial holes, and the planning in association with John Balfe.

Meanwhile, the Interdepartmental Working Group was nearing the end of its deliberations close to Christmas 1980, and the Department of Finance was arriving at the conclusion that the TAI study had been found to be seriously deficient in several important aspects. So much so in fact that it believed the approval in principle, announced by Minister of State Flynn on 25 September, could not reasonably be regarded as a binding commitment which had to be followed through with a financial allocation.

And alarmed at newspaper reports that work was to start shortly at the site, Finance warned that the promoters had no authority to award contracts or incur expenditure without prior consent. Battle lines were being drawn.

CHAPTER SIX

1981: RTÉ asks what's going on here? – Civil servants' chagrin –
Cabinet approval – Go kill some sheep – First Board meeting – Aer
Rianta fears – Archbishop's concern – First sod cut and the story of
the spade – Galway gets tongue lashing – Aer Lingus flight hijacked

We're building an airport but
don't tell them!

THOUGH contracts had not been awarded, Frank Harrington, on the
Monsignor's say-so, started work on a proper road into the site on 6
February, 1981. Drainage work had to be done, and a parking place for
the heavy machinery had to be prepared. Bog was on average 2m thick,
lying over rock.

It did not deter Harrington: "It was great ground really. There was
no money on the table but, knowing Horan's reputation as a doer, I
knew it would be coming." Based on trust, millions of pounds worth of
equipment trundled onto the site.

The Working Group issued its findings to appropriate
departments on 4 February 1981.

"Their conclusions differed quite considerably from the TAI study
on a lot of things. There were differences over costs between the reports,
length of runway, staffing, losses, etc. The TAI were talking about a
break-even situation, while the Working Group were predicting losses of
about half a million pounds per year in certain circumstances," recalls
Padraig Flynn who had been keeping a very, very close eye on the
emerging recommendations!

"The Working Group's conclusion was that no option justified it
on purely economic terms but that other issues did and should play a
role and that was the socio-economic and political issues, and of course
we had already given a commitment for regional development.

"The involvement of the State became a key issue too. It was
important that neither the State directly nor through Aer Rianta were
to be closely associated with the on-going management for economic
reasons, that there would have to be tremendous flexibility in the
operation of the airport," added Flynn

The Working Group reported that the suggested location seemed
to meet the catchment area criteria well. It also noted that of the six

sites selected by the promoters, the Barnalyra site was aeronautically the most acceptable.

The Group also confirmed the view of the Meteorological Service that operationally disruptive conditions due to low cloud and poor visibility would be more disruptive than in Dublin or Shannon because of the altitude, but added that operationally disruptive conditions might not be as common as at Cork.

Broader questions as to whether the country needed a fourth full-scale airport were not addressed at all. The development of a new local aerodrome in Sligo was also excluded from their reckoning.

It also reported that visits to the site by Aer Rianta personnel indicated that the Barnalyra site was a difficult but not impossible one, due mainly to the massive earthworks involved.

In relation to the capital costs likely to be involved, the Working Group disputed the TAI study which estimated that the airport runway of 6,000 ft could be built at a cost of between £5m and £6m at 1980 values.

It also did not agree with John Balfe's costings for a 7,500 ft runway and apron space with accommodation for three 737s which Balfe estimated would cost £7.5m, a sum the Work Group said did not make provision for navigational aids (£0.5m), the acquisition of fire and general services equipment (£0.3m), or for security fencing of the airfield (£90,000).

The Working Group estimated that a 6,000 ft runway (which Aer Rianta and Aer Lingus said was adequate for 737s), together with apron space for one 737, taxiway connection, airfield lighting and visual navigation aids would cost £7.2m. Additionally, fire and general service vehicles and navigational aids would cost a further £700,000 to £800,000. In their eyes, therefore, the total cost for a 6,000 ft runway and facilities would cost in the region of £8 million at 1980 prices. Of that sum, over £3 million would be in respect of earthworks.

Furthermore, construction of a 7,500 ft runway, based on Aer Rianta estimates, would cost £12m, it said, pointing out that the difference in their estimates and the Balfe costings was due to calculations of excavation quantities, Balfe citing a lower figure.

The Interdepartmental Report estimated that the annual cost of servicing a capital expenditure of £8 million (for a 6,000 ft runway) would be in the region of £1.3million p.a. at an interest rate of 15.75% over a 25-year amortisation period, though it admitted there were no direct charges in the Aer Rianta accounts for interest or depreciation at the State airports since all capital assets were vested in the Minister for Transport.

The Working Group found it hard to quantify the potential of the religious tourism market, but stated it was of the view that development of a large pilgrimage market centred on Knock Shrine could well be the key issue which would determine the viability of the airport.

However, the Working Group put its estimate in relation to numbers of passengers on a scheduled Connaught Airport-London service at an upper limit of 26,000 a year, and set a lower limit at a mere 13,000. These figures contrasted sharply with the TAI estimates of 36,000 passengers in 1983 (the projected year for commencement of operations), rising to 40,000 to 50,000 passengers per year for all destinations through the airport. But, the Group conceded, forecasting passenger numbers was an inexact science. Cork Airport, for instance, had been projected to have 30,000 passengers in its first year and it in fact achieved 76,000, it pointed out.

Referring to cargo traffic, the Working Group mentioned that live animals and meat products were usually exported by air freight in larger volumes and over longer distances, and aircraft normally used in such trade required a runway of about 7,500 ft. However, it added that the extra £4 million to provide a 7,500 ft runway could not be justified for this traffic alone. We will return to this central point later in this chapter as it probably explains in part the rationale behind the Monsignor's insistence on pushing for the longer runway.

In terms of operating costs, TAI pre-supposed achievement of the maximum degree of flexibility in working arrangements and manning, with the primary aim of a break even position within a total revenue range of between £140,000 and £250,000; the Government Group accepted that flexibility in manning would be crucial if the airport was to achieve break-even. It warned that, if the Airport was to have staffing on the lines of the existing State airports, costs would exceed £1 million per year.

And where TAI and the promoters were projecting a break-even situation on operating costs, the Working Group said the best that could be hoped for was a £20,000 profit, with no account taken of costs of State services like Customs, Immigration, or capital charges of £1.3 million. But the downside was that instead of a profit on day-to-day operations, the losses could be in the region of £30,000.

Judgement on the viability of the Knock-to-London flights was even more pessimistic in the eyes of the Working Group. It predicted losses to the operating airline were likely to be between £150,000 and £500,000 a year. The annual loss expressed in terms of cost per passenger would be in the range of £70 to £90, meaning in effect that every passenger using the airport would have to be subsidised by that amount.

Summarising, the Working Group found themselves in somewhat of a dilemma. Going ahead with the full-scale facility as proposed by the promoters was 'fraught with unattractive financial prospects'. But on the other hand, irrespective of where the airport was located the prospects of mounting viable air services and operating an airport on even a break-even situation were 'remote'. Against that background, the Working Group reported it was unable to formulate any clear-cut recommendations.

The 'approval in principle' pledge was acknowledged in passing by the Working Group. While not necessarily sharing the validity of that commitment, the Group conceded that it would be difficult to visualise the promoters accepting a shorter length of runway (anywhere in the range 2,000 to 5,000 ft) incapable of extension beyond its initial length as being in keeping with the spirit of the commitment.

So the Working Group left the door ajar in its final comment: "Overall, our work has shown that there is no option which, in the view of the Group can be justified in purely financial/economic terms. Decisions on the nature of the facilities and the scale of operations to be provided, will, we suggest, have to take account not only of the financial/economic aspects on which our study by its nature had to concentrate but also on wider issues of a socio-economic and political nature." That final sentence, allied to the unquantifiable potential of the pilgrimage traffic, provided the gap in the fence through which the project escaped the bureaucratic net.

Albert Reynolds recalled the report as being neutral enough. "You could read it any way, but when the word got out there were plenty of recommendations from all over the place, including the Shannon Airport people who expressed concern."

It was known within the Civil Service that Minister of State Flynn had not been happy with the initial draft report but was meeting stiff resistance from Departments other than his own who sought, naturally, to preserve their own independent line. The Minister of State, according to reports at the time, wanted the Group to produce a report which was acceptable to him. Some members of the Work Group saw that request as both 'irregular' and 'outrageous'and used those words in urging the Department of Finance to put down its foot. In fact the Department of Finance was insistent that the Department of Transport secure a Government decision on what type of airport was to be built before funds would be released.

To many in the West it boiled down to the classic case of who was running the country, 'faceless' civil servants or ministers elected to do a job of work. Flynn's ramrodding of the proposal, which, remember, clearly had the unspoken imprimatur of his Taoiseach, was following in a well established ministerial custom of looking after one's home base, and that practice is still widely followed today throughout the land, despite tighter controls - and ministerial denials!

Concern within Finance was to escalate still further in mid-February when Monsignor Horan stood in front of the RTÉ cameras at the busy airport site and was asked by an incredulous Jim Fahy: "What exactly is going on here?"

Monsignor (laughing): What do you think is going on? We're building an airport. And I hope the Department of Transport doesn't hear about it. Now don't tell them. We're going to have it built in a very very short time. You see the activity that's going on here. There's another load coming. I think it's marvellous, don't you.

Fahy: Are you being absolutely serious about what's going on here?

Monsignor: And we've no money, but we're hoping to get it next week, or the week after.

Fahy: You don't really have permission? And you don't have money?

Monsignor: Well, I'm not sure whether I have permission or not, but I'm going ahead anyway – just taking a chance.

Fahy: Are you trying to call somebody's bluff, or what exactly are you up to?

Monsignor: I'm trying to build an airport, and have it soon, because Connaught needs an airport very, very badly. See all the people that are unemployed around this area here. We have 600 on our list, and we're bringing them in and putting them to work as soon as possible.

Fahy: Monsignor, it seems absolutely incredible that you and a handful of other people here would jump the gun as it were, go ahead and start seriously talking about building an airport, definitely, certainly building the approach road at the moment, without having the government's full approval, without even being certain that this is a suitable location for an airport, and certainly having no commitment as . . .

Monsignor: I have met the officials from the Ministry of Transport and they've liked me very much and I know they won't let me down.

Fahy: You have to be bluffing!

Monsignor: Ah no, no, no, I wouldn't, no. I mean I'm very sincere, you know. I'm a very sincere person.

The programme might have made for great television. It was typical Horan, humorous and self-deprecating, and in Horan-speak, winking at the politicians who were onside and were prepared to push the project through a less-than-pleased bureaucracy. He was saying what was underway was no big deal, that the Mayos were taking it all in their stride, that they had to help themselves out of the morass. But no doubt in retrospect the usually canny media man privately regretted his performance given that it was being beamed out to a wider and more critical audience unaware of his whimsical sense of humour.

Those who knew him recognised it as vintage Horan; those that did not thought an ageing priest had lost the run of his senses.

And given that the project had only outline planning permission and government 'approval in principle' the programme was certainly enough to give some politicians and some civil service mandarins apoplexy. And they were not alone. Those who begrudged the new-found Mayo 'assertiveness', as John Healy termed it, were about the place and could hardly believe their eyes, most especially the more envious regional competitors who had been beaten to the punch by a wily old priest. Now on film Horan was 'hamming it' as Healy observed some years later.

"The Dublin establishment knew nothing of that Haughey decision (to build the airport) and less of the Monsignor's exuberance, his weakness for hamming and it was all to fall on that piece of (RTÉ) film," Healy was to recall in *The Irish Times* on hearing of the Monsignor's death in 1986

A caustic article in *The Irish Times* of February 24 (1981) probably encapsulated the feelings of many outside Mayo who had watched their screens in disbelief. The Monsignor was lashed; the programme makers were lashed, the writer, conceding that while the Monsignor's motives were selfless, he should not have been excluded from the journalistic standards that could be applied in investigations of, say, a Knock businessman.

The article went on: "The interview was conducted in an extremely light vein, as if Monsignor Horan was engaged in a piece of entertaining whimsy of little importance to himself and none to us.

"Admittedly, an opponent of the airport scheme (referring to a Ballina businessman and Junior Chamber member) was given the opportunity to criticise the operation. He pointed out that Aer Rianta had to subsidise Cork and Shannon airports as it was. Would Aer Rianta end up subsidising an airport it did not build? one asked.

"Building airports is a serious matter best left to airport builders. It is not the job of clergymen, no matter how well-intentioned. Monsignor Horan assured us that he had the Government's favour in the whole matter. That work is well underway on a project that has just outline planning permission without the Irish people or the experts being consulted is an extremely serious matter. The Catholic Church is already well enough established in this country without it deciding on when and where to build airports."

The article was to set the tone for much of the media criticism that was to follow.

Finance Minister Gene Fitzgerald had been appraised of the television programme, and the fact that work appeared to be underway annoyed him. He thundered off a letter to Transport Minister Albert Reynolds expressing his alarm, and again urged his colleague to bring the Working Group's findings before Government.

Albert Reynolds recalls the sequence of events: "First of all the Department of Finance did not want to hear about it, but then what's new? They wrote me a letter after it was made public that the Monsignor had bought over 500 acres. I got a second letter saying there was no Government decision and 500 acres had been purchased and I wrote back a sharp letter saying if some private individual decides to buy 500 acres in Mayo it is his business, nothing to do with me. I didn't pay out any money for it.

"I remember getting another letter from the Minister for Finance after the Monsignor was on RTÉ with Jim Fahy. That letter complained the project was going ahead without any approval. I replied to the effect that when the Government approved it, it would be handled in the normal way, that the details of the project would evolve before we were asked to give a decision. I also wrote to Monsignor Horan pointing out that no approval had been given by the Government, and any work carried out in advance of approval might not be subject to grant monies thereafter.

"I was aware that the promoters had improved access to the site which was their private property. That's all that was done. No work whatsoever was undertaken on the apron, the runaway, or the taxiway prior to the Government decision," he asserts.

When the Cabinet met on April 15 1981 the Airport was on the agenda and the Department for Transport, Posts and Telegraphs brought its memorandum to the table. Finance had been given only two days' notice and complained that time should be given for proper consideration of the issues. That view was swept aside.

Minister Reynolds told the Cabinet he was satisfied that the best course of action was to proceed with the construction, built to ICAO (International Civil Aviation Organisation) standards, with a 6,000 ft runway and supporting facilities, including navigational and landing aids to enable operations under Instrument Flight Rule conditions. Aer Lingus had indicated that a 6,000 ft runway would be adequate for Boeing 737 services. The cost (at 1980 prices) was estimated at £8 million.

In relation to financing the operation, the Minister proposed that it be funded by way of Exchequer grants from the Vote for the Department of Transport. As the special Budget Subhead was a new one, monies could not be released until after the Vote had been passed by the Dáil and the promoters would have to make temporary arrangements to cover expenditure in the interim. It was likely that expenditure on the airport in 1981 would exceed the £0.5 million subhead provision.

The Minister indicated ownership of the airport was to be vested in a private company established by the local promoters, with representation from Departments of Transport and Finance on the Board of Directors. The ownership issue was later to become another controversial aspect of the airport with detractors claiming there was not a precedent in the whole of Europe for a public facility to be financed out of public funds and yet remain under private control. But, as we see here, the Government decided ownership was to be vested in a private company already incorporated . . . 'with a view primarily to ensuring adequate control of Exchequer funding of the project'. {Note: The promoters incorporated Connaught Airport Development Company Ltd as a private company on December 1 1980, before Government approval was granted but subsequent to the approval in principle accorded on September 25, 1980.}

The Government further decided that supervision of design, tendering process and construction work was to be undertaken by Aer Rianta on a commercial basis, with the local company to be a legal entity which would acquire the land, employ consultants, place contracts, etc. And the Minister proposed that, in the interest of keeping operating costs to a minimum, day-to-day management of the airport was to be left in the hands of the local promoters.

Though Finance Minister Fitzgerald advised the cabinet that the scheme hadn't been properly evaluated, and objected strenuously that the project was being rushed through without proper consideration, the Government approved the Minister's proposals. Monsignor Horan was over another hurdle.

But within the permanent government, i.e. the civil service, there was fairly widespread agreement with the Finance view that the 'artificial air of urgency which had attached itself to the project needed to be called to a halt if costly mistakes were to be avoided'. The Department of Finance, which would ultimately have to pick up the tab, knew that potential national expenditure excesses of over £300 million had already been identified by April, so it was in its own interests – and the national interest as it saw it – to ensure that anything that would aggravate that position further should be resisted.

Of course, in the West of Ireland, where communities had existed on crumbs since the founding of the State, that argument cut very little ice. Sure wasn't money being found every day of the week to shore up various propositions and dead ducks elsewhere while the emigration drift from Connaught was again turning into a torrent ran the counter argument from western interests.

Padraig Flynn had no qualms: "The Government did decide that the responsibility for the airport project would rest with the Department of Transport and half a million pounds was included in the Budget under the Department's Subhead. We were determined that Knock was going to be funded directly," he says.

It was a view shared by his Minister, Albert Reynolds: "Yes, there were an awful lot of people who thought it was daft. But I took the view then that Connaught needed an uplift and the money that appeared to be involved was not outlandish. It was a lot of money for that day but for an investment of that kind and for something that was going to service the area, I did not see it as outlandish. But we all knew that if you had the fixed costs that Aer Rianta would have brought to the project it would have dragged it down before it started."

Former Taoiseach Reynolds, who had got to know Horan well in the old showband and ballroom days of the '50s and '60s, says he remembers clearly the Monsignor offering the first £1 million on the table for the project after it had been agreed to by the government. "I told him I wanted to see it done, so you keep your million. You run the airport, we won't be involved in the running of it and it won't make money for some time so you will need your million to cover your losses. We will put the airport there; you manage it."

Where that million pounds was to come from is an intriguing question, but finding it would not have fazed Horan who had a long and successful history of raising funds for various projects. As matters transpired, he had to raise multiples of that before the airport opened.

The Department of Transport's advocacy of Knock was opposed all over the place, including from within Government where ministers were looking for approval for proposals much nearer to their own hearts, recalls Reynolds.

Amongst the most vehement public opponents was Shannon Airport Advisory Committee which, in behind-the-scenes meetings, told the Minister that Knock, in the elaborate format proposed, was not to their liking. The Group's PRO Kevin Reynolds was reported in the *Sunday Press* on March 22 saying that while they would accept that 'the proposed terminal would be mainly catering for invalids, we would see it as a threat to Shannon'.

But back to the Monsignor's desire for a 7,500 ft runway. He always knew that to take wide-bodied aircraft, to facilitate transatlantic flights and to link up with Marian Shrines around the world he needed a decent runway, and he knew if he didn't get it now he never would. However, another powerful reason was the potential for air freight and especially for meat products. And the source of that potential lay just down the road at the Halal Meat Packers' plant in Ballyhaunis.

Sher Mohammed Rafique, originally from Pakistan, had arrived in Ballyhaunis in the seventies and had quickly established a thriving meat processing business. By 1980 he was employing 150 staff and was processing 50 per cent of the total lamb kill in the Republic and had a foothold in the beef processing sector. He was just about to embark on phase two of an expansion blueprint on a 250-acre site and had set a turnover target of £150 million and a doubling of his workforce by 1985. Halal was then the only Muslim-owned processing business in any of the EEC countries and had access to Middle East markets because all animals were slaughtered in strict accordance with the Islamic ritual as prescribed in the Koran.

Apart from their business acumen, Horan and Rafique were to have something else in common: the Knock parish priest had built

Ireland's biggest church, the Pakistani businessman was to go on to build Ireland's first mosque, in Ballyhaunis, opposite his meat plant.

And the two men saw eye to eye. Rafique speaks fondly of his 'old friend': "I was air freighting meat through Shannon and he knew it, and when he came to see me in the late 1970s he knew more about my company than I did myself. He knew I was giving jobs to people, that I was buying up lambs and helping the farmers. He said, 'What would you think of an airport at Knock that you could export from?' and I said, 'Why not!'

"I forgot about it until he called again, probably in 1980 and he told me he had bought the land for an airport. He said to me: 'Don't ask me how much I paid for it, but I got the land.' We went to see the site, up the bog in the middle of nowhere! It was very rough terrain, but he pointed out the possibilities: 'This will be for industry, this will be for the runway, this will be for...' I replied, 'An airport is one thing, industry is another. Who do you think will come here to set up a factory?' And he replied, 'You never know!'"

Horan asked Rafique to join him. "I told him I was too busy, I was living in England and commuting. I said I would talk in support of the airport, would use the airport but could not afford the time to get involved to that degree. The rest is history, nice history," says Rafique.

Rafique knew a few politicians in Dublin, and went to talk to them to see what they thought about an airport in Mayo. "They said it was a crazy idea! I remember leaving the highest office in the land one day and the occupier (whom he did not name, but it was clearly C.J. Haughey) said: 'You are crazy. Go and kill some sheep!' I said it was not my doing!"

But he did promise Monsignor Horan that he would use the airport rather than go to Shannon which they were using three or four times a week at that time.

As we have seen from the Government Working Group deliberations of 1980/81, aircraft normally used in such trade as meat shipments required a runway of about 7,500 ft. So here was another powerful imperative for Monsignor Horan to push for his 7,500 ft: the potential for catering for Halal's growing export was clearly in the back of his mind.

Back in Dublin in May, the civil servants were trying, as they saw it, to bring some order to the headlong development in Mayo. But backers of the airport had another view: they saw the mandarins as 'getting in the way of the development'. With the first meeting of the new company due in June, the issue of funding began to crystallise. Civil servants were at pains to point out that the £500,000 allocated to the Budget Subhead for small airports was quickly dissipating. Minister Reynolds had already promised £150,000 for Farranfore Airport in Kerry and a further £90,000 to Abbeyshrule Airport in Co. Longford, leaving a mere £260,000 in the Subhead, while the work done at the Connaught Regional Airport site, including purchase of land, already exceeded £500,000.

On the home front, too, Deputy Paddy O'Toole of Fine Gael was locking horns with political opponent Padraig Flynn over what he saw as the lack of financial commitment to the project so far and he suggested the Government was holding it back as 'an election goodie'.

Flynn dismissed the claims 'scornfully' according to the *Western Journal*. He said provision had been made in the Subhead under his Department's estimates for £500,000, the first time in the history of the State that such a subhead had ever been introduced. "It is a contingency figure, a starting point to which other cash is added when needed. Normally such subheads are for amounts like £5 or £10," he retorted. Political sensitivities were being rankled on the home front!

By now Aer Rianta was making it quite clear that they did not want any involvement in the ownership or management of the airport, pointing out, not unreasonably, that it would be a much more expensive undertaking if they were seen to be involved. In other words, construction costs would go through the roof under the State body, a fact very well understood back in Mayo where the reaction was one of relief.

Michael O'Leary, Chief Executive of Ryanair, reckons the admission by Aer Rianta was a lucky escape for the Monsignor. "We'd all be terrified they'd be appointed to run anything. Put Aer Rianta in charge of a group of hotels during the greatest boom in tourism in twenty years and they manage to run it at a loss. Put the public sector in charge of anything and they will make a balls of it. They can't run anything properly and it's always run by unions."

MEP Jim Higgins agrees with the Aer Rianta comment. He says if the State agency had gone in and built the airport it would have cost ten times more than what the Monsignor did it for. "A lot of the work was done on a voluntary basis, he managed to get FÁS schemes and so on, he used every kind of device, and the net result was that we ended up with an international airport for a fraction of the cost of what the State would have done it for. It is the finest example of private enterprise that you could come across."

Back in 1981, Monsignor Horan was finalising the first Board of Connaught Regional Airport. John Healy was invited to the Presbytery with a few others where he reviewed the list of nominees. Some years later Healy wrote in his column in *The Connaught Telegraph* that one person declined the honour for personal reasons 'which James accepted in an understanding way'. The person was in fact Healy himself who told the Monsignor he could be of more help from the margins.

The name substituted for Healy was Sligo businessman Seamus Monaghan, a close acquaintance and business partner of Healy and

Castlebar garage proprietor Cathal Duffy through their joint shareholding in the *Western Journal* which was set up in 1978. In fact Duffy proposed that Monaghan – 'Ray MacSharry's side-kick and bagman' according to Healy – be appointed a director when Healy declined.

Seamus Monaghan has a very vivid memory of when he was asked. "I was sitting in my office one morning and a phone call came through from Monsignor Horan. I had never met him. I didn't know who he was really. And he said 'Hello, how are you doing?' I said, 'Great, what can I do for you?'

He replied: 'It's not what you can do for me, it's what I can do for you; would you like to join the Board of Connaught Airport?'

'I said we have our own airport in Sligo and I am a shareholder. What's this about Connaught airport?'

And he said: 'Yes, we are building an airport in Connaught for Connaught.'

I said, 'lovely.' I agreed to join just like that.

"Cathal Duffy then phoned me and said he had hoped to get to me before the Monsignor rang.

"The Monsignor wanted a representative from Sligo and he got me! He wanted all Connaught represented, and as far as I understand it he invited a Galway politician of Fianna Fáil persuasion to nominate someone in that county, and the reply was, "No, we want it in Galway."'

The founding Board consisted of nine directors: Monsignor Horan, Chairman; directors – Cathal Duffy, Archbishop Joseph Cunnane, Seamus Monaghan, Mayo County Manager Michael O'Malley, Roscommon garage proprietor P. J Casey, three civil servants nominated by the Government, Patrick Ryan and James Vincent Feehan (Transport), Stephen O'Neill (Finance). Jim Ryan was appointed Board Secretary/Director.

"The Board had as its objective the creation of a viable piece of lasting infrastructure in the West/North West of Ireland," says Cathal Duffy. "The vision of the Board was not alone to provide air services to the UK and beyond for the people of Connaught to have ready access to the region for business people and tourists but it was also their belief that such a regional/international airport would attract, in due course, significant inward investment and form a solid base for sustainable employment."

With all the comings and goings, all the meetings, all the deputations, growing media interest, and a full workload in his Knock parish and at the Shrine, Monsignor Horan was belying his years. His zest for the job amazed all about him. "The more he did the more energy he seemed to generate," recalled Fr. Colm Kilcoyne.

A source of huge support in all the unfolding challenges was his great friend, Archbishop Joseph Cunnane. Said airport engineer John

Balfe: "The Archbishop's support was crucial to the whole undertaking. Really, without that support Horan couldn't have moved."

But the Archbishop worried about his friend's onerous, energy-sapping workload and commitment to the task at hand, and when work commenced on the project the senior churchman turned to Balfe and said, "Seán, don't let him break the law."

"I knew he didn't mean it in the strict sense, for the Monsignor would never knowingly break the law. It was just that he had an issue with paying VAT on work done at the Shrine. People who made donations to the Shrine had paid their taxes already and he couldn't see why the State was taking a second bite, especially as the money was being spent on a national Shrine.

"So we had to keep the whole thing above board and that was the only alert the Archbishop gave me – 'don't let him break the law'. In his enthusiasm to get the job done he wouldn't consider everything, he wouldn't consider he was breaking the law. He was an incredible person, totally faithful and loyal. His word was his bond. He was a true priest, his vows were solid."

A few days before the first meeting of the Board, Monsignor Horan wrote to the Department of Transport making the case for a longer runway than 6,000 ft on the basis of talks he had had with the Boeing aircraft company in the USA. This prompted one civil servant to observe that the people in Cork would not take too kindly to the provision of a much bigger runway in Mayo than was available to them!

The inaugural meeting of the Board of Connaught Airport Development Company Ltd took place in the Department of Transport in Dublin on June 8, 1981 at 2.30pm. All the Board members, apart from Mr Vincent Feehan of the Department of Transport, were present. Also in attendance was the Board's accountant Michael Cosgrove and solicitor Ward McEllin. Monsignor Horan was in the chair and the civil servants present got a very quick indication that here was a man, and indeed a Board, not for turning.

The civil servants advised that the Board not acquire the site and the liability attaching to that date (circa £540,000) on the grounds that the company had not yet been assured of long-term funds through the passing of the estimate for the Department of Transport. Their advice was overruled.

The Board also resolved to appoint the contractor (Frank Harrington & Co Ltd, Kilkelly) to carry out the earthworks on the site. The contract was for £3.6 million and the work was estimated to take 52 weeks. The figure included price variation clauses and for some PC sums, so that the final cost for that phase was estimated to be in the region of £4 million, with approximately half of that likely to be spent in 1981. This meant that the Board would require £2.5 million in 1981, including the £540,000 already expended.

The Board had come under strong political pressure to award the contract to a Fianna Fáil contractor, as Frank Harrington, it was pointed out, had strong Fine Gael leanings. Sean Balfe says he was present when the overtures were made but the Monsignor refused to entertain such representations. "We kept it straight down the line and fought them off."

Back at the meeting the civil servants argued against the decision to place the contract immediately, but were again overruled. They did acknowledge, however, that as the contractor was highly recommended, that his price was very keen, and that Aer Rianta had approved the bill of quantities and the contract generally, the Steering Committee would have no option but to approve the tender.

It is understood the civil service representatives also warned of the risk inherent in incurring commitments before Dáil approval for the expenditure was given. However, it was the Board's view that the risk that the Dáil would not approve expenditure on the project was very small and they decided to push ahead. Shortly afterwards the Board arranged bridging finance of £750,000 from a commercial bank.

The Board of Connaught Airport had got off to a decisive and confident start, even if civil service feathers had yet again been ruffled. It was going to be full steam ahead at the airport, and that was good news for the many hundreds who had already applied for work on the site. The country's rising unemployment figures – 126,039 according to *The Irish Times* in March – were giving increasing cause for concern.

The storm clouds and the political implications looming on the horizon were forgotten, however, on May 2 when Minister for Transport Albert Reynolds, arrived to cut the first sod at the site. Five thousand people gathered on the high plateau for what was, according to Monsignor Horan, the most historic event in Connaught for over one hundred years. Clearly, the two main Sunday papers did not acknowledge the magnitude of the occasion for they had made no mention of an impending ceremony – nor indeed had radio or television. The airport was not yet in the controversial zone!

Minister Albert Reynolds, wielding a silver spade, sliced through the turf and sent a sod spinning into the air with gusto. He was flanked to his left by Monsignor Horan and Archbishop Cunnane, while on his right stood Deputy P. J. Morley. All four beamed for the *Western People* front page photograph, under the heading 'Yes, Faith Can Move Mountains!'.

Minister Reynolds had been invited to do the honours by Monsignor Horan who rang him weeks earlier to set up the date. "I remember him saying to me, 'We are going to make it worth your while the day you turn the sod for this. We are making you a nice presentation, and I hope you keep it in a place of honour. It's a lovely silver spade.'

"So I went down, turned the sod, and someone made off with the spade!" he laughed.

The story of the spade has made it into local folklore around Kilkelly, a village which has given its name to the epic 'Kilkelly Ireland' ballad on emigration.

Local businessman Stephen Tarpey, who was a staunch and early supporter of the airport, put a special request to the Monsignor.

"What's that?" Horan asked.

"I'd like to supply the spade to dig the first sod."

"Well now," he replied, "you are the first person to mention that so you can carry on with it."

Tarpey went across the village street to Joe Fagan and secured an ordinary spade, free of charge when the cause was explained. He then went to Tim Snee who lives just out the road and who won an All-Ireland medal at full back with Mayo minors in 1966 when Tarpey was a selector. Snee worked in Basta in Tubbercurry and Tarpey asked him to take the spade there and dip it in chrome.

'I will of course,' said Tim, and he had it back the next evening. The spade was sparkling and looking like silverware. Tarpey brought it over to Eddie Egan, jeweller and engraver in Castlebar, and got him to inscribe a band to fit around the handle 'Presented by the people of Kilkelly'.

"When Albert Reynolds arrived I handed him the spade and afterwards I got him to sign it, and then the Monsignor. I put it in a black bag and took it home for safe-keeping. I didn't know Albert Reynolds had been promised it. Later when Charlie Haughey came to perform the official opening in 1986 he signed it too, and on the day of the flights to Rome in 1985 the crew of the first Aer Lingus flight signed their names on it also."

In 2005 the precious, much-signed and still gleaming spade was presented to Joe Kennedy, chairman of the Airport Board, and it is now mounted behind glass for public scrutiny at the airport, adjacent to Fr Peter Quinn's selection of Mayo and All-Ireland GAA medals.

But we digress. Minister Reynolds said in a lengthy speech at the sod-cutting that the airport would do as much for Mayo and for Connaught as Shannon Airport had done for the Mid-West. Paying tribute to the drive and enthusiasm of Monsignor Horan, he said he regarded the Government's decision to approve the Connaught International Airport project at a cost of £8.5 million, at 1980 prices, as proof, if further proof were needed, of the Government's commitment to developing the West of Ireland. (Note: the Government commitment had been nudged up in the press release by £0.5m.)

The Minister referred to faint-hearted people who had cast doubts on previous aviation undertakings in Ireland, and he said he looked forward with great optimism to what the future held for the airport.

Monsignor Horan in his speech had a word for the cynics. They were for some time trying to make up their minds as to whether the airport would be a white elephant or a monster to gobble up Shannon, he said. "They need not worry, for nowadays, with modern technology, we can give the white elephant a lovely blue rinse. For after all, who can say that Connaught is not entitled to their airport, and I can assure you, Connaught will make good use of it. We are not casting envious eyes at Shannon or posing any threat whatsoever. We are, on the other hand, convinced that with co-operation and goodwill, we can be a great asset to Shannon and Shannon's Transatlantic traffic will be a great boon to us."

He praised Minister of State Padraig Flynn who was in attendance, still on crutches following his crash in December, and who, he said, had been given special responsibility by Taoiseach Haughey to get the project moving as quickly as possible. "Thank God that we had the right man in the right place and at the right time we made our move for an airport," he asserted.

The Monsignor expressed his deepest appreciation for the understanding, sympathy and enthusiasm that the Taoiseach had shown for the project, from the very first occasion that it was mentioned to him. He had given the people of Connaught the greatest break that they ever got during the past century, and he was certain the people of the province would not forget him for that.

He had praise too for local Dáil deputy P J. Morley and Minister of State Seán Calleary for their assistance. "It makes me very happy to know that the Government have approved of it and that they have the full support of the main opposition party," he added.

He also singled out the Fine Gael leader Garret FitzGerald who had visited the site a few months earlier: "And he told me that he was fully in favour of Regional Airports." Horan was keen to stitch that into the record, for in politics one never knew.

In the crowd was a strong Mayo Fine Gael representation including Deputy Paddy O'Toole, Senator Myles Staunton of Westport, former deputy Tommy O'Hara of Foxford, and Councillor Martin Finn. Also present were the Minister for Agriculture Ray MacSharry, and Minister of State Denis Gallagher, who had a few months earlier gained some recompense for losing his senior post in Haughey's 1979 Cabinet reshuffle.

Minister of State Flynn had by then been nicknamed the Messiah by Monsignor Horan according to Stephen Tarpey, and in keeping with that lofty elevation, the Castlebar man told Michael Finlan of *The Irish Times*: "There is something supernatural in this (project)." No doubt the civil servants and political opponents who had been rolled over in the Mayo *tour de force* had another word for it!

Bishop Thomas Flynn of Achonry performed the blessing, the

airport being in his Diocese. Political representation from Galway was noticeably bare, so much so that John Healy in his Sounding Off column in *The Irish Times* of May 4 let loose on an old hobbyhorse of his, regional equity or the lack of same.

"For close on two decades now the policy of regionalisation has been carried through by various Governments and that has meant that Ireland West is Mayo lumbered in with Galway. The two counties are Ireland's second and third biggest and while there is supposed to be equity in facilities and development, the sad experience is that when it came to locating personnel and office facilities and regional headquarters, Galway vacuumed everything into that city.

"Galway wanted – still wants – the province's regional airport and resents Mayo's assertiveness in ramrodding the project into the county. Sligo and Roscommon, however, see the regional benefit and had their political Ministers there to mark that approval," observed Healy from a Barnalyra vantage point overlooking his ancestral home in Charlestown.

Healy, with his dander up, also had a rattle at his friends in the civil service: " . . . the Reverend Horan of Knock bulldozed a new international airport out of the thin snipegrass soil and through a Dublin Civil Service which might have wished to gamble on his departure to his Heavenly reward but reckoned the odds against them because the Horans live to be a good age." (And if proof were needed for that assertion it could be found in the bright and sprightly frame of the Monsignor's proud 94-year-old mother, Catherine, who was at the ceremony.)

After the sod-cutting ceremony the guests repaired to the Beaten Path in Brize, Claremorris, for lunch. Outside the venue Minister Reynolds and the Monsignor were having a quiet chat in the sun when they were interrupted by a Garda Superintendent who took the Minister to one side.

"He informed me that an Aer Lingus 737 with 113 passengers on board had been hijacked en route to London and ended up in Le Touquet Airport in France. So I never got to the lunch. I had to head back to Dublin immediately," says Reynolds.

The trip back would have taken three hours by car but Airport Board member Cathal Duffy rang Castlebar Airport which was about 20 minutes away and by the time the Minister got there a small plane was fuelled and ready: 55 minutes later the Minister with responsibility for transport was at Dublin Airport to catch a plane to France to deal with the incident.

Remarkably, the hijacking had a connection with a Marian Shrine much admired by Monsignor Horan. The hijacker was an Australian, Laurence Downey, a former Trappist monk, who ordered the pilot to fly to Tehran. He was holding test tubes he claimed were filled with explosives. Bizarrely, his demand was that the Third Secret of Fatima be revealed. (Later it transpired that the secret foretold the gun attack by Turkish gunman Mehmet Ali Agca on Pope John Paul 11, who had been in Knock less than two years earlier. The Pope subsequently donated the bullet dug from his body to the sanctuary at Fatima where it was placed in the gold crown of the Madonna.)

The hijacking incident, which ended without loss of life or injury, was enough to ensure that the sod-turning ceremony for Connaught Airport was again pushed off the front pages of all the daily newspapers! But the airport was to be back centre stage within weeks, for Charlie Haughey was about to call a General Election.

CHAPTER SEVEN

1981: Charlie Haughey's cv - Fine Gael pledges £10m - Barry Desmond onslaught begins - Experts' thumbs-down - Union row - Government pulls out - Charlestown protest meeting - Minister attacked - Whore's kiss

Plug pulled after non-stop bombardment

CHARLES James Haughey had become Taoiseach and Leader of Fianna at the end of 1979. Both his parents were from Derry. His father was an officer first in the IRA, then in the Irish Army and he served in Ballina and Castlebar. Not long after Haughey's birth on September 16 1925 at Mountain View in Castlebar – he was delivered by legendary midwife Mrs Minch, a grand-aunt of Fine Gael leader Enda Kenny – his father developed multiple sclerosis and had to retire from the army. The Haughey family moved to Dublin.

After qualifying as an accountant he became actively involved in politics. His wife, Maureen, was daughter of Taoiseach Seán Lemass. On the fourth attempt, in the 1957 General Election he was elected to Dáil Éireann for the first time as a Fianna Fáil TD. He quickly worked his way through the ranks becoming Minister for Justice in 1961. He was of a new breed of politician, one of the 'men in mohair suits' brigade and close friends were Donogh O'Malley and Brian Lenihan. To John Healy they were a breath of fresh air after decades of civil war politics; he admired their style and ability and became a close confidant.

The political upheaval in the North in the late 1960s almost led to the end of Haughey's political aspirations. The Nationalist community was under attack and the Government set up a fund of £100,000 to provide aid. However, Haughey and his ministerial colleague Neal Blaney were accused of using the money to import arms for use by the IRA. Both ministers were sacked from the government by Taoiseach Jack Lynch.

By 1975 Fianna Fáil was in opposition but Haughey had rehabilitated his power base and won a recall to Lynch's Front Bench. Haughey was appointed Spokesman on Health & Social Welfare, and two years later, when Fianna Fáil returned to power with a massive majority thanks to a 'give-away' budget of reckless proportions, he

67

returned to the Cabinet after an absence of seven years. He was appointed Minister for Health & Social Welfare.

Following covert moves against him, Jack Lynch resigned and in the ensuing battle for leadership Haughey beat off the challenge of George Colley. On 11 December 1979 he was elected Taoiseach and leader of Fianna Fáil, almost ten years after the Arms Crisis nearly destroyed his political career.

By the time Haughey took over the reins of power the country was heading down the slippery slopes and into economic crisis. The profligate manifesto, which ensured the party's return to power in 1977, had grossly exacerbated an already worsening situation, and Haughey correctly identified the looming crisis.

The nation got an indication of how serious matters were when he went on RTÉ television on January 9 1980 and outlined a stark and disturbing economic scenario:

" . . . the figures which are just now becoming available to us show one thing very clearly. As a community we are living a way beyond our means . . . we have been living at a rate which is simply not justifiable by the amount of goods and services we are producing. To make up the difference we have been borrowing enormous amounts of money, borrowing at a rate which just cannot continue. A few simple figures will make this very clear . . . we will just have to reorganise government spending so that we can only undertake those things we can afford . . ."

But as the nation got ready to tighten its collective belt Haughey did a complete U-turn. Amazingly, he boosted public spending, which was soon out of control and led to increases in borrowing and taxation at an unwise level. Perhaps he was already looking to a General Election and a personal mandate? Whatever, circumstances conspired to take the choice of dates on which to go to the country in 1981 out of his hands. One was the H-Block hunger strike by IRA prisoners seeking political status. The other was the Stardust nightclub inferno on St. Valentine's night in which 48 Dubliners lost their lives. The Fianna Fáil Ard Fheis which was to take place the following day was cancelled.

Haughey eventually announced the dissolution of the Dáil on May 21, two weeks after Albert Reynolds had cut the sod to signal the start of work at Connaught Airport. The General Election was scheduled for June 11. It was to be the first of five general elections in the 1980s, and in many of them Connaught Regional Airport – or Knock as it was more commonly known by now – would be a political football many liked to kick. Indeed, the level of political instability was to dog the airport over the following five or six years.

However, for the June 1981 election both Fianna Fáil and Fine Gael supported the airport project, Haughey and Fine Gael leader Garret FitzGerald separately visiting the site and expressing support. The Fine Gael Leader even trumped Fianna Fáil when his East Mayo TD Paddy O'Toole promised not alone money for the airport, but an additional

£10 million to build a huge international sports complex adjacent to the site. The bidding war had started!

Paddy O'Toole remembers that the country was in election mode, and the Fine Gael front bench had discussed the project as it had become an election issue with local spokespersons demanding commitments to the project. "Our fear was that the airport would become a non-viable 'white elephant' unless additional elements of business could be created. It was in this context that the idea of a major sports complex was brought forward. It was felt that a 'sports centre of excellence' could be established that would appeal to international athletes in training.

"There was ample space in the vicinity of the proposed site and facilities could be provided for a training centre of world class that would result in putting Knock Airport on the map. It was felt within Fine Gael that while, politically, we had to support the concept we should ensure that it would be viable and some creative thinking had to go into establishing how additional revenue flow could be created. There was a general consensus that a 'stand-alone' transport facility would not be a viable proposition," he says.

The General Election saw Fianna Fáil take 45.3% of the first preferences to secure 78 seats, six down on where they had stood. Sympathy for the Anti-H-Block candidates who took two seats, and attractive tax proposals put forward by Fine Gael, cost FF dearly. Fine Gael gained 22 seats to stand at 65, while Labour, under Michael O'Leary, lost two seats to come in on 15. Failing to secure a majority in the 166-seat Dáil, a Fine Gael-Labour Party coalition came to power under FitzGerald. It was going to be a precarious foothold with the Independents, on 6 seats, holding the balance of power.

Contractor Frank Harrington began work on the airport runway proper on July 1. That same week the Coalition Government took office and discovered that the State's finances were in a perilous state. Dr Garret FitzGerald, when interviewed for this book, said after he received the seals of office on 30 June 1981 and before he got back to the Dáil to announce the members of his government, he was informed of the gravity of the State's financial situation. It was much worse than was publicly known, or had been known to him. He was told that current spending was running almost one-sixth above the budgeted spending level in addition to which a number of loss-making State enterprises required capital injections for which no budgetary provision had been made.

He said based on the current rates of spending and likely revenue receipts, the rate of borrowing likely to be required in 1982, exclusive of funding of the capital needs of State enterprises, was estimated at 21% of GNP as compared with the 3% borrowing rate that was considered prudent. "I had to call an immediate emergency Cabinet meeting and to bring in an emergency Budget three weeks later," he said of the perilous predicament his government inherited.

Paddy O'Toole was appointed Minister for the Gaeltacht, and Paddy Cooney got the Transport portfolio. Cooney's appointment was not taken as a good sign back in Knock, given that, while a FG Front Bench spokesman, he had declared that the airport was 'arguably one of the greatest white elephants in the western world.'

O'Toole recalls that on entering Government that July, Knock Airport was an item on the Cabinet agenda. He discovered it had been on the previous Government's agenda but had not been dealt with.

"The item before us sought that payment (the first State payment) from State funds would be made to meet the then accumulated costs incurred. Within a number of weeks the payment was made and I recall there was no major problem with my Cabinet colleagues. Within a short time of entering Government we had discovered, for the first time, what the real state of finance was. I recall we were appalled at how serious the situation actually was."

On July 7 Transport Minister Cooney supplied Government with a number of options in relation to the airport, and two days later the Department of Finance recommended the immediate cancellation of the project without the compensating building of a smaller airport. The Department of Finance acknowledged that its recommendation would almost certainly raise the issue of compensation for the contractor and would raise questions as to the ownership of the land. The Coalition government rejected the Finance recommendations and approved a grant aid allocation of £2.5 million.

But the Airport issue was quickly to prove very divisive. Back in Mayo the political heat was turned up full blast on O'Toole, as reflected in a trenchant piece in *The Irish Times* of August 4 by John Healy. He wrote that the bulldozers were one third of the way up with the runway and the job was going a bomb - "and had better be finished, or the dogs of the street won't drink O'Toole's blood if the airport and the sports complex aren't finished by the time Garret goes for the next election."

A minister on the government side knew how to play rough, too. Monsignor Horan was driving back to his presbytery late in September after being over to the site to see work progressing at a most impressive rate. The news came on the radio, and one of the main items was a blistering attack by Labour's Barry Desmond on Charles. J. Haughey. "It was the flash-point, the signal for a protracted, concerted, relentless attack on what Desmond insisted on calling 'Knock' Airport," the Monsignor retorted.

In his onslaught Desmond—who was Minister of State in the Department of Finance with responsibility for Economic and Social Planning – called on his Taoiseach to suspend all expenditure on the project pending a full review.

Desmond had, shortly after being appointed, asked to see the departmental files on Knock Airport in which he said he discovered serious reservations. In September he was given some estimates of the likely cost of the project. Including interest and essential services, it was estimated the cost would come to £20.5 million. And that at a time when Cork Airport had lost £961,000 in 79/80, and Shannon a whopping £1.85 million in the same period.

In an interview for this book, he remembers that when he went into Finance in 1981 the senior officials in the Department informed him that the International Monetary Fund was taking a very hard look at Ireland and on various capital projects, so much so that they were worried about the monetary stability of the country in the light of what happened from 1977 onwards. "There were massive debts, public expenditure deficits, and the over-expenditure of the State in its Budget amounted to huge money. In the light of that I began to look at all capital projects throughout the country. My responsibility had a very broad remit which I had sought and I wasn't just homing in on Knock Airport, but all projects of a capital nature."

He began to develop grave doubts about whether an airport could be built in Knock for the projected figure and eventually came to the conclusion it would require £20m. "Actually, it worked out at about £14m. by 1984/85, so my projections were not that far off when interest was taken into account. The figures were given to me by very eminent public servants who had no axe to grind, and many of whom incidentally were from the west of Ireland," says Desmond.

His onslaught on Haughey over the airwaves, followed up by a comprehensive press release – in which he called the spending 'outrageous' and questioned how the go-ahead decision had been arrived at by the Fianna Fáil government – brought an immediate rebuttal from Msgr. Horan. Refuting the claims, Horan said it would cost £8 million to £10 million, at 1980 prices, to provide the airport unless there was further inflation. "And that is something," he chided, "over which Mr Desmond has more control than the airport promoters."

In the end Horan's figures were to be much nearer the mark than Desmond's. Horan was to later claim he came in on budget and on time, which is not something that could be said about the more recent Port Tunnel and Luas in Dublin where the overruns alone would have built Knock Airport many times over.

But Desmond had his adherents. His no-holds-barred press release of September 29 won support on the Dublin doorsteps, and from TDs in all parties. One Fine Gael TD wrote to the Minister: "Good to hear you try and expose the scandal of the proposed airport at Knock, Co. Mayo, but it appears that our Government is lacking the guts to knock the project."

On that same date Junior Minister Desmond received at Dáil Eireann a postcard from Knock replete with a colour picture of Monsignor Horan holding the Golden Rose presented by the Pope to the Shrine. The unsigned message simply read: 'Prayed for you today'. In his book of political memoirs, *Finally and in Conclusion,* published by New

Island in 2000, Desmond observed: "At least he (the Monsignor) had a sense of humour about taxpayers' monies."

Sorry to spoil a nice story, but Desmond was mistaken in believing the postcard came from the Monsignor. Horan's handwriting was well known to the author and, having seen the postcard, it can be categorically stated it was not written by the builder of Connaught Regional Airport! Back in June 1982, Bruce Arnold, writing in the *Irish Independent*, made the original mistake by claiming the postcard had come from Horan. Those who knew the Monsignor also knew it was not his style to send the Golden Rose of Knock postcards with sarcastic comments to anyone. Horan refrained from refuting the erroneous claim, but told friends it was a pity Arnold did not visit the Airport and see for himself the good it would bring to the area.

Minister Paddy O'Toole, on behalf of the Government, rejected Desmond's 'pull the plug' demands. He pledged the project was going ahead as planned, with Government backing, but the words were no sooner out of his mouth when Desmond again attacked the project publicly. Looking back to those momentous events of the '80s, O'Toole says Desmond tended to indulge in 'doomsday' scenarios and not even his own party colleagues took much notice of his pronouncements. Be that as it may, the Labour minister had the bit between his teeth.

Taking advantage of the spat between the two men, Fianna Fáil leader Haughey nipped in and asked the Government to make its position on the airport clear, and he criticised it for rounding up the projected cost figures.

Picking up on the Desmond attack, the *Irish Independent*, in its editorial of October 1, questioned the need for the airport. "Can we, in times of black recession, afford to spend such sums? Does the region need an airport at all?" The attack did not come as a surprise to Horan who had by now come to accept that the paper was not 'friendly'.

A day later the *Irish Press*, in its leader, said whatever about the merits or demerits of the decision to build, Cabinet decisions should mean that – and at one time did mean – even junior Ministers accepted collective responsibility for them, whether or not they personally agreed with what had been decided. "Does Mr Desmond now accept the Cabinet decision that Knock airport goes ahead?" it asked.

Senator Jim Higgins, from nearby Ballyhaunis, was also highly critical of Desmond's remarks, but Dublin TD Nuala Fennell told a national Family Reconciliation conference that the money should instead be spent on family issues. Horan hit back, saying the church was spending much money providing such services.

Predictably, the Mayo papers rounded on Desmond's stance, the *Western People* of October 6 being fairly typical of the response: Under the heading 'Airport Begrudgers,' it stated: "If it (airport) were being built in his Dublin constituency – or, for that matter in the bailiwick of Galway's Deputy Michael D. Higgins – there wouldn't be a whisper of protest from those same sources. Indeed, Mr Desmond might ponder on the silence of the Western lobby with regard to the electrification of the Dublin rail links: no protest have been raised from this side of the country because the project is believed to be a worthy one, even if it is being carried out at the expense of rail users from this region."

But there were dissenters in Mayo, too. At a meeting of Mayo County Council a former chairman and controversial figure, Frank Durcan (Fine Gael) lashed what he termed the 'wasteful' airport proposal. *The Connaught Telegraph* of October 21 carried the report in which Cllr Durcan charged: "It will be the jobless in this region who cannot afford fresh meat for their children's dinners once a week who will pay for this scheme in years to come. There are people who will live to see the grass grow up through the middle of the strip."

He also declared that the airport was under the control of a private clique who were never elected by the people.

However, the council agreed to support the project.

The following week, in the same paper, the Mayo County Manager, Michael O'Malley, who was also a member of the Airport Board, defended the project. He said it was one thing for economists to make an analysis of the position and say that an airport was not justified.

"In general, economists would usually, if asked for a solution, tell us we have an interesting problem. But that is not a solution and it is necessary to provide a quick means of communication into Connaught and County Mayo in order to develop the total potential which is there," he maintained.

That same week, in the *Western People,* reporter Michael Ronayne made the case for the airport and quoted Charlie Haughey's reasons for backing it. Haughey told him he supported the project because it was important for Mayo and the West of Ireland generally. "It is more important than any physical, economic or commercial consideration in that, in my view, the airport represents an investment in individual inspiration, dedication and enterprise. You have people there who are going to make the project succeed no matter what happens," said Haughey.

Transport economist Dr Seán Barrett, a lecturer in economics at Trinity College, Dublin, entered the debate with a two-part series in *The Irish Times* in October. He argued that the TAI feasibility study commissioned by the promoters did not justify the £10 million capital expenditure they were demanding, and said even an expenditure of £5 million was not endorsed unequivocally by the study.

Saying former Taoiseach Charles Haughey had admitted the cost of the project could reach £10 million, whereas TAI had estimated a cost of £5 million to £6 million, he made an observation which the promoters found ludicrous: "There has been no explanation from the promoters why the cost has doubled although it has been claimed that the highest cost estimate of £20 million includes the Minister for the

Gaeltacht Mr Paddy O'Toole's international sports centre at the airport."

He questioned the TAI findings, the projected passenger and staffing numbers, operational costs, and the 'secret costs' which he itemised as a halt to the development of other small airports, a running down of rail services to Mayo and Sligo, and an annual loss of £150,000 on the Dublin-Knock air service. "It is apparent the airport has no chance of covering its running costs," he asserted.

In terms of the depressed economy, he held that diverting £10 million to £20 million from other investments under the capital programme would have a cost implication for the taxpayer. He pointed out that almost 90 per cent of PAYE income tax was being devoted to paying interest on projects on which politicians had bestowed capital write-offs.

Describing the growth of public-sector borrowing as an unwelcome aspect of Irish finances in recent years, Barrett said public-sector attempts to arrest it should be public knowledge, and it was, therefore, he argued, regrettable that the strong views within the public service against the project had not been published. His bottom line was that 'in a decade of reviewing public expenditure in this country, this is the worst project I have seen. It should not proceed'.

Dr Ken Holden, author of the TAI report, responded to the issues raised by Professor Barrett and other critics in an article in the *Irish Press*. He stuck to the main findings of the TAI report, saying the airport would be viable if run in the manner recommended, with flexible work practices and the waiving of interest charges (which was already being done in the case of State airports in Dublin, Shannon and Cork). He also stuck to his guns in maintaining that direct scheduled 737 flights to London would be commercially viable.

And he summed up his defence with a brave prophesy: "If the airport is run in the manner envisaged, I personally believe that the construction of this airport will eventually be seen to have been one of the most significant developments in Connaught in recent times, while the promoters will one day be looked on as men and women of outstanding foresight and vision."

Early in November the *Irish Press* reported a call from Michael Cox, general secretary of the National Association for Transport Employees, who thought building an airport to accommodate jumbo jets was 'really stretching the imagination'. Instead, he wanted the money invested in a rail link to Knock.

However, the Monsignor in response said that such a rail link would do little for the vast majority of the people of Connaught.

There was also plenty of media sarcasm about, and the *Sunday Press* of November 8 typified that with a colour piece which stated, in part: "Paddy O'Toole, whose political career might suffer a crash-landing if anything happened to the project, made a spirited defence of the airport plan at last week's Cabinet meeting. His Mayo colleague, Enda Kenny, said little. As secretary to the parliamentary party, he was too busy taking notes."

The story of an airport in a rural Mayo setting was spreading its wings internationally. *Time Magazine* of November 9 featured the airport under the double heading, 'Knock, Knock, What's There?' followed by its answer 'A $32 million airport, that's what, for a village of 400.' It re-ran all the old arguments, saying on the face of it the idea was absurd. It quoted two views, one from an anonymous official: "Fine Gael don't dare stop it." The second came from the Mayor of Sligo Eugene Henry who was purported to have said: "A good bus service would be better."

No one missed the chance to air their views. One of the most absurd comments originated at a public meeting of the Mayo Branch of the Campaign for Nuclear Disarmament in Ballina where it was claimed the airport would almost definitely be the target for a nuclear missile attack in the event of another world war breaking out!

* * *

But the *Irish Press* of November 12 rolled out much heavier gunfire when it reported that a Government adviser, UCD Transport economist Dr James A. Crowley, a consultant to the Department of Transport, had described the airport as 'defying credulity'. According to the report, he urged the Government to cancel the project, accusing the promoters of allowing their ambitions to 'run wild'. He also dismissed the notion of flexible labour practises offering the solution to viability as it would be 'impossible on a sustained basis under current Irish work practices'.

However, a day earlier Dr Crowley had delivered a lengthy and reasoned paper to the South-West Section of the Chartered Institute of Transport in Ireland, entitled 'The Crisis in Air Transport' and it contained very little of the emotive language quoted in the *Irish Press* the next day.

In his paper he set out to attempt three things: (a) to outline the forces at work in international aviation to give an understanding of where Ireland stood, and how the country fitted into the broader scene; (b) to analyse the precise financial situation of Aer Lingus and the options it faced, and (c) to assess the assessment procedures which should have been followed in relation to the Knock airport proposal, and for future proposals of that nature.

Dr Crowley pointed out that Aer Lingus was in deep financial crisis, and in 1980/81 had sustained a net loss of almost £17 million and he argued State investment of between £29 million and £54 million was needed to restore its equity-to-debt ratio to prudent levels.

Halfway through his paper he referred to Knock specifically, saying: "It seems particularly ironic, in the midst of Aer Lingus' problems, and those of Irish airports (Shannon and Cork in particular, where traffic needs boosting) that some £12 million to £20 million is to be spent on a project to build an airport which the country does not need and in circumstances which in any other country would defy the law of credulity. Maybe 'credulity' is another word for faith, but even so it must be realised that faith is a subjective thing. In a democracy, such as ours professes to be, there have to be procedures for objectively weighing up major investment opportunities."

He went on: "Pinning one's hopes on the uninformed beliefs of optimistic individuals may have a certain amount of appeal from a romantic/political point of view. But the harsh economic reality is that the rest of the world demands value for money, both with regard to the £20 million we borrow from it, and with regard to the services and products we sell to it using the facilities we create with the borrowed capital."

He believed the country could do with a debated and written-down airports' policy, if for no better reason than to state the ground rules and appraisal procedures to be followed in the event of another proposal such as Knock which, he conceded, was now water under the bridge.

Crowley said he was not particularly opposed to the development of Knock airport as such, nor was he suggesting that the Knock project should be singled out for his recommended approach to investment appraisal. In other countries such procedures were commonplace in all major investment and divestment decisions, not just in the transport sector but also in other sectors, such as health, education, energy, he argued. But, because of the absence of a proper overall appraisal, two important questions remained unanswered about the Knock project: first, whether an airport was the best way of spending money to develop the Knock and Mayo regions; second, whether the nature and size of likely returns was such that Knock was top of the list of potential areas for this level of expenditure in the country.

*   *   *

On November 11 the *Western People* published a lengthy article penned by Monsignor Horan in which he set out to clear up the 'misrepresentation and distortion' of the facts in many of the newspaper reports.

He said it would come as a surprise to many that some people living in Connaught were up to 220 miles from any airport. He wrote of the need for an airport in the region, and pointed out that the ESRI had shown average income of a family in the West to be 25 per cent lower than that of a family in any other part of the country, and that the unemployment percentage in Mayo was twice the national average.

"Why the hue and cry over £10 million?" he asked. "Haven't the people of the West been paying their taxes for thirty-five years without getting any air service whatsoever?"

He said that if some of the airport critics were smokers and drinkers they should remember that we were spending £2 million a day on drink and cigarettes, not to mention the £150 million that had been spent on gambling in 1980. He reminded his readers that the gas pipeline from Cork to Dublin was also being funded by taxpayers in the West – without any suggestion to bring it to Galway or Mayo.

And turning to those who had criticised him for dabbling in politics he retorted: "I can honestly say that I have never taken part in politics. If striving for equal rights and opportunities for the people of Connaught makes me a politician, then I am a politician. This is not the first time in my life I have made an effort to help the people of the West, especially in the parishes where I have worked. I worked with Fr. James McDyer in the Save the West campaign. I played a leading role in bringing electricity and water to the homes in the parishes where I worked. I helped to provide local employment and amenities by promoting afforestation, drainage and road construction. I helped in the building of new houses and in the reconstruction of run-down houses for the poor and the needy. I have been active in all kinds of social work, especially in arranging for the payments of grants and allowances to eligible people. In carrying out this work, I have to admit that I have made representations to all politicians and for this I make no apology to anybody. With a history of this kind it is not surprising that I would be involved in the construction of an airport to relieve the great western problem of unemployment. I always felt that a priest's work should include corporal as well as spiritual works of mercy."

When *Business and Finance* called to do a cover story interview they found Horan being interviewed by Hong Kong Radio, and by Donncha O'Dualing for his popular *Highways and Byways* series on Radio Éireann. He was much in demand.

The magazine described him as a master of the 'I come to bury Caesar, not to praise him' technique, defending his airport by reference to other uses of the taxpayers' money while declaring solemnly that neither he nor the people of Mayo begrudged the lucky recipients one penny. He professed himself as being glad that the £45 million for the Cork to Dublin gas pipeline had been found. He was glad for the people of Dublin that they were going to get an electrified commuter train system.

"And neither were we unhappy at the decision of the Government to save jobs by giving the contract for a new ship at Verolme Dockyard in Cork at a cost of £24 million – a ship that could be built in Japan for £12 million. And we did not complain when the jobs of the NET industry were saved by the Government last May, with an injection of £50 million."

And Horan wondered if it was not excessive to be spending £18 million on a new women's prison at Clondalkin to house 60 women. Unless there was some conspiracy known to the Government for women to go on an extraordinary rampage of crime, and to get caught, why was it necessary to provide accommodation at a cost of £300,000 a unit?

"We never look with envious eyes at you people in Dublin, so why should you resent Mayo's £10 million?" the Knock parish priest asked.

Those who knew him well were steadfast in saying Horan never held grudges and went out of his way to meet and talk to people who did not agree with him. Tom Neary remembers going to Castlebar one night with him to attend a *Today Tonight* programme on RTÉ which had Barry Desmond on the panel.

"The Monsignor said to me, 'I never met this guy. Should I shake his hand or say hello to him?' and I said, 'Sure, it might do no harm.' So up troops the Monsignor to the table where Desmond was sitting and said, 'How are you, Barry? You are welcome.' But Desmond was as cool as a breeze. He didn't react towards him. There was no warmth or anything. He kept straight-faced."

*   *   *

Towards the end of November another row blew up. This time *The Connaught Telegraph* predicted that union action could cripple the site. Union representatives claimed the contractors, Frank Harrington and Company, had refused to negotiate with them. Castlebar-based Union Secretary Michael Kilcoyne, wrote to Barry Desmond on behalf of the ITGWU and the Bricklayers' Union (UCATT) to see to it that discussions on a normal site agreement were concluded, given that such an amount of public money was being spent on a non-union site.

Kilcoyne recalls that in the '70s money became available for regional airports, and he remembered setting up meetings with representatives of Congress, including John Carroll, Monsignor Horan and a few other people, to tap into those funds. At the time Waterford Regional Airport was being planned.

He felt that his union (ITGWU) had been helpful and Congress had been supportive, although he conceded the airport the Monsignor had in mind then was probably different to the regional airports people were talking about at that time.

"When work at the airport started Harringtons were the builders, and it was a non-union company. Some of the workers complained about their conditions, their bad pay, that they weren't in the mandatory pension scheme, etc. On foot of that I took the line that the unions should be in on the site. I can't recall being prevented from going on the site. Bear in mind these guys that were contacting me about their poor conditions did not want to be identified to Harringtons or the Monsignor and hence I could not walk up to them – they would be gone.

78

That was the era that was in it at the time. There was no such thing as the Industrial Relations Act to follow procedures."

Kilcoyne's letter, and representation from ITGWU President Carroll, were forwarded by Desmond to Transport Minister Paddy Cooney on November 17. In his cover letter Desmond expressed the fear that if a worker was killed on the site it seemed that there was no mortality cover for the widow and dependants given that the contractors were not in the pension scheme. He proposed the Government should withhold further subvention if the contractors failed to enter into immediate negotiations.

Horan replied to Kilcoyne telling him he had no objection to the men joining the union. According to sources, there was, however, the feeling that the Monsignor did not want unions involved, not because of conditions but because he was afraid there could be costly hold-ups which would have screwed up his projections. It should be remembered that 1979 had been the worst year ever for industrial disputes in Ireland. The Army had to be called in during a nationwide bus strike. A national postal strike lasted for over four months. And the situation was not much better in the early 1980s. Strikes were leading to serious over-runs in costs . . . and that was something Horan was determined to avoid.

The union issue rolled on for some years and, when the government finally pulled the plug on the project, Kilcoyne pointed out that there was a 49% unemployment rate in the area and called on Congress to support moves to have government backing for the airport restored. Carroll retorted that the application should be thrown in the bin.

Horan was not best pleased with that attitude. He described it as a scandalous response in the light of hundreds of jobs at risk. But he praised Kilcoyne for his support, saying he had the courage to change his mind about the airport and to say so publicly. He added that, irrespective of unions, workers were workers and work should be provided for them

Kilcoyne, now an Independent member of Castlebar Urban Council and Chairman of the Consumers' Association of Ireland, has great admiration for Horan, and it has not diminished over the years. "He was a man who cut through red tape and it is a pity we did not have another person like him. It would have made such a difference. He should really have been a politician, and if he was we would not be how we are in the West of Ireland today. As I see it myself on a local council, we are strangled by red tape."

He summarised Horan's philosophy as being much better to ask for forgiveness than permission. "In other words do it. If it is wrong ask for forgiveness. But if you ask for permission you won't get it. The Monsignor used to say he was an old man in a hurry and that is why he had to cut through the red tape."

Ironically, virtually from its becoming operational Knock Airport has been unionised. "At the end of the day my aim was achieved; there are a lot of workers there now, being paid decent wages and enjoying good conditions of employment," says Kilcoyne.

He also acknowledges Charlie Haughey's role in the development of the facility. "I'd say this, and it is probably controversial, if Haughey had continued in government as Taoiseach at that time, I believe he would have secured tax-free industrial status for the airport and that would have attracted jobs. He had the same kind of philosophy as Horan, which was 'get on with it'. You have to recognise the good points also in a person."

However, back in late 1981, Monsignor Horan was more concerned that the attack initiated by Barry Desmond was followed on by what he saw as a concerted, planned and persistent campaign of denunciation, vilification, misrepresentation and downright lying. West was pitched against East, and the Dublin media relentlessly pursued the story.

The government, through media leaks, let it be known that a scaling-back of the project was on the cards. And at two Steering Group meetings an official of the Aeronautical Section of the Department of Transport suggested that perhaps a 4,000 ft runway might suffice in the circumstances.

Desmond said at the time he was of the view that an airport of modest dimensions could have been built. "I had no particular objections at the time to 4,000ft, but when I saw a NATO style 7,500 ft airport being built in a location which was open to question to say the least, and on the basis of pilgrimage traffic which was very highly hypothetical, totally unproven, I began to have very serious doubts," he says.

Monsignor Horan and his Board rejected suggestions for a 4,000ft runway out of hand for they knew that such a limitation would spell commercial doom for their project.

Michael Finlan, writing in *The Irish Times* on the morning of December I, described how he had found the 130 men working on the site preoccupied with rumours of a drastic cutback as they continued the massive operation of laying down a jet runway across the bogland.

The quantity surveyor on the job, Aidan Calleary, told the paper's Western correspondent: "As far as we're concerned, we have heard of no cuts. We are working as though there will be no cuts but we are disturbed by all the rumours. Naturally enough, it has made people on the site nervous, and it has also disturbed our back-up people, who are putting pressure on us, and I mean the banks."

Finlan reported that the men on the job were particularly proud that they had done a massive job of earth-shifting at a fraction of what it would have cost elsewhere. "Never again in the history of aviation will they get an airport built as cheaply as this one," said one of the workers,

P. J. McDonnell. "If they don't allow us to finish it now, it will be the greatest shame of all time. The amount of money that's being saved by having the airport built now instead of in ten years' time is unimaginable. It would be madness to halt the work now when we have so much done and when, in fact, this airport will be not just an asset to a particular locality but will be a national asset."

He added: "An awful lot of those people out on that site have gone to the trouble and expense of purchasing equipment to tackle the task. They now have very heavy commitments with monthly repayments for their purchases. If they are to be laid off they will have no place else to go. It will be the end of the road for them."

That very day Monsignor Horan was in Dublin for a meeting at the Department of Transport and for over two hours they tried to persuade him to accept a 4,000 ft runway, suggesting that perhaps a longer runway might eventually be achievable. And if he did not accept, he was warned that the entire project might be axed. He refused to budge.

The next day the axe fell with a sickening thud. A phone call from Transport Minister Paddy Cooney conveyed the news: "The Government has decided when the present earthworks contract has been completed to cease its involvement with the Connaught Regional Airport project. Its involvement in the completion of the process will be renewed when financial conditions indicate."

At that time £4m had been paid out by the Government, and a further £2m remained to be paid over between December and the following March.

And with 'the postponement' decision went the promised £10 million international sports centre, though the hope was that that too would be built – eventually. John Healy in his *Irish Times* column of December 7 played with that word 'eventually': Paddy O'Toole would deliver - eventually. Senator Jim Higgins would speak up – eventually, he teased.

Healy put to flight the notion doing the rounds that the Permanent Government (i.e. the civil service) was to blame for pulling the plug. If the politicians didn't have the clout to bring the permanent governors to heel then they shouldn't be there, he argued.

As for Healy, well, he was of the firm opinion 'that any doubts about the airport being built can now be safely shelved. It has been so thoroughly politicised now that its building is inevitable'. That assessment was a brave one. However, had Fine Gael/Labour remained in power for an uninterrupted run of five years it is difficult to see at what stage they could have resurrected the project in the economic circumstances that prevailed, and what for instance the costs for the restart would have been in say, 1987?

On December 4 former ministers Albert Reynolds and Padraig Flynn visited the site to express their solidarity with the workers and the

Monsignor and his team. Reynolds saw the decision as a betrayal of the West and the western region.

Looking back on that day, Padraig Flynn recalled a pre-election pledge had been made by all concerned and Paddy O'Toole and Garret FitzGerald, and all political parties in the area, made the pledge. "So when Paddy Cooney made the pull-out announcement it was very distasteful to some of us that they were only concerned about wealth and job creation and that Knock did not comply.

"That was almost like saying the West of Ireland did not feature insofar as any possibility of economic revenue was concerned. It was tantamount to economic and social withdrawal from the West. These were difficult times – Tuam Sugar Factory was for the chop and the whole question of decentralisation was put on hold, so it seemed like provincial Ireland was shutting up shop. This project had a commitment and had an approval and was at an advanced stage and was being cut off at the knees and all it warranted was two sentences from Paddy Cooney," says the former Minister.

Flynn said the Monsignor was pragmatic about the decision. He said he was disappointed but not surprised. He was very resigned. He was very calm. "That smile on his face knew something that we didn't know . . . it wasn't going to die, it wasn't going to fail. He was very prayerful about it and he told us it was going to be finished," revealed Flynn, adding that when Desmond was asked about the decision he said he was pleased. "It was almost like a concerted East of Ireland attack on the West," is his abiding memory.

"A lot of people had come back to work on the site, it was big time – small by present-day standards – and they couldn't understand how agreements and commitments and Dáil approval for money could be cancelled. The Monsignor made it quite clear to us that he regarded the commitment as a promise and that it would have to be honoured. We agreed with that, Albert and I saying it would be finished, even if we had to wait for a change of Government.

"Charlie Haughey at the time was quite adamant, irrespective of what it had cost us in the election, and it did cost us electorally in some parts of the city because of the continuous barrage of suggestions that it was profligate. Haughey's attitude from the start was that it was going to be a success," Flynn says.

On December 6 1981 the *Sunday Tribune* interviewed Flynn who said opposition at the highest level of the civil service had resulted in the Government decision to scrap the project. He said that while Minister of State at the Department of Transport he 'speeded up the bureaucratic process' to have the proposal accepted by the government. In rail-roading the proposal through he succeeded in having the project approved for grant-in-aid government funds in less than a year from its inception.

"This project was resisted from day one by higher echelons in the Department of Finance," said Flynn. "They were going to do nothing about it but they were alarmed that I could speed up the bureaucratic process, and my reasons for pushing the project towards approval were based on my reckoning that the £8 million it would cost at 1980 prices would rise to £25 million by 1985," he told the paper.

*   *   *

Monsignor Horan told Michael Finlan of *The Irish Times* on December 5 that he had no plans to raise the money to finish the project. "I did my best to have it finished. Now I hope that the people of the West will speak up for themselves and make their feelings known to the Government." He was adamant it was the Government's responsibility to come up with the money and no one else's.

Within Mayo the people were ready to stand up and speak for themselves. Fianna Fail activist Frank McCullough, chairman of the recently formed Connaught Airport Action Committee, warned that they were going to start a protest the likes of which had never been seen. "It's not going to be a flash-in-the-pan protest, but it will go on and on until the Government reverses this shameful and monumentally stupid decision," he warned.

He pointed out that all that was needed to finish the job, including the terminal building, was another £5.5 million. "It's insane to go so far and then not finish the job," he said.

Within days the protest bandwagon was rolling. Fine Gael councillor Sean McEvoy called for the resignation of his colleague, Gaeltacht Minister Paddy O'Toole; the Connaught Airport Action Committee called a public meeting for Charlestown; Ballina Urban Council convened a special meeting and called on the Government to reverse its decision; Killala Community Council and Ballyhaunis Chamber of Commerce came out in support of the airport.

With so much grist at its doorstep, the Claremorris Fianna Fáil Cumann whipped up anti-government fervour by listing a range of issues which the Coalition had abandoned, including the extension to the County Hospital at Castlebar, the building of a unit for mentally handicapped in Swinford, decentralisation of Government offices to Ballina; the building of the Letterkenny airstrip, while the Government had also failed to take any action on saving Tuam Sugar Factory, the closure of the maternity wing at Grove Hospital in Tuam, and the loss of jobs at Payne (Ireland) factory at Ballindine. The list of grievances was endless and emotive.

With his back to the wall, Minister O'Toole admitted he was fighting for his political life. But he maintained the decision was only a 'temporary postponement' of the project. He also told the local papers that it was both 'totally and highly irregular' for a Government to pump millions of pounds into a private development that would be owned and controlled by a private company – The Connaught Regional Airport Committee – when the airport was eventually completed. "Not one penny of the many millions it is expected to cost will have been put up by that committee," he charged.

John Healy had a clear view of what was happening: the country was back in two-dimension land, he declared in his *Irish Times* column of December 12. "For three long decades up to the '60s, we had a country which was a freak among nations in that it had only two sides: The North and the South. The North-South axis dominated verbal politics and allowed the other dimension of the nation, the East-West axis, to go about the business in which the West was slowly bled to death to swell the urban East."

But after a bit of action, tokenism even, the normal order had been restored, opined Healy. He listed some home-truths as he saw them:

- The natural gas pipeline was not going anywhere near the province of Connaught. The gobdaws in the West, of course, accepted the assurances from the 'experts' that it would not be economical to pipe it into, or through, the West.
- The Tanaiste was spending days trying to save Clondalkin Paper Mills. Would he jump into a helicopter to hustle to Kilkelly or Charlestown and try to see what he could do to provide jobs for the 150 families whose employment would end next March when work was chopped at the airport site?

"We had," declared Healy, "made bloated Dublin the employment hub of Ireland. All the experts and Rent-a-Mouth Brigade who were so good at costing the Connaught Regional Airport might care to quantify the social and economic cost of moving 150 families from Mayo into Finglas or Cabra or Renelagh or Tallaght, housing them and keeping them on social welfare payments until such time as they can find work."

*　　　*　　　*

There was no lack of heat – or tension – in the Parochial Hall in Charlestown on the night of December 8 when 1,100 packed in for what was to be a stormy and, at times, hostile exchange of views between Connaught Airport Action Committee Campaign chairman Frank McCullough and Senator Jim Higgins of Fine Gael. The hall was a bubbling cauldron of emotion and seething anger.

The charged atmosphere was so explosive Higgins is never likely to forget that night. His recall of events is vivid: "I drove down from the Seanad and Charlestown was absolutely packed. I had to park my car way out the road before making my way into the Town Hall. It was like a Land League meeting. I could feel the crowd parting like the Dead Sea as I walked up the hall. You could feel the bristling hostility, or maybe it was psychological on my part, but the chasm opened and I made my way right up and sat at the top of the hall."

"The speakers were hammering the Government and all this business of collectively beating the drum and getting everyone behind it was the order of the night. The battle-cry was that the airport was going ahead, and they were condemning Barry Desmond, Garret FitzGerald and so on."

When the chairman asked did anyone want to speak from the floor, Higgins mounted the podium and took the microphone. "I spelt out the reality of the public finances, but on the other hand pledged I would do all I could. I said I felt this was only a temporary cessation of work and that when the public finances improved the airport would go ahead. At the same time I pledged my undying fealty and loyalty to the project itself. But you could feel the naked hostility. As a matter of fact it was so hostile that I was advised not to leave until such time as the hall had cleared."

In a report of the meeting the *Western People* gave a blow-by-blow account of the exchanges. Senator Higgins accused the Action Committee of taking a political slant and ignoring Minister O'Toole and himself. He accused the Action Committee of remaining very quiet as the situation evolved. "Paddy O'Toole and I were left on our own, fighting on our own," he charged. At one stage, with the temperature rising, the Chairman of the Action Committee threatened to cut him off if he continued to bring politics into the discussion!

The meeting was also addressed by Deputies Padraig Flynn and P. J. Morley, and after two hours of discussion it ended with the Chairman pledging to bring the campaign to every town. A petition would also be drawn up. A spot collection raised £437 for the fighting fund.

Looking back on the events of that time, Paddy O'Toole said feelings were very obviously running high. "Senator Higgins and myself were in the line of fire. An Action Group took over the promotion of the Airport; it was made up of both sensible people and an extremist element. Like all such groups the extremist element tended to be more vocal and less restrained. There was a mixture of political and religious zeal at work and this at any time is a dangerous mix. These people did not wish to hear anything about the economic state of the country and expenditure on the Airport took precedence for them over all other projects. I felt the serious criticism was affecting my political position but I could do nothing to defend my position even though at all times I was backing the project."

Little more than a week before Christmas, Ballina and Castlebar Urban Councils held special meetings to discuss the worsening situation. There was unanimous support in Ballina for the airport, the members also proving sympathetic towards Minister O'Toole, and expressing the view that the Government had 'pulled the mat from under his feet'.

There were dire warnings too that the Coalition would pay for their mistake at the next election. Deputy Seán Calleary (FF), Vincie Troy (FG), Gerry Ginty and Gerry Moore (FF) all supported Minister O'Toole and called on the Government to rescind its decision.

However, in the county town, Castlebar UDC witnessed some fiery exchanges. Dick Morrin (FF) led the attack on Fine Gael, saying it looked as if the Dublin government had put gates up at the Shannon so that development could not infiltrate Connaught.

But Cllr Christy Tynan said Monsignor Horan gave his blessing to one party in the last election and Haughey only thought he wanted a grass strip. He said the Fianna Fáil motion condemning the government decision had as much sincerity as 'a whore's kiss'.

Cllr Martin Hopkins (FG) called on the directors of the airport to chip in the money themselves, or raise it to finish the job and show there were more people in Connaught than 'cribbers, grousers and grumblers'.

The sparks really began to fly when Cllr Frank Durcan said the airport would not benefit the people of Mayo, it was a private operation and they had no say in it. "This would mean that in ten years' time they could sell it to a foreign body," he declared.

He said Our Lady of Knock would be more concerned with people living on the side of the road, in sub-zero conditions, than having an airport. "It is an attempt to make it (airport) into a Fianna Fáil Shrine. And I as a Catholic take exception to that. We have a moral duty to look after the majority of the people in the county," said Durcan.

Chairman Cllr Johnny Mee (Lab) said it was time the lunacy stopped and they got their priorities right. "If it is a toss-up between the Airport and the (proposed) Regional Technical College or a new hospital, then I am on the side of the hospital," he said, reflecting the local community priority at the time.

The amended proposal that the Airport Company match the Government's £6 million pound-for-pound was carried on a vote.

But at least the man at the centre of the row, Monsignor Horan, showed he had not lost his sense of humour. Asked by *The Irish Times* for his New Year resolutions, he said he had learned a lesson: never to start another airport in an economic crisis!

And giving an insight into his deepest thoughts and battling qualities, another of his resolutions was: 'Remember that to lose a battle is not to lose the war.'

How prophetic those words were to prove!

CHAPTER EIGHT

1982: GUBUS all round - Mayo County Council support - Fianna Fail 'can of worms' - Horan threatens Minister - Contract for runway signed - NATO fears - Blood-curdling tales of the béiceadán - Heated moments in corridors of power -Mitchell's open mind

GUBUS all over the place

AT the end of 1981 the Organisation for Economic Co-operation and Development (OECD) painted a grim picture of the economy for the following 18 months. It predicted that Ireland would be attempting to support 'a prince's standard of living on a pauper's income' yet again in 1982.

The balance-of-payments deficit was expected to stand equivalent to 10% of Irish national income, and that would mean that the country would have lived beyond its means for the fourth year in a row, reported *The Irish Times* of December 23 1981. In fact, the OECD anticipated the country's balance-of-payments performance in 1982 would be by far the worst in the Western industrialised world. Inflation was projected to rampage ahead, with prices expected to rise by an average of almost 19%.

January opened to the worst winter weather for fifty years. December had been the coldest since records began, with Malin Head hitting -4.5°C; Claremorris -8.3°C; Galway -6.5°C; and Belmullet -5.2°C. Then, on Friday, January 8 1982 most of the country, and especially along the eastern seaboard, was brought to a standstill by snow blizzards. Roads were impassable, there were ESB power failures, trains and buses were cancelled, Dublin airport was closed and shipping services badly affected. Snow drifts measured up to 10 ft deep in places. Several people died in accidents.

As the situation worsened the government was lambasted for its lack of preparedness and response. Rattled by media atacks, the Government established a Crisis Emergency Committee and the Army, Air Corps, Gardai, Fire Brigade and Civil Defence were called out.

Taoiseach Garret FitzGerald returned from holidays in the Canary Islands to take charge of the Emergency Committee under the chairmanship of Tanaiste Michael O'Leary. Bread and milk shortages were reported, 25,000 homes along the eastern seaboard suffered blackouts and schools were closed nationwide. Abandoned vehicles were pilfered and set alight in Dublin while in the countryside livestock perished.

The Army was called out to clear icy Dublin streets 'in defence of the citizenry's life and limb'. It had not been called in earlier because the City Manager had not requested their assistance, said Defence Minister James Tully as the Government felt the pressure.

Ray Burke, Fianna Fáil environment spokesman, said the fact that the national road network was only barely functioning was the sign of lamentable failure on the part of the Government. Nearly a week after the blizzards the Government's overall co-ordination of emergency services must be called into serious question, he said.

The crisis gave rise to 'rip-off plumbers', *The Irish Times* reporting that one Dublin plumber had admitted charging £1 a minute for domestic jobs and pipes burst in the freeze-up.

When the weather cleared, in Dublin's RDS the airport in Mayo was featuring in the Young Scientists' Exhibition, with Geraldine and Seán Beirne, students from St. Joseph's Secondary School, Charlestown, making the case for the project continuing. Their entry was illustrated with a detailed model of the airport – the buildings, the control tower, and the 7,500 ft runway.

At Knock presbytery hundred of letters of support were pouring in to Monsignor Horan, who had by this time, according to Cormac MacConnell in the *Irish Press* of January 8, sought legal opinion on behalf of the Company as to the validity of the Coalition's 'postponement' decision in December.

MacConnell wrote that the former Attorney General Colm Condon, SC., was of the opinion that the Government could be liable for up to £8 million damages because of its failure to complete a contract entered into for the construction of the airport.

The article went on: "In relation to the Government decision to cease funding the project when the £2 million earthworks phase is completed this spring, the report cites Mr Condon's view as being that the Government, like a private individual, could be bound by the law of contract."

In fact, the Board had discussed the matter earlier that day, and Monsignor Horan told MacConnell that he felt the company had no intention of taking legal action.

Padraig Flynn, in an interview for this book, said the legal advice the Board received was that the commitment would have to be honoured by the Government. "It was always our intention that any money given would be grant-in-aid," he pointed out.

However, Paddy O'Toole told the author that the legal position enunciated by Condon in 1982 did not worry the Government. "The question of liability would only have become an issue in the event of the abandonment of the project. At no time was it proposed to abandon the project," he says, referring back to Paddy Cooney's statement of December 1981.

In Galway, negotiations had concluded for the acquisition of four acres of land, allowing the runway at Carnmore, eight miles outside the city, to be extended from 585 metres to 1,200 metres. It was predicted that, once completed, Aer Arann would operate flights to London, Manchester and Birmingham, as well as Dublin.

But there were much bigger issues on the horizon back at Dáil Eireann. On 27 January Finance Minister John Bruton stood up to deliver his Budget and rocked some left-wing Independent TDs, including Jim Kemmy of Limerick, by attempting to put, in effect, VAT on children's shoes.

The Taoiseach Garret FitzGerald dissolved the Dáil when Kemmy refused to vote for the Budget, and a general election was called. Monsignor Horan smiled. "The government had fallen and 'Knock Airport' might live again," he recalled some years later.

Connaught Regional Airport again became a soft political target. And the flak did not just come only from Labour or Fine Gael. Dublin Fianna Fáil Dáil candidates Sile de Valera and Niall Andrews also questioned the wisdom of the party's policy in continuing to support the airport. Andrews wanted £50 million for ring roads around the capital. Their party colleague in East Mayo, P. J. Morley, called for disciplinary measures against both.

As the battle at the hustings raged, Mayo County Council called a special meeting to discuss a Fianna Fáil motion for Government support for the airport. The local papers carried the ensuing report in full in their first editions of February. Councillor Frank Durcan called for a sworn public inquiry into the matter, saying planning permission had been granted in three days without the submission of plans relating to sewerage, etc. However, later in the debate, he caused a ripple of surprise when he reversed his previously stated public stance and said he was for the airport, though not at the present time as there were more pressing needs in the county.

In reply to the planning allegation, Senior Planning Officer Seán Dunleavy said permission had been granted because of the 'urgency' of the project. Interviewed for this book, he recalls he completed the work in one day. "Everything was in order. The law allowed it at that time; later it required fourteen days before permission could be sanctioned. After I dealt with it, the application went to County Manager Michael O'Malley and it was approved that very evening."

At the meeting County Manager O'Malley said he had already declared his interests and he would make a further statement at the next meeting of the council. It will be recalled that O'Malley was a director of Connaught Airport Company, and that had led to accusations that he therefore had a vested interest in the project.

Deputy Padraig Flynn and Senator Jim Higgins were among those who took part in the debate. Deputy Enda Kenny proposed an amendment to the Fianna Fáil proposal. He asked that the necessary finance be provided for the project 'as soon as public funds allow'.

When it came to the vote there was a surprise outcome. Fine Gael, which had a majority on the council, could muster only 12 votes. Fine Gael's Martin Finn of Claremorris voted for the Fianna Fáil motion and Councillors Durcan and Sean McEvoy (both FG) abstained. The Fianna Fáil motion was therefore carried 14-12 in support of the restoration of the project.

With rumours doing the rounds that some Fianna Fáil candidates were privately admitting that the party had opened a 'can of worms' by getting involved in the airport in the first place, party strategists at national level issued its candidates with a briefing document giving 'five facts to dispute any criticism of the Fianna Fáil pre and post-election position'.

Realising that the Party's support for the airport would be highly unpopular on Dublin doorsteps, the internal memo pointed out that the airport would cost the equivalent of 7 miles of roadway; that at all times the position was that the airport was to be taken over and operated as a private company. It also said that the 'Regional Airport at Kilkelly' would provide for short-haul jets and not Jumbos; that the grant-in-aid of £8 million as costed in 1980 was a once-off; that the project was a viable proposition. And it reminded its candidates that Fine Gael had supported the proposal on two occasions, and the supplementary estimate of £2.2 million prepared by the Coalition in mid-June 1981 had unanimously passed through the Dáil.

While he had probably anticipated the bureaucratic resistance to the airport proposal and had moved to outflank that opposition while in power, Charlie Haughey was surprised by the widespread political and public opposition the project encountered and agreed that the internal memo be issued to help defuse the controversy.

On the doorsteps in East Mayo Gaeltacht Minister O'Toole was also meeting a hostile reaction. Under intense pressure, and an admission that he was fighting for his political life, he turned on his critics as he went about his canvass: "Do they want me to build the damn thing myself?" he demanded when confronted by the media.

Journalist Tom Rowley, in a constituency profile on East Mayo for the *Irish Independent*, predicated that outgoing Fianna Fáil TDs Seán Calleary and P. J. Morley were well positioned to retain their seats while Paddy O'Toole was under pressure on two fronts, from his airport critics and from party young lion Jim Higgins of Ballyhaunis who was expected to score heavily at the polls.

Monsignor Horan found it unbelievable that Fine Gael had again included the airport in its election manifesto for East Mayo. He observed that as the only representative of the people of the West in the Cabinet, O'Toole should have done the decent thing and resigned. "If he had done that he would have been a hero in the West for all time, his political future guaranteed," he was to later observe.

With tensions between the two Mayo men at a new high, O'Toole admits he was walking a veritable tightrope. "I was being blamed for

Government decisions, whether I supported such decisions or not. I was in a 'no win' position," he concedes. Their relationship went back to 1974 when O'Toole was elected to Mayo County Council. At that time Knock was being developed, stalls were being removed and a new road development was planned together with the building of the Basilica.

"On becoming a TD and subsequently a Minister I had various close encounters with Monsignor Horan. As he became more deeply involved beyond his depth in the airport development, pressure began to build up. The undertakings he gave to contractors could not be delivered because of lack of finance. He tended to blame others for the predicament in which he found himself. We had our private conversations where he became very political and threatened to use his influence against me. I became aware of the efforts he was making to divert support away from Fine Gael and from me in particular in elections around that period," says the former Minister.

The Airport Action Committee approached all the candidates in the run-up to the election on February 18, and secured pledges in writing from candidates that they would, if successful, resign their seats unless the project was completed. The pledges, the *Irish Press* revealed, were collected in Mayo, Sligo, Roscommon and Leitrim. It was believed that some, but not all of the deputies who signed the pledge, deleted the question containing the resignation pledge before signing.

The *Irish Press* reported that all the Fianna Fáil TDs in the three constituencies – Messrs Flynn, Calleary, Gallagher and Morley in Mayo; Sean Doherty and Terry Leyden in Roscommon, and Ray MacSharry, Mattie Brennan and John Ellis in Sligo/Leitrim had signed the pledges.

In Sligo outgoing Minister of State Ted Nealon confirmed to the paper that, in response to each of the questions on the form, he had replied: "I support entirely my government's position on the project and agree with Desmond O'Malley's statement that the airport project does not have economic priority."

The campaigners also revealed that Paddy O'Toole had flatly refused to sign the pledge, while his West Mayo colleague, Enda Kenny, was 'missed out' by the Action Committee because he was on the campaign trail when they called.

Fianna Fáil emerged as the largest party with 81 seats, an increase of three, while Fine Gael dropped two to end up on 63, with Labour holding its 15 seats. For the second election in a row, Mayo yielded up four of its six seats to Fianna Fáil. Haughey was then threatened with a leadership challenge which did not materialise and he was elected Taoiseach with the support of Dublin Independent Tony Gregory, and three Workers' Party deputies. Gregory achieved national prominence through the famous 'Gregory Deal' which he negotiated with the Fianna Fáil leader, and which guaranteed a massive cash injection for his inner-city Dublin constituency.

But John Healy was a happy man, as he told his readers in *The Irish Times* of March 22: "The man who championed the airport, and its role

91

as a growth centre for the West is now back in office as Taoiseach. I have news for the economic experts and the Rathgar Set in Fianna Fáil: Charlie is finishing on schedule the Connaught Regional Airport at Knock as part of the infrastructure to revitalise the western region. It will have an industrial estate on the perimeter. It will be an integrated operation and as needed for the region as the development of Dublin's Inner City, and a lot less costly."

There was, too, a pleasant surprise for the airport promoters. They found that the Coalition had allocated £4.5 million for the project in the Budget. Taoiseach Haughey and his Finance Minister Ray MacSharry gave a commitment that the airport would be finished. The newly appointed Minister for the Gaeltacht Padraig Flynn announced on March 19 that the project was to be allowed to proceed without a hitch and on target. Ironically, Fine Gael had provided the largesse but had taken the flak during the election, losing seats and again getting none of the local credit for bankrolling the airport. It was hard to discern the party's strategy; indeed, local Fine Gael activists were later to admit that the party's approach was shoddily handled.

John Wilson was appointed Minister for Transport in the new Cabinet but he did not prove to be as accommodating to Knock as Albert Reynolds had been in the previous Fianna Fáil administration. Indeed efforts by the developers to secure sanction for bringing water and 3-phase electricity to the site hit a stone wall. The Monsignor blamed Wilson for curbing progress at the airport from February to November, and for delaying the opening.

Tom Neary remembers that John Wilson was quite 'anti' the project. "He blocked the terminal building, the water and the electricity; he was not helpful which was rather strange." It was on occasions such as this that Horan would turn to Cathal Duffy and say, somewhat ruefully: "You had better go and see your Uncle Charlie. This is not right what's happening here!" A Fianna Fáil insider at the time observed some years later: "Within the party they were not all with us, you know."

Work raced ahead at the site, the workforce earning praise from Monsignor Horan for their intelligence, skill and dedication in the face of a consistent campaign that could have killed their jobs. But there was more flak from Galway, with businessman Thomas McDonogh telling a meeting of the local Chamber of Commerce that the Mayo regional airport was a waste of public money which could be put to better use on infrastructure and communications.

McDonogh was quoted as saying in the *Irish Independent:* "We're a misgoverned country when we are prepared to sink £16 million in a boghole in Mayo."

But after that the media onslaught on the airport subsided. Now the focus for attention became Charles J. Haughey who seemed to be perpetually fighting off leadership challenges or being questioned about his economic policies. Unemployment continued to rise, hitting 148,000 by April, with commentators projecting it would rise to 200,000 by the end of the year. It was already beyond the threshold Jack Lynch, a few years earlier, had said would be acceptable for a Fianna Fáil government.

On May 24, huge crowds of people across the country marched in protest at burgeoning income tax and PRSI changes. The PAYE sector was far from happy and gave vent to its feelings.

There was by now a noticeable decrease in public utterances from the Airport Board which, the previous November, had passed a resolution declaring that all press statements had to be cleared by the Board and made by the Chairman. The resolution was in line with what the Government nominees on the Board had been seeking, but Monsignor Horan felt it was merely caving in to demands and tying the hands of the Board members in refuting criticism. Effectively, he had been silenced by his own Board.

P. J. Morley concedes that Monsignor Horan had a tendency to give interviews to the media which did not go down well with some members of the Fianna Fáil party. "They would complain about money being wasted in the West. Charlie Haughey used to tell me to tell the Monsignor not to be so vocal in his media utterances."

Journalist Michael Ronayne remembers covering the 1982 general election campaign when Haughey visited South Mayo: "I mentioned the Monsignor to him and he told me to tell the Monsignor to keep his mouth shut as it was not helpful to the cause!"

During that campaign Horan happily posed with candidate PJ Morley for a photographer. "Unfortunately the picture did not come out because there was a glitch with the camera," recalls Ronayne.

The 'media gag' on Horan was picked up by Frank Byrne in the *Sunday Independent* of 22 August 1982. The directors of the airport, he observed, appeared to have taken a vow of silence. At that time, he said, light planes were capable of landing and taking off from the partially completed runway.

*   *   *

The next airport tussle saw Taoiseach Haughey and the Fine Gael Leader Garret FitzGerald locked in yet another battle of words over a new contract, this time for 1800 metres of runway and taxiway

Minister John Wilson was by then proving more helpful and he told the Dáil that construction work on the runway phase would be completed by September or October of 1983, allowing for an official opening in 1984, and that the entire cost would be around £12 million.

The row ignited when Geraldine Kennedy, political correspondent with the *Sunday Tribune,* revealed, on September 12, that the promoters of the airport had signed a legal contract for £2.7 million, and that the contract had been signed by Monsignor Horan and the contractor Frank Harrington on August 27.

It was a cast-iron contract. No chances were being taken this time round. "Monsignor Horan signed the contract after he had received a letter from the Minister for Transport and Tourism, Mr Wilson, indicating his consent to the placing of the contract subject to the provision of a satisfactory bond by Frank Harrington Ltd and provided that an overdraft could be used to meet expenditure in 1982," Kennedy wrote.

Ms Kennedy said she understood that the document had been referred to the Chief State Solicitor's office in Dublin to give the promoters and the contractor an assurance that whatever government was in power, it would be obliged to pay the money. It was intended that the £2.7 million would be paid out of the next year's estimates.

Garret FitzGerald retaliated, telling the *Sunday Tribune* the government was putting its predilection for 'strokes' and 'deals' before the fulfilment of its obligations as an employer and before the maintenance of the health service, to give but two examples. However, the Government Press Secretary Frank Dunlop, on behalf of the Taoiseach, said not one single penny was allocated or approved other than the funds provided by the Fine Gael/Labour Coalition in that year's estimates, and Mr MacSharry's budget. He further added that the Government had no knowledge of the new contract.

It was all semantics, of course. Four days later the *Irish Press* tried to get to the bottom of the confusion. Transport Minister Wilson called on FitzGerald to withdraw his allegations that the Government had signed the contract, saying that a secret contract had not been signed by the Government. However, he confirmed the promoters and the contractor had signed the contract for £2.7 million on August 27. Dr FitzGerald said it was obvious from what the Minister said that he had authorised the signing.

What really happened was that the minority Fianna Fáil government, pressed by the Airport Board, sought to safeguard the future of the airport by pencilling in the funding in such a way that the commitment had to be honoured by whatever government was in power in 1983.

The Board was acutely aware that a change of government could scupper their hopes, and a wink was as good as a nod. The Board had four or five tenders in for 6,000 ft of asphalt runway and was ready to move. With a Board meeting scheduled for the following Monday, Horan decided not to hang about.

John Balfe already had the tender report prepared and legal opinion had been received that the Board could sign the contract with the contractor. Frank Harrington was again the most competitive tender.

Monsignor Horan rolled up his sleeves, drew all the parties to the contract together and ironed out any remaining issues. In preparation, the lights in Knock burned late into the night. The signing took place over a weekend of frantic activity. When the Board assembled on Monday in Knock, the Monsignor stood up and said he was delighted to inform the meeting that he had signed the contract with Frank Harrington, his being the lowest tender for the 6,000ft runway in accordance with the recommendations.

A source close to the scene recalled that the civil servants on the

Board were taken aback but could do nothing about the new contract even if they wanted to.

"The Monsignor sat there and smiled. He had finalised the contract in two days and had signed it and was now sitting there with an innocent face on him, saying in effect, sorry lads, you know the tenders had been received and the way was clear to sign," the source said.

They were the two days that made the difference in guaranteeing phase two, and were key in ensuring that the runway was not later chopped to around 4,000ft, according to authoritative sources.

Years later, in his memoirs published posthumously, Monsignor Horan did not delve into the particular circumstances of the signing of the contract. He simply recorded that before the minority Fianna Fáil Government fell in November 1982 it had prepared its capital expenditure programme for 1983 which contained £2.7 million for contract no. 2, and that contract had been signed between the contractor and the company on August 27, 1982.

Between the Monsignor's prodding and Haughey's acquiescence, funding for the airport was guaranteed for another while, at least. It was a valuable assurance at such a volatile time politically.

*   *   *

Meanwhile Charlestown-based Peter Walsh, secretary of the Connaught Regional Airport Development Association (CRADA), told the *Western People* a new car would be raffled to raise funds, and trips were being planned to America to raise awareness, membership and badly-needed money.

The airport was at the centre of a war of another kind in early August when rumours began to circulate that NATO had its eye on the runway. Deputy Enda Kenny raised the matter with External Affairs Minister Gerry Collins, pointing out that the strategic position of the airport would make it a vital asset in war activities. The suggestion was dismissed by the Minister who reiterated the Government's stance on neutrality and said they did not intend to make any airport, or other facility within the State, available for military use. The rumours had their origins in the recently ended Falklands War which had raged through March, April, May and June.

Christy Moore was later to immortalise the NATO rumours with two telling lines in his song about the airport (Note: see Chapter 10):

Did NATO donate the dough, my boys? Did NATO donate the dough?
Did NATO donate the dough, my boys? Did NATO donate the dough?

Another crisis had much greater relevance back in Dublin, however. On August 16, the Attorney General Patrick Connolly resigned after wanted double-murderer Malcolm MacArthur was found staying on his property. Mr Connolly was unaware of any links connecting MacArthur with the murders of Nurse Bridie Dargan in the Phoenix Park and a Co. Offaly farmer. The ensuing scandal was later described as 'grotesque, unbelievable, bizarre and unprecedented' by Charles Haughey, and the word GUBU was entered into the lexicon by perennial Haughey opponent, Conor Cruise O'Brien.

Towards the end of August, Barry Desmond, now on the Opposition benches, was telling the *Sunday Independent* that 'even at this late stage work should be halted on the airport'. He said medical card holders and lower paid workers in the civil service should come before 'this kind of expenditure' and while his remarks resonated along the east coast, in most parts of the West, where the dole queues were growing and emigration was rising again, his words fell on bemused ears.

Supporters of the airport were wishing Desmond would bury his battle-axe as had been done at the historic Barnacuige airport site some 2,500 years earlier. Tom Carney of Shanvaghera, Knock, had come across a perfectly preserved axe head as he walked the airport site in October. Much folklore attached to the site, and an ancient burial mound had been identified during construction work.

A man who knows all about the history and folklore of Barnacuige is John Finn of Kilgarriff, Charlestown. Now in his eighties, he lives a few hundred yards from the airport. Like so many more in the region, he had gone off to find work in England when he was a boy of sixteen, working with farmers in Lincolnshire, and then in construction with Wimpeys. When work on the airport started he carted stone, dug trenches, and whatever. "It was great compared to what work had been there before," he says.

He had always been aware of the history of Barnacuige and as a boy had seen a big burial mound, with stones all charred by fire. "Archaeologists came from Dublin and dug up bones and brought them away and estimated from the jawbones and leg bones that the ancient people buried there stood at least over 7 ft. tall," he claimed.

He said one of the most grisly stories told of olden times related to happenings in a 'half-way house' at the back end of the runway, near Barnalyra Wood. "It was really a rough boarding house, and one night a man travelling by horseback from Sligo to Claremorris for a fair stopped over," he related.

"The weary traveller had to share the bed with the son of the house, but during the night he heard some conspiratorial whispering going on and suspected that he was going to be robbed . . . or worse. He moved to the inside of the bed, inside the sleeping son of the house. Within minutes the parents entered the room armed with an axe but in the dark they mistakenly cut the head off their son who was now on the outside of the bed. In the ensuing confusion the man got on his horse and rode away.

"The next night mad roars rolled across the hillside, calling out until daylight, and continued on for years and years. It became known as the Béiceadán (meaning the yeller or the bawler) until there was a Mass said on the spot, and then it stopped," said the local historian.

"Tradition has it that people used to rush to their houses at night before the 'Béiceadán' would start," said Mr Finn. With Barry Desmond at full flow in condemnation, wits around the area likened his non-stop rantings to the blood-curdling yelling of long ago!

*   *   *

On September 14, Ireland mourned the death of Princess Grace of Monaco, following a car accident on a winding road in the principality. News of her death came as a great shock to her Kelly cousins in Newport, Co. Mayo. Some years before she had paid a visit to her ancestral home, and plans were afoot to conserve the building.

For another person of Mayo roots, October 6 was yet one more testing day: An Taoiseach Charles Haughey emerged with a majority of 58 votes to 22 in an open but bruising ballot on Charlie McCreevy's motion of no confidence in his leadership.

On October 15 Cork Airport celebrated its 21st birthday. The airport had yet to make a profit. However, Shannon Airport, which had lost money over the previous three years, indicated it was on target to return to profit, mainly due to the doubling of Russian Aeroflot flights. The airports had been supported by many millions from State funds.

In November the second general election of 1982 took place a mere nine months after the first one in February of that year. While it had not been the shortest Dáil in history, it was unusual in that there had never before been three general elections in eighteen months. The election was called by Haughey after Independent and Workers' Party TDs withdrew their support when the government insisted on introducing substantial budget cuts.

Back at Knock, the fall of the minority Fianna Fáil government set off immediate alarm bells. Airport Board director Seamus Monaghan takes up the story: "One of the payments was due to us and an anxious Monsignor Horan gave me a letter on the very day the Government fell, and I was asked to go to Dublin immediately and get Ray MacSharry, the Minister of Finance, to sign the letter of approval for payment before he went out of office.

"So I was standing there in the corridor in Dáil Eireann when the door flings open and out come Haughey and O'Malley, arguing between the two of them, and I am standing there with my mouth open looking for MacSharry. Haughey was like a raving demon and so was O'Malley. I didn't know what was going on. MacSharry brought me in and on the way Haughey snapped, 'What the hell do you want, Monaghan?' I nearly shit in my pants. And the letter shaking in my hand, and the words of the Monsignor ringing in my ear, 'Don't come back without getting it signed'. When Haughey cooled down he told MacSharry to sign it and I came back with everything in order, much to the relief of everyone at Knock!"

Within days weary politicians raced to the doorsteps again. Confronted by the press on a visit to Mayo, Garret FitzGerald refused to give a commitment to the airport, and would make no call until he had seen the exact nature of the State's finances. However, a Fine Gael candidate in East Mayo, school-teacher Sean McEvoy, nailed his colours

97

to the mast by declaring that he would throw his full weight behind the campaign for completion if elected. His speech was immediately disowned by the Party's organisation in East Mayo.

But there was backing for a 'scaled-down' airport at Knock from Martin Dully, chief executive of Aer Rianta. He told the *Irish Press* on November 18 he found no difficulty in accepting the logic behind the project, but would question the decision to establish a £21 million project at Knock whereas a scaled-down version, perhaps in the order of £8 million, did make sense. Where he got his £21m estimate from puzzled the Mayo promoters, though.

Padraig Flynn felt the media were very disingenuous at the time, particularly the *Irish Independent* which declared 'the whole thing has been a political ploy for votes' to save Morley's seat. "Of course, it had been a political decision and activity to try and rejuvenate the West which had been neglected. But the *Irish Independent* at that time supported the withdrawal and I recall that a journalist from that paper wrote that Knock Airport was 'an absurd dream' and that the 'kiss of death' had been given to an over-ambitious regional project," he said. "In actual fact, analysis will show that the airport cost us votes around the country," he asserts.

At the hustings the electorate was tired of all the political rhetoric in relation to the economy and Fianna Fáil in-fighting and Garret FitzGerald got a ringing endorsement to get on with sorting out the economy. His party romped back with 70 seats, up 7, to record its biggest ever election triumph, coming to within a mere five seats of Fianna Fáil. And Labour, under Dick Spring, gained a seat. Between them FG and Labour had 86 seats, a clear majority, and they agreed on a programme for government. Paddy O'Toole withstood the challenge in East Mayo and was appointed Minister for Fisheries and the Gaeltacht.

While it was a national triumph for Fine Gael it turned out to be a PR disaster for the party in Mayo and the adjacent region. "We ended up going back into government in 1982 and picking up the bill for it and having to honour the commitment made by Charlie Haughey and Albert Reynolds, so effectively we got none of the credit, but all the blame, having paid for the project," said Jim Higgins, a FG senator at the time.

Dublin TD Jim Mitchell took over as Minister for Transport. Asked about Knock Airport by the *Irish Press*, he said he had an open mind. He said he would look at all the financial implications and would approach the issue without prejudice for or against.

Over on the Opposition benches, Charlie Haughey had to endure yet another heave against his leadership by Charlie McCreevy and others: he survived yet again. For another Fianna Fáil politician things were a little easier: Patrick Hillery was installed as President of Ireland for a second term on December 3.

Meanwhile, at the top of windswept Barnacuige, rock was being blasted, vast amounts of peat were being removed, and the runway was being laid down by busy but worried hands.

CHAPTER NINE

*1983: No more cash for Knock – Tribute to workers – Work at site –
Kilkelly buzzing – Financial Journalist to rescue – Keeping good
side out – Preparing for Gay Byrne and Morley Safer –
Dealing with the media*

Facing up to Gaybo and Morley Safer

IT wasn't to be a particularly great year on a number of fronts. Industrial
unrest and factory closures were to dominate the news. Jobs were to be
lost when Ranks and Dunlops closed. It was also the year top racehorse
Shergar was to be snatched and businessman Don Tidey kidnapped.

On the political front there were to be revelations of 'bugging'
conversations and 'tapping' of journalists' phones which would drag
Fianna Fáil through the mire and have long-term implications for Charlie
Haughey.

But before all of that transpired, the year opened none too brightly
for Monsignor Horan's creation. The constant media-knocking continued
where it had left off, and the Christmas trees were barely down when the
Evening Herald and its sister paper, the *Sunday Independent,* talked of
Minister Jim Mitchell presenting 'scarifying reports' on the airport to the
Cabinet. Worse, the 'divide' within the Cabinet over the issue was
widening.

The *Irish Times* of January 17 carried an even more worrying
headline – 'No more State cash likely for Knock Airport' – over a story by
Michael Finlan who, from soundings, was of the opinion that the
Government would withdraw financial support from the airport. Instead,
it was speculated, the Government would give backing to a more modest
proposal for developing the airport at Carnmore, outside Galway city.
That option, if pursued, would cost only £1 million compared with a
minimum £12 million for the completion of Knock and, in the view of
some, as much as £16 million, he mused.

However, Finlan pointed out that some sources claimed the
Government would be bound by the watertight contract put in place by
the outgoing government for phase 2. In fact, the new administration had
checked out the contract which had been signed between Horan and the
contractor and found it to be legally binding.

There was really no option other than to honour the contract and
the money allocated. It was a line picked up by Bruce Arnold in the *Irish*

Independent of January 19. Attacking the 'appalling behaviour of certain members of the Fianna Fáil Government in sanctioning the project in the first place,' he said, "They acted irresponsibly, outrageously so. They ignored, treated in a perfunctory fashion, and, in certain instances, actually sought to change the professional reports and documents on which their decisions were to be made. From the start it was clear that Knock would be a permanent drain on public finances. All that was needed then was for the government to say 'no.' Now it is rather different. Ironically it may well be foolish for the present government to do other than go ahead," Arnold wrote.

After sustained knocking from economists, one man stood out from the herd and pointed out that the airport was not such a wild idea after all. Colm Rapple, writing in the *Irish Independent*, gave this refreshing view: "Hopefully, however, the Government will be careful about where the axe falls on capital projects. Capital spending creates a lot of employment – even sometimes when it appears wasteful. By all means cut back on imports or expensive machinery whether it be for hospitals or ESB power stations. But do not cut back on employment-creating construction work. There might even be a conversion to the view that laying the runway at Knock Airport was not simply throwing money into a boghole. Those employed would otherwise be on the dole. Instead of drawing state funds, they are contributing to the coffers. Most of the materials are domestic so the firms supplying them are paying extra tax. There is less leakage of money from the Irish economy from that spent at Knock than from many other supposedly wise investment decisions."

Here, at last, was someone from a financial background, standing up and saying what Monsignor Horan had been singing off the rooftops for the previous two years: up to 120 workers were employed on the site; they were paying their taxes; they were pumping money back into the local economy; building houses; sending their kids to local schools which had been under threat of closure. The raw materials were coming from the locality.

In fact, the Monsignor was a stickler for insisting that all materials should be bought in the region. "He absolutely insisted on everything being procured West of the Shannon if possible," says John Balfe. "For instance, we were ordering the gully gratings, and the nearest supplier we could find was Limerick Foundry but they were importing them. Horan instructed me to find someone else, and eventually we found a foundry which had no problem in making the items, but revealed they had been prosecuted for making hand-grenade casings for the IRA. I knew if I told the Monsignor he'd tell me to keep looking, so we got the gulleys there without filling him in further," Balfe relates.

Meanwhile, as feelings against the government worsened in the locality, Mayo sources were quick to point out that it could find £2m to secure 35 jobs at Clondalkin Paper Mills. Projects were being bailed out where the political numbers stacked up: it was a scenario familiar to the West.

Fr. Paddy Kilcoyne, who was then curate in Kilkelly, remembers that many locals came back from England to get work on the project. He was present one particular day when lorry owners were bringing gravel up to the site and there were 30 or 40 lorries queued up to get the material delivered. "The sense of rush and activity was palpable as the drivers were on so much a load. The contractor set up a rock-crushing plant right beside the runway and also a tarmac plant adjacent to the site. It was great. There was so much happening; people were working and they had hope."

Main contractor Frank Harrington knew a time when scarcely a load of building blocks would be sold in Kilkelly – a small village a few miles from the airport – in a year. "Now 200 to 300 houses have been built. The airport gave hope. The Monsignor saw the bigger picture; he knew that infrastructure would lead to progress," he says.

With a new government firmly in place and a new minister in charge of transport, the Airport Board took stock of their situation at length at a meeting on 15 February. It was agreed to furnish Minister for Communications Jim Mitchell with a complete overview of the position. They drew up a comprehensive profile of the traffic expected through the airport, running costs and total cost for completing the project. The Minister was invited to come and see the work for himself. He accepted the invitation, but it would be some months before he eventually got to Mayo and Barnacuige.

Of more immediate Cabinet concern was the overall state of the country and the stringent efforts needed to knock it into shape. The sharp edge of Government efforts to get to grips with the balance of payments deficit was felt by motorists in the first week of March when petrol shot up by 14 pence a gallon as increased VAT charges began to bite. Petrol was now costing the Irish motorist £2.80 a gallon, making it very close to the most expensive in Europe.

On March 10, the *Irish Times* reported the closure of the Ballina-based *Western Journal* newspaper, after five-and-a-half years in existence: John Healy's local sounding-post was no more. Jobs were lost in Ballina and Sligo.

*　　　　*　　　　*

EEC funding for the airport had been discussed and sought by the Board, so in April Monsignor Horan was 'delighted and thrilled' when MEP Sean Flanagan, former TD and captain of the Mayo All-Ireland winning teams of 1950/51, brought news of the Commission's recognition of the Mayo airport.

The Commission recommended aid totalling 25 million ECUS – less than £18 million – be provided for the development of three airports, including the Connaught facility, Flanagan announced.

But some place along the way that particular money promise ran into a cul-de-sac. The Government was to announce within days that under the criteria laid down by the EEC, the Knock development was unlikely to qualify for any such grant. However, John Lichfield, in a report filed for the *Irish Press* from Brussels on May 26, said the EEC Commission view was that if the government decided that it wanted part of its share of the 1983 regional fund allocated to Knock the Commission would almost certainly agree.

The conflicting media reports and government statements were interpreted back in Mayo as meaning the Government wasn't really interested in seeking EEC funds for the airport. A few years later Monsignor Horan was to claim that, unknown to the Board, Minister John Wilson had withdrawn the Board's application to the EEC for funds in late 1982. He alleged the Minister did so on the advice of the department officials who considered it not to be a worthy project. The civil service interpretation differed from that assessment: it was their understanding that during informal discussions, the European Commission representative had asked that the application not be pressed as, if it were, the decision would be a negative one. Nowadays, that might be classed as 'spin'! (See Chapter 15 for EEC application saga.)

However, the Monsignor was never short of uplifting moments. An Englishman, living in Dublin, called on him one day and said: "Monsignor, I don't want to take up your time but I really could not pass without telling you something. I visited the airport today. I saw for the first time, a team of Irishmen doing a wonderful job in their own country, that they have been doing in other countries for generations. They deserve an airport."

In the third week of July Minister Mitchell eventually visited the Airport and had lunch with the Board of Directors. It was not his first time in Knock; he had been a regular pilgrim to the Shrine over the years. He said he was very impressed by what he saw, though he did not make any pronouncements. However, Monsignor Horan said he got the view the Minister was favourably disposed.

It was a view shared by contractor Frank Harrington: "It was a beautiful day as the Monsignor, the Minister and myself walked the runway. You could see Croagh Patrick and Nephin and Charlestown below. Jim Mitchell said to us: 'I am delighted, I have seen your picture now and it's a lovely sight'."

The work went on, the *Western People's* Michael Ronayne reporting on September 21 that the 6,000 ft runway has been completed during the week, with provision for an extra 1,500 ft should the need arise. The building of the runway and apron was an enormous job. Contractor Frank Harrington says he had to get men back from England who had the knowledge and experience of big projects. "We got twenty or thirty such men, and most of them are still with me, twenty-five years on. They included Mick Ruddy from Foxford, who is now our general foreman and a great organiser; Pat English, a chartered engineer from Kiltimagh, is also still with us and runs the whole contracts section; John Corcoran, a specialist in tarmac is also still with me; Paddy McDonnell, one of the first men on site, came from the Board of Works; and Jim Henry whose expertise on lifting and moving the vast amount of peat was exceptional."

Massive quantities of peat, granite rock and unsuitable material had to be removed to achieve the design levels, and excavation equipment worth millions of pounds trundled in from all over Ireland to expedite the works. Principal quantities of peat and rock excavation and gravel filling involved included: Peat excavation 1,200,000m³; Soil excavation,

500,000m³; Weathered rock, 75,000m³; Solid rock, 80,000m³; Imported fill, 1,333,000m³; Soil recompaction, 350,000m³.

The gravel filling came from nearby gravel pits and the company also opened and operated a rock quarry situated 0.5 km to the north of the runway. The work on the initial 1,800m runway commenced in September 1982 and was completed in August 1983. A Parker 353 mobile tarmacadam plant was also set up close to the runway and was capable of producing up to 100 tonnes per hour of bituminous products. Another quarry of limestone rock was opened six miles from the airport site and produced most of the blacktop material. The surfacing operations, complete with friction course, started on June 2 1983 and were completed on 27 August of the same year.

The concrete apron was laid and completed between September 1983 and April 1984, and the reinforced concrete frame terminal building and four-storey control tower were also undertaken in 1984. The extension of the main runway from 1,800m to 2,300m in length was carried out in 1984/1985. Duty Officer Matt Macken, who worked on the construction phase, remembers that Horan would arrive unannounced in his brown Ford Cortina and drive slowly around the site. "You wouldn't be aware he was here at all, unless you heard his car revving up. He always seemed to have an entourage of people with him, politicians, business people, journalists, God knows."

One day along came Sir Matt Busby, the former and fabled manager of Manchester United, who had visited the Shrine: some years earlier he had been made a Knight Commander of St Gregory, one of the highest civil honours in the Roman Catholic church.

Busby and several others had been invited to Ireland for a quiet weekend by Joe Kennedy and they met Monsignor Horan in the Parochial House in Knock. Kennedy and Horan knew each other, and the Manchester businessman often sang with the Monsignor in Kennedy's pub in Doocastle during his fund-raising sessions.

Recalls Kennedy: "After lunch he asked us to go down and see the work in progress. He put myself and Matt Busby in the back of the car, drove down the runway, doing about 70 mph, and I remember his flake of hair on the one side and it flying out the window of the car as he pointed out the development work."

Matt Macken recalls that workers on the site had the feeling that they couldn't let him down. "He was killing himself, not for himself but for everybody else; all the hard work, all that stress he was under. We understood the importance of the project, that was our attitude."

A building site under such pressurised conditions is never all sweetness and light, of course. Workers remember Horan exploding one day in 1985 when a lorry drove over freshly laid tarmacadam as he watched apoplectic from the control tower. "He could get very very cross and if you stood up he wouldn't be long telling you. You had to keep going," admitted Macken.

Looking back on a job well done, Frank Harrington acknowledges they could have backed down and cut back on the runway. "We didn't and we were proved right. You could not do a mile of roadway nowadays for the money spent on the airport. It has become a roadway to the world, great value for the money spent."

The runway was built to last. On its rock-solid foundation, it has never needed repair work since it was built. "Twenty years later and there's not a mark on it, never a hand put to it since we left," says Harrington proudly.

The cheap media shots continued, however, the *Sunday Tribune* of November 6 being fairly typical: it referred to the project as the 'airport that gave shrines a bad name'.

However, if Jim Mitchell was perceived to be favourably disposed during his visit, a letter from him arrived at Knock on December 14. It contained no pre-Christmas cheer – the project was being axed, and this time the decision was final. The last pay-off was to be £650,000 to meet 'existing contractual commitments', and there would be no further exchequer support to subsidise running costs (which the Board had told the Minister it hoped to meet from its own resources). Almost £10 million in state funds had been sanctioned for the project, and that was the end of it, the Government decreed.

That night journalist Michael Ronayne and schoolteacher Colman O'Raghallaigh drove from Claremorris to see Horan and cheer him up. He was-off limit for media calls, but he knew his visitors well and welcomed them.

"We were talking over the issues, giving him a bit of moral support, when the RTÉ news came on and up flashed some archive footage of Garret FitzGerald in relation to some other story," remembers Ronayne.

There was a fellow in the background whom Horan thought he recognised.

"Who's that fellow behind FitzGerald?" he asked his guests.

"I told him it was Dan Egan, the Fine Gael press officer, and that he was actually an in-law of mine. Nothing more was said about it then," chuckled Ronayne.

"But later, when we were leaving, he said, 'So he's (Egan) related to you. It's time you threw some Knock holy water on him'!"

Horan kept his counsel to himself for a few days, and when he finally spoke in public about the government's decision he said he believed it had a legal and moral commitment under the grant-in-aid agreement to provide funds to complete the airport. Remember, in April 1981, the Fianna Fáil Government had sanctioned the project to the tune of £8 million at 1980 prices and now, over two years later, less than £10 million had been sanctioned, so allowing for inflation and delays caused by the political shenanigans what had originally been pledged was probably just about honoured.

But Minister Paddy O'Toole was not holding out any further hopes when he told the *Western People* the nation's financial health was so poor that they had to take tough decisions. "In better times, the decision would have been different," he said.

Looking back, O'Toole remembers that Cabinet decision as being the outcome of a long and acrimonious discussion in which six or seven options were considered and various degrees of Government action and expenditure over a two-to-four year period were discussed.

"This discussion took place at a time of a worsening financial position. I was absolutely opposed to this letter being sent and met with Monsignor Horan who was in a very threatening and belligerent mood," he says. Horan in a rage was a fearsome sight, as several confronted by his wrath could attest! "At the time the pressure to cut back on expenditure and allocate funds to those projects which had a chance of success was very much part of the decision-making process," O'Toole added.

After Christmas Monsignor Horan was adamant the airport would be finished, and was hopeful the Government would provide the necessary £3 million to add the terminal building, water and sewerage, fencing and electronic equipment to the main runway, taxiway and apron now nearing completion. He ruled out, however the possibility of a campaign in Britain and the US to raise funds. Obviously, he wanted to maintain pressure on the government to deliver.

Even with the pressure mounting on his shoulders, very few saw Monsignor Horan down-hearted. Contractor Frank Harrington recalls that he never saw him down in the dumps, though he undoubtedly must have been at times. "He was under huge strain, but he always kept the good side out, always kept the flag flying."

And keep it flying he did. Journalists from all over the world flocked to his door in Knock: *Time, Newsweek,* the *New York Times* and *The Times* of London were amongst those to interview him. And television programmes in the US and Ireland wanted to have him as a guest. Morley Safer of the CBS flagship programme *Sixty Minutes* pursued him for his coast-to-coast broadcast.

Monsignor Horan was suitably impressed when he heard that a thirty-second advertising slot on the programme would cost $340,000. Doing his sums, he estimated the worth of the programme to Knock and the airport would therefore be $13 million. The Monsignor was not someone to look a gift horse in the mouth.

Safer found him a very worthy adversary with a rapier-like wit, a ready smile and poker-like ability to discuss his plans without giving away an iota of privileged information. The programme was syndicated through the English-speaking world and was transmitted in Ireland by RTÉ after it had gone out in the US.

Journalist and old acquaintance Michael Hand was later to comment on Horan's sparkling performance . . . "I remember the twinkle in his eye as he stone-facedly answered the interviewer's questions which endeared him to the capitalists of that country (America)."

Gay Byrne also sought him for the *Late Late Show* which the Monsignor considered the most daunting challenge of all television engagements. He studied Gay Byrne's techniques for weeks, and even had a stand-in Byrne look-alike pose difficult questions. He concluded that he was lacking in humility in his approach, and reckoned if he had the proper attitude it wouldn't really matter if he made a fool of himself or not. He was happy with the outcome. The reaction was most positive, the level of support appreciable, he concluded.

His curate at Knock, Fr. Colm Kilcoyne, himself a media expert, says Horan had something in dealing with the media one would pay big money for. "He told me one time you never win an argument on TV or change minds by logic. But you persuade, by your manner, that this is an ok guy, reasonable, likeable and then, having bought the person, you may buy his point of view. But the essential thing is to sell your own reasonableness. You never buy from someone you dislike. That, and when under pressure admit you have a wild dream and then laugh and say, 'Sure I'll give it a try anyway and if it fails, so what?"

Before undertaking tv appearances the Monsignor consulted widely. Albert Reynolds remembers one particular call when he was not in Government. "He rang and said he was going on RTÉ and asked for advice on how he might handle the estimates of what it (airport) would cost. I said there is one very simple answer. You are talking about £12m or £13m for a project in the West, and at that time bus services were costing £13m per year in subsidies. I said there's your figure now, the price of the airport, and surely the West is entitled to its share of the national spend."

Through all the knocks and the cross-examinations Horan's irrepressible humour and ability to get what he wanted did not let him down. Lord Altamount Jeremy Browne of historic Westport House recalls being asked to do a programme on RTÉ television with the Monsignor and of the two of them travelling to Dublin by car for the recording. First they had to visit each other's houses.

John O'Donoghue, who was doing the programme, had asked them to attend a showing of John B. Keane's 'The Chastitute' so that he could ask them what they thought of it, amongst other things.

However, on the way to Dublin the Monsignor said he had no interest in seeing Keane's production. Instead, he said he'd like to attend the musical 'Annie' which was playing to full houses in the Gaiety.

"I had read rave reviews in *The Irish Times* and knew it was booked out well in advance," recalled Lord Altamount, "but nevertheless he asked me to drive to the theatre, and we arrived as the crowds were flocking in. It was like a rugby scrum outside the door," he said.

"Wait here," Horan told Lord Altamount and vanished into the middle of it, his head bobbing up now and again.

Minutes later he reappeared, waving triumphantly aloft two tickets.

"How did you do that?" enquired the amazed peer.

"Oh, I just told them I had the Lord waiting outside in a car – I didn't say which one," laughed Horan.

Lord Altamount once asked Horan what his next project was going to be after the Airport. "I am going to build a big deep-water port off the coast of Mayo. I am absolutely serious because if we do all the big ships will call," he had replied.

Meanwhile, Horan needed all his resilience for these were tough times in Mayo. Ceimici Teo at Corroy, near Ballina, was to close and the jobs transferred to Cork. Min Fheir Teoranta had already closed in Erris, and Bellacorick power station was under threat. And he was still the guts of £3m shy of completing his airport.

Divine intervention was desperately needed!

CHAPTER TEN

1984: Ladies of the night – That foggy boggy hill remark – Holy smoke in Knock – Big money on way – Kenny clashes over churchgate signatures – Christy Moore song takes off – Shaggers lost heart – Money in tea chests – Government hands over airport

Ladies of the night, Foggy, Boggy Hill and Holy Smoke!

ON January 1 Galway City began celebrations marking its mayoral status granted by King Richard III in 1484. A wide-ranging programme of events was planned to mark the year in the City of the Tribes.

Elsewhere, it was announced President Ronald and Nancy Reagan were coming to Ireland on a four-day official visit. And a Dunnes Stores worker refuses to handle South African goods.

Another difficult and uncertain year for workers dawned at Knock Airport. With money rapidly running out, workers who had placed their trust in – indeed invested in – the project were facing into a very precarious future. The Airport Board had to plan the orderly winding down of operations. There was no other option but to lay off staff, and gradually the hectic pace and din of activity began to abate and fall silent.

The Monsignor told the media he was sad but not disheartened. He still believed the Government should complete the project so he held back from conceding that the promoters would have to raise the shortfall and finish the job. After all, the estimated amount needed, approximately £3.4 million, was a huge sum in 1984 terms. Throughout the community there was the sense that the West had been let down again by government.

Underneath the surface, there was a welling of anger, but more so resolve. The feeling was 'we have come this far; let's show them'. Offers of support came readily. One that made the local and national headlines was tabled by the chart-topping Royal Blues Showband of Claremorris who had romped to the top of the charts in the '60s with 'Old Man Trouble', sung by Doc Carroll. The band offered to undertake a three-weeks coast-to-coast tour of the US to raise funds. Band manager Andy Creighton was reported in *The Connaught Telegraph* of January 18 as saying

107

that they hoped to collect up to £500,000 from their performances and to offer the cash to the airport company.

Creighton, one of the great band managers of that era, told the paper the band would work with Irish exiles from the West of Ireland. "I can see the venture proving most successful," he said. However, Monsignor Horan, rigidly maintaining the government should honour its commitment, turned down the band's offer. He appreciated the goodwill and the offer of support, 'but I don't want the airport to be associated with a dance band'. He could probably see the headlines if he agreed to the offer: 'Monsignor dances to new tune!' or even: 'Band Helps Old Man out of Trouble.'

Around that time, John Mahon, a Charlestown businessman and Fine Gael supporter, got a call to meet the Monsignor at the site. He found Horan sitting waiting in his car with Jim Ryan.

"I got in and the Monsignor quickly got to the point. 'You know the money has been stopped, I'd like you to go to Fine Gael people in the county to get up a deputation to see if the decision can be changed,' he said.

"Monsignor, it's a waste of time. It's gone," I replied. "You have done so much work up to now, keep going. What I would do is clear the bog out in front of the runway and fill it, but don't surface it, and then you can go to the people and raise the money to tarmacadam it, bit by bit," Mahon advised.

Taoiseach Garret FitzGerald certainly had no intention of relenting. On a visit to the West he informed the media the promoters should take a leaf out of what was happening in Galway where people were investing private funds to develop their own facility. "Over 90% of funds for regional airports in the country has been used on the Connaught Regional Airport and this has created problems elsewhere," he told newsmen. It seemed pointless pointing out to the Taoiseach that not too many people in Dublin, Cork or Shannon had dipped into their pockets to get an air service!

During this time Charlie Haughey continued to take an interest in the airport and he advised some members of the company to make sure that the two civil servants appointed to be board be retained as they were a vital link between the Board and the Government of the day. The advice was taken.

*　　　*　　　*

Just when he felt he needed time out, the Monsignor got a call from Queensland, in Australia, to attend the opening of a new airport at Cairns. The promoters there, who had been having the same regional airport difficulties with government as the Monsignor was experiencing in Mayo, had seen the Morley Safer CBS programme and wanted him over for the opening. They also wanted him to talk to the media about the benefits of opening up the regions to air transport.

The invitation covered tickets for himself and his trusty lieutenant Jim Ryan who had just been given three months' protective notice at the airport as the necessary retrenchment moves began to bite. Also on the trip was airport engineer John Balfe who paid his own expenses. They set off in March.

Balfe recalls that the Monsignor relished being away from all the controversy, meeting friends and people who had heard about Knock Airport. On the way out they visited Singapore, and called on the Monsignor's cousins in Sydney, Balfe's relations in Perth, and Jim Ryan's many friends down under.

"The Monsignor absolutely came alive in front of a camera and was at his best in Australia. At Cairns he had to give a speech to all the travel agents and the minute he got in front of the mike he was beaming and he was brilliant. He got a massive reception; they just loved him."

Today, Cairns has a thriving international airport and in the manager's office is a crystal memento brought by the party from Mayo all those years ago. They stopped off in Brisbane and people were coming up and shaking the Monsignor's hand. "He was a huge success there; everyone seemed to know him. He is not an easy man to describe. He had an element of ego but not ego for himself. Everyone we met in Australia he charmed. He was a charmer, and they recognised him as the underdog who could make things happen," Balfe says.

Horan was, of course, the consummate media performer and was much in demand on radio and television. But it was not all work, as Balfe acknowledged. "We were having a great time seeing the sights and one day we were to go on the Murray river but the tour operators we booked with let us down. The Monsignor went to them and said, 'I am never going to travel with ye again,' knowing full well he'd never be there again! We all laughed."

Balfe has particularly abiding memories of Melbourne. They had booked accommodation along the way through an agency and everything went fine until they reached that great city of the trams and panoramic river views in Victoria.

"As it happened the hotel we were booked into was in an area much frequented by American soldiers on leave from Vietnam and in search of some R&R. Inevitably, ladies of the night flocked to the area as rooms were available, and we ended up booked into a hotel which was of doubtful character on a Saturday."

Jim Ryan, who had travelled the world and had worked in Australia, raised alarm bells with Balfe when he heard they were staying in that particular area, and those fears were confirmed when Balfe saw the room he was staying in.

"Jim and I knew we could not stay there and I went down to the Monsignor and told him we'd have to move on. I must have spent an hour on the phone trying to get hold of the travel agency that afternoon, and eventually I got Quantas who arranged alternative accommodation.

"Of course, the Monsignor knew what was going on but he had this ability to close his mind out. Once I got the new hotel address, I explained to the lady receptionist that we had an Irish monsignor with us and couldn't stay. She said, grudgingly, she understood.

"But as we waited for our taxi, the receptionist was giving out under her breath and as we beat a hasty retreat through the door, she couldn't resist a parting shot and exclaimed, in a loud voice, 'Even the Lord forgave Mary Magdalen, you know,' nodding after the retreating Monsignor."

*   *   *

While the trio were still away in Australia, Connaught/Ulster MEP Seán Flanagan was claiming the headlines back home in the *Irish Press* of April 4 with a story suggesting that $40 million of a planned investment of $500m was heading for the West within days, and a sizeable chunk of that – £20m – was for the airport!

The advance cash, the paper claimed, was part of a proposal announced the previous week by Flanagan in Strasbourg. The projects were being fronted by a company called AGM Holdings of Maryland. Hundreds of jobs were promised over the next ten years. That extraordinary proposal and other subsequent investment proposals for the Airport industrial zone are dealt with in Chapter 21.

*   *   *

Indicative of the political sensitivities that the airport aroused at that time, another spat flared on the home front when Deputy Enda Kenny objected to signatures calling on the government to support the airport being sought at churches. A petition had been got up to exert pressure on the Coalition Government to have a rethink on the axing. His call was promptly slammed by Stephen Tarpey, a whole-hearted member of the Airport Action Committee, who reminded Kenny that he had no objection to political parties taking up financial collections at the same locations.

Kenny, now Leader of Fine Gael, says he felt at the time that the collecting of signatures involved the greater Church in what was essentially a political issue though being promoted by a priest. Kenny, based in the neighbouring West Mayo constituency, had been accused of keeping a relatively low profile as intensifying criticism rained down on the heads of his East Mayo colleagues, O'Toole and Higgins.

However, the Fine Gael leader points out that as a backbencher in the early 1980s he really had little influence over the Cabinet decision of 1983. "I expressed the strong opinion that this was the wrong decision," he says. He concedes that his party was outmanoeuvred by Fianna Fáil, and believes Fine Gael should have handled the controversy in a better way. When appointed Minister for Tourism in the late '90s, Kenny was to do much to advance the airport's cause, as we shall see.

Back in Ireland again in April, a much refreshed Horan quickly had the bit firmly between his teeth. Impatient of the political impasse, he sought meetings with Minister Mitchell. The Minister turned down the first invitation, but on receipt of the second letter asked the Board to submit proposals for the completion and operation of the airport.

Monsignor Horan submitted the proposal on June 18 in which he asked (a) if there was any point in the Board expecting further State aid. (b) would the government seek financial aid from the EEC to complete the project? (c) what future role did the government plan to take in relation to the airport? (d) in certain circumstances, would the government hand over, free of charge and without conditions, full ownership of the project, as completed to date, to the company? (e) would the Government consider in principle establishing a Duty-Free Zone in the vicinity of the airport, and (f) if the airport was completed in accordance with acceptable standards, would an airport licence be issued, and would authorisation be given for scheduled international transport requirements?

What the Board was saying in effect to the Minister was: "Hand over the airport to the Board, license it, authorise scheduled flights and we will take it off your hands once and for all."

It was an offer the Fine Gael/Labour Government could hardly refuse, but the way of politics is strange. Instead of grasping the opportunity to get rid of the Knock monkey on his back, the Minister took himself off to Galway a few days later for the opening of the Cranmore Airport and let fly at the Knock project. He called the airport site a 'foggy, boggy hill' and said it was ill-advised in the extreme to build it in a location far from big towns and cities. He also charged that the promoters built the airport against the advice of experts.

Horan immediately rounded on the Minister for his 'outburst'. In a lengthy statement published in the *Western People,* he said: "It is a pity the Minister should have used the occasion in Galway to sow the seed of enmity between the different counties in the West. His aim seemed to be to 'divide and conquer'. Why should the decent people of the West be asked to suffer the humiliation of fighting amongst themselves for crumbs from the Government's table? From the comments I have heard the people of the West would resent anybody trying to divide them and especially a politician from outside the province.

"The Jim Mitchell that made the speech in Galway is certainly not the Jim Mitchell that visited the Connaught Regional Airport last year and was most impressed by it. I met Jim Mitchell on that occasion and I have great respect for him as a person and as a Minister. I was disappointed, very disappointed, with the Galway performance."

Monsignor Horan went on to say that the Minister had given the impression that £13 million had been spent on the project. If £13m had been spent the airport would be completed. "The truth is that less than £10 million has been spent to date. If the Department had allocated sufficient funds each year and had not refused the company permission to proceed with the work on schedule the airport might have been built for £9 million," he retaliated.

Later the Monsignor was to contrast the actual amount spent to that date by the State (£9.8 million) with the estimate for the new runway at Dublin airport, £32 million at 1983 prices.

In many respects Mitchell's 'foggy, boggy' speech marked a turning point for the airport. Supporters of the airport were appalled that the minister would so denigrate the efforts of the community and the promoters, and even people who had been critical of the project, felt the Minister had gone way over the top. So taken aback were Mitchell apologists that the word went out that the speech had been written by civil servants and the minister had not read it in advance. It was a fanciful, naive notion.

Mitchell's ministerial colleague, Paddy O'Toole, says he could not comment on the circumstances of how the statement came to be made. "I can say that Jim Mitchell later expressed regret at having made the statement and was fully reconciled with the Monsignor prior to the latter's death."

By now the airport people loved to love and loved to hate was racing up the charts with Christy Moore's pithy song 'The Airport Up in Knock'. The balladeer recalled how it came to be written. He was staying in a house in Hagfield, near Charlestown, after a gig in the area and a few were sharing Horan tales late at night when the idea took hold. He drove his van up and down the half-built runway looking for inspiration.

Charlestown County Councillor Gerry Murray recollected the circumstances in which the song was composed. "Christy had been playing in Ballina the previous night and he had a few verses written. He called to see me on the way back to Dublin. He had another few verses written by then. So we drove up in his van to the site and he was expecting a small grass runway. But when he got there it was like looking out to sea in Enniscrone: what he could see was a sea of tarmacadam going to the horizon!

"We came back down and added a few more verses, and I came up with the 'Nato supplied the dough!' lines," says Murray.

Christy Moore says the song earned him great kudos from the Monsignor who sent him a sacred scapular. "I was also invited on the inaugural flight to Rome but I had to demur for I had a hot gig in Kentish Town to fulfil and I knew the Monsignor would understand!" he recalls with a smile.

Courtesy of Moore, here are the opening lines of a song that will forever be associated with the airport:

"At the early age of thirty-eight, my mother said, "Go west!"

"Get up," says she, "And get a job!" Says I, "I'll do my best."

I pulled on my wellingtons to march to Kiltimagh
But I took a wrong turn in Charlestown and I ended up in Knock.

Once this quiet crossroads was a place of gentle prayer
Where Catholics got indulgent once or twice a year.
You could buy a pair of rosary beads or get your candles blessed
If you had a guilty conscience you could get it off your chest.
Then came the priest from Partry, Father Horan was his name.
Ever since he's been appointed Knock has never been the same.
"Begod," says Jim, "'Tis eighty years since Mary was about.
'Tis time for another miracle," and he blew the candle out.

From Fatima to Bethlehem and from Lourdes to Kiltimagh
I've never seen a miracle like the airport up in Knock."

Ironically, Ryanair Chief Executive Michael O'Leary holds that one of the great mistakes Ireland made was not joining NATO at the end of the Second World War! "The Americans would have built about six international airport along the West coast of Ireland. Now, a lot of Ryanair's expansion throughout Europe is coming through airports initially built by the military," he opined.

Moore's song was not the only one to be written about the airport. In fact, according to 'Songs of Past and People 2'[8] it gave rise to dozens of verses, including 'The Ballad of Knock Airport' by Louis Gunnigan of Lurgan, Aughamore; 'Monsignor Horan' by Michael O'Grady; 'The Airport in Banc Dubh' by John Byrne and Tom Duffy of Coill Mór, Kilkelly, a village directly under the flight path of the airport; and by Tóm Waldron of Crossard, and Paddy Walsh of Kiltimagh. Paddy's brother, Gerry Walsh of the Raftery Room, Kiltimagh, also penned verses. Even Monsignor Horan himself composed a parody 'I'm Dreamin' of a Great Airport' which he sang at many fund-raising events and indeed on television.

Before May was out the Airport Board had decided to go it alone, to raise the money to complete the job. The Monsignor had made up his mind, and his Board backed him.

Tom Neary recalls the seminal moment, going down one evening with Horan in the car to the airport site.

"We'll have a look and see what way is it looking," the Monsignor had said.

"At that time the site was wide open. You could drive right in and down the runway. We drove down the tarmac and eventually the tarmac ended at a barrier and all that was after that was gravel and stone. The Monsignor looked over the barrier and said, 'This is where the . . . lost heart, but we will finish it ourselves!'

---

8   '*Songs of Past and People 2*' is a second collection of songs from East Mayo and nearby West Roscommon, with a companion booklet of the same title compiled by Joe Byrne in 1995.

Journalist Michael Ronayne, who knew the Monsignor well, reckoned he most probably used the word 'shaggers' which was a great word of his when the Fine Gael/Labour Coalition drew his ire.

Be that as it may, Tom Neary said in the twenty-one years he had spent working at close range with Horan, he never before encountered such determination and willpower. "His face said it all," remembers Neary. "All of £3.5 million was needed to finish it; it sounds small today but it was a lot of money back then, but it didn't daunt him," says Neary.

"And you can take it the money is not coming from Mr Flanagan, MEP, or his followers," an angry director Seamus Monaghan told the media when the go-ahead-alone decision was taken. "No one is going to say that we left £10m. lying in the ground and walked away from it just because Mr Mitchell wanted to play politics with the airport," he charged.

One day, during the political U-turns, when work had stopped on the site, Frank Harrington recollects getting a call from the Monsignor asking where were the trucks. "I told him they were all over the place. 'Well,' he replied, 'a tv crew from England is arriving at the site in an hour and we need to show them that work is continuing.' And within an hour the trucks were there and work was underway again."

He fondly recalls another day when Horan called to his office in Kilkelly, anxious to get the runway finished amidst all the uncertainty. We went outside to talk. 'Are you going to finish the runway or what, Frank?' he asked.

'I am, no problem,' I replied, and we went off and had a cup of tea. We had that type of working relationship. He was a great man to work for. He always held to his end of the deal.

"He used to say to me with a flourish of his arms: 'Frank, in twenty or thirty years' time Monsignor Horan won't be thought of but the airport will be here, playing its part in the development of the region.' Today, when older people see a plane in the sky over the airport they say, 'There's Monsignor Horan.' Only for him it would not be there," is Harrington's firm conviction.

Seán Balfe reckons Harrington went into debt for around £600,000 if not more, to keep the project going. "He took a huge risk, he trusted the Monsignor and the Monsignor said he would get the money."

Former FG Minister Paddy O'Toole said it was commonly understood during the course of construction that contractors were taken on on the understanding that funding would be available, if not by the State by the Church.

"It then became clear that the Church would not or could not deliver the funding and the Monsignor came under pressure to find money for work done. Some contractors visited Cardinal O'Fiaich to check out the veracity of the promises made about the Church backing and found they didn't stack up," he maintains.

Contractors who were worried went directly to Horan for their money because they were under pressure from their banks. A story is told that one such sub-contractor told Horan he had to get funds into his bank account before close of business to avoid cheques not being honoured.

The Monsignor regretted that he did not have any, that there was nothing in the kitty at that time, and asked his caller if anyone else owed him money. When it was acknowledged that that was the case, the Monsignor is reputed to have said: "Go to them and meanwhile I will pray for your success." When the hard-pressed sub-contractor went to the first client on his list, the man said, "The very person! I have a cheque here for you." This was typical of the sub-contractor's day and by the close of business at the bank he had collected enough to satisfy his bank manager.

*   *   *

Though the fund-raising campaign had not yet opened officially, envelopes containing donations for the airport started coming into Knock Shrine. A fund-raiser told Cormac MacConnell of the *Irish Press* on May 25 that the money was going into tea chests. "There must have been up to £100,000 going into those tea chests," he was told.

In June the Mayo Association in Dublin raised £5,000 for the airport fund and pledged to raise another £10,000 to £15,000.

And, unknown to himself, Barry Desmond was a powerful generator of money for the airport: the more he gave off about the project in the media the more people responded to the Monsignor's cause.

Seamus Monaghan, a Board member, admitted Desmond – whom he referred to as the Elder Lemming – used to get up his nose with his on-going onslaughts. He recalled one particular day when he was driving to Knock to meet the Monsignor and Desmond came on the radio.

"He was giving me a terrible headache. He was driving me up the walls, and when I got to the Presbytery I rushed in to the small room on the left-hand side of the door. The fire was lit, a few turf in it and the smoke curling up the chimney. The Monsignor was sitting there reading his office and I came through the door and blurted out, 'Monsignor . . . !' But he pointed to the chair across from him for me to sit down. When he finished his office he said: 'Now, what is it, Seamus?' I said 'Monsignor, we have to do something about this fellow. We just have to do something.' And he is sitting there quietly and I'm giving out yards.

"He just put his finger to his lips to silence me and he caught me by the arm and brought me to another room and there were people there counting money, and he said, 'Seamus, the more Mr Desmond speaks out against us on the radio and the more publicity he gives us, the more envelopes come through that door, so don't even bother worrying about it,' and that's fact."

To the Monsignor there was no such thing as bad publicity. "The Monsignor knew all about that maxim and he never, ever said anything about Barry Desmond, and Barry Desmond defied him on several occasions, and I was all on for answering him, but the Monsignor would say, 'No, no'," says Monaghan.

Monaghan's evaluation of Desmond is earthy: "He was an asshole. He was building up his own profile. He gave the airport more crap than anyone. They talk about Jim Mitchell, but Barry Desmond was a Labour man determined to get to Europe, and he got there eventually. It appeared he wanted nothing to happen in the West of Ireland. He couldn't see beyond the Pale."

To help raise the enormous amount of money required, Horan gathered a small group of people in his sitting-room in the Presbytery in Knock. Present were Jim Ryan, Secretary of the Airport Board; Marie Page, a key member of the Knock Shrine staff; James O'Donohue, then of Allfresh Products, Charlestown; and Tom Neary, Chief Steward of the Shrine. "This small committee was to become the powerhouse to drive the fund-raising campaign," recalls Tom Neary.

It was decided to run a series of international Jumbo Quiz raffles with prizes being donated by business people and others. "The prizes included cars, sites for houses, bullocks, hoggets, tons of coal, fills of oil, sums of money, holidays and so on. Two Knock stewards gave us big pieces of land near towns and they fetched goodly sums that enhanced the funds," says Neary.

Monsignor Horan revealed to the media that a large farm had been donated to the cause by an anonymous benefactor. That benefactor was in fact James O'Donohue, who had been listening to the radio one day when the Monsignor announced he was pressing ahead to finish the project, and appealed for helpers. As a steward at Knock Shrine, O'Donohue knew the Monsignor only to see, but he had kept his distance because he felt Horan was a cross man. The two were quickly to get to know each other much better.

O'Donohoe had been left a farm in Co. Sligo by a relative and offered it to Horan for the airport at their first meeting. "But," responded the Monsignor, "you are a married man – how many children have you?" I had four at the time. He said, "You will need that farm." But I said, "Look, Father, as far as I am concerned I am interested in jobs for the area, I brought Fr. McDyer here in the '60s in his Save the West campaign. Look at Shannon. If you have one person working you help support twelve more," O'Donohue told him.

O'Donohue sold the farm, about 30 acres, and gave Horan the proceeds, about £40,000, for the airport. It was a lot of money then but think what it would be worth today! The Monsignor asked O'Donohue to join his fund-raising team, and he agreed, as did his wife, Mary. Identifying contributors to the fund was James O'Donohue's first task. He got out the Golden Pages and started going through the list of likely donors, doctors and professional people, but Monsignor turned to him and asked: "What are you doing? You are wasting your time. It's the poor people who always help me."

O'Donohue recalled a particularly poor fund-raising month, November, when subscriptions were going down. "I was getting worried and feeling really down about it, but he barked at me 'James, Providence will provide.' He put his whole trust in Providence."

There was a question of legality over major raffles at the time because they began to exceed the limit of what could be paid out in prizes under the Lottery Act. There had been an issue around that time when bookmaker Barney Curley raffled his big house.

After getting legal advice, the Knock fund-raising team added a question to the raffle, making it a game of knowledge rather than a game of chance. "We checked it out with the lawyers and were given the green light," said O'Donohue. The money rolled in.

Mary O'Donohue said most mornings after the Jumbo Quiz was launched she'd go up to Knock Shrine to give the girls there a hand sorting out the post. "There used to be sackloads and there were four or five of us there, opening all the envelopes and putting the money in a tea chest which quickly used to be full and overflowing. And then we'd count it and Monsignor would look in and say 'God bless the work' and ask for the final figure each day. We were working like beavers, counting all this cash. There was magnificent support.

"Whenever we had accomplished something special, raised maybe £10,000, he'd say, 'Ye did great. Now what's the next thing ye have planned?' He wouldn't turn around and have a show and thank everyone. He'd clap his hands, say, 'Ye are fantastic people. Now on to the next thing.' The Monsignor was really charismatic during that time. He was unreal."

Then one day, while in America raising funds, James O'Donohue rang Monsignor Horan from Boston. The Monsignor told him people were saying the draws were illegal. 'You are in charge, James,' he warned and O'Donohue conceded he was and would deal with it when he got home. When Horan delegated he delegated!

When O'Donohue got home the local garda sergeant said he had to take a statement. "It appears there was a complaint made to the Chief Superintendent. I said, 'Sergeant, I am within my rights to remain silent and silent I remain. I'm giving you no statement'."

Mary O'Donohue said the legal uncertainty came to a head just before the final draw when Monsignor Horan got an anonymous – and inaccurate as it transpired – tip-off that the gardai had been ordered to search the Shrine offices to establish if the Lottery Act was being breached.

Mrs O'Donohue says one day the Monsignor rang looking for James. "I said he was in Dublin. He said, 'Can you come up straight away? It's urgent.' When I got there he brought me into a room and said,

'Mary, we are in trouble. They are going to do a raid on Knock Shrine. Imagine on our only national shrine. They are going to raid it!

'What do you think we will do?' he asked.

'Monsignor, if there is no evidence there is nothing they can do!'

"We scratched our heads. We were talking about getting rid of all the fliers, all the promotional material for the Jumbo draws," she says.

She says within a short time the Shrine's furnace was stuffed with promotional draw material, except the counterfoils for the final draw. The 'incriminating evidence' went up in smoke. "It was like the Queen Mary sailing out of port. You could see the smoke rising over Knock," she recalls.

Then all the counterfoils and the draw drum were loaded in the back of a van and taken to a place of safe-keeping. Some claim it was covered over with a big Foxford woollen rug.

Mary O'Donohue says they could not afford not to have the draw. "We had sold a lot of tickets by that stage and there were three or four really big prizes, a house, a big cash prize. There was no way we could abandon it but we could not afford to be caught up in a legal wrangle either."

On the night of the raffle a small body of organisers travelled to a secret venue in the area known as the Cloontias in West Roscommon. Different cars were used. Some took the back roads because they were afraid of being followed. In the paranoia that existed, several swore there were garda cars at every crossroads. The draw was held in a safe house. The Monsignor was not present.

Garda sources confirmed to the author that a complaint about the draw had indeed been made, but dismissed reports that cars were being followed. The fact that a garda car was spotted was purely coincidental, the source said.

After the draw was made the contents of the drum and other draw paraphernalia was carried outside and piled on the ground as the pale moon was rising over the countryside. "It created a Nephin-like mound and a match was struck and up rose the flames like a lark in the clear air. You've heard of Dante's inferno! That was it but the result of all the dedicated labour was gratifying," recalls Tom Neary.

The top prize was £30,000 and was won by a Cork subscriber who gave some of his winnings back towards the airport. Another big donation boosted the coffers: it came when a South of Ireland horse trainer rowed in with a cheque for £10,000, a not inconsiderable sum at that time.

And Mary O'Donohue remembers the Monsignor telling her of the day a man called to him at the presbytery. "He looked like a knight of the road. The man said he had two accounts in the AIB 'and I'll give you what's in the lesser one because I want to help the airport.' He insisted on doing so. And what was in the lesser one? THIRTEEN GRAND!"

When an RTÉ television crew arrived on September 24 they found a stream of money coming in to complete the airport. Since the appeal was launched to finish the project, more and more donations were arriving at the airport office in Knock, and a source indicated as much as a quarter of a million pounds had been raised by then.

Monsignor Horan told RTÉ that support was coming in from not alone Connaught, but from Cork, and Kerry, and Monaghan, and Waterford, and Louth, you name it, and from Northern Ireland and from across the seas. "The sums could be anything from £1 to £10,000. We get in £100, we get in £20, we get in £5. It varies. We get in four or five hundred letters every morning." RTÉ reported that twenty volunteers were present almost every night of the week, mailing literature, answering enquiries and organising speakers to attend fund-raising meetings.

Tom Neary says the Stewards and Handmaids of Knock were key to the success of the Jumbo Quiz. There were 1,200 of them and they sold an enormous amount of tickets in their own areas all over the country. He said various members of the Shrine staff also worked to sell tickets to pilgrims attending Knock. "They spared no effort to swell the coffers. I recall especially, the late Mary Concannon, who had a special knack when it came to selling tickets. She was mother of Pearce Concannon, one of the original staff members at the Airport and now Head of Emergency Services," he recalls.

One of those to help count the money as it came in and send out letters of thanks in return was John Carty, now a Fianna Fáil Deputy. "The people wanted to see the airport up and running and they gave generously," he said. It was Carty, too, who took a young Bertie Ahern, then Minister for Labour, down to the site of the airport. "Work was only in its infancy. You could hardly get around. We were up hills and down hollows, and the car had to be washed afterwards, it was in such a state. I think Bertie thought we were all mad: a lot of people did at the time!" he recalls.

The campaign was also taken overseas: RTÉ reported that Mary and James O'Donohue were organising a fund-raising visit to the United States and had set a number of prime contacts in each city. It was hoped to raise $100,000. Equipped with press cuttings, footage from RTÉ, promotional material and raffle tickets, they embarked on a busy schedule and did many press and radio interviews. While successful, the tour to cities such as New York, Philadelphia, Boston, Cleveland and Chicago did not raise anything near the anticipated target, though in follow-up visits Monsignor Horan received generous contributions.

Mary O'Donohue told of some disappointments. "We had appointments to see high-profile emigrants in a few cities, but we were kept waiting and got the run-around. One wealthy businessman whom we had an appointment with did not even show up. Courtesy was out the window! However, in Philadelphia, Charlestown native Attracta O'Malley was really fantastic; she did so much for the fundraising effort," Mary O'Donohue recalled. They addressed 1,500 at the Philadelphia Mayo Ball which was one of the highlights of the social calendar there.

Sources in Mayo estimated that exiles in America contributed between 35,000 and 50,000 dollars to the circa £3.3m raised by Horan and his tightly knit team. The political bickering over the airport denied the project 'official blessing' while the question of who owned the airport also had an adverse effect Stateside, according to sources.

As already stated, the key to generating funds over 1984/85 were the Stewards and Handmaids of Knock Shrine, and shortly before his death in 1986, Monsignor Horan had publicly acknowledged their role. "No other group of people in this country have worked so hard to raise funds for the completion of the airport after it had been abandoned by the present Government (Fine Gael/Labour Coalition). After the withdrawal of the Government from the Airport a special committee of Stewards and Handmaids was set up to organise the gathering of funds. Fund-raising still continues, and I want to acknowledge publicly the wonderful part that the Stewards and Handmaids have played and are playing in this operation. I thank them and all the friends of Knock Shrine for the great help they have given. That the airport has reached the present stage of completion is due entirely to the efforts of many people in this country and abroad," he said.

Minister of State Noel Treacy, TD, Minister for European Affairs, Department of Foreign Affairs, saw Monsignor Horan's fund-raising skills at first-hand. He was chairman of Galway County Council when he got a call from the Monsignor one Sunday night. "He said he'd be in Galway in the morning and would meet me. We arranged to meet at 10.30am in the Imperial Hotel. He said he needed contacts in Galway city. I put on my thinking cap and picked out all the Mayo names that I knew were in the heavyweight division in commerce here. I gave him the list. I met him again for lunch at 2pm and he had 27,000 punts collected. He was some man, a wonderful man with a warm smile who had a vision and would bring you with him under his umbrella no matter how bad the situation was."

On October 12 the Airport Board submitted another memorandum to Minister Mitchell, repeating again the points made in earlier correspondence, essentially asking the Government to hand over the airport to the company. The *Irish Press* on December 6 reported that the Minister was expected to recommend the proposal to the Cabinet for approval.

A week later the media reported that the Government had agreed to hand over control of the airport, so the way was now clear for the company to take charge of its own destiny. By that time the Government had much more serious issues to concentrate on. And one of those was the unemployment rate which, according to *The Irish Times,* was running at 16.4% with 214,517 out of work.

Elsewhere, Ethiopia was in the grip of civil war and famine and Bob Geldof was lining up Band Aid to release the fund-raising chart hit 'Do They Know It's Christmas'.

CHAPTER ELEVEN

1985: Mayoman of Year award – Tractors and planes – Pious rogue –
Pushing it out to over 8,000 ft – Vital beacon goes on blip –
US offer of £2.5m causes controversy – Police escort in Boston –
Eighteen conditions to be met

Board tensions over Rome priority

REMEMBER the phenomena of the moving statues? Well, 1985 was the year with reports of weird happenings emanating from Asdee in Co. Kerry, and from Ballinspittle in Co. Cork. It was also the year Bob Geldof organised Live Aid at Wembley with Ireland emerging as the highest 'per capita' donor. It was the year, too, that U2 had a hit with 'The Unforgettable Fire.'

In Mayo, the closure of Travenol Laboratories in Castlebar early in the New Year with the loss of hundreds of jobs came as a savage blow. The company had been a major employer in the county with plants also in Belmullet and Swinford.

The reversal increased Monsignor Horan's resolve to provide the vital piece of infrastructure he was working on with all his might. "You can't expect industrialists to stay here if infrastructure is not developed," he said.

But the news was not all bad. Within days he was chosen as the Mayo Person of the Year by the Mayo Association in Dublin, and the date was announced for the first flight out from the Airport. It would be in October and would be to Rome and Loretto for the Knock Shrine's stewards and Handmaids' Golden Jubilee.

In early February the Burlington Hotel in Dublin was full to overflowing to celebrate with the Monsignor as he received his richly deserved Mayo Person of the Year award, and there to see him honoured was his proud 97-year-old mother, Catherine, who was one of his greatest supporters. Loyal fans of the doughty parish priest travelled from Britain and the US to share the night with him. It was one of those great community occasions, with over one thousand people rising to acclaim their champion.

Meanwhile, the Airport board continued to press for a letter from Minister Mitchell officially dissociating himself from the project. There was a thaw in relationships: in a memo before Government the Minister proposed that his department's involvement with the company should be terminated but that the state should maintain a 'contingent claim' on the airport's property for a period of 20 years.

Mitchell pointed out to Cabinet that withdrawal of government involvement would require an amendment to the company's Memorandum and Articles of Association to omit the control referred to in the first paragraph of the document. "It would be this amendment that would effectively give the company full autonomy over the running of its affairs, except in respect of licensing which would shortly be sought on completion of the airport," wrote Colman Cassidy in the *Sunday Press* of February 10. At that stage, the paper estimated that the fund-raising drive had reaped £750,000.

"But perhaps the saddest feature of all has been the Coalition government's unwillingness – on purely ideological grounds – to pick up the £3m or £4m for Knock Airport that is literally lying on the table in Brussels for the development of peripheral EEC regions," commented Cassidy.

In an RTÉ *Today Tonight* programme a few weeks later Horan acknowledged that £750,000 had indeed been raised and another three quarters of a million would make the airport operational. They did not intend to embellish everything, concessions would be offered at the airport and the minimum amount of staff would be employed initially to ensure costs were kept fully under control. He said for every £1 being spent on the project, the company was getting £5 in value in return. Public works contracts might have been traditionally costing multiples of their original estimates – and up to recent times massive overruns were common – but under Horan's stewardship no such waste was being countenanced.

Asked did he not foresee industrial relations problems arising, "No," he replied. "Surely the unions would welcome 15 or 20 jobs?"

The interviewer asked him how he would react to a Bishop, an admirer of his, describing him as a 'pious old rogue'?

To which the Monsignor responded: "Well, I might be a rogue but I don't think I am pious," followed by a typical peal of laughter.

He steadfastly maintained during the interview that in years to come the critics of the project would all be answered.

On the same programme, director Seamus Monaghan was asked did he think the airport would have come about if a Coalition government was in place in 1980.

He didn't mince his words in reply: "Well, I think you should ask the people in Shannon or the people in Cork that. Would there have been a Cork Airport or would there have been a Shannon Airport if it wasn't for a Fianna Fáil Government? We wouldn't have an airport in Sligo if it wasn't for the Fianna Fáil Government. So as far as I'm concerned now, there wouldn't have been an airport at Knock."

Then the interviewer raised a question about a possible conflict of interests for Monaghan: would the Sligoman's electrical firm be in the running for the installation of the lights and related work?

Monaghan: I will definitely be pricing that contract. Definitely in the running for it. I can only say when the prices are in and you know, tenders are in and that's it.

Interviewer: Would you see any conflict in the fact that you're a member of the Board and also tendering for what after all could be a million, million and a half pounds worth of business?

Monaghan: Well, while I'm a director of the Airport, I am only a director of my electrical company. There are other directors involved in my company. So I'm in, it would be very bad taste if I couldn't price a job because I am the director of that company. I see no conflict of interests whatsoever. In fact while that decision would be going on I'd resign from the board or step down until that decision was made.

Interviewer: You don't think the fact that you are, have been involved in it, you have a head start on anybody else?

Monaghan: No.

The national media had a habit of whipping up ridiculous scenarios in relation to the Airport, and the *Today Tonight* programme could not resist asking: "Will the airport be run on proper lines in the sense that, I mean there had been a lot of talk about suggestions of local farmers sort of coming in to take Jumbo jets down, and tractors pulling planes around?"

The picture was being painted of a country bumpkin operation for suburban viewers. Can't you just imagine the picture being portrayed: Mayo farmers with hay behind their ears and mucky wellingtons up to their knees running around the runway in their old smoky Massey Fergusons attached to gleaming hi-tech Transatlantic Jumbos! The Dublin chuckles could be heard in Belmullet.

Monaghan assured viewers that only proper tractors and proper fire engines would be used, and proper safety regulations would be in force and people with expertise would be employed.

*   *   *

To mark his Person of the Year award, the local community in Knock gathered in the Rest and Care Centre in early March to make a presentation to their parish priest. And it was on that night, reported Michael Commins in *The Connaught Telegraph*, that the Monsignor ended the long-running saga relating to the name of the airport.

"It will be Knock Airport," proclaimed the Monsignor, "apart from some legal matters where Connaught Regional Airport will probably prevail," he told his delighted attendance. The 'Knock' description was for purely local consumption, however, for he made known in the *Pioneer* magazine of the following month that he was always careful to call it

'Connaught Regional Airport'. And one of his typical poses for the camera was a smiling Monsignor with a Connaught Airport bag held aloft. (See also Chapter 20 re various airport names.)

As Mayoman of the Year Horan was in much demand at social events which were a healthy source of funds for the airport. A generous response was forthcoming from the expats in Boston when Monsignor Horan and Jim Ryan visited there in March 1985. Over 1,000 people turned up in Mosleys on the Charles, in Dedham, Mass. Ciaran Staunton, a native of Louisburgh, was one of the organisers and all the stops were pulled out. Horan was met at Boston Airport by the Chief of Police and given an escort to City Hall to meet Mayor Ray Flynn. A recording of his appearance on the *Late Late Show* had been flown over in advance and was shown on a giant screen at the venue. Amongst those to meet him were Mary Staunton and Mary Morley who had originally contributed funds to Tooreen Hall in the late 1940s. Coincidentally, Charlie Haughey was also being honoured in Boston that weekend.

The Monsignor sang a few songs and for hours afterwards posed for photographs and signed autographs. Private donations were made to him for the airport, and while he refused to say how much had been donated his smile confirmed a generous response, said Staunton.

"I think he was primarily in the area looking for investors and was trying to interest airlines to fly to Knock from New York," recalls Staunton who now runs O'Neill's Pub on Third Avenue 45th St, Manhattan, New York, and is vice-chair of the Irish Lobby for Immigrant Reform. It is estimated that over 60,000 Irish are undocumented in the US and Staunton and those on the Irish Lobby for Immigrant Reform scored a notable success on May 25, 2006, when the Senate passed a Bill progressing moves towards citizenship. Mayo Fine Gael TD Michael Ring was roundly praised by Staunton for his support for the campaign.

*   *   *

The national media loved any Knock story with an angle, and Des McEvaddy provided one when he dropped out of the Mayo skies one Sunday for an enjoyable event. Brother of Ulick, he was also a shareholder in Omega Air.

Michael Hand, writing in the *Evening Herald* on April 23, related that in a telephone conversation with his mother, Margaret – who was the first woman chair of Mayo IFA – she mentioned she had a lovely joint of roast Mayo beef in the oven for lunch. Would he join her in the family homestead on the Charlestown road outside Swinford?

"Into his own private Cessna, parked at Iona, bachelor Des skied it to the West in the sunshine of the day. He had planned to land at Castlebar, but strong crosswinds made it a little bit dodgy.

"So Des McEvaddy headed for Knock – or the Connaught Regional Airport as it was officially known. He landed nicely – much nearer Swinford by the way – and parked his plane beside a caravan.

124

"A young girl was in the makeshift 'arrivals' building collecting subscriptions from Sunday drivers, who, incidentally, use the runway to teach young men and girls the art of driving a car in comparative safety.

"Des asked the young girl how much the landing fee was. The girl – never having seen a plane land before – didn't know. McEvaddy paid twenty pounds, and got a receipt to prove that the Airport is open to traffic from the clouds."

Michael Hand knew the Monsignor well from the old dance-hall days and commented: "Horan would have been a captain of industry were he not a man of the cloth. His entrepreneurial skills were nurtured in the old days when parish dance-halls were in fierce competition from private enterprise in the days of the big draw-bands. And he made Tooreen one of the best venues, moneywise, in the land."

Apropos Hand's comments about young girls learning to drive on the runway, one such learner was Elaine Harrison from nearby Kilkelly. She knew the airport site like the back of her hand. She had attended the flag-raising ceremony back in 1980, and got to know the runway very well, learning to drive on the wide band of rolled tarmac. "I think everyone from the area learned to drive on the runway when it was being built. It was one of the things you did at that time – it was part of growing up near an airport, and there were regular reports of crashes on Sunday afternoons," she recalls.

Now Elaine Harrison-Grealy, she was amongst the first to take up employment at the airport in September 1986, and she currently works in the office section.

Fencing and landscaping around the airport were just some of many issues to be resolved in 1985, but help was on the way when Senator Jim Higgins announced in April that a year-long FÁS social employment scheme had been sanctioned.

Attracting investment to the industrial zone continued to be a key objective of the Monsignor and his Board, and in May it was revealed that an expert group had been engaged to draw up a plan to realise that potential. However, in June, when Horan was in the United States with Archbishop Joseph Cunnane and Fr. Tom Shannon word reached him that his mother, Catherine, (97) had died. She had been his firmest supporter and accompanied him to many of the official functions he attended. Friends recalled that the news affected him badly. He openly wept at her funeral and missed her dearly over the rest of his life.

The first official touchdown at the new runway was recorded on June 24 when two aviators, taking part in a successful attempt to establish an aviation record and get their names in the Guinness Book of Records, landed their single-engined Cessna 182. They were Iona National Airways pilot Terry O'Neill and national school teacher Jim Duggan, and they landed at 52 Irish airfields within a 14-hour period. Funds raised from the attempt went to Our Lady's Hospital, Crumlin. Permission had been given by the Department of Communications.

By the end of July interest in the inaugural commercial flights to Rome in October had captured the imagination of the public. The 8-day trip, according to Chief Steward Tom Neary, would cost in the region of £420, which covered hotel with full board, coach tours, etc. An audience with the Pope had been arranged, and the trip would also take in Loretto and the home town of Padre Pio, San Giovanni. So strong was the demand that a third Aer Lingus 737 had to be chartered.

A new appeal went out for funds to finish off the extended runway, which had by now been pushed out to 8,100 feet, with a turning circle beyond that again. Monsignor Horan again explained that a minimum of 7,500 feet was necessary to meet standards for a fully laden and fuelled Boeing 737 to take off. He was just making assurances doubly sure.

There was another huge response to the fund-raising appeal, an example being the Tample (Charlestown) Sports and Pattern which raised over £7,000 and expected that figure to grow to perhaps £10,000 before the fund closed. Some local school children pledged they would raise £500 each through the sale of raffle tickets.

Sticking to the Monsignor's maxim of making a little money go a long way, the company did a deal with the liquidators of the controversial John de Lorean car factory outside Belfast, buying the ultra-modern broadcasting and paging system. The high fidelity sound system had originally cost the British taxpayers up to £100,000. It was snapped up by the company for an undisclosed bargain sum.

When Deirdre Purcell and Gerry Byrne of the *Sunday Tribune* landed at the airport in late August to do a news feature they were greeted by the Monsignor in person. Their subsequent report (Sept. 1) marvelled at the extended runway nearing completion, saying it was longer than Dublin and Cork. They also revealed that the new instrument landing system being installed in time for the Rome flights would be superior to the faulty Dublin Airport system. Cork Airport, by contrast, did not have an instrument landing system, the report stated.

A radio beacon enabling pilots to locate the new airport electronically would also be installed in October, it added. Although no one knew it then, that beacon was to cause quite a scare! The *Sunday Tribune* flight also caused its own scare.

Byrne and Purcell had chartered an aircraft from Iona Airways and flew down to interview the Monsignor. Getting clearance had been like a game of Ping-Pong. "First of all we had to negotiate a battle of wills and wits between the Monsignor and the Department of Transport over whether or not the flight would be allowed. The pilot almost lost his licence because the flight should not have been allowed. There had been a lot of problems with light aircraft doing 'touch and goes' on the runway and causing danger to the construction workers. The Department had issued a *Notandum* and refused to lift it unless the Monsignor agreed. The Monsignor said he would agree if the department lifted it first and that's where the stand-off remained. It was symptomatic of a battle for control of the airport," says Byrne.

The aviation journalist claimed on arrival their plane 'almost killed' an old woman – it might even have been a nun – who rushed out to greet them and risked running into the propellers.

The 'near miss' was obviously not too close for it did not put them off their lunch with the Monsignor in the Presbytery. Horan reckoned they were the first paying passengers to land there. "Afterwards, as Horan got his car out of the garage I noticed some golf shoes and a golf bag lying in the corner and I asked him if he played golf. 'Ah, those, I don't think I'll ever be using them again,' was his reply. Life had got much too busy for one of his favourite pastimes."

There was a time when Monsignor Horan had looked forward to his game of golf. Monsignor Grealy, who played with him for the best part of thirty years, recalled that he was not a great golfer. "But he had this great knack of putting you off at the top of your swing when he'd mention something or other and then chuckle away as your ball headed in a direction you did not quite intend!" he recalled with a rueful smile.

Working under so much pressure and with so much to be done, it was obvious to observers that the stresses and strains were impacting on and between the promoters. A good weather vane was John Healy's offerings in the *Irish Times*, and on September 9 he raised more than a few eyebrows in his Sounding Off column when he led with the headline 'Why Mayo is puzzled by the Monsignor'.

Referring to comments made by Horan that overtures from an American company based in Chicago to take £2.5m equity in the unfinished airport had been turned down, and that a British proposal had not been chased up, Healy lashed into the Monsignor, saying in effect he had lost sight of the ball in a scramble to get his high profile flights to Rome launched. Monsignor Horan privately dismissed Healy's unexpected onslaught. As far as he was concerned the proposals could wait, or maybe he believed they did not amount to a whole hill of beans when analysed anyway. And he was just not taken by the British proposal to build a golf course on land that could be better used for an industrial park. (See Chapter 21 for details of that particular skirmish.)

Anyway, the company was now on the cusp of the much-heralded flights to Rome, and Department of Communication officials were expressing concerns that the airport would not be up to international licensing safety and technical standards by the departure date. Much work lay ahead, and the company did not even have a management team in place.

In fact Minister Mitchell, the *Irish Press* reported on September 25, was concerned that his 18 conditions might not be met. The paper reported a source close to the Department saying 'with a bit of luck and good weather' most of the conditions could possibly be fulfilled in time. "If everything goes right they can meet the conditions by the date," a Department spokesman said.

The article, written by Tim Hastings, also referred to the ownership issue, revealing that the Minister was understood to have insisted in talks with the company that the State interest in the airport be held in trust in any new ownership arrangement. "The Minister is understood to be agreeable to the existing two ministerial appointees being withdrawn on this basis to help encourage any new outside financial investment in the project," he wrote.

In the lead-up to the Rome flights, Aidan Quigley, a retired Air Lingus pilot and a native of Foxford, Co. Mayo, was appointed to oversee the final critical arrangements and to ensure that all regulations were fully met. He had flown the Pope to Ireland six years earlier, and had volunteered his service free of charge. It was a godsend in the absence of local expertise.

In talks with the Department of Communications and the Board of Directors of the Airport, it was agreed that Quigley be appointed acting General Manager from October 10 to November 10 1985 to cover the critical period of the flights to Rome. He recalled he had been briefed in some considerable detail by the Department with regard to his responsibilities, and had also been assigned the task of supplying the vast amount of technical data required by them to license and open the airfield for the operation of the special flights.

He met immediate and total co-operation from every member of the engineering staff and the workforce. "I knew I was dealing with a group of men and women who were highly motivated and were eager to assimilate knowledge of the complex business of operating jet aeroplanes," he said.

A vital piece of equipment, a radio beacon on the approach to the runway, had had to be commissioned. It had been installed by a Dublin company in a little hut built with a projecting radio aerial. It was imperative that it was up and working when the Department officials came to do their tests in the weeks before the flights to Rome.

Ballaghaderreen businessman and electrical contractor Brian Kelly, who was also a fund-raiser for the Airport, related there was great commotion the day before the crucial test. Aer Lingus were to do an approval run with an inspector on board from the Civil Aviation Authority.

Said Kelly: "Our beacon was supposed to send out a signal, all the time bleeping out the call sign. I was up in the control tower at the airport listening to the OK signal coming in and it going 'beepidy beep', 'beepidy beep', all the time. Everything was fine. The next thing the signal failed on the monitor. It was gone! There was no call sign. The lads up on loan from Shannon Air Traffic Control said, 'Where's it gone to? Did anyone knock it off?'."

An anxious Kelly drove over to the beacon hut a few miles away, and saw the radio was on and the red indicator light confirmed that. "It

Pope John Paul I I with Monsignor Horan and Archbishop Cunnane in Knock in September 1979. Photo: Henry Wills, Western People.

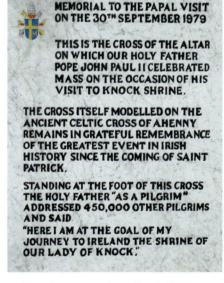

An enduring reminder at Knock Shrine. Photo Michael McCormack.

The Golden Rose at Knock. Photo: Michael McCormack.

Three Mayo-born archbishops of Tuam, all associated with the Airport. Front, Most Rev Dr Joseph Cunnane, and back, from left, Most Rev Dr Michael Neary and Most Rev Dr Joseph Cassidy. Photo Henry Wills, Western People.

1981: Cutting the first sod: Minister for Transport Albert Reynolds does the honours in the presence of Monsignor Horan, the Archbishop of Tuam Dr Joseph Cunnane and Bishop Thomas Flynn of Achonry. Western People photo.

Terminal clock, prior to installation, 1986: Included are Alo Reddington, Paddy McDonnell, Eugene Waldron and Brian Kelly. Western People photo.

December 1980: At the blessing of the airport site and the raising of the Connaught flag. Photo courtesy Fr Paddy Kilcoyne.

Pointing the way: Monsignor Horan shows the way with his long runway, 1985. Western People photo.

Ancient and modern: The new basilica rises on the Knock skyline, 1970s. Photo: Western People.

1980: Taoiseach Charles J. Haughey speaking outside the house in which he was born in Castlebar. To his left is Monsignor Horan, and to his right, Cathal Duffy,. Archbishop Joseph Cunnane and Judge John Garavin.

Knock Shrine: the chapel built onto the Apparition gable at the Church, with the white marble statues commissioned on behalf of the Church by Judy Coyne. Photo: Tom Campbell.

The first 'official' aircraft to land on the new runway, June 24, 1985. Photo courtesy Fr Paddy Kilcoyne.

Checking out progress on the runway in July 1983, from left, Frank Harrington, Pat English and Mick Ruddy. Photo courtesy Fr Paddy Kilcoyne.

1982: From small beginnings: G. Gourlay and M. Harrington at the site caravan. Photo courtesy Fr Paddy Kilcoyne.

July 1983: Minister Jim Mitchell, Monsignor Horan and Jim Ryan walk the runway. Photo courtesy Fr Paddy Kilcoyne.

Members of the first Airport board pictured in July 1986 with a giant Transamerica jet in the background. From left, Vincent Feehan, John Dillon, Michael O'Malley, Monsignor James Horan, Jim Ryan, Seamus Monaghan, Cathal Duffy and Patrick Ryan. Photo: Frank Dolan.

Cardinal O'Connor of New York being greeted at Knock Airport by Archbishop Joseph Cassidy when pilgrims flew in on a peace pilgrimage in 1988. Photo: Frank Dolan.

2005: Make a Wish: David Moran (7), Swinford, on the steps of an aircraft at Knock with Pearse Concannon, Head of Fire and Security; Gardai Brendan Walsh and John Ruane, Swinford; and Noreen McKenzie, West of Ireland Wish Granting Co-ordinator, Make-A-Wish Foundation. Photo: Michael McCormack

Workmen pictured with Monsignor Horan at the airport in 1985, and underneath, almost the same group pictured with the bust of the Monsignor in the Airport in May 2006: Henry Garvey, Tom Grennan, Gerry Murray (standing in for his brother Peter David), PJ Harraghy and Paddy Moran.
Photo 2006 Michael McCormack

Staff at Knock in 1996, front, from left: Helen Higgins, Elaine Harrison-Grealy, Ann Marie Murphy, Michael McGrath (Manager), Eilish O'Connor, Maura Hughes, Majella Walsh. Middle: Pearse Concannon, Gerry Niland, Matt Carney, Catriona Flatley, Rose Lynn, Jim Corry, Helen McGrath, Ann Caulfield, Aidan Horkan, Edward Scanlon, Jimmy Harte. Back: Owen Durkin, Sean Donlon, Paul Morris, Jimmy McNicholas, Paul Hughes, Michael Grealy, Matt Macken. Western People photo.

1996: The fire service crew at the Airport, from left: Matt Macken, Jimmy McNicholas, Pearse Conway, Eddie Scanlon, Michael Grealy, Paul Morris and Paul Hughes. Western People photo.

1983: Inspecting the new runway, from left, Jim Ryan, Pat English, Mick Ruddy, Paddy McDonnell, Clerk of Works, Monsignor Horan, Frank Harrington (main contractor), Sean Balfe (engineer), Chris Lycett, Paul Crowe and P J. Durkin. Photo: Western People.

Terminal Building, 1985: Foreman Willie Muldowney supervises progress. Included are John Foley, Padraig McNicholas, Ted Gallagher and Peter Murphy. Photo: Western People.

Ander Blom and Peter Flatley working on the instrument landing gantry at the end of the runway, 1985. Western People photos.

The house at the end of the runway. Photo: Western People.

1985: Piper Paddy Walsh leads Monsignor Horan, Connaught Airport travel bag held aloft and accompanied by Mayo County Manager Michael O'Malley to his waiting Rome-bound plane. Western People photo.

Aer Lingus First Officer Paddy Judge from Ballyhaunis and Monsignor Horan share a joke before boarding for Rome, 1985. Western People photo.

The Knock Shrine banner, Monsignor Horan, the Bishop of Elphin Dr Dominic Conway, and Stewards on the steps of St. Peter's in Rome, 1985.

137

Aer Lingus jet returns from Rome, November 1, 1985. Note the banks of turf in the foreground, adjacent to the runway. Photo courtesy Fr Paddy Kilcoyne.

October 25, 1985: crowds throng the approach road to the Airport to see the flights to Rome take off. Photo courtesy Fr Paddy Kilcoyne.

Knock pilgrims on the steps of St. Peter's in Rome, 1985.

1985: The Gilvarry family from Killala wave before heading off to Rome. Western People photo.

Aer Lingus air hostesses on Rome duty.
Western People photo.

Airport contractor Frank Harrington and his
wife, Patricia, pictured with Monsignor Horar
before boarding the Rome flight.
Western People photo.

Following the piper as Rome awaits!
Western People photo.

The women— and the men— behind the wire,
as passengers bound for Rome are giving a
rapturous send-off. Western People photo.

Order of Malta personnel on duty.
Western People photo

1985: Seven young people from Tample, Charles-town, who helped raise £7,000 for the Airport: included are Robert O'Connell, Sinead, Maura and Patrick Grimes, Brian O'Donnell, Mark O'Donoghue and Damian Groarke.
Photo: Western People.

Checking in for Rome. Western People photo.

All set for Rome as the crowds below cheer.
Western People photo.

Television camera roll: RTE's Thelma Mansfield interviews some of the Rome-bound passengers.
Western People photo.

Above: 1985: Rome-bound pilgrims are led
to their plane as they wave to the crowd.
Photo: Western People.

Left: "Here we go" – a delighted Monsignor
Horan acknowledges the cheers
Western People photo

Below: One of the many banners on display
to celebrate the Rome flight, 1985.
Western People photo.

"We did it together." Charles Haughey and Monsignor Horan claim the moment as the crowd looks on below. Western People photos.

1986: Charles Haughey, Monsignor Horan and Cathal Duffy at the opening. Western People photo.

1982: Site foreman, Mick Ruddy, and Aidan Colleary.
Photo: Fr Paddy Kilcoyne

1986: Umbrellas up on opening day. Western People photo.

144

1986: Some of the crowd compressed in front of the terminal building on opening day. Western People photos.

Charles J Haughey and harpist Frankie Forde-Waldron who performed on opening day.
Western People photo.

1986 and it's thumbs up! Maurice Buckby, the first airport manager, Monsignor Horan
and Jim Ryan in the control tower. Western People photo.

Part of the musical swirl on opening day. Western People photo.

146

Opening day and surrounded by well-wishers, Monsignor Horan waves.
Western People photo.

Charles J Haughey cuts the tape to open the Airport, May 1986. Western People photo.

Mother Teresa of Calcutta who flew in through the airport en route to Knock Shrine, 1990s.

Famous Mayo priests meet in Knock: Fr Patrick Peyton, the Rosary Priest, and Monsignor Horan. Photo: Tom Campbell.

English cricket legend Ian Botham and British chart topping rock star Eric Clapton with Marcia Pearson Evans of Ryanair at the Airport., early 1990s. Western People photo.

John Healy waves as he greets the first transatlantic flight into Knock, July 1986. Western People photo.

Minister Mary O'Rourke pictured with Cathal Duffy and Monsignor Dominick Grealy in the Airport Boardroom. Western People photo.

Hollywood star Robin Williams and young fans. Western People photo.

Irish soccer star Kevin Moran and fans.
Western People photo.

Soccer star George Best and Western People reporter
Liam Horan at the Airport, early 1990s.
Western People photo

Charles J Haughey and Cathal Duffy pose in front
of the bust of the builder of Knock Airport, Monsignor James Horan. Western People photo.

British Prime Minister Tony Blair being greeted by
Airport Manager Michael McGrath and staff.
Western People photo.

Airport Manager Michael McGrath greets
Woody Allen, 1990s. Western People photo.

Prince Charles and Airport chairman Cathal Duffy at
the Airport, early 1990s. Western People photo.

1996: Archbishop Joseph Cunnane leads the congregation in prayer as the remains of Monsignor Horan are brought home. Western People photo.

Order of Malta personnel take the coffin from the aircraft at Knock Airport. Western People photo.

Monsignor James Horan is laid to rest in the shadow of Knock Basilica, August 1986. Western People photo.

Former Taoiseach Charles J. Haughey, Cardinal Tomas O'Fiaich and Minister Jim Mitchell, with Monsignor Grealy and Papal Nuncio Dr Gaetano Alibrandi in the background, at the funeral of Monsignor Horan at Knock Shrine, 1986. Western People photo.

Handmaids and stewards of Knock Shrine ring the apron with the huge crowd in the background as Monsignor Horan's coffin is brought back into Knock, 1986. Western People photo.

Monsignor Dominick Grealy blesses the inaugural Knock to London Ryanair flight, 1986, from left: Jim Ryan, Brian Flynn, Ann Geary, Michael O'Malley, Martin Finn, John Mahon, Eugene O'Neill, Tom Beisty, Jim Higgins, Maurice Buckby and Bishop Thomas Flynn.. Western People photo.

1987: John Mahon and Maurice Buckby being weighed in for Slimathon by Eddie Riddle of BAI. Photo: Western People.

Inaugural Ryanair service to London, 1986: Monsignor Grealy with Minister Paddy O'Toole, who launched the service and Eugene O'Neill of Ryanair. Western People photo.

Vast crowds turned up to see the first plane from America touch down at Knock, July 1986. Western People photo.

A warm Mayo welcome is accorded passengers on the first transatlantic flight into Knock, July 1986. Western People photo.

"Here she comes": the first transatlantic flight from New York to Knock about to touch down, July 1986. Western People photo.

Five week-old Thomas McHale of Philadelphia who travelled with his parents, Mary and Bill on the first transatlantic flight into Knock, July 1986. Western People photo.

Helen McGrath and Ann Caulfield serving up good cheer at the Airport Lounge, 1990s. Photo: Henry Wills, Western People.

"I'm home": Foxford-born US travel agent Brendan Ward is greeted by Monsignor Horan as he alights from the Transamerica jet in July 1986. Western People photo.

2006: Pictured at the launch of the new fleet of fire tenders were fire-fighting crew (Back, from left): James Tanner, Marcus McDermott, Brendan Grogan, Des Groarke, Declan McCann and Andrew Sweeney; (Front); Andrew Dockery, Michael Monaghan, Michael Grealy, Robert Grealis, Minister Eamon O Cuív, Pearse Concannon, Liam Scollan, John Maloney and Noel Jennings. Pic Peter Wilcox.e

2006: Best regional airport - receiving award from Minister of State Pat the Cope Gallagher is Michael Greally, while also pictured are Cormac Sheils, General Manager of Penauille Servisair Ireland; Dan Loughrey, Chair of Chambers Ireland Air Transport Users Council; and Robin O'Sullivan, President of Chambers Ireland. Pic Grainne Duggan

2006: Looking good! Ireland West Airport Knock/Ireland West Tourism's co- sponsored entry in the BMW Round Ireland yacht Race.

2005: Robert Grealis, Kevin Heery, Pearl McIntyre, Michael O'Leary and Liam Scollan celebrate another Ryanair route. Photo Michael McCormack.

Rugby star Ronan O'Gara and Kevin Heery at Legends of Rugby promotion at the airport. Photo Michael McCormack.

Thomas Hewitt greeted by his wife Anne and grandson Daniel from Athlone on his arrival from peacekeeping duty in Kosovo in 2005. Photo: Michael McCormack.

Bernie Kearney of County Roscommon who has amassed over the years a large collection of newspaper cuttings on the Airport, pictured at the 20th anniversary celebrations. Photo Michael McCormack.

Michael O'Leary of Ryanair with (front) Maria Horan, Phil Cassidy, Ann Caulfield, Bernie Horan, Pearl McIntyre and (back) Bernie Morris, Kathleen Towey, Robert Grealis and Kathleen Regan. Photo Michael McCormack.

A typical scene at the Check-in Desks at Knock. Photo Michael McCormack.

2005: easyJet Top Customer Services Award, from left: Pauline Cowley, Julia Brooks, Sheila Cannon, Maria McGrath and Sarah Casserley. Pic Michael McCormack.

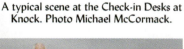

Carmel Keegan and John Kilcoyne of the Connaught Aero Club which is based at the Airport. Photo: Michael McCormack.

Ireland West Airport Knock Staff Charity Fundraising Committee, from left: Anne Caulfield, John McCarthy, PJ Rochford, Pearse Concannon, Breda Walsh, Sheila Cannon and Jimmy McNicholas at the Staff Charity fundraising night in Belmont Hotel, Knock in 2005. Photo: Michael McCormack.

2006: Clio Watson, Castlebar, the first passenger on the Durham Tees route, receives recognition from Desmond O'Flynn and Annette Kearney. Pic Michael McCormack.

Above: One of the great rugby legends of all time, Gareth Edwards welcomed by the Managing Director Liam Scollan in 2005. Photo: Michael McCormack.

Left: Margaret Gordon, Moylough, Tubbercurry, signs the Book Of Condolences for the late Charles J. Haughey at the Airport in June 2006. Photo: Michael McCormack.

2006: Members of the Horan Family pictured at the commemorative bust of their relative, Monsignor James Horan, which stands inside the main door of the terminal building, from left: Aisling Grimes, Claremorris, Jimmy Horan, Kilmaine, Anne Grimes, Ballinrobe, Bernadette Horan, Kilmaine, Marian Diffley, Ballymahon, Jean Horan, Abbeyleix, Bart Grimes, Ballinrobe, Paddy Diffley, Ballymahon, Pat McLoughlin, Claremorris, and Flo Ruane, Crossmolina. Photo: Michael McCormack.

2006: Former taoiseach Albert Reynolds being presented with a photograph of himself turning the first sod in 1981: from left, Dr. Pat O'Hara of the Western Development Commission, Liam Scollan and Martina Burns of Ireland West Airport, and Lisa McAllister, CEO, Western Development Commission, during at 20th Anniversary Celebrations. Photo: Michael McCormack.

2005: Robert Grealis and Gillian Buckley of Western Development Commission sign grant deal. Pic Michael McCormack.

1989: Minister Seamus Brennan greeted at Knock by Cathal Duffy, Seamus Monaghan and Michael O'Malley. Western People photo.

Gareth Edwards, one of the great rugby legends of all time after his arrival at Knock International Airport with many other Welsh rugby stars who were in Ireland to play the Legends of Rugby Charity Golf Classic in Galway in 2005. The group includes Bob Norster, Gareth Davies, Ieuan Evans, David Richards, Bleddyn Bowen, Mark Wyatt and Bleddyn Taylor. They were welcomed at the Airport by members of the staff. Photo: Michael McCormack.

2006: At 20th anniversary night, Liam Scollan, Minister Brian Cowen, Joe and Kathleen Kennedy and John Carty, TD. Photo Michael McCormack.

Knock Shrine chief steward Tom Neary addressing the 20th anniversary night. Photo Michael McCormack.

Michael O'Leary of Ryanair does a flying change of jerseys at Knock. Photo Michael McCormack.

Ulick McEvaddy and Padraig Flynn at the 20th anniversary night. Photo Michael McCormack.

Roscommon football team supporters Marty Groarke, Ballaghaderreen, Senator Frank Feighan, Boyle, and Noel D. Walsh, Ballaghaderreen, off to London to see their team play in 2005. Photo: Michael McCormack.

Capt Fred O'Donovan from Castlebar returning from duty with 29 Infantry Group KFOR meets his triplet daughters, Anna, Sarah and Katie and wife, Patricia. Photo: Michael McCormack.

2005: Mrs Margaret Hawksworth, née O'Shaughnessy, Ballintubber, Co Roscommon who was the 3 millionth passenger to pass through the Airport, with Liam Scollan, CEO. Photo: Michael McCormack

Pearse Concannon of the Airport charity fund-raising committee , presents a cheque to Cynthia Clampet of Mayo/Roscommon Hospice. Photo Michael McCormack.

2006: Paul Claffey of Mid-West Radio congratulates Mary Croghan of Castlerea on being the 4 millionth passenger to pass through Ireland West Airport. Photo: Michael McLaughlin

Rachel Hughes, Greg Hughes and Emma James from Ballina welcomed by Santa at the Airport, Christmas 2005. Photo: Michael McCormack.

'This way, Minister': photographers Henry Wills and Frank Dolan line up their shot at the 20th anniversary celebrations. Photo Michael McCormack.

Airport MD Liam Scollan hits the right notes at 20 anniversary bash. Photo Michael McCormack.

Joe Kennedy, Minister Brian Cowen and Liam Scollan cut the 20th birthday cake. Photo Michael McCormack.

Tommy Moran of the Connaught GAA Council and Liam Scollan tieing up a hurling sponsorship deal. Photo Michael McCormack.

Monsignor Joseph Quinn and Terry Gallagher, London-Mayo Association, addressing the 20th anniversary celebrations. Photo Michael McCormack.

2006: Section of attendance at 20th anniversary celebrations night. Photos Michael McCormack.

was going 'beepidy beep' but there was nothing coming in on the speakers over at the tower. We then got on to Shannon and asked an Air Traffic controller there if he could read our signal. He said he couldn't, so he asked a transatlantic flight 35,000 feet up to tune into the Knock signal; the Canadian pilot came back saying he could get us, but very faintly."

Something was obviously amiss. That night Kelly could not sleep, twisting and turning as he tried to figure out what the hell was going on. He got up early on the day of the test and revisited the outer marker hut again. "It was then pouring rain and I was there looking into the hut and saw the aerial coming out the jamb of the window and could see this spark coming from the wire where the insulator was broken. It appears that when the hut had been plastered, the wire going out through the window got a slight nick, and that was sufficient to disrupt the signal."

He had a two-way radio and rang the airport and asked how far out was the incoming inspection plane? It was now heading towards the West. Kelly knew that meant the pilot wouldn't have looked for the signal yet as he wouldn't have swung around.

As luck – or maybe it was divine intervention again – would have it, there was a farmer coming down the road on his tractor and Kelly frantically waved him down.

He noticed a yardbrush with a timber handle and a shovel in the back of the trailer. "Come here quick, get that brush and hold that wire up against the edge of the concrete until it stops sparking – there's a plane going to pass over here any minute now and if you don't hold that wire up they're going to crash!"

Perhaps a bit dramatic, but the farmer got the point. He was wearing wellingtons and he held the wire up with the yard brush. Within minutes the plane went zooming over.

"I said, 'Good man yourself,' and got in my car and hared back to the airport. By the time I got there the plane had landed and there was this reception committee greeting the pilot. The Monsignor blessed the pilot and wished him safe flying.

"Within what seemed like minutes the farmer comes rushing in in his wellingtons and said: 'Did ye land all right?'

"He had followed me down in the tractor. I was afraid to say anything because there were fellows there from the Department and the first excuse they got they'd have pulled the plug! And if the Dublin papers had got hold of that story at the time they'd have made a right skit of it," related Kelly with a smile.

On October 22 the airport was given the all-clear by the government inspectors for the flights to the Eternal City. Monsignor Horan paid tribute to his erstwhile opponent, Jim Mitchell, saying the Minister had indeed, both verbally and in writing, done everything in his power to assist the airport in its initial venture.

Aer Rianta were supplying the control tower personnel for the day in addition to fire-fighting equipment, tenders and trained personnel, to be paid for at cost price. Customs staff were being seconded from Ballina to handle passport control. The runway and turning circles were completed and passed. Seven miles of perimeter fencing had been erected. Civil Defence, Order of Malta and Mayo Fire Service personnel were lined up . . . and a security firm had pledged its services free of charge for the big day.

Media interest was immense. RTÉ, the BBC – which had a six-man team in the region for several days previously – and ITN indicated they would have camera crews present and journalists from many countries sought and secured accreditation.

And to put the icing on the cake, the *Western People's* lead story on October 23 told readers that the Pope would be invited to fly into Mayo the following year for the official opening. A source close to Horan told the paper: "We are sure that while in Rome it will be suggested to his Holiness that he make the trip, and it is not beyond the bounds of possibility that he will accept."

And generous people continued to come forward. The day before the flights to Rome the Monsignor received a call from his solicitor and this time it was good news. He had been willed £17,000 for his own use. "And where do you think it's going?" he asked James O'Donohue. "It's going into the airport."

Better still, an aviation inspector gave the arrangements for the Rome flights a clean bill of health. "The Board," he acknowledged, "met every condition meticulously. It was an astonishing performance in the circumstances."

After almost six years of uphill slogging, the open skies finally beckoned.

CHAPTER TWELVE

1985: Dublin gets everything- Rome flights take off - Pope invited back to Knock Shrine - In international aviation league - Fund-raising gigs and songs in the night - Sobering bill for services - Predictions of death!

Look up Rome, it's Knock!

AFTER all the setbacks and after the political football that was Connaught Regional Airport had been kicked up and down the east coast and further afield by an assorted band of politicians, a cynical press and economic gurus, Friday October 25 1985 marked the best of days.

It was the day when the iron will of an ageing priest, backed up by his growing community of believers who had had their bellyful of begrudgery, faced down their detractors. Against all the odds, the dream was about to be turned into reality.

An estimated 15,000 well-wishers crammed the airport complex from early in the morning as the haze cleared to bright sunshine. It was, as Monsignor Horan said, 'a day that God had made'.

And there on the apron that day were to stand three Aer Lingus Boeing jets, two 737s and a 707, all ready to make the inaugural flights from Knock to Rome to mark the Golden Jubilee celebrations of the Knock Shrine Society. Ahead lay a Papal audience with Pope John Paul 11, the man who had come to Knock Shrine only six years earlier.

To get three aircraft from Aer Lingus had proved to be another struggle for Horan. "He had filled three planes, and then they told him he could have only two, so he said he'd call the whole thing off; he couldn't disappoint so many people. He put them over a barrel and they had to guarantee the third flight," said James O'Donohue who was one of the pilgrims.

Leading the pilgrimage was the Archbishop of Tuam, Dr Joseph Cunnane. He knew the Monsignor better than most, and recognised the tough steel that ran through his fibres, having seen the Partry native in action as parish priest of Knock and in particular in such monumental undertakings as the building of the Basilica and the planning for the papal visit to Knock Shrine in 1979.

Other West of Ireland bishops in the party were Most Rev Dr Thomas Flynn of Achonry and Most Rev Dr Dominic Conway of Elphin, and Rt Rev. Monsignor Thomas Finnegan, PP of Roscommon, and later Bishop of Killala. Four-hundred-plus pilgrims prepared to board the three flights, and hundreds more who tried to make the historic trip were disappointed: travel agent John Dillon of Ballyhaunis said he could easily have filled another plane.

Matt Macken, now a duty staff officer at the airport, set out from his home in nearby Crossboyne in the early morning darkness to get to where the action was to be that day. "I will never forget the beam of light from the Control Tower sweeping out across the countryside. That, for me, was the realisation that the airport was up and running, that a new dawn was being heralded for the region," he says.

The first Boeing, the *St. Eunan,* touched down at 10.08am to scenes of great jubilation. Flags were waved, car horns sounded, and school-band music wafted into the air. After all the doubts and all the set-backs, seeing was believing, and there could be no mistaking those big jets dressed out in the livery of the national airline standing where men had cut turf only a few years earlier.

Mary O'Donohue remembers the Monsignor turning to her as the first Aer Lingus jet touched down in Knock and saying, "It's there now, Mary, and they cannot dig it up again."

There had been frenetic activity to get this far in the intervening, turbulent months. Money was being raised by the busy fund-raising team, and the Monsignor had attended many social events, particularly in singing lounges around the region.

He was the star turn though it was widely conceded he couldn't sing for nuts. But he always loved entertaining people. "I sing a song, tell a yarn. I have been invited all over the place, sing a few songs, tell a few yarns. I sign autographs for people. I'm in a kind of film star class," he once chuckled in an interview. Adding, "Thank God, it doesn't go to my head because in a few years I know I will only need a 6x4 (grave)."

Mrs O'Donohue said members of the fund-raising team used to take it in turns to accompany him to the concerts. "Fr. Porter would go too from time to time, and he had a great tenor voice. I recall coming home one night the Monsignor asking, 'Now Mary, who sang best tonight?' and all I could do was reply, "Do you think I am going to answer that!'"

The 'gigs' went on weekly, often happening after a gruelling and stressful day. "But," wrote his curate Fr. Colm Kilcoyne in a *Sunday Press* tribute, "they were important to him, not for the money they raised but because they raised spirits and because they kept reminding him of the people for whom he was building the airport in the first place. He'd sing a few songs – not always using the notes the composer had in mind. He'd tell a few jokes and tell them well. Then he'd thank the people for turning out and for being faithful to the airport. Nothing too heavy, nothing too long. Then he'd encourage them to coax another song – which was usually 'If I Can Help Somebody' – and with that he'd hop down off the stage, talk, laugh and argue the toss with every man, woman and child in the place.

"This was much more than a harassed man going the rounds of the lounges of Mayo collecting a few bob for his pet project," said Fr. Kilcoyne. "This was a happening as old as Parnell and Davitt. It was the visitation of a man who knew and felt for the tribulations of a people who lived with unfulfilled aspirations. He knew, from whatever sources I don't know, the passion that small western farmers have for their own place. We may be the greatest wanderers on earth but home is home. We want to be sure we could stay if we wished, could marry, bring children into the world and grow old there.

"He never said these things in his on-and-off-stage banter but the Mayo people who flocked to the lounges and who supported the airport knew he was aware, knew he respected this in them and they loved him for it.

"After such a night he'd meet me with a glint in his eye. I think that he suspected that I frowned on such shenanigans and would favour the more intellectual approach to western problems. So he'd ask how I thought he did. In another this would be arrogance. Not him. He was a pro and wanted to know – just as anyone who sings, performs or writes in public want to know so that it will be better next time," added Fr Kilcoyne.

All the money went towards completing the runway, the control tower and the departures lounge. The Department of Communications had been approached for a licence and Minister Jim Mitchell, while he wouldn't give another penny to the project, pulled out the stops to clear the way for the flights.

Given the controversy that had surrounded the airport, a huge attendance was guaranteed and had to be marshalled. The man in charge of the airport for the occasion, Captain Aiden Quigley, very much aware of the demarcation issues at well established airports throughout the world, was thrilled to see the people who had built the airport, men and women, double up as duty or security officers, caterers, message runners, PA announcers, baggage handlers and loaders, mobile patrol staff, whatever was needed.

They dovetailed with gardai, Civil Defence, Knights of Malta and Mayo Fire Brigade and ambulance personnel to provide the necessary hands to the pump and to meet all the security and safety regulations, backed up by experienced personnel from Aer Lingus and Air Traffic Control.

Monsignor Horan was in great form. He greeted the dignitaries and aircraft personnel and in between conducted countless interviews and posed for the photographers, waving a miniature version of an Aer Lingus jet over his head to create photo opportunities. The crowd pressed to the wire fence overlooking the apron on which the jets had parked. They loved it and they cheered him to the echo on that lovely morning. Messages of goodwill from Minister for Communications Mitchell and from Charles J. Haughey, Leader of the Opposition, were read to the press: both wished the airport well.

Cormac MacConnell of the *Irish Press* could not help noting that amidst all the jubilation there was much comment around the airport at the failure of any member of the Government to attend, and contrasted that 'stay-away' policy with the high profile of Fianna Fáil, represented by former Tanaiste Ray MacSharry, MEP, and front-bench spokesmen Padraig Flynn and Denis Gallagher. When planning work for the airport started Fine Gael had blamed Fianna Fáil for hijacking the project; now it was very much on the outside.

In an editorial in the same issue there was much praise for Monsignor Horan and his latest achievement. Said the paper's leading article: "To many people in Dublin, and indeed in the present Government, Knock has become a symbol of all the grant rip-offs and squander-mania that bedevilled Irish public standing in recent years – in rather the same fashion some people in rural Ireland will point to DART as an example of how 'Dublin gets everything'.

"Monsignor Horan has been at the centre of some pretty searching criticism over his airport, his claims for it and his fund-raising, even to the extent of being the subject this week of a hard-hitting – and hilarious – BBC *Newsnight* programme which concluded after the interviewer had done his worst, with the obviously amused anchor-man commenting on the likelihood of 'buying a second-hand airport from That Man! "The BBC comment, though done in a light-hearted fashion, infuriated Horan supporters: the comparison with artful dodger Arthur Daley of the British television series *Minder* was not appreciated.

The *Irish Press* defended the project: "The point is, Knock Airport is there, a monument to what a man with a dream can do, and whatever its detractors in academia or Cabinet may say – and of course their sayings and dire predictions may yet be all proved true – the fact is that in comparison with some of what has gone on in the Irish public sector recently, Irish Shipping for example, Knock Airport looks a damn sight better than a number of the projects that have swallowed taxpayers' millions."

Fittingly enough, there was a hefty complement of personnel from the locality 'crewing' the three jets out of Knock that October day. Everyone then, it seemed, knew someone who worked in high-profile Aer

Lingus and stewardesses and pilots who succeeded in joining the national airline usually earned honourable mention in the local press. There was an unmistakable glamour attached to a job with the national airline then.

While the *St. Eunan* was piloted by Captain Jack Bagnall from Dublin, most of the crew were from the region, and included First Officer Paddy Judge from Ballyhaunis, and hostesses Carmel Freyne-Bourke (Ballyhaunis), Marianne O'Shaughnessy (née Sweeney) of Achill Sound, while the Senior Hostess was Catherine Hynes of Galway. For pilot Paddy Judge it was an especially memorable occasion: it seemed not so long ago when Horan was in Tooreen and Judge was going to Mass there. "Then he was a Father and I a schoolboy in Carrownedan NS. Now we were having our photograph taken together."

The crew of the *St. Canice* Boeing 707 included First Officer Ray Moran of Westport; senior hostess Julie Kenny of Louisburgh, and hostesses, Kay Glavey (Glenamaddy), Linda McEnroe (née McGuire) of Ballyhaunis, and Maria Martin (née McGrath), a native of Knock. The Captain was Bud Boyce and other crew included pilot Kevin Caffrey, and two air hostesses from Dublin, Ann Hillery and Niamh Killodan.

Padraig Flynn, who had, as Minister for State in the Department of Transport, played a key role in steering the airport through the bureaucratic maze and who went on to become Minister for the Environment and later still EU Commissioner, delighted in the buzz of the occasion. "The Monsignor was ebullient that day. The twinkle in his eye was marvellous and he had a great chuckle. I recall him saying it would take years for the airport to reach its full potential but it would play a central role in the development of the province."

Monsignor Horan, looking back a few months later on that great day, recalled: "That, for me, was the official opening, an occasion when strong men cried, when three aircraft rose majestically from a site that was formerly a bog."

And, yes, strong men did cry that day. Tears of joy and pride were everywhere as we boarded our jet and headed off for the three-hour flight to Rome. A typical comment of the pilgrims was 'imagine it, we will be Rome, the Eternal City, in three hours!'.

And those realisations were coming from a people, many of whom had had to emigrate to England in search of a job and knew what it was to take the 'cattle boats' from the North Wall. They had endured a tortuous sea crossing, and then had boarded a train for another long journey to Euston Station in the heart of London. Or Manchester. Or Leeds. Or Birmingham. Or Coventry. Or Oxford. Or Scotland. Now they would be in Rome three hours after setting out from Knock! Talk about empowering people and changing mindsets forever!

John Healy watched on from the sidelines at what he described as 'the birth of a new region' and next day in *The Irish Times* had a right go at External Affairs Minister Peter Barry, who had, a few days earlier in a speech in Luxembourg, called for a stronger regional policy for the EEC.

"How much ECUs (EU monetary unit) went into the building of the Connaught Regional Airport, Peter?

"Not one single ECU, Peter. Not as much as one brass ha'penny did the project get from Europe.

"You know, as I know, Peter, the money is there if you and your government look for it," accused Healy.

Those who travelled on the inaugural flights will remember well the euphoria as piper Paddy Walsh, son of Gerry of the Raftery Room, Kiltimagh, led pilgrims to the steps of the aircraft, which they ascended, to the background of a musical selection that included 'Step Together,' 'West's Awake,' 'Let Erin Remember', and the 'Wearing of the Green.' As they reached the aircraft door they turned and looked back, marvelling at the size of the wildly-enthusiastic, flag-waving crowd which had taxed the confines of the site. Once on board the pilgrims were settled in by the Aer Lingus hostesses, and Knock holy water was liberally sprinkled about by devout believers and anxious travellers. Before long the aircrafts were cleared for take-off. One by one they trundled from the apron.

As they taxied down the virgin runway the sun danced on the metallic fuselage. Inside was an eclectic mix of young, middle-aged and senior citizens hitting off on an historic adventure from the heart of Connaught, full of awe and wonderment. For some it was their maiden flight. The first plane roared down the runway, hit 160 mph and rose into the air at 11.17am, the second shortly after 1 pm. The third, en route to Dublin for refuelling and disembarkation of Aer Lingus staff, lifted off before 3pm.

Ballaghaderreen businessman and airport activist, Brian Kelly was on the same flight as the Monsignor and his party. It was a memory that will endure. "I recall the Monsignor standing up and making a speech as the aircraft took off, and the hostess saying, 'Please sit down' . . . and him saying, 'Indeed I will not. I have started talking and I will finish' . . . he was just so delighted."

First item on the agenda after take-off was the Rosary for our safe journey, and it was fervently recited. Within no time we were out over the Irish Sea, over Wales and on to the English coastline, flying out over Brighton and the Cliffs of Dover, skipping over the English Channel, on over France, our pilot indicating that Paris was not far away, a dizzying 33,000 ft below, then over mighty Mont Blanc and the Alps and Lake Geneva. Then we were informed Pisa lay not far away, and thoughts of the Leaning Tower filled our minds, but those quickly gave way to preparations for landing at Ciampino Military Airport, not far outside Rome.

There was a great cheer and rounds of applause as our jet caressed the sun-drenched Italian runway – ironically, shorter than the one we had come from – and rolled to a halt. Again first impressions of the pilgrims: considerably warmer that even the beautiful day we had left back at Knock – ancient Rome had just enjoyed its hottest summer in 120 years – and the strict security that prevailed, no-nonsense-looking police patrolling with guns strapped to their hips. Three hours had brought us a long way from the carefree, joyous, gun-free atmosphere back in Mayo!

We were taken to our hotels, all seven of them, adjacent to Rome's bustling Termini rail and bus station, and over the next eight days we were to get to know all the famous sights, including the Piazza della Republica, the Via Nazionale, one of the city's most renowned shopping centres, the Trevi Fountain where coins were tossed in, wishes made, and in the process Rome's poor were assisted in some small measure. Once a year the fountain with its magnificent streams of cascading water is switched off and a quarter of a million euro is swept up and goes to the orphans of the city.

Our pilgrimage, our adventure, was expertly organised and we saw all the sights, the Colosseum, the Circus Maximus, the white monument of Victor Emmanuel 11, the Tiber, the Catacombs, all the great landmark churches including the glorious Parthenon, built in pagan times and later converted to a Catholic Church. And of course the Vatican and the marvels of the Sistine Chapel. Archbishop Cunnane and Bishops Flynn and Conway and fourteen others concelebrated Mass in St Peter's, under the shadow of St Peter's Chair, an awe-inspiring Bernini creation. Beforehand, the Knock pilgrims had posed on the steps of St. Peter's for the official photograph.

Other highlights included a visit to San Giovanni Rotondo, high in the Gargano Mountains where Mass was offered at the tomb of Padre Pio; the Holy House of Loretto, high on a hill overlooking the Adriatic Sea; and Assisi of St Francis fame, three hours north-eastwards in Umbria.

Another memorable highlight was the visit to the magnificent gardens and fountains of Tivoli, about an hour outside Rome. Tivoli is rich in history and has many links with Emperors, Cardinals and Popes and we mingled for hours with some of the one-and-a-quarter million visitors who saw its attractions that year, and every year. Perhaps what made this day stand out in the minds of the pilgrims from the West and North-West of Ireland was our evening meal at a nearby restaurant where Monsignor Horan was the life and soul of the sing-song afterwards. The resident musicians struck up an immediate rapport with the Monsignor and backed him as he sang with gusto a retinue of old Irish favourites, including 'When Irish Eyes are Smiling' and 'Danny Boy'. Irish eyes were damp by the time he had finished the latter. One occasions like these one witnessed the motivational skills of the Monsignor in full play: he had the pilgrims in his hand.

He was in his element, away from all the hassle, endless Board meetings, pressure to raise money, and the expectation he generated in people. He could joke and laugh and be himself.

But, of course, the real goal of our journey was the audience with Pope John Paul 11 on the Wednesday in the newly opened audience hall of Paul V1, to the left of St. Peter's as one looks up the famous Square. We joined with pilgrims from many countries, the Knock group led by Shrine Stewards dressed in blue sashes and white gloves and Handmaids in their white uniforms. The atmosphere was indescribable, a whole mix of wonderful emotions which welled and multiplied as the Pope moved through the hall and shook hands here and there. He welcomed especially the Knock Handmaids and Stewards, and was introduced to Chief Steward Tom Neary and Mrs J.C. Coyne who in turn presented him with three personal gifts – a picture of Knock Shrine, a stone from the Apparition Gable at Knock and a book entitled 'Mayo,' a compilation of Mayo writers edited by Bernard O'Hara, a native of Killasser, Swinford.

Bishop Conway of Elphin introduced Monsignor Horan as the man who had built an airport and the Holy Father exclaimed – "Airport!" It was instantaneous recognition. Yes, he too had heard about the airport at Knock!

Monsignor Horan embraced and shook hands with the Holy Father and thanked the most-travelled Pope in history for the audience. He told him: "I hope you will come to Ireland and Knock soon again."

The Polish Pope nodded. He had been there only six years previously and had – much to the disappointment of the half million or so who had gathered – to cut his visit somewhat short due to his schedule over-running, so it was very much in the minds of all the members of the Knock Shrine Society and indeed Monsignor Horan and West of Ireland bishops who had determined that this unique opportunity to extend a new and personal invitation would not be lost.

Airport contractor Frank Harrington said he never saw the Monsignor happier than during those days in Italy. "He was in great form, leading the pilgrims in song and in prayer. He was out among his people, he could talk to everyone, and he was so happy then."

After a few more days of stunning sightseeing it was time to get our planes home. And there, amid the international travellers gathered in the busy departures hall at Ciampino Military Airport, were two Knock giants, Monsignor Horan (74) and Mrs Judy Coyne (84). They, more than most, had put the Mayo Shrine on the map, she over fifty frustrating but rewarding years, he over twenty action-packed years.

They both, in turn, walked up and gazed at the monitors which showed the sequence for our return flights, and both were quietly satisfied. Between them, they had taken on apathy, frustration, the Church, governments and disbelievers. Now they had come from a Shrine the Pope had prayed at to the Pope's seat in Rome and they had flown there from their own back garden.

And at that moment both shared another common dream: the building up of pilgrimage traffic to Knock, and from Knock to Marian shrines around the world, and they would do it through a great new facility i lar Condae Mhaigh Eo.

For the rest of her years, Mrs Coyne would pray daily for the success of the airport.

Monsignor Horan spoke of the network of shrines that existed, and of the potential there was to develop that precious tourist business. And he revealed that he intended to build a housing complex in Knock Village, with a mix of accommodation for old and young. It was very important to keep the age-mix right, he said: he was already planning another facility to help regenerate Knock.

Now, however, sitting on the flight-deck with Captain John Clegg as the 707 prepared to land in Mayo, Monsignor Horan put other projects aside as he surveyed the landscape underneath. "What I saw below was a beautiful airport, not a foggy, boggy plateau as they said," he recalled.

He was delighted to learn that the pilots of the three aircraft had praised the standard of the runway, Captain Jeremiah Hill classifying it as 'the finest in Ireland, absolutely superb'.

Tom Neary, who had done much to organise the trip, recalled: "In three short hours we had touched down at Knock, tired after eight days, but happy and refreshed. We were grateful for the privilege and felt a sense of achievement. All-in-all, the pilgrimage was a wonderful experience, an outstanding success. Our memories of it will never die."

It was an undertaking that undoubtedly portrayed what could be done and gave the confidence necessary to take the project another step forward. And that other step was being lined up by the Monsignor and his Board even as the pilgrims were in Rome: Ryanair, the fledgling airline which operated the Waterford to London service, had applied to the Department of Communications for a licence to run a daily scheduled service from Knock from April 1 1986, the proposed opening date for the airport.

Meanwhile, however, 4,000 people and several school bands turned up again at the Airport to greet the flights home on November 1. Just before boarding in Rome the Monsignor had called John Mahon over and confided, "I hate going home to all the fuss."

And the fuss was not very far away. Within a few days of the return flights the media was revealing, almost gleefully, that the State aviation services bill for the two days of the outgoing and incoming flights was to cost the fledgling company without a penny to its name all of £10,000.

Maybe, just maybe, Europe might come to the rescue? The thorny question of EEC funding was now back on the burner, and Dermot Walsh of the *Irish Independent* reported that EEC Regional Fund Commissioner Varfis had confirmed in June (1985) that available Knock money was being held up because the Government had not responded to questions from the Commission on aspects of a Department of Communications study on Knock. That row, as we will see, was set to continue: no immediate relief was in sight from that source!

Back at the Airport boardroom table there were again signs of a strained relationship. *The Irish Times* reported conflict within the Board in two reports, in November and December. These reports had as their genesis John Healy's critical and unexpected attack on Monsignor Horan in September. (See Chapter 11, and also 21 where matters relating to the Industrial Zone are dealt with in detail.)

Michael Finlan of *The Irish Times* filed a report on December 18 revealing that the airport was encountering serious financial difficulties which had forced the official opening in 1986 to be deferred from April to June. And even then, a well placed company source suggested to him that it might not be possible to open the airport on which work had now practically come to a standstill.

"The company source disputes the contention of the managing director, 74-year-old Monsignor James Horan, that only £1 million is now needed to complete the airport. In fact, allowing for inflation, the total projected cost of the airport now stands at £14 million, which means that £3 million is required for its completion," wrote Finlan.

Finlan's informant estimated that £1.2 million had so far been raised through raffles and appeals. "Now, according to the company source, the money has dried up. He (source) says that a second raffle turned out to be a disappointment because, in his view, 'the Live Aid appeal has cleaned out this country of charity money, and the recession has not helped either'."

The source also believed that another reason for the public not now responding to appeals for contributions to the airport was because of the heavy publicity that surrounded the pilgrim flights to Rome. He maintained that when people saw the planes taking off on television and read about it in the newspapers they concluded that Knock Airport was successfully completed, 'which is not the case at all'.

Finlan's source also confirmed an earlier report in *The Irish Times* that tensions had developed in the company boardroom over the best way to make the airport viable. He also confirmed that there had been criticism by some Board members of the 'cult of personality' that so far had dominated the public relations image of the airport.

Those Board members, disclosed Finlan, wanted a more pragmatic approach to the development of the airport, and were placing much faith in a £2.5 million offer from American business interests which the Minister for Communications was examining. (See Chapter 21.)

The Airport company, added Finlan, had now engaged an English firm of aviation consultants, British Airport International Ltd, to carry out a six-month market and feasibility study. Meanwhile the only work going on was a FÁS Youth Employment scheme which had some 20 young people engaged in landscaping the area around the terminal building.

In between those two reports a director at the airport, Seamus Monaghan had refuted the allegations made by Finlan's source. He was, he told the *Western People*, furious at the attack on the Board, suggesting it was a case of sour grapes, and he was disgusted at the utterances.

There is absolutely no doubt that relationships were at stretching point at that stage. Sources interviewed for this book spoke of the enormous pressure on the Monsignor with bills to be paid and decisions to be made.

However, Seamus Monaghan said the Board had the greatest respect for the Monsignor. "We thought there was no one like him."

But he instanced occasions when some big expenditure was being discussed and the Monsignor wanted to go ahead. "We were worried that we could all be sued if the thing went belly-up and I said to the Monsignor at one meeting, 'Look, we are all married with families and if you died you'd have the Church behind you, but we'd be left holding the bag,' to which he replied, 'Are you predicting my death?' What could I say to that!"

Monaghan also saw another more accommodating side to the Monsignor. "There'd be an important meeting coming up, and he'd arrive down in Sligo with Jim Ryan. One day, with the snow thick on the ground, they came down and he marked my cards for the meeting coming up. No doubt I was not the only member he visited. He knew how to get around something; he did not believe in walking on people."

John Mahon said the Monsignor was aware that the publicity waves he was making did not always go down too well. "He told me himself that he was warned he was making trouble for several ministers by looking for this and that in public and was advertising himself too much and they were all telling him to keep a lower profile."

The clashes between the Monsignor and some Board members over his 'raffle ticket' fund-raising methods did not go down well with the people actually raising the money to finance the completion of the project. While some Board members' views on fund-raising methods had been given a public airing by Healy, the fund-raisers themselves saw the Board as 'utterly useless' at raising money. "They talked all day and argued and criticised while we went out and raised the money to complete the airport and help the Monsignor," one source recalled.

Another source said some Board members made it hard for Horan. "He'd have an all-day Board meeting and come out looking ten years older. The pressure on him was enormous. His backroom staff of girls and Tom Neary and others were key to the fund-raising. The Board had no hand, act or part in raising money. He knew he had the Stewards and Handmaids who would help out in selling tickets, and the O'Donohues and others who gave freely of their time to get the money in."

So while there was undoubtedly the element of Horan being exceptionally good at motivating people and getting things done, his frustration at being tied down by lengthy and trying Board meetings was understandable. Conversely, there was the view within the Board that Horan was on a solo run, that he was taking the credit for making the whole thing happen on his own, and was not perhaps keeping his eye on what some felt were the key strategic priorities. Simply put, they saw the flight to Rome as a distraction and the purveyor of a message that the job was done and dusted when in fact nothing could be further from the truth.

For his part, Horan told journalists he could take the pressure because he made an act of humility every morning and didn't care what people said about him.

"If you trust in God you don't mind what people say as long as your conscience is clear," was a stock-in-trade answer of his.

There was something for Horan to smile about before the year was out, however. *Aspect* magazine, in a feature on the airport, and referring to the likely cost of the project, showed that the original TAI feasibility study had indicated a capital investment expenditure of £6 million at 1980 values. Applying the CPI escalator, that worked out at £10.5 million by 1985 prices, the magazine calculated. And that estimate was based on a shorter 6,000ft runway.

Although the writer of the article did not extrapolate further, the Monsignor no doubt did his sums, again using the CPI escalator, and was pleased to see that the government pledge of £8 million in 1980 would have equated to just a shade under £14 million in 1985, and that was the figure that finally completed the project one year later!

But in the run-up to the official opening day the embers of controversy were to be fanned again when it came to deciding who would open the airport. Or, to quote Horan, who would play the fiddle on one of the most auspicious occasions in Mayo history.

CHAPTER THIRTEEN

*1986: Management contract signed – Opening day washed out –
Most flights cancelled – Charlie's wind-tossed flight – How lone
London flight touched down – Getting back VAT money – Paul
Durcan's epic poem – First US flight lands – Monsignor in hospital*

There is only one fiddle to be played!

THE year was to bring many crises. Seven people were to die on board
the Challenger space shuttle, and the world was to learn of the
Chernobyl nuclear reactor explosion and loss of life. It was the year, too,
that the Irish Sweepstakes closed after 56 years, and our jobless figure
reached 250,000.

In the charts, Chris de Burgh's 'Lady In Red' was to race to the top.

And if only Pope John Paul 11 had made up his mind and agreed
to return to Knock again he probably would have been asked to cut the
ribbon to open the airport, and thereby would have been avoided yet
another controversy. That is, of course, if Popes actually open airports!

The hot-potato issue of the opening lay some months away,
however. Meanwhile, the Board was pushing to have scheduled flights to
London tied down as the service was critical to the viability of the
operation. Aer Lingus did not want to know and Ryanair was trying to
get to its feet after its first tentative steps the previous November.
During January the Airport Board was in negotiations with Kiltimagh-
born ex-Aer Lingus pilot Danny Higgins whose company, Celtic Air, was
anxious to step in and run two flights a day to London from May 15, at
a one-way fare of £75. The ambitious young company executive told the
media other flights to the UK were being examined.

On February 11 Jim Farrelly of the *Irish Independent* reported that
a £1m ILS system providing electronic navigational aids had been
installed, and that consultants British Airways International had
predicted passenger figures for the first year could be as high as 270,00
and worth £40 million in revenue.

Their projections estimated the potential from the North
American route to be in the order of 120,000 passengers for

scheduled/charter flights, with European scheduled/charter routes having the potential for over 80,000. Potential was one thing, finding interested carriers and laying on scheduled flights to such destinations in the year of start-up was a horse of a different colour, so the BAI reported projections were wildly optimistic to put it mildly. Yet, BAI was to get the contract to manage and run the airport, at a reputed fee of £100,000 sterling a year. The company had been formed in 1978 and had international experience. In 1984 BAI had taken over the management of the UK Regional airports of Exeter and Southampton and had just entered a ten-year contract to manage Southend Airport.

In Dublin for a press conference, Monsignor Horan confirmed that the BAI contract had been awarded. He also revealed that Aer Lingus had told him they could not provide scheduled services without a subsidy and Aer Rianta had told the Board they could not operate the airport. BAI was a subsidiary of British Airports Authority which ran Heathrow and other UK airports. Horan announced that Maurice Buckby would be BAI's Irish project manager, in effect manager of the Connaught Regional Airport. While it solved the immediate management issue for the Board, the contract was to have serious repercussions.

Another pressing issue in need of resolution was of a financial nature: funds were desperately required to install vital facilities and one of the fund-raisers Brian Kelly recalls an occasion when fund-raising chairman James O'Donohue called a crisis meeting to see how the money could be raised.

The meeting kicked around a number of ideas as to how and where the money could be found. Kelly asked whether the building company (the promoters) were registered for VAT. If it was, money could be claimed back.

The Monsignor's eyes lit up. "What's that? We're not, we're not registered, are we?" he asked, looking around the room.

No one in the room knew for sure so they decided to check it out with the financial people. Kelly sought advice from his own accountants in Athlone. The news was positive. And within days the accountant was before the Monsignor in Knock, explaining how VAT worked and the benefits of being registered.

After the position had been fully thrashed out, the Monsignor beamed: "So they owe me money, so."

"And we said they do but you have to be registered. Then you will get your money back," explained Kelly.

"Who, who won't give it back to me?" asked the Monsignor.

The accountant explained they would have to go through the formality of registering and then wait for approval of registry and satisfy any queries there might be.

"That could take ages and our need is great," responded Horan. "Who's in charge of all that kind of thing?"

Tongue-in-cheek, someone volunteered: "Well, the man at the top is Patrick Bedford, the Collector-General of Revenue."

"Paddy Bedford," beamed the Monsignor. "I know him well. He is a great friend of Knock Shrine. He comes here every month. Margaret, get Paddy Bedford on the phone for me." So he talked to the top Revenue man and said, "Paddy, I have a few fellows here and they say you owe me money and if I make the proper application you will get it for me. It's quite a considerable amount of money and if we send in the application, will you look after it? Fine, Paddy, fine. I'll tell them."

When he came off the phone the Monsignor told his small audience that the documentation had to be prepared and put through the normal channels and if everything was in order the refund would indeed be made.

According to Kelly, the accountant was flabbergasted at the direct approach! It was a classic case of Horan going to the man at the top as was his form. But within a short period, when all the application forms and other relevant documentation had been sent in and approved, they got a cheque for about £375,000 in VAT refunds. It was a nice little windfall for the airport, and the Monsignor was thrilled.

Those who knew Horan knew he always took the direct route to achieve his aims. Tom Neary accompanied him on many visits to Dublin, and knew the form well. "Maybe we'd be visiting some Government department, and he'd always want to see the boss. Sometimes they'd send down a young person to see what this man wanted, and immediately he would say, 'I want to see the man in charge here.' When the person went off to report back, the Monsignor would turn to me and laugh and say, 'We might have a bit of bog on our boots but we are able to do our business at the same time!'."

"Invariably," said Neary, "he'd eventually get through to the boss and make his case. He'd say there was no point in beating around the bush or going the long way around unless you had to. And he was always well prepared for such meetings, he'd be as many steps ahead as he could. It was just that he was a very organised man, he didn't believe in wasting time, and he had every day's work set down on paper. He'd say there is far too much talk and not enough action. He was also great for giving people a little bit of encouragement, wasn't afraid to delegate and knew that people would take on responsibility. He believed you had to involve people to get them interested."

Meanwhile, the Mayo Association in London was making sure its members would be there in numbers for the opening day. *The Connaught Telegraph* reported the exiles' hopes of flying in 370 well-wishers for the tape-cutting jamboree, while the Mayo team, due to play London in the senior football championship in Ruislip, would fly out from Knock on the return leg. All nice and dandy, but hadn't Robbie Burns a poem about the best laid plans of mice and men!

Through all of this, dealings between the Government and the Airport Board continued to be of the knife-edge variety. While a working relationship existed between the two parties, the Coalition's political nous told them that their role at the launch would be a secondary one. Their suspicions were confirmed when it was announced in early April that Charles J. Haughey, Leader of the Fianna Fáil Opposition, would be invited to open the airport.

The *Irish Independent* revealed that Haughey had been proposed by Seamus Monaghan and seconded by Cathal Duffy, with Monsignor Horan, Michael O'Malley and Jim Ryan supporting the proposition Against the proposal, speculated the *Independent*, were directors John Dillon and the two Department of Communications representatives, Vincent Feehan and Paddy Ryan.

"It was believed," added the newspaper report, "that BAI had advised against inviting Haughey to perform the opening, on the grounds that it would politicise the event and cause a rift with Bord Fáilte."

According to a source, Charles Haughey had thought perhaps the opening might have been done in 1985 on the day of the Rome flights, but the Monsignor pushed that aside, saying it might look too triumphant a gesture on that occasion. The clear implication was that Haughey would have been prime candidate to open the airport from that occasion, if not before.

James O'Donohue was also aware that Haughey was the preferred and only choice of the Monsignor. "I recall," he said," there was a Garda day at Knock and I happened to be there, and the Monsignor had the top brass and other guests in for lunch. They were all talking about the upcoming opening of the airport and I heard the Monsignor saying, 'Garret is now in power. I'll ask him to open the landsite and Charlie to open the Airport.' And one of the guests said in surprise: 'Sure Garret won't play second fiddle to Charlie' and the Monsignor replied in a fit of laughter, 'Well, there is only one fiddle to be played.' He was like a big child with the burst of laughing. Oh, Charlie had to open it: he'd swing for Charlie!"

Seamus Monaghan says Horan had always promised Charlie that he would do the opening. "Charlie had not asked, it was just the Monsignor's way of thanking him for his support, and the Monsignor never went back on his word. He was a man of honour. There was a Coalition in government but the Monsignor wanted Charlie to open it because he had given his word, kinda 'sure on the day you will open it' kinda thing.

"There wasn't even a brick laid at that stage, just a big pile of rock and I was wondering how it was going to look myself. We were at a meeting in Dublin just before the decision was taken on the official opening and Jim Mitchell was there with a few Civil Servants and he wanted Garret FitzGerald to open it.

"We told him we had already decided who was going to do the honours, and that was it. Garret can be there, no problem," we said.

"But," he claimed, "the Government actually got Bord Fáilte to send a telex to the Monsignor telling him that if Garret FitzGerald opened the airport all the meals would be paid for, the expenses of journalists would be paid for by Bord Fáilte, and if not the Government wouldn't pay a penny towards the day.

"When the telex came in the Monsignor handed it to me and I could not believe what it indicated. I read it and it was grabbed out of my hand and copied. The story appeared in the papers the next day," he added. Bord Fáilte immediately denied the claim.

Tom Neary said there was no doubt in his mind that the Monsignor would invite the Fianna Fáil leader to open the airport. "The Monsignor had his own way of looking at things, politics and politicians. Deep down he had no interest at all in whether you were a Fianna Fáil man or a Fine Gael man or a Labour man. He had no real interest in party politics. He would say, 'The politicians are there and we have to go with them because we can't get anything done if we don't.' He felt from the start that Charlie was with him and that he signed on the dotted line when it was necessary and therefore why not invite the man even though circumstances had changed, CJH no longer being Taoiseach."

One thing the Monsignor admired in Haughey was his ability to make a decision, according to Neary. "He'd say to me there are an awful lot of people unable to make decisions about anything, and he'd say that's a terribly important consideration if you are attempting to do anything. He'd say if you are not able to make decisions you will never get anywhere. That was one of his very strong points. He could decide like that, this is what's to be done, we are going with this and there are no two ways about it. And then this downright determination, arising from the decision: nothing would put him off. And he could bring people with him. I often heard it said you'd do things for James Horan that you wouldn't do for others. He could win you over and he had the bit of fun and humour and he'd give you the feeling this is worth having a go – you will get a kick out of trying this. He had that little knack and that is why so many people came out and helped him."

Another endearing thing about the Monsignor, recalls Neary, was that he wouldn't fall out on a permanent basis with anyone. "You could have a battle today with him and he'd shake your hand tomorrow. He'd say.' You know me well, I don't hold anything against people. I make my point. They might not agree with it but so what?' Deep down he had the bit of the old republican spirit in him."

Senator Jim Higgins, who believes his party was caught offside from the beginning of the project, says in an effort to try to depoliticise the occasion he had proposed to the Board that President Paddy Hillery perform the official opening. "However, the company wouldn't buy into it, and said they were not having it."

Cabinet Minister at the time, Paddy O'Toole recollects that Taoiseach Garret FitzGerald received a letter from Monsignor Horan outlining details of the official opening. "He invited the Taoiseach and all the Cabinet to the opening which, he said, was to be performed by the Leader of the Opposition, CJ Haughey. In the circumstances, a decision was taken that no Cabinet member would attend."

If the Government had been bloody-minded enough it would have prayed for rain on the opening day parade. In the circumstances, it did not have to. 1985 had produced a really bad summer in the West, and the portents for the summer of 1986 didn't look much better. In fact, conditions were so bad on the land in the West, the *Western People* reported in May that there was a farm fodder crisis. In response the Government called in the Army to deliver 1,500 bales of hay deep into North Mayo. The hay, ran the report, was a welcome addition to the thousands of bales ferried into the Erris region by the local Co-operative Society, and it was snapped up like 'hot buns' by farmers 'stunned and facing ruin' as the crisis deepened.

Tim Quinn, Manager of the Erris Co-op, said the hay was being made available by farmers in the south of the country at the generous price of £1.50 a bale. However, he estimated that sheep valued at about £350,000 had died in the North Mayo area as a result of the bad weather and the shortage of fodder. Cows, calves and other cattle had also been lost, he reported.

*   *   *

Back at the airport, where the official opening day had been fixed for May 30, Monsignor Horan was pressing his bank to sanction a letter of credit for the runway lighting. He rang Albert Reynolds, who was then on the Opposition benches, looking for advice, saying the bank wanted him to sign personally for the loan.

Recalls Reynolds: "He told me they wouldn't give it to him any other way. I said I presume you don't have the money – about £400,000 or £500,000, I think – and he said, 'No I don't.'

'What's your problem then about signing for it? You are signing for it personally. You are not signing it on behalf of the parish.'

"So he signed, and only weeks afterwards he died," said Reynolds. That letter of credit was to have a telling sequel as we shall see.

Days before the opening, anticipated passenger numbers for the year ahead were given a timely boost when Senator Jim Higgins announced that the Blue Army in the US would fly 7,000 pilgrims to Knock every year. The man behind the commitment was the Senator's cousin, Daniel J. Lyons, whose father hailed from Skeghard, Ballyhaunis.

Meanwhile John Healy, on holiday in Australia, found the airport was very much of a media 'joke' there. Referring to a television programme which he had seen in Brisbane, he wrote: "The Connaught Regional Airport must be the best-known airport in the world inasmuch as, before it opens at all, it is known from Sydney to Singapore, from San Francisco to Strasbourg. The latest Australian (tv) effort didn't miss a cliché. Why it was a 'joke' was not explained. This, it seems, is taken for granted. It was built single-handed by Monsignor Horan, yet the joke was that although it may never know, or see, an international tourist, the Irish taxpayer had to cough up 20 million Australian dollars.

"We had Seán Barrett, the Coalition's licensed economic guru, to dismiss the airport in the bog as a waste of money and if it ever became operational it would only have 20 part-time workers and would lose money. Think about that one.

"I have to admit to cringing a little bit more than somewhat at Seán Barrett doing down the Irish for what can hardly be a great appearance fee. I don't mind us washing our dirty linen – or clean linen which the Barretts of the world may choose to regard as soiled – at home. I have a fair track record in that department. But when it comes to the international scene I am all in favour of using any bit of exposure which I can get in any of the media to sell the country as best I can," rapped Healy in his *Irish Times* column of May 17.

Horan was at one with Healy in decrying journalists who exported copy to the foreign press which was derogatory to the Irish people, the Church and State institutions. He was from the old school in that regard, believing that anything that made a laughing-stock of the country, its traditions and culture outside these shores, was to be opposed. He saw the airport as a good example of that kind of abuse and railed against 'fabricated stories' which were exported by journalists and reappeared in the *New York Times* or *The Times* of London. "A foreign saboteur could not do more damage to our country than this irresponsible journalism," he recorded in his Memoir. It depended on perspectives, of course.

Meanwhile arch-critic of the airport, Minister for Health Barry Desmond declined an invitation to attend the laying of the foundation stone for a £10 million extension at Mayo General Hospital in Castlebar, but it had nothing to do with his pet flogging horse; he rejected the Castlebar invite because he was not asked to officiate at the hospital ceremony. That honour was to go to the Fianna Fáil chairman of the Western Health Board, Senator Mark Killilea, and the Minister said it was an insult that the name and office of the Minister of the day would not be jointly inscribed on the stone with that of Senator Killilea.

Nine days before the opening ceremony, Minister Mitchell granted a temporary licence to Celtic Air to operate scheduled services on the London and Manchester routes, using a 44-seater Fokker aircraft. It was good news: an essential service was in place, or so it seemed.

The count-down was now well and truly on and the media interest ate up the column inches in the local and national newspapers. The choice of ribbon-cutter was still making the news but an unrepentant Monsignor explained to the *Irish Press* that he had invited CJ Haughey to open the airport for two reasons, one Haughey was a Mayoman, and two, "We wouldn't have the airport today unless he had given it to us in the first place when he was Taoiseach."

Shortly before the opening a Government Press Service spokesman announced officially that Government members would be unable to attend because of 'other commitments'. The timing of what was seen as a 'sour grapes' comment was unfortunate for it coincided with an announcement by Pierre Mathijsen, the Director-General of the EC's Regional Policy, who flew into the airport on his way to attend a major conference in Ballyhaunis organised by Gerard McGarry's Enterprise Connacht/Donegal group. He raised the temperature by commenting that the Government's withdrawal of financial support from the airport would make it more difficult for the EEC to channel funds into the development. If the Government changed its mind, he indicated to the author, the Airport's application for EEC funds would be considered in a favourable light.

"If this is the attitude, it is terrible," Monsignor Horan responded when asked to comment. EEC funding, or the lack of it, had been a long-running issue between Government and the Board with the EEC caught in the middle of the sandwich. .

On May 28 the *Western People*, which had been a staunch supporter of the project from day one, produced a souvenir supplement to mark the opening. The headline on the front page, over a full colour aerial shot of the runway, proclaimed: "And they said it couldn't be done!" Well, it had been done. An old man dared dream and had put a piece of infrastructure in place that would justify his conviction.

On the morning of the opening, airport manager Maurice Buckby was quoted as saying the young staff recruits at the airport – with an average age under 25 – 'are absolutely outstanding. They are incredibly adaptable. We could not possibly make it pay otherwise'.

However, the weather did its best to spoil the party atmosphere. It teemed from the heavens and the dark clouds sat down on the new runway. It was as if someone was weeping at the folly of it all, though devout people in the huge crowd reminded those around them that it also rained cats and dogs the night of the apparition at Knock back in 1879!

Tom Neary had driven the Monsignor to Dublin to do interviews and recordings at the RTÉ studios the day before the opening. "The next day we came back down through the Frenchpark route. It was absolutely belting rain, a horrible day in fact," he recollects. "The Monsignor wondered if anyone would turn up." In the West, the rapidly worsening conditions were causing grave concern and the awful spectre of flights being cancelled on opening day was turning into a probability as the minutes ticked by. The control tower was anxious.

Meanwhile Charles J. Haughey and his wife Maureen were arriving at Dublin Airport to fly westwards. In the capital, too, the dark rain-clouds were gathering. The small party flying out for the occasion included Brian Lenihan, P. J. Mara, the Government Press secretary, and poet Paul Durcan who had been commissioned by Haughey to write an epic poem to mark the occasion. It was going to be a bumpy ride!

Poet Durcan, whose parents were from Mayo, recalled in an interview in *Magill* magazine a month later that their plane flew incredibly low and was bouncing around in the air, and when they got over Mayo the rain was bucketing. They could see cattle huddled for shelter, and at one stage the weather was gusting so much the plane was actually on its side in the air, Durcan told the magazine.

"Tell the control tower we're coming in," Haughey instructed his pilot as they spotted the rain-lashed runway. Clearly, he was not for hanging about in a small wind-tossed plane! Monsignor Horan strode out to greet his guests on the apron as the excited, rain-drenched crowds pushed to the perimeter fence overlooking the apron to snatch a view of the warm handshake between the two Mayo men.

Meanwhile a plane-load of happy Mayo exiles was heading across the Irish Sea from Southend in Essex oblivious of the threatening weather conditions. The Mayo Association in London had chartered four aircraft from Island Airways after Alice Rouse, wife of Association chairman PJ, had done the spadework with travel agent John Dillon in Ballyhaunis acting as logistics link man. On one of the flights was Mayo Association member and Safe Start founder Tom Beisty who says they didn't realise that three Knock-bound flights had already been diverted. "Our flight would have been too but myself and Jim Beisty were talking to the pilot up in the cockpit when he apologised that he had left the drinks trolley behind to save weight. He remarked how he appreciated there was not one word of complaint."

What the pilot wasn't aware of was that the duty-free had been opened and the party had begun in the rows of seats behind the cockpit. Someone's efforts with the rosary were soon drowned out as the craic and banter swept the plane as the drink flowed. "He had no need to apologise. The Mayo lads had found an answer," recalls Beisty with a smile.

But there was a change in the mood when the pilot informed the Mayos on board that his orders were to land in Dublin. He explained to his crestfallen passengers that he had no precise map co-ordinates for Knock Airport nor had he confirmation that fuel was available to him there for his return flight.

"Earlier, during our heart-to-heart with him he told us that he had once been an RAF bomber pilot and that he did not wish to go back to the times when he had to fly across the Channel with a map strapped on his knee looking for the Cliffs of Dover and other landmarks that would lead him back to Biggin Hill RAF Station," says Beisty.

But the Mayo-bound passengers were not taking no for an answer on this most auspicious of days in the history of their county. "We reminded him that he would be the first airman to fly passengers from England into the brand-new Knock Airport, and assured him that a pilot of his calibre could easily follow the N4 and N5 roads down from Dublin. Then he could bear right at the creamery tower at Ballaghaderreen which, we told him, was every bit as good a landmark as the Cliffs of Dover. We guaranteed him there would be fuel there and begged and pleaded with him for what seemed an eternity."

The pilot must have got caught up in the moment because, amid wild cheers, he swung away from his approach to Dublin Airport and headed west – only to find the weather was awful. "We could hardly see a thing. But by this time he had very little fuel to go anywhere else, so he set us down in torrential rain to the consternation of the Knock airport authorities who obviously did not expect us to land," says Beisty.

The London passengers were held in the Arrivals Hall until a 'Customs Man' arrived from Charlestown, but in happy spirits, the ex-pats gave vent to their feelings. Many of them kissed the ground like the Pope and really relished the moment as others took pictures. "I remember the customs officer was so pissed off he tried to confiscate Michael Durcan's camera. Needless to say, he got no camera. We emerged into the main hall to wild cheering with the Agnes O'Connell pipe band from Romford in Essex playing a mighty welcome for us – it really was something special and I know everyone on that flight was proud to be there," recalls Beisty, summing up the euphoria of the occasion.

On that historic flight was Mayo heart-transplant recipient, Johnny Kilgallon (47) of Church Road, just outside Ballina. The Kentish-town resident was marking the first anniversary of his operation at the famed Harefield Hospital in London.

In all, nineteen small planes landed for the opening, including flights from Abbeyshrule in Co. Longford which got to Knock by following the railway tracks because visibility was down to 100ft. in places.

On the platform Charles J Haughey (61) was addressing the attendance of about 5,000 people who braved persistent wind and rain and bitterly cold conditions. He looked out on a banner held bravely aloft with the message: 'Mayo for Sam, Monsignor for Pope!'

"The control tower of the airport," he said, "will send its beam of light across the lovely landscape of Connaught, a flashing beacon of hope and encouragement, symbolising a new phase of progress and development."

Raising his voice to compete with wind and rain, he continued: "It is good to be here today because this is a day that will be long remembered in the West. We are making history here. This represents a triumph over the straitjacket of negative establishment thinking.

"The Monsignor's dream was equality of opportunity for the people of his beloved Connaught. Persistent and resolute, this extraordinary man overcame all difficulties, swept aside all obstacles and succeeded in the seemingly impossible task he had set himself.

"Few parts of Ireland have suffered more cruelly from the lack of economic development and the scourge of emigration than this area," said Haughey, adding: "The economic, cultural, social and even political significance of this addition to the modern infrastructure to the province of Connaught is truly enormous."

That Bank Holiday weekend, on national radio, Haughey was to pledge that the airport industrial zone would be granted duty-free status if Fianna Fáil was returned to office. However, he hoped the Coalition government would agree to the application already submitted by the Airport Board. "I think every airport with an international dimension automatically has a duty-free zone now," he said.

There was a great cheer when the Monsignor moved to the microphone, first with a jocular apology: "As a matter of fact, I was in Dublin this morning and if I had been here I can assure Charles J Haughey that we'd have no rain!" But then he had always claimed Knock had a direct line to the Man Above!

Expressing his pride that the project had been completed, he proclaimed, "This is the greatest thing that has happened in Connaught in the last 100 years." He said Haughey's faith in the project had never wavered. It was through loyalty to him that the people of the West continued to work on the project when all seemed lost.

Thanking those who supported the project, he continued: "The people are the salt of the earth and I could not have achieved anything at the Shrine or the Airport without them."

Referring to the fund-raising campaign that had made it possible to complete the project, the Monsignor said, "There's Live Aid and Sport Aid and Self Aid: the people of Mayo have been practising self aid for generations, otherwise they would have disappeared."

Master of ceremonies Michael O'Malley described Monsignor Horan as 'the greatest Mayoman that ever lived' to thunderous acclaim. Then it was poet Paul Durcan's turn to engage the crowd, by now growing restless in wet clothing as the main phalanx of the media watched through the fogged-up windows of a bus park near the platform.

"Can you imagine what it is like to wait there in the middle of a storm on the top of a mountain while Mr Haughey speaks and then cuts the tape, knowing that you have to hold these drenched people with a long poem," Durcan later told *Magill* magazine in an interview with Colm Tóibín.

"The poem," wrote Tóibín, "was in sections full of the mystery, incantation, mockery, irony, pity, humour, naivety, risk and sorrow which fill Paul Durcan's poems."

185

Durcan sought the blessings of Our Lady of Knock, of Barnalyra, Ballyvary and Portacloy amongst other Mayo locations.

Charlie Haughey was later to observe that he was particularly taken by the verse which envisioned Raftery the poet sitting at the airport, contentedly drawing on his pipe as his heart soared with the aircraft.

As the poem wended to a conclusion, keen observers saw Haughey's hooded eye mysteriously flash at Padraig Flynn who was, in his own words, 'half liaison man' between the Monsignor and his Leader. Refusing to comment on Haughey's flashing glare, Flynn confined himself to saying he would never forget the historic occasion.

Harpist Frankie Forde-Waldron rounded off the official ceremony with a rendition of 'The West's Awake.'

Haughey unveiled a plaque which carried a carefully crafted set of words. It read: "The establishment of this international airport was authorised by An Taoiseach Mr Charles J. Haughey, TD, on 25 September, 1980, and was officially opened by him on 30 May, 1986." The wording was clearly inclined to the interpretation that Haughey was still Taoiseach in 1986. As far as some members of the Board were concerned, there was still only one real Taoiseach!

The attendance included future Taoiseach Bertie Ahern and most of the Fianna Fáil Shadow Cabinet. The airport was blessed by Bishop Thomas Flynn of Achonry and Church of Ireland Bishop John Neill. The attendance also included Archbishop Joseph Cunnane; Charlestown-native Bishop Joseph Cassidy of Clonfert; Bishop Eamon Casey of Galway; GAA President Dr Michael Loftus of Crossmolina; and Mr Michael McNulty, Director General of Bord Fáilte.

There was no representative from the Government present. Minister of State Enda Kenny did not arrive until late afternoon, 'due to duties in Dublin'. Senator and MEP Jim Higgins views his party's 'stay-away' as a big mistake, compounding other errors in relation to the airport. "Not attending the official opening was not an astute thing to do. We should have been officially represented; the party should have been officially represented. I was there but I was only a bit player in the Fine Gael party at the time. We should have bitten our lip and gone to it," is still his assessment.

The Mayo team, en route to play London in the Connaught SFC in Ruislip, had waited at the airport for hours for a plane that could not land because of the worsening conditions. Eventually they were bussed from Knock to Shannon at 6.30 that evening, and their flight to Southend did not take off until 12.15 a.m. on the Saturday morning. They got to their hotel at 3 a.m., but their ordeal did not deter them from beating London on the Sunday afternoon. For football star Liam McHale it was a special occasion: he celebrated his 21st birthday that day.

However, the team's ordeal was not yet over. A bomb scare (which turned out to be Coke cans left in a plastic bag) at Southend delayed their return flight and with no landing lights fitted at Knock they had to divert to Dublin. They were then bussed back to Knock. Many in the travelling party of players and supporters did not reach their homes until 5 and 6am the following morning.

Mayo football legend Willie Joe Padden was to term it a long journey into night – and day! Castlebar businessman and staunch Mayo supporter John Hanley was one of hundreds caught up in the frustration. He lashed out at the 'cock-up' arrangements and demanded a full investigation into what he described as 'a disgraceful mess'. "We were kept in the dark about everything, in Knock and in Southend," he said on arrival back home after the marathon ordeal.

But for Monsignor Horan and his Board it had been a great day: they had built and opened the airport against all the odds and had seen to it that a vital piece of infrastructure had been provided for the region, largely on time and within budget, based on 1980 figures. That evening not even the disappointment of finding out that Celtic Air's plans for scheduled flights to the UK had been deferred until the autumn due to delays in securing necessary licences could dampen the elation around Mayo, though the awful weather which fouled up the opening day drew knowing tut-tuts.

It was a point latched onto by the media. "In Dublin," reported the *Sunday Tribune*, "aviation experts, economists and senior civil servants shrugged knowledgeably. What else could you expect!"

By now the Airport had its own Aero Club. Monsignor Horan was anxious to have the facility operational as much as possible and he approached John Kilcoyne who was a member of the Mayo club flying out of Castlebar.

"There was very little aviation activity around Knock at that time but we soon changed all that," he recalls with a smile.

With just three members, two instructors and a paltry £300 bank loan, Connaught Aero Club leased a plane and took to the skies. With membership rapidly increasing, a loan of £17,500 was subsequently secured from the Aviation Council of Ireland and a plane bought by the club. Today five instructors operate out of the Club, and many who have passed through its rigorous training programme have secured top jobs with top airlines, though most members use it for recreational purposes.

Much bigger planes were coming, though. On June 16 a jumbo jet from United Arab Emirates landed at Knock on a training flight from Shannon, and just a month later, with still no sign of a scheduled service to the UK, the *Western People* reported that Coventry-based group 'Destination Knock' was to operate a service from Luton every Saturday, using a 44-seater charter.

*   *   *

Another momentous occasion dawned on Tuesday, July 29 July when the first flight from New York touched down on the runaway carrying 254 passengers.

"This is a great day for Connaught, the day when we have established communications with Kennedy Airport. In fact this airport, Knock Airport, is as well known now as Kennedy Airport or Heathrow," said a delighted Monsignor Horan. In another era he might have been referring to the successful laying of the transatlantic cable between Newfoundland and Kerry in the 1860s as he realised the enormous significance of what he and his team had achieved in connecting New York with Mayo by air.

The passengers included 81-year-old Mrs Beatrice O'Brien (née Cassidy) of Barnacuige. She was born on a farm just two miles down the road and had emigrated 62 years earlier. She was met by her brother, Michael, and told reporters she intended to walk the few miles to the place of her birth. The flight from Kennedy Airport, under pilot William Boyd, had taken 5 hours and 35 minutes. Operated by Sceptre Charters, the Super 73 DC-8 jet off-loaded 900 pieces of luggage and this caused a certain amount of congestion and delays as the airport's luggage carousel had not yet been fitted. Amongst the passengers were many elderly Mayo exiles and they were warmly welcomed by over 5,000 people who turned up to see the giant Jumbo land.

First man down the steps onto Mayo soil was NY tour operator Brendan Warde, a native of Foxford, who organised the historic charter, and there to greet the arrivals was a happy Monsignor Horan. The youngest passenger on board was 5-week-old Thomas McHale of Philadelphia who travelled with his parents, Mary and Bill.

Several passengers had some difficulty in renting hire cars with the leasing companies charging £50 for delivering a car from Shannon to Knock, in addition to the normal charges. However, the travelling party got a great Mayo welcome, laid on by the Monsignor who had his reception committee in place. Recalls Mary O'Donohue: "At that time there were really no facilities, so he wanted to lay on the hospitality, and he asked me to organise it. There was plenty of help from Knock and women friends, and we did up the arrivals area in the Irish and American colours, and put on a great reception and he was delighted. He said 'Mary, this is how I want things done in Knock Airport, done properly'."

The O'Donohues were to run the downstairs restaurant at the airport for ten years, first on the invitation of Monsignor Horan, and later on the insistence of his sister, Nancy.

Monsignor Horan was a very proud man as he greeted the visitors from New York. However, those who knew him remarked he looked a little drained. One old friend thought he looked dreadful. Not too many, though, realised that he was just out of a Dublin hospital after an operation some weeks earlier. Within days he would be dead.

CHAPTER FOURTEEN

1986: Monsignor dies in Lourdes – First coffin into Knock – Had picked out burial spot – Thousands pay tribute – Monsignor Grealy takes over reins – Drive to wipe out debt – Ryanair start London service – Great sadness as exiles return to UK after Christmas

If she wants me I'll come . . .

EARLY in 1986 Monsignor Horan had sought to have some of his considerable pastoral duties lightened. He had not spared himself over his life, and the previous ten years or so had been particularly onerous on him as parish priest of Knock: he had transformed the village and the shrine, built a £1.8m Basilica, planned the papal visit and, subsequently, had embarked on the building of a major airport and all the anguish that that entailed.

Now approaching his 75th birthday, he had had discussions with Archbishop Joseph Cunnane on several occasions and also with his successor-to-be and old friend, Fr. Dominick Grealy, on setting aside some of his responsibilities. Their friendship had begun forty years earlier, back in Tooreen. Shortly before his own death, Grealy recalled with a smile: "Imagine me being Parish Priest of Knock with Monsignor Horan as Administrator!" The clear implication was that there would still be only one boss.

In June 1986 Archbishop Cunnane announced his Tuam Diocesan changes which paired the two friends together: Monsignor Grealy was to become parish priest of Knock on September 1, with Monsignor Horan becoming Administrator of the Shrine on the same day. Monsignor Horan saw that, no doubt, as giving him more time to concentrate on getting the Airport up and running and to attract the many pilgrims he envisaged flying in from all parts of the world to the Marian Shrine.

A short time before, Horan had underlined the dream he had for the Airport servicing the Shrine. "Looking into the future I can see thousands and thousands of pilgrims landing there every year. Standing at the airport they will be able to see another great Shrine, Croagh Patrick, peeping majestically over the far distant Partry mountains. Who knows that one of the most famous pilgrims in the world, Our Holy Father, Pope John Paul 11, may one day land at Knock Airport and pay a second visit to Ireland's Marian Shrine. Stranger things can happen. What a wonderful treat it would be for all the pilgrims who were so disappointed because they could not see the Holy Father at close range during his first visit," he said.

He had a clear vision: finish the airport, get the international pilgrimage traffic flowing through the airport, and have the Holy Father pay a return visit, but this time in through Knock Airport as it had by now become universally known. This 'old man in a hurry' had his goals firmly set.

In June he was in discussions with the fledgling Ryanair about providing a scheduled service to London after it emerged that Celtic Air's plans were encountering major difficulties. That same month he also celebrated the Golden Jubilee of his ordination. To mark the occasion Seamus Monaghan sent him a personal cheque for £500. "I had noticed," observed the Sligo businessman and Board member, "that his clothes were getting threadbare. He lived a very frugal life and spent nothing on himself, so I gave him the cheque. I said to myself, surely after 50 years a priest he deserves a good suit."

"But he never kept anything for himself, and I got a return letter of thanks dated June 18 in which the Monsignor wrote: "I am most grateful . . . but on second thoughts I decided to put the money into the airport funds and I know that it will bring us a lot of good luck. Anything I get in that way is put to the same cause. I can assure you that I appreciate your kindness very, very much."

After his Golden Jubilee celebrations and meeting once again many of his old Maynooth classmates, Horan was admitted to hospital in Dublin for what was reported to be a hernia operation on July 1. He had been complaining of remittent stomach problems for a few years.

His closest clerical friends, Archbishop Cunnane and Monsignor Grealy, travelled to Dublin to call on him after his operation. Monsignor Grealy said it was then that his friend's oft-used description of himself as being 'an old man in a hurry' really struck home.

"Well, he actually was in a hurry, and it was very obvious to me in the last year of his life that the Airport was taking its toll on him, all the meetings, all the pressure, and then he went into hospital. During our visit he said to me three times, 'Dominick, there is nothing wrong with me' – by that time I had agreed to go to Knock on September 1 – and the third time he said it, I replied, 'I know that.' When we left the hospital I said to the Archbishop, 'There is something very wrong here'." Grealy suspected the prognosis was not good.

After a two-week period of convalescence at his sister Nancy's home, the Monsignor was reported to be in good spirits and confirmed he would be travelling to Lourdes on a pilgrimage from Knock at the end of July. His sisters, Mary, Margaret, Bridie and Nancy had already booked their flights. Tom Neary, Chief Steward at Knock, organised the flight after suggesting to the Monsignor that he'd like to test the water. "At first the uptake was very slow, but he said, 'We will fill it' and we did," says the retired Balla secondary school teacher.

In the interval the Monsignor attended a fund-raising concert in the Orena Hotel in Knock, and discharged some duties at the Airport, the most important being the finalising of documents in connection with the signing of the contract for the approach and runway lights. A letter of credit had been signed with a local bank to fund that crucial project.

Taoiseach Garret FitzGerald visited Mayo towards the end of July: local FG councillors expected him to announce freeport status and 'chawed' him off for not doing so. "He has left it to Haughey who won't be back in office two days before giving Connaught Airport duty free and every other facility that wouldn't have cost us a ha'penny to give," said an annoyed party man, Councillor John Martin Flannery of Charlestown.

On the day of the Lourdes flight Padraig Flynn journeyed across to the Airport to discuss some matter with the Monsignor. He found a busy scene. "There was a great crowd there, a wonderful event, great excitement and James and myself were talking over in the corner, reflecting on things that had happened, and where it was going and all that sort of thing.

"The tannoy system was calling for him to board the flight and he said, 'Oh, I must go, Padraig'.

"And I kept saying 'Ah, take your time.' We were still talking a few minutes later when it boomed out again, more excited this time. 'Oh, I must be off. I must be off. They are waiting for me,' said the Monsignor.

'Listen James, take your time. They'll be calling you home soon enough'. And that was the last time Flynn saw Horan.

"In a way it was a one-man show for years before that. He had seen the Shrine develop through all the hardships, ups and downs. He knew exactly where he wanted the Airport to go. He always conveyed the impression to me of the Cardinal physique. He was also full of devilment, that twinkle in his eye," recalls Flynn.

Journalist John Healy was deeply perturbed when he saw Horan at the Airport a few days earlier as the first flight touched down from America. "I was shocked when I saw him and when I shook hands, the only thing I could stammer was, 'James, your job for the next few years is to live. You have a few more of those days to see yet'." Yet, that very day Horan was to shake the hand of every one of the 254 passengers who came down the steps and put in a three-hour stint as front-of-the-house man par excellence, posing for pictures and chatting to the arrivals. Later, he skipped a Board meeting to slip home to rest.

A few days later Mary O'Donohue was standing at the door of the Airport restaurant when he went over to her before catching his final flight to Lourdes. "He took my hand and shook it so hard that his grip actually squeezed the rings into my fingers. He thanked me for every single thing – something he had never ever done before and I thought this is strange. I just knew I was not going to see him again."

Accompanying the Monsignor on the pilgrimage were all the Shrine staff. "He brought them all with him. It was almost as if he knew he wasn't going to come back," recalls Tom Neary.

The signing of the lighting contract was uppermost on his mind that morning, recalls Neary. "He said, 'I can't go on the plane until I do this,' and he did. Afterwards, I remember he walked through the departure area and looked around and was kind of crying and I said, 'What is wrong with you?'

'I've signed the last document now. They can take it or leave it,' was his reply as he walked out onto the plane. "He was the very last person to board the aircraft," recalls Neary

The party checked into their hotel in Lourdes and the Monsignor, according to Neary, was in sparkling form, having taken a nap.

"Some of us went for a walk and when we got back to the hotel James was dressed in a báinín sweater and standing beside the piano and singing the whole repertoire – 'He's Got the Whole World in His Hands', 'I'll Walk Beside You', 'We Won't go Home until Morning', 'Moonlight in Mayo', 'If I Can Help Somebody As I Pass Along the Way', and 'Old Lang Syne' at the end.

"He was enjoying a very rare glass of wine – something I had never witnessed before – and we had a lot of banter, good fun and chat. I rarely saw him in such good form, even though he was a man without moods. But he seemed to be very happy, and I think he really enjoyed his glass of wine. Before he retired he went over and sat down and chatted with his sisters," says Neary.

Next morning, when he failed to appear for breakfast, his sister Nancy, a nurse, went to his room. She found him dead. "He died apparently one hour after going to bed. He was just lying in the bed, not a ruffle or a stir on the bedclothes or himself," says Neary. An inquest revealed that he had died of a blood clot.

To Neary fell the task of informing the Knock pilgrims gathered at the hotel. "They wept openly when I broke the news to them and I could only share in their grief. For all of us knew that it was the passing of someone very special, a sort of prince among people. It was hard to break the news to them, his friends."

Neary, his trusted lieutenant over many years, said it was just the way the Monsignor would have wanted to go. He always said he hoped to die peacefully, without a long illness. That was how it happened – peacefully. His wish was answered. He always said, in quiet conversations, that he did not want to be lingering in hospital, causing trouble or anguish to anyone.

"He had his wish – it was as if the Virgin Mary transported him here to Lourdes so that he would go painlessly and as he would have wished himself. And the way he would want people to react to his death would be to rejoice, not be sad, to be happy for him," added Neary.

It was in Lourdes that Neary the schoolteacher saw the special relationship between the media and the Monsignor unfold. "Despite all the stories, all the criticisms, the Monsignor never held any bitterness towards any of them. He'd say, 'Well, you know, the people that are with you and for you, you can understand that. It's the other side and I think they do what they do, maybe they believe in what they are doing and they don't see our point of view. But they have a job to do as well.' And even though the criticism would be negative enough he'd reason 'it won't do us any harm,' and I don't think it did. I'm not sure there was any kind of badness behind it at all. And I'll tell you why I think that: when he died in Lourdes and the news reached Ireland an awful lot of journalists and media people, and I know some of the hardest of them, came to Lourdes straightaway, and, do you know, they were crying. Behind it, they had a kind of respect and admiration for him."

Deirdre Purcell, writing in the *Sunday Tribune*, was one of those to fly to Lourdes and in an interview with the Monsignor's brother, Bart, she learned that Horan always went to the French Shrine in October each year. "No one knows why he came in July this year, except himself. He always said she would come when she was ready for him. He always said, 'If she wants me I'll come'."

Now his body was being flown back to the airport he built, on a plane carrying the first coffin into his creation. His four sisters, and two brothers, Bart and Pat, accompanied his remains on the homeward flight.

The Irish Times, in its editorial of August 2, paid this tribute: "He (Horan) gave hope and inspiration at a time when emigration, unemployment, distressing economic statistics and general gloom have been our daily fare. The Monsignor, with staggering confidence, put heart into his own people. He exhorted them to action, and apologised to no one for standing four square for his own province. It had had bad times more than most parts of the country. James Horan made them stand up and they rose to his appeal. As the preacher had it, to everything there is a season, and a time to every purpose under the heaven: a time to be born and a time to die . . . yet he might have gone on to even more ambitious and heartening developments in the region of his airport had he been spared a few years. For a leader, undoubtedly a leader, has gone."

Seán Balfe, who had served the Monsignor faithfully for the previous fourteen years at the Shrine and the Airport, had one last task to do: arrange for the reception and parking of the aircraft so that the coffin could be unloaded facing the terminal to give those who came to pay their respects a clear view.

As the jet taxied to a halt, the Handmaids and Stewards of Knock Shrine formed a guard of honour and the coffin, draped in the flag of the Order of Malta, was carried from the plane and placed on a dais. Piper Paddy Walshe, playing 'Hail, Queen of Heaven', led the short procession, followed by members of the Board of Connaught Regional Airport, with mourning relatives walking behind the coffin.

Archbishop Cunnane and Bishop Thomas Flynn blessed the coffin and prayed for 'James, who has faithfully fulfilled his ministry'. The scene was overlooked by the statue of Christ the King at the edge of the apron. Mourners joined the cortège along the nine-mile route to Knock and followed the hearse to the Basilica where 5,000 people filed in to pay their respects that evening.

The remains were received by Monsignor Grealy who, a few days earlier, had been doing his First Friday rounds in his Tuam parish when he got a call from Archbishop Cunnane telling him the sad news and asking him to go down to Knock immediately to take charge.

"Monsignor Horan showed great understanding by dying outside the country and giving us two or three days to prepare for what was the biggest funeral in Ireland for years. Fr Grealy's joke is tinged with poignancy. He would have had a laugh at that himself," Justine McCarthy reported in the *Irish Independent*.

Now in the Basilica built by his friend and predecessor, Monsignor Grealy delivered a short homily in which he likened Horan to the Curé d'Ars. "The Curé d'Ars spent his years pouring out love in various forms. He went around doing good and he became a saint. The Monsignor loved people and loved meeting them. His great gift was his attitude towards people. Almost everyone who met him afterwards felt that he had a personal interest in them. He was ordained for love of God and man and his whole life was given to that." It was a theme Fr. Pat Munroe, Monsignor Horan's cousin, had touched upon at Requiem Mass in Lourdes the previous day.

At the funeral, the Minister for Defence, Paddy O'Toole represented the Government, and the leader of the Opposition was represented by Brian Lenihan. People filed past the coffin for hours, mothers lifting their young children so they could see through the little glass window in the coffin lid.

Young and old attended, and Fr. Colm Kilcoyne, a curate at the Shrine, was particularly taken by four young Dubliners who arrived in the village shortly after 6am 'looking the worse for wear' as they inched past the coffin.

Asked why they had made such an exhausting journey, one replied simply: "Because we liked your man."

On Tuesday, August 5, 7,000 people attended the Mass of the Resurrection, attended by Cardinal O'Fiaich and the Papal Nuncio, Dr Gaetano Alibrandi. 310 priests and 14 bishops were in attendance. Rt Rev John Neill, Bishop of Tuam, Killala and Achonry, represented the Church of Ireland.

Archbishop Cunnane read a message of condolence from Pope John Paul 11, and then delivered a powerful and moving homily in which he paid tribute to his life-long friend. He described Horan as 'an inspired and inspiring leader for whom no task was too difficult, no effort too great, in the promotion of Knock Shrine and its pilgrimage'.

The Archbishop said the late Parish Priest of Knock believed passionately in his mission and his work for people. "If his efforts led him into confrontation with those who disagreed with him, as they did in the case of an airport, he never shirked the consequences, though they were not of his seeking," he said.

Dr Cunnane said the airport project was the fruit of long and mature reasoning based as were all the Monsignor's schemes, on his perception of the needs of the West of Ireland.

Tracing his commitment to various parishes in which he had served, the Archbishop said, "Horan was very conscious that the priest in rural Ireland, and especially in the West, should be a man of the people, prepared to work and, when necessary, to fight for better conditions for them in their homes, their farms, their families," he added.

Dr Cunnane said it was the toughness of character and the courage developed in these lesser efforts that prepared him for the much bigger challenge and opportunity that came his way with his appointment as Parish Priest of Knock. The congregation burst into applause when he finished his tribute.

As the funeral procession from the Basilica to the final resting place proceeded, traditional musicians played the lament for 'The Earl of Mayo'– 'a fitting tribute for a leader of men who injected a new vitality into the West of Ireland', wrote an *Irish Press* reporter. As the cortége passed by, roses rained down on the coffin, thrown by those unable to reach the grave.

Burial took place in the shadow of the Basilica at the spot Horan had indicated to Tom Neary several years earlier. One day they were walking the Shrine grounds when Horan said, "Come over here. I want to show you something." Near the statue of St Thérèse, he said 'You know now there's a lovely piece of ground here and I'm telling you when I am gone you'll know."

The day before interment took place ground staff at the Shrine had to cover over the grave as people had insisted on throwing money into it "We took £300 out of the grave in £10 and £5 notes and silver," said staff member Brian Egan. There had been no tradition of throwing money into a grave in the region: it was as if people still wanted to help Horan out. Michael Finlan of *The Irish Times* wrote that the spontaneous act was akin to saying, "We'll finish your airport for you."

The Government was represented by Communications Minister Jim Mitchell who described the Monsignor as 'a magnificent man'. "You could not dislike him, he was absolutely infectious and nearly impossible to resist. I thought he was wrong about the airport – and I still do – but I was very fond of him," he said.

Senator Jim Higgins recalls there was a lingering anti-Fine Gael hangover at the ceremonies: "Jim Mitchell came down to represent the Government and, normally, you would expect the Government minister to be accorded all due protocol. There is a helicopter pad right beside the Basilica and he was not allowed to use it for whatever reason so the Government helicopter had to touch down in a field maybe 300 to 400 yards away. I went up in my car and collected him, and again at the actual funeral itself there was no reference to the fact he was there or anything like that.

"There had, of course, been a building of bridges between the Monsignor and Mitchell, but Fine Gael never really recovered from the political fall-out." He added, "Though obviously over time it dissipated, an example being the 1997 election when we had a five-seat constituency in Mayo and Enda Kenny, Michael Ring and myself took seats."

Paddy O'Toole recollects that from conversations he had with Jim Mitchell in the mid-1980s and indeed after they left government, he got the strong impression that Mitchell had developed admiration for Horan in the persistence he had shown during his campaign for the airport. "I also think the Monsignor Horan developed a certain respect for Jim Mitchell and ultimately began to understand the difficulties under which the Minister was operating," he says.

Fr. Colm Kilcoyne said he had seen one particularly revealing insight into Irish politics a few years earlier. "The Monsignor had one long session with Jim Mitchell. Hard going. Nobody giving an inch. Then going out the door Jim Mitchell asked him to say a Mass for some intention."

Fund-raiser Mary O'Donohue said the Monsignor had his knife in Mitchell. "But, you know, the funny thing is, when it was all over, he had great time for Mitchell. I was in the office one day and Mitchell was talking to him and it was a really nice conversation, and he respected Mitchell at the end of the day."

Minister Mitchell was subsequently to pay fulsome tribute to his old adversary in the Dáil on January 21, 1987: "By any standards, he was an exceptional man. To be truthful, when I first met him there was a certain antagonism but we quickly became very good friends. I came to respect him very much indeed. I often said to friends and to officials of my Department that I would have loved to have had him as chairman of one of my troublesome State companies because he would have been the man to sort them out. I said that with great sincerity. He was truly a great man. Apart from his ability, he also had other magnificent qualities which were rare. Certainly the combination of his qualities was rare and his death is a great loss not only to Knock, to Mayo and Connaught but to Ireland. I am sure he is now resting in Heaven which he much deserves."

Fianna Fáil leader Charles J Haughey, who was also present at the Knock obsequies, and who was in fact assigned the Shrine's sole helicopter pad, told journalists: "I will put it quite simple – we will never see his like again."

Other dignitaries present included former Fine Gael Taoiseach Liam Cosgrave, and Oliver J. Flanagan and Seán Bedford, both representing the Knights of Columbanus. Three Ministers of State attended, Ted Nealon, Paul Connaughton, and Enda Kenny, but they were vastly outnumbered by the large number of Fianna Fáil TDs, MEPs and senators present.

Writing in the *Sunday Press* on August 3, Fr. Kilcoyne, who had known the Monsignor for over 20 years, described his real legacy. "History books will talk about basilicas, papal visits and airports. And they ought to. The real legacy of Monsignor Horan, and I know how much of a cliché this sounds, is in what he built in people. All through his parishes in Connemara, Cloonfad, Tooreen and Knock, he urged and pushed for rural electrification, group water schemes, land reclamation, road improvements and better houses, not so that these things would be there but so that people would live richer, more dignified lives."

*   *   *

So now, a month earlier than he had expected, Monsignor Dominick Grealy (59) found himself overnight not alone parish priest and administrator at Knock but he was also about to be asked to take on the huge burden of becoming caretaker and fund-raiser of an international airport without a penny to its name.

Grealy and Horan were like chalk and cheese. Horan was outgoing, loved the limelight, the action and the arguments. Grealy never saw himself as a public personality figure and had no intention of trying to fit Horan's shoes. "When I came here to Knock I said I would not even try on his shoes – they were always too big for me," he said on taking up his new duties.

For the previous two years Monsignor Horan had been fund-raising most successfully for the completion of the airport which now employed 28 people. But there was no consistent commercial revenue stream and the money had to be raised throughout Ireland, in Britain and in the US, and voluntary contributions had flooded in.

By the time he died he had raised more than £3 million, and the back had been broken on the debt, but there was still a mountain to be climbed. There were no scheduled flights lined up of any consequence and aviation facilities had to be improved before any carrier could be approached with confidence.

And it quickly became obvious that Horan's name and his ability to raise money were prime reasons why banks loaned money to the airport. His track record in creditworthiness was unblemished and the banks usually had faith in him to repay any loans.

But when he died the rules changed. Having signed the contract for the runway lights the day he left for Lourdes, on foot of a letter of credit from the bank, the deal was suddenly taken off the table when news filtered back home that he had passed away.

Seamus Monaghan, whose firm had been awarded the contract, had ordered the lights from GEC on foot of the letter of credit. However, he claimed within days of the Monsignor's death the Board was informed that the bank had cancelled the agreed facility.

"The man wasn't cold and they cancelled the letter of credit. They cancelled the cheque immediately, and they told GEC they had cancelled it. I had to go back to GEC and tell them to keep the stuff on order and I sent a cheque out of my own account to keep the thing clear," he said.

Banks had, of course, good reason to be jittery, as illustrated by a front-page lead story in the *Sunday Independent* of August 10 which proclaimed in a triple-deck headline: "Board not yet told of £200,000 shortfall: £7,000-a-week loss at Knock Airport." The predictions of the doomsayers were looking more credible.

The Board members had met in Knock on the morning of the Monsignor's funeral. Seamus Monaghan said, "Someone asked, 'what are we going to do now? Then someone said, 'We will have to elect a new chairman' and someone else said, 'You will do.' They wanted me to be the chairman."

The meeting was adjourned until after the Monsignor's Month's Mind Mass without taking any decision, although it is likely there was a discussion about the pending interlocutory injunction scheduled for the High Court the following Friday requiring Celtic Air Handling Ltd to vacate the airport. The injunction was granted on the basis that Celtic Air had failed to meet a number of ground handling commitments.

The Board reconvened again on 11 September, and in the absence of the two Government representatives – who were directed to absent themselves by Minister Jim Mitchell – Seamus Monaghan (47) was installed in the chair. However, within hours the Minister made it known that he opposed the appointment as the election did not correspond with his understanding of the proposed arrangements.

The Minister's statement added: "It is important moreover that all directors should have sufficient time to consider all issues involved and the election of a chairman should proceed on the basis that would ensure there could be no future suggestion of a conflict of interest."

The 'conflict of interest' point raised by the Minister referred to the awarding of the lighting contract to Safeway Electrical Contractors of which Monaghan was managing director. The contract, for £300,000, was awarded before Monsignor Horan's death and was understood to be the lowest tender submitted.

Seamus Monaghan said he figured the only reason the Board wanted him to be chairman was because they weren't sure it was going to work and they didn't want a Mayoman to fail. "That's my opinion and I have always said that and I will say it, because a Mayoman did everything: a Mayoman built the airport, the Monsignor was a Mayoman, everyone was a Mayoman. I was the only Sligo-man and I always think the only reason they picked me was because I was not a Mayoman!"

Immediate pressure was exerted at government and church level to get the Sligo man to step down. "The Church came to me and said, 'Look, the controversy, Fianna Fáil and all this kind of stuff, it's not doing the airport any good.' I remember we were at a Board meeting in Knock and a director said to me, 'You stick there, boy. You stick there,' and shortly afterwards the phone rang on the wall and I went over to answer it. I said, 'Hello,' and the response was, 'Charlie Haughey here,' and I said, 'Yes sir.' How are you doing, Boss?', and he said, 'You stick there and don't let them move you'."

He said after the call he spoke to Monsignor Grealy who had joined the Board in place of Monsignor Horan. Grealy committed to do the job for a specified period so that the debt could be tackled and commitments undertaken. Monaghan agreed to step down – his reign, first time round, had lasted a mere five days.

"In actual fact, Monsignor Grealy was a very big contributor to the airport. He stuck his head out and raised the money, to be fair to him," recalls Monaghan.

Monsignor Grealy's take on the chairmanship controversy was that he joined a politically split board, that he had no knowledge of running an airport, and so did not want to get involved. However, the two Department nominees came to him and implored him to take the job as chairman, which he did. On RTÉ radio he praised Monaghan's 'wonderful gesture' in standing down to end a controversy which, he said, could only damage the airport.

"I knew straightaway how accounts were at the Airport, and the Archbishop was very worried at the time. He had good reason to be. I found the Airport was way, way down, something like £400,000, and there was 28 of a staff, a manager and £12,000 in wages that had to be paid out each week. The runway lights – costing in the region of another £400,000, including engineering works – had not been installed and there were no scheduled services and the terminal building, costing another £400,000, needed to be finished. The opening had been rushed by 'an old man in a hurry' who clearly knew he was nearing the end," Monsignor Grealy revealed in an interview for this book before his death in December 2005.

There was another powerful argument for him taking over, and that was to discharge any perception there was that the Church was in the background providing a financial safety net. Said Monsignor Grealy: "I really wanted to separate the Church from the airport, and I knew it could not go on as it was. There was a big sense out there that the Church had a responsibility to discharge the debts, so I was going to be up to my neck in it anyway. But I said once the debt was cleared and essential work done I would get out of the Chair. I set a definite deadline for myself, and I told the Board so.

"Immediate expenditure for the infrastructure required back in 1986 was estimated in the region of £400,000 and, of course, the running costs were mounting up by the day. We had no money," recalled Monsignor Grealy, "and we needed £1.5m quickly."

In fact, money was so scarce in 1986/87 that when it was decided to impose a 50p per car parking charge, the supervisors' hut at the exit gate was a recycled confessional box from Knock Shrine. And one of the longest-serving staff security officers at the airport, Seán Donlon, remembers that collecting money from motorists was a slow process because so few were passing through.

He'd get his petty cash in the morning and worked off that throughout those slow days. One of his most vivid recollections of those straitened times relates to a day when some workers came down from the airport terminal to his hut looking for money to buy a bottle of gas.

"It probably did not cost more than a fiver but, unfortunately, I had not collected that much and told the workers, who went back to the manager Maurice Buckby. He rang me and told me to hand over the petty cash in the hope that by the evening I would have made up for it. I handed over the money and the men went off to buy the bottle of gas. That's how scarce money was," says Donlon.

Sleeves were rolled up again. Monsignor Grealy, the 'caretaker' who knew nothing about running an airport, drafted an appeal. He sent out a letter in August to thousands of people throughout Ireland, 'indeed the very same people who had already given more than £3m to Monsignor Horan'.

The appeal, sent to 200,000 homes, read:

‘Dear Friend of Knock,

Monsignor James Horan died on August 1 in Lourdes. Everyone who knew him is still shattered by his death. He was, as you know, a man of extraordinary faith, vision, determination, courage and friendliness. He was of the people and for the people – especially the people of the West of Ireland. It has been well said that the epitaph of the great architect, Christopher Wren, might be that of Monsignor Horan, too: 'If memorial you seek, look about you'.

Yes, look about you at Knock, in Mayo! His work, indeed – the Basilica, the range of facilities, Knock village, the Airport – enshrines his memory. But he lives on, too, in the hearts of all the people he loved to call 'friends of Knock'. Without them, he knew well that all the work he did would never have happened.

One part of his plan, however, remains uncompleted. Before the Airport becomes what he hoped for, prayed for and worked for; before it's in a position to fly in the hundreds of thousands of pilgrims who want to come from all over the world to Knock and to the West, an expenditure of £1.5m is required – urgently.

For that we must again turn to you – there is no one else to turn to. It may seem soon after his death to make this appeal. But Airports don't wait; they must work or deteriorate. I, as his close personal friend for forty years, know that he would want me to ask for your help NOW because it would be his dearest wish to see the Airport he fought for completed. Anything less he would see as failure, and Monsignor Horan did not like to fail.

So, I make this appeal in his name and on his behalf – to finish for him the work he began and to which he gave himself so generously and so totally. The cause is special. It is a salute to a special man and his dream, a memorial to someone who gave to his people in the West of Ireland – and indeed to all of us – new hope.

For any help you give, I feel sure you will hear the echo from a far distant shore of that soft western voice, once again saying: 'May God bless you.'

Monsignor Horan is dead: God rest him after his labours! As a final tribute to him, let's finish the Monsignor Horan Memorial Airport! May God bless you.’

The appeal, signed by Monsignor Grealy, was an immense success. On a tide of great emotion, money flowed in. £850,000 came in small and large contributions. Not very long afterwards, with the help of the loyal Stewards and Handmaids of Knock Shrine, a church-gate collection was organised in Connaught and the catchment areas of Donegal, Cavan and Longford. It yielded £350,000 from many people who will never even see Knock Airport, said a delighted

Monsignor Grealy. He praised especially the organisational skills of James O'Donohue and Tom Neary, and the goodwill of the clergy.

Tom Neary estimates the money raised through voluntary contributions, Jumbo raffles, overseas visits and Monsignor Horan's Roadshows and various appeals under Monsignor Grealy came close to £4.5 million- an incredible sum by any standards, perhaps the equivalent of £18 million in today's terms! Could it be done today? Unlikely!

*   *   *

Meanwhile recruitment and training of staff got underway. Majella Walsh (née McDonnell), from Swinford, remembers her first week in the autumn of 1986, being trained by an English company. "One day the trainer turned to us and said 'Years from now you guys will be famous because you have been the first staff to have worked at this airport.' I remember being dropped off for work the first day. I was so excited. My father, Paddy, had worked on the building of the airport."

Jim Corry from Co. Clare was a student in a radio school in Limerick when he heard there were job opportunities for technical personnel at the new airport. He took the bus from Ennis, did an interview with Maurice Buckby, the then Airport manager, and was offered a contract there and then. He has been at Knock ever since.

With personnel being put in place, paying passengers became an absolute priority and there was some good news on that front. Ryanair. which applied in August for permission to run scheduled services from Luton to Knock, announced it would be commencing service in December. That application was to prove decisive in turning the fortunes of the airport around. The Board also agreed to name the airport 'Horan International Airport' and before the month was out the Department granted the airport its full licence.

In October, Minister Mitchell appointed Charlestown businessman John Mahon (49) and Omega Airlines director and Swinford native Ulick McEvaddy (34) to the Board in place of his Department nominees Paddy Ryan and Vincent Feehan. And the Minister for Finance, John Bruton, appointed Michael Honan, MD at the Japanese Asahi plant, near Killala, as his nominee.

Honan, formerly of Clondalkin Paper Mills, had been appointed by Alan Dukes to the Board of the Industrial Credit Corporation after helping to pull Asahi around. He said he was apolitical, but when he joined the Airport Board that October he was seen as coming from the enemy camp by some of 'the flag bearers of the soldiers of destiny'.

He said the Airport Board reminded him of a sort of parish council, with a membership of vested interests, all trying to do their best. He struck up an almost immediate rapport with Seamus Monaghan, a straight talker with a lot of guts. "We stood together and started the process of setting up proper accountancy procedures," he said.

By now the Government had moved to regularise ownership of the airport. Paddy O'Toole recalled that by April 1986 Exchequer funding had amounted to £9.8m. The ownership of the airport was in the hands of a private company, The Connaught Airport Development Company Ltd incorporated by local promoters in December 1980 – prior to State involvement but subsequent to Minister of State Padraig Flynn's approval in principle granted on September 25 of that year. The Company owned the site to the value of £9.3m. In order to protect the asset and the State's investment, Minister for Transport Mitchell proposed, on legal advice from the Attorney General, to set up a Trust. It was proposed that, in the interests of continuity, the existing Board members would be nominated as Trustees.

"But because this was being done without the safety net of legislation the Minister had to undertake discussions with Board members whose co-operation was essential in the absence of legislation. All this took some time and the delay was misrepresented as sinister by certain elements who set out to cause difficulties. The Board gave the Minister their full co-operation," said O'Toole in an interview for this book. It was to take several years of negotiations before the Trust was finally settled, however.

In mid-November Ryanair got the licence to operate Knock-Luton flights three days a week, beginning on December 16 and using a 44-seater BAE 748 apply named *Spirit of Monsignor Horan.* Return fares were quoted at £139. Ryanair had been founded on 28 November 1985, and, like Knock Airport, it was almost written off before it started. Like Knock, too, it was to have a difficult passage.

At around the same time, the US-based Blue Army pilgrimage group sought permission from Government to allow direct flights from the US touch-down at Knock instead of having to land at Shannon first, a restrictive mandatory procedure, while New York travel agent Brendan Warde reported that he planned six charters from the US in the summer of 1987. "We are having no difficulty in filling seats," he said. The mandatory government stopover at Shannon was to prove problematic, costly and inconvenient, however, and that issue was to develop into another long-running saga.

On December 16 Defence Minister Paddy O'Toole inaugurated the Ryanair Knock-Luton service. Over the busy Christmas period the airport recorded a throughput of 1,200 passengers. Television cameras were present to capture the sad face of emigration when passengers checked in for their flights back to England after the festive period. Mothers hugging their sons and daughters, tears shed, despair and pessimism everywhere. It was a sight not seen before in one place in Mayo, a sight that Monsignor Horan had set out to change.

Ground-floor bar manager John Glavey of Aughamore has seen the scene change since 1987 when he first took up duty. "Originally, the arrival door and the departure door were just across from the bar, so you could see all the comings and goings . . . huggings and kissing, cheering, tears, sad farewells, people coming to meet people," he said.

Retired Duty Officer Aidan Horkan remembers the first New Year he worked at the airport, seeing the men returning to England and leaving their wives and young children at the departure door. "The scenes of sadness would bring out the goose-pimples in you," he said.

Such sad scenes also left an indelible imprint on Pearse Concannon, Head of Emergency Services, who said he hated working the days after Christmas at the airport in the early years. "I can still see young children holding onto the leg of their father's trousers as he said goodbye and prepared to leave for England. It was heartbreaking to witness it and I know those scenes will stay with me until I die. I never knew the country was in such a state."

CHAPTER FIFTEEN

1987/88: – FG penchant for kicking sleeping dogs – Church responsibility at an end – New chairman elected – The saga of EEC application for grant – Management company sacked – New manager appointed – Dáil watchdog pleased but Desmond unrepentant

Airport fights off predator Aer Lingus and ends BAI contract

THOUGH no one saw it coming as they pondered the year ahead, 1987 was to be the year of Black Monday when world financial markets suffered huge losses. In fact it was to be the worst stock market crash in history. On Monday, October 19, the Dow Jones Industrial Average fell 508.32 and closed at a record-breaking low of 1,738.40 points. The 22.9% loss almost doubled the percentage lost in the Wall Street crash of 1929, which was 12.82%. Stock market analysts believed that the crash was set off by a number of events, including the poor choices of portfolio insurance professionals and program trading.

The impending crash was not going to make it any easier for the struggling aviation industry or fledgling airports like Knock, but that was some months in the future. Meanwhile, buoyed up by traffic figures over the Christmas period, Eugene O'Neill, Chief Executive of Ryanair, gave the Board of Connaught Regional Airport some really welcome news.

It would take Knock only five years to break even whereas it took Cork 25 years to reach that stage, he confidently predicted. For an airport struggling to get on its feet and with its figurehead Monsignor Horan no longer guiding its destiny, the Ryanair projection marked a positive start to the New Year. What people generally did not know was that Ryanair itself was losing money hand over fist!

However, Airport Manager Maurice Buckby felt the Knock performance could be appreciably better if the Government relented on the Shannon stopover clause which, he estimated, could lose the airport up to 7,000 passengers from the US that year.

Within days, Ann Geary, Chairperson of Ireland West Tourism, rounded on Minister Jim Mitchell's decision not to grant direct flights from the US to Knock. She declared his ruling as 'unbelievably callous' and said it made a mockery of the concern being expressed by some politicians about the airport and the great facility they believed it to be for the West.

Mrs Geary of Pontoon Bridge Hotel, near Foxford, did not pull her punches: "His (Minister) decision will mean a loss of 20,000 US visitors and £10 million in tourism earnings," she predicted.

There were losses elsewhere, too. On January 20 the Fine Gael/Labour coalition fell when Labour withdrew support in a row over Budget proposals. In the subsequent General Election, Fianna Fáil took 81 seats, an increase of six, Fine Gael lost 19, and Labour lost 4. Big winners were the PDs who surged up to 14 seats, two more than Labour. Fianna Fáil formed a minority Government, and Charles J Haughey was back for his third and final time as Taoiseach. Outgoing Minister for Defence Paddy O'Toole lost his seat in East Mayo.

O'Toole readily acknowledges that the rows over the Airport cost him his meteoric political career. "The reaction locally, in the vicinity of the Airport, was one of opposition to me and while the Ballina electoral area backed me fully as before, the extra 10% needed outside the area was not forthcoming."

He blamed what he called certain sections and personnel in the media for the part they played in inflicting the maximum damage on Fine Gael and, by inference, on him, he being a Cabinet member at the time, and the most identifiable local Fine Gael cockshot.

He recalls that at the time he felt bad about the political reversal but with hindsight believed he had been done a good turn. He quickly put politics behind him and got on with living, he says pragmatically.

Senator Jim Higgins, who was subsequently to succeed O'Toole in the Dáil, has no doubts as to the political message to come out of the Airport saga: "The late John Kelly said once upon a time, 'if there's any sleeping dog lying around Fine Gael are sure to kick it'. This was one sleeping dog that we kicked and paid the political price for long enough."

The battles were not only of a political nature. The State airline, Aer Lingus, weighed down by demarcation and a burgeoning cost base, resisted threats to have its flanks exposed to private enterprise. It tried to kill off Ryanair before it rose too far off the ground, especially having noted the success Ryanair had attained from a cold start-up over the Christmas period at Knock. Aer Lingus zoomed in on Sligo and Galway to offer cut-price fares to Dublin with onward connections to foreign destinations. Now, for an extra £10, passengers could get on board at Sligo and Galway to link up with outward connections at Dublin Airport. The pincer movement was obviously planned to undermine traffic out of Knock.

Ryanair, founded in November 1985, was particularly vulnerable, racking up losses of £3 million by the end of its second year of operation on its routes, but its interest in Knock was a life-saver for the new airport – and for itself.

Ken Holden, the man who had done the TAI feasibility study back in 1980, says Ryanair knew the potential of Knock. "At the time Ryanair saw a great opportunity: the airport was there, passengers: were waiting to jump on board, there was no competition."

Aer Lingus had made it clear it would service Knock to Dublin only if it received major subvention. It was not interested in flying direct to London and was therefore of little use to Knock. With Ryanair offering fares from Knock to Luton at less than half the £300 average cost Aer Lingus was charging from Dublin to Heathrow, people from the West of Ireland working in England quickly realised that they could fly home more regularly to be with their families for weekends. In 2003 Aer Lingus Chief Executive Willie Walsh was to admit that the national airline had been ripping off its customers for years through its fares policy.

Airport Duty Officer Aidan Horkan feels the true social impact of the Airport has never been fully understood. "In the 1980s/1990s the West was ravaged by emigration, and when the airport opened it did two significant things: it provided a fast means of transport and travel, and it removed the stigma of emigration. It played a huge social role. Workers in England got travel coupons from their employers to come home every six weeks, and the stigma thing changed. Confidence grew. Those who had to find work in England were no longer cut off from their families," he observed.

The growing Ryanair business was especially welcome, given that hopes pinned on the expansion of the Blue Army pilgrimage charters from America were not being realised. In fact in early February Airport Manager Maurice Buckby announced the proposed flights had been deferred to 1988. Yet again, the mandatory stopover at Shannon and the consequent extra costs involved were advanced as reasons for the change of plans.

In Seanad Éireann, Jim Higgins was pressing the case for cessation of the obligatory stopover, reiterating that 20,000 pilgrims would be lost to the area unless a concession was granted.

By March critics of the stopover felt vindicated when the *Irish Press* reported that 26 staff at the Airport were now on short time, working week-on, week-off, in a cost-cutting exercise to rearrange finances and get a more suitable working routine up and running. The bottom line was that the Airport was struggling for business.

In reply to charges by Barry Desmond that the Airport had

already lost £1 million for the first seven months of operation, an airport spokesman denied the claim, saying the loss was £140,000, but defiantly indicated the intention was to show a profit at the end of the first 12 months of trading.

Television sets around the region were tuned into RTÉ I on the night of April 22 when an hour-long documentary on the life and times of the late Monsignor Horan was transmitted. Entitled *A Simple Country Priest,* it traced his life from boyhood days in West Mayo right through to the Papal visit and the opening of the Airport. The Monsignor recalled his people were driven out of Wicklow in Cromwell's time, and settled on a small farm in the village of Partry.

*   *   *

The success of Ryanair was key to attaining a firm foothold in scheduled services, and morale received a timely boost when Tony Ryan's company announced it was increasing flights on the Luton route from three to four times a week, with plans also to open up routes to Manchester and Birmingham.

Seamus Monaghan has no doubts about the role of Ryanair at Knock. "We were very beneficial to Ryanair, and they were very beneficial to us. They were sent out of heaven. Aer Lingus controlled the skies over Ireland; Danny Higgins of Celtic Air and others had tried before Ryanair. The new airline was a blessing to the airport."

Cathal Duffy, who was to succeed Monaghan as Chairman, is adamant that Ryanair formed one leg of the Knock Trinity. "The story of the airport is quite simple: Monsignor Horan had the dream, Charles Haughey authorised the funding, and Ryanair made it a reality," is his succinct summation.

The extra flights meant extra passengers and extra revenue, and at the end of the first eleven months of trading the airport company revealed that there had been 2,612 movements and a total of 14,167 passengers. And for the year 1987/88 projections were for 50,000 passengers. The much-derided TAI estimates were already being borne out.

In May, the *Western People* reported that the first freight flight out from the airport had departed for Canada with an unusual cargo – 30-ton load of tyres!

Monsignor Grealy got out of the Chair on 1 June '87. In moving aside, but remaining as a member of the Board, he underlined that the Church's perceived responsibility for the Airport had been discharged in full. "I had to do that because if I stayed as Chairman I would still be seen as representing the Church and in the eyes of the public, the Church was running it. It was all right in the beginning but I knew it was bound to cause problems later on, especially when it began to make money. Imagine what they'd be saying if I was still in the Chair: where was the money going and inferences that I was making thousands!," he said when interviewed for this book.

He had been Chairman of the Airport Board from August 1986. In that short period the people had responded magnificently once again, this time contributing £1.2 million. The job, essentially, was completed, and at extraordinarily great value. It is opportune now to recall that one of the key conclusions of the Transport Analysis International (TAI) study commissioned by Monsignor Horan in early 1980 was that a minimal acceptable 6,000 ft runway airport could be built for £5-£6 million (in 1980 money). Factually, the Airport reportedly cost £12.5 to £13 million when completed in 1986, or just over twice TAI's prediction for a lesser specification. The huge amount of excavation required by the site added some £1.5m to the cost while building an 8,200 ft runway to full ICAO international standards would have added another £2.5m approximately. Additionally, inflation combined with the decline in the value of the Irish pound from near parity in early 1980 to below 0.8 accounted for much of the remaining overrun.

Monsignor Grealy later acknowledged the exceptional kindness and generosity of so many people towards the Airport and towards Monsignor Horan and himself. "They voluntarily contributed over £3 million in Monsignor Horan's time and in my ten months as Chairman and fund-raiser they gave £1.2 million. The latter, I think, was the people's most outstanding tribute to Monsignor Horan. He was dead but, especially because he was dead, they wanted to finish what he had started," Monsignor Grealy later recalled.

Within days of stepping down Monsignor Grealy gave an interview to Raidio na Gaeltachta which blew up into a minor controversy of sorts. Grealy said the radio report was not correct and blamed the translating of what he had said for causing a misunderstanding between himself and the new chairman, Seamus Monaghan, who had immediately expressed dismay at the report.

Grealy said his statement that the Airport needed funds had been changed to imply that he had said the Airport was in dire need of funds to survive. "That is not true. I have great hope for the Airport," Grealy, in a clarifying statement, told the *Western People* on 24 June 1987.

He acknowledged that the debt on the Airport was down to £400,000 and said he had no doubt it would be paid off.

Monsignor Grealy also took the opportunity to refute persistent rumours that Knock Shrine funds had been used to ameliorate the Airport debt. Shrine funds had never been used for the airport, he said, and he refuted any such impression the Raidio na Gaeltachta report had given to that effect.

Rumours of funds donated for the Shrine being diverted to the Airport had also been current in Monsignor Horan's time, but James O'Donohue, one of the main fund-raisers, says Horan was always very straight about where the money went. "If you were giving a subscription for the Shrine it went to the Shrine, and it was the same with the Airport," he recalls.

Seamus Monaghan said he always felt as long as Monsignor Horan was there the Church would somehow pick up the tab. "However, the minute he died all that changed. I remember a few months after his death meeting the Archbishop and I said the Monsignor wouldn't have done such and such, and he replied, 'Listen Seamus, the Monsignor is gone.' I was a bit shocked at that. To me he was a great man, the things he would think of and could do. He knew everyone. But what I suppose the Archbishop was doing was bringing closure to the perception there was of Church responsibility." Now that Grealy had stepped down as Chairman that closure was complete, though he was to remain as a highly valued member of the Board until his death in 2005.

The Sligo businessman finally stepped into the hot seat previously filled by two Knock parish priests. He assumed control just around the time Minister for Tourism and Transport John Wilson was, in reply to Patrick Cooney (FG), informing the Dáil that Knock's Connaught Regional Airport owed his Department £117,000 – £80,000 for air traffic control services and £28,000 for flight checking of navigational aids. The Department was pursuing the outstanding bills with the Company, he said.

Monaghan was soon to discover that fund-raising promises made to Monsignor Horan were not always kept now that he had gone to his eternal reward. He remembers particularly a prominent businessman coming into the Airport in 1985 and asking Monsignor Horan what he could do to help. The Monsignor agreed perhaps he could organise a fund-raiser. The businessman promised he would help. "Later, when I was chairman Jim Ryan came to me and said we should check out the offer and we went and met the man. Ryan introduced me, we shook hands and I said, 'We'd like to follow through on what you promised Monsignor Horan.' But he replied, 'Sure the King is dead. What can you do?' and he walked away with a nod of his head!"

While the Board was scraping around for money to equip the airport, there did not appear to be a problem feeding insatiable over-runs on Dublin's DART system, according to Joe Rea, President of the IFA. He came out strongly in support of Horan International Airport in September when he lashed the Dublin overruns. He told the *Irish Press* that the DART network had cost £106m since it began operations in 1984 and had clocked up losses of £75 million, bringing the total cost to the taxpayer to over £180 million.

"This is the equivalent of 18 Knock Airports. The conservative wisdom of the Dublin jet set is that DART is a wonderful thing and that Knock Airport is not. The comparison illustrates well the blind spots in discussing economic issues in Ireland where the marshmallow soft-centred economic theories operate," said the farm leader. In a swift reply, Iarnrod Éireann accused him of using distorted figures and said the rail system had lost only £7 million in 1985 and would break even by 1990!

*   *   *

While DART was gobbling up big money, back in Knock it was estimated that the airport would make a profit of £50,000 for the 12 months to May 1988. It was a modest profit projection, but was well ahead of what the doomsayers had predicted. There was further good news in that the government had lodged an application with the EEC for an ERDF grant for the Airport.

The row between the Airport company and the Coalition government over the application for EEC money had been long and bitter. Up to now it had never been seen by the Fine Gael/Labour government as a priority.

Back in 1985 the *Sunday Independent* had reported that EEC Regional Fund Commissioner Grigoris Varfis had confirmed that 'available funds' for Knock Airport were being held up because the Government had not responded to questions from the Commission on aspects of a Department of Communications study of the project.

The EEC application saga for European Regional Development Fund (ERDF) support had taken on a life of its own. The background to the case was as follows: the company submitted its application on 30 July, 1982, when Fianna Fáil were in Government. The Commission responded on 19 August 1982 asking for information on the estimated number of persons to be employed at the Airport and the expected traffic through the Airport.

The Government replied to Brussels on 3 September 1982, saying the estimated number to be employed at the Airport was 18, assuming maximum flexibility in managing and work practice.

And it put business and pilgrimage traffic together at an upper limit estimate of 26,000 per year; lower limit 13,000. The volume of general air freight which could be expected was small but specialised cargo carriers for such items as fish, live animals, and meat products was also a possibility, responded the FF Government.

In November 1982 Haughey's minority Government fell. But before it did Minister John Wilson had inexplicably withdrawn the

211

EEC application. It was done without the Airport Board being informed. Monsignor Horan later said he understood the Minister had acted on the advice of department officials who felt it was not a 'worthy project' for EEC aid. Horan added that the department officials were of a mind that it was a foolish venture. The relationship between the Airport and John Wilson had always been frosty, and Horan had been critical of the Minister on a number of occasions.

The issue lay pretty dormant until September 1983 when the Commission was asked about the current status of the application by the Coalition Government. In response the Commission outlined the reasons it had difficulty in supporting the application, which were:

(I)   The Airport did not fall within the framework of the Irish Regional Development Programme.
{Note: The project was not mentioned as a specific development measure in the Regional Development Programme because the RDP which was current at that time had been drawn up in December 1981 at which time the Coalition government had decided to defer completion of the airport project until the financial position of the country improved.}

(2)   The feasibility study of the project by Transport Analysis International (TAI) had rejected the case for an International Airport at Knock.
{Note: This view went apparently unchallenged by the Coalition FG/Labour Government. The TAI case from the outset was premised on evaluating routes to and from the UK and Europe. And the conclusions were crystal clear: the success of the airport was predicated on a Knock to London scheduled service. The TAI study also mentioned – but did not build the case on – the potential for additional charter services from mainland Europe, in particular, Belgium. It could be argued a very narrow interpretation of 'international' was taken to play down that aspect of the TAI report and thus weaken the case.}

(3)   The estimates supplied for business/pilgrimage/freight traffic would not appear to justify the project.
{Note: Maybe so, but in the report by the Government Interdepartmental Work Group in 1980, the unquantifiable potential of pilgrimage traffic had been the clincher in not rejecting the TAI feasibility study.}

Back at Knock, the belief was that all three points raised by the EEC could have been easily addressed had the Coalition government the inclination to press the application.

On 12 June 1985 MEP Ray MacSharry raised the matter in the European Parliament with Commissioner Varfis, and from his reply it was widely interpreted that the Commission was laying the blame for the lack of progress at the door of the Irish authorities for not supplying the requested information.

Minister for Finance Alan Dukes wrote to Commissioner Varfis on 21 October 1985 in an attempt to 'put the record straight', pointing out that there had been 'no shortcoming' in Dublin.

Responding, Varfis acknowledged his reply to MacSharry was not intended in any way to imply a shortcoming on the part of the Irish authorities. However, his letter went on to state that as no comeback had been received from the Irish authorities to the three difficulties listed by the Commission in 1983 the matter was put in suspense.

In response to the Commissioner, Dukes pointed out that the difficulties in question, which were essentially of a fundamental nature related to potential demand for the services to be offered by the Airport, were not of such a kind as to enable them to be solved through action by the Irish authorities, and accordingly, that the question of comeback did not arise. Commissioner Varfis was asked to confirm that this was the case.

His reply to Minister Dukes, dated December 12, 1985, was intriguing:

> "You express the opinion that the Commission's telex of 26 September 1983 which summarised the considerable difficulties experienced by the Commission's services in evaluating this application for Community aid, raised queries of such a fundamental nature as not to reasonably expect a reply from the Irish authorities. May I explain to you that this does not appear to be the case. The telex in question addressed three issues:
>
> I. The Regional Development Programme (RDP): Not only has the airport in question not been included in the RDP, but no explanation as to its omission from the programme was been provided to the Commission.
>
> 2. The potential impact of the Airport on development of the region in question: No adequate evaluation of this has been provided.
>
> 3. The use of the Airport: Independent estimates of the viability of the investment have not been provided.

"Therefore, you will understand I cannot give the confirmation you request in your letter. It was always open to the Irish authorities to reply on the three points mentioned above, although I do recognise that, as I said in my original letter of 25.11.85, it would be difficult, if not impossible, for them to reply positively to these points.

"You will, of course, realise that, from the Commission's viewpoint, it is incumbent upon the Irish authorities, if they wish to pursue this application, to supply the justification for the project, in the absence of which it cannot be endorsed for European Regional Development Fund financed by the Commission," explained Commissioner Varfis.

On January 11, 1986 Varfis received a letter from Dukes which brought the passing-the-buck correspondence to an end: "I am glad to note that you accept that it would have been difficult, if not impossible, for the Irish authorities to reply positively to the points raised in the Commission telex of 26 September 1983," wrote Dukes.

The Coalition Government therefore had a number of options: it could press the case, withdraw the application, or leave it on the table. It chose the latter.

Critics of the Government claimed the Irish administration was leaving money on the table in Brussels, but that impression was not entirely accurate either. The records show that Ireland collected its full ERDF allocation for 1982 and subsequent years.

And apart from obviously wishing that the whole contentious Knock Airport rumpus would go away, it would have surely been in the Government's mind that, if they pressed the application and succeeded, Knock would merely displace 'preferred' projects for which Regional Fund monies had been sought. And that would have placed the Government at the centre of another dilemma: the promoters would have demanded that any money so granted would go to the Airport. For a government which had already decided to end all monetary aid to the project that might have proved hard to stomach!

In June, 1986, just a few weeks after the official opening of the Airport, Minister Jim Mitchell strongly rejected claims that his government was not pressing the EEC claim. In a statement carried in the *Western People* of June 18, he said when he met the Airport Development Company in September 1985, he explained the position that there was not, in the view of EEC officials, adequate cost-benefit justification or economic argument which would meet the EEC criteria. "I told the Company if it gave some additional justification the matter would be looked at again. I have not since received any additional justification," Mitchell said.

However, a spokesman for the Company replied that they had supplied all the facts to the Department of Finance, but their application could get nowhere unless the Government stated they were backing the airport. Given the atmosphere that prevailed, it would have taken a lot to persuade the Airport Board that the Government was favourably disposed towards their claim.

The company sent one of its directors to Brussels in an effort to convince officials there of the validity of their submission. However, it did not succeed because the application did not have Government backing, the director was told.

Around that period Commissioner Mathjisen had attended a major seminar in Ballyhaunis and in interviews with the local press made it quite clear that the Government would be pushing at an open door if it wished to actively pursue the application.

And that was essentially the case. At best the Coalition took a very passive approach to the application to the EEC for regional funds for the Airport.

However, Paddy O'Toole has another view. He was on a Cabinet subcommittee which handled the issue, and said statements that the Government was unwilling to pursue finance in the EEC was mischievous and false. "The legal position was that ERDF monies are not committed to a project until such time as the Commission reaches a decision on the granting of ERDF assistance to that specific project. The Commission did not approve ERDF funding for Knock Airport," he says.

Semantics apart, the breakthrough was to come the following May (1988) when the new Fianna Fáil government successfully backed the application.

Before that, in January 1987, Minister Jim Mitchell of Fine Gael had circulated a memorandum proposing that Knock Airport should be designated a free port under the Free Ports Act 1986. In June 1984 the Airport Board had requested the Minister to grant such status. The Minister said the granting of the special status would be 'a magnanimous attempt by the government to assist the promoters in securing some return on the project'. His announcement came a day before Labour walked out of the Coalition with a General Election looming, and Barry Desmond told the author it smacked of a rush of blood to the head. "I was flabbergasted, for it was a major concession and came at a time when every penny in the State coffers needed to be protected. It is strange how ministers go out of focus just before they leave office. Had the proposal leaked, all the airports would have been looking for it. The whole country would have become one big free port," he said.

Possibly so, but while it had all the appearances of a 'death-bed' conversion by Fine Gael in the lead-up to the General Election, it also underlined Mitchell's growing goodwill towards the airport. Whatever, it did not save the political career of Ballina-based TD and Minister, Paddy O'Toole.

*   *   *

Signs of a no-holds-barred price war at Knock between Ryanair and Aer Lingus loomed large on the horizon in early December (1987) with Aer Lingus again attempting to grab some of the action. It was a move that caused great concern within the Company which felt that any undermining of Ryanair was not in the best interests of Knock. In a direct challenge, Aer Lingus sought permission to fly Knock-Dublin for £39 return, and that led to another confrontation between the national carrier and the Board.

Seamus Monaghan says the minute Ryanair began to tick over on the route, Aer Lingus wanted to muscle in. "I remember going to a Board meeting and there were Aer Lingus people putting up signs all over the place. Ryanair said, 'What's going on here? Aer Lingus are going starting to fly to Dublin'."

Monaghan said his Board didn't know anything about such plans. "I got onto Aer Lingus and I told them 'No Way'. I was on the radio and said, 'No way are you going to fly in' and the Aer Lingus spokesman said, 'Oh yes, we have a right.' I said, 'You have no right, and I will block the runway if you come in'. And those were the kind of arguments that went on. All they wanted to do was sink Ryanair, and I remember telling them, 'I'll put blocks across the runway if you attempt it.' We made them take down every sign. That's the kind of mentality there was then, and that's the mentality Ryanair had to get around, and these were the frustrations we had to go through."

On December 12 the *Irish Press* reported that the Aer Lingus application had been shot down by the Government because there was not 'sufficient traffic to support two carriers on the Dublin route'. Another deep sigh of relief could be heard around Knock. The unfriendly predator had been beaten back.

But Aer Lingus retaliated. It tried to open up a chasm between the airport and tourism interests by arguing Knock was missing out on an opportunity to bring in tourists from a wide range of Continental cities, and, further, that travellers would not be able to avail of the low fares which were already being offered out of Shannon and Cork.

Chairman Monaghan had the last word in the row: he said they would welcome Aer Lingus opening new direct routes to Britain or the Continent from Knock. That was in 1987 – the challenge had not been taken up by 2006! It would be two years before Aer Lingus got permission to service the Knock-Dublin route. Meanwhile John Healy, writing in *The Connaught Telegraph,* said if the people of Mayo had to depend for the establishment of the Airport on the good wishes of the national carrier, Aer Lingus, Horan International would still be a sick joke and a white elephant.

He continued: "The terms on which they were willing to run a scheduled flight to London were so outrageously high and demanding that not even Paul Getty and his millions could countenance the demand. It was the Company's polite way of telling Mayo to shag off and forget its delusions of an international airport. The officials knew a quarter of the traffic though Dublin Airport came from the West, travelling on CIE's bone-rattler. That would do them. No point in getting involved.

"Ryanair came in. Ryanair surprised Ireland and Mayo by carving out a lucrative flight to Luton. Aer Lingus, red-faced and acutely embarrassed because its arch-rivals had made its management team look like duffers, had not the graciousness to accept they'd made a mistake and goofed badly: the company merely added to its resolve to 'shoot Ryanair out of the skies', the company's buzz phrase." It was typical Healy, going for the jugular.

*   *   *

One of the most difficult tasks confronting Chairman Monaghan and his Board was an escalating behind-the-scenes row with British Airways International which was contracted to manage and run the Airport, at an annual charge of £100,000 sterling.

It was to prove a very acrimonious relationship. The Board was unhappy with the British company's performance in several areas, and felt particularly that projections made and commitments undertaken had not been delivered upon. BAI was far from happy also; it was out a lot of money and was demanding its pound of flesh. The relationship worsened rapidly.

Newly-appointed Board member Michael Honan, Managing Director of Asahi near Killala, who had been nominated to the Board by the Department of Finance to help sort out the financial mess at the Airport, said he found a very difficult situation. "I had enormous respect for Monsignor Horan; he had put in place the finest piece of infrastructure the North West will ever have, but when he died total chaos existed," he says. Sorting out the BAI contract was one of the first priorities.

Seamus Monaghan remembers the culmination to the dispute. "We owed bills and BAI were pressing for their money and it seemed to us they were trying to take over the Airport. We attended a meeting in Luton. It was a rough meeting. They were going to do this and that to us."

With no sign of a resolution emerging, the parties agreed to meet again in Knock in a few weeks. In the meantime, it emerged that

217

BAI's parent company was going public and also that a lawsuit had been lodged against the British company by Cyprus airport.

"So when they came into the Knock meeting they told us they were going to pull out and laid down the law about what they were owed, what they were going to do. I said, 'That's fine, but we are going to sue you for £2.5m.'

'What are you talking about?' the stunned BAI chief negotiator demanded.

"I said, 'the way you have run the airport, you have not delivered on the terms of your contact.' The BAI man said, 'You cannot do that.' So after about two hours of heated argument, around 12 midnight, they said they were pulling out the next morning. I said, OK, how is it going to appear in the London *Times* tomorrow that you are being sued for £2.5m and ye going public?"

Honan weighed in by saying that if BAI wanted to avoid a second Cyprus scenario they had better sit down and talk business. "We said if we couldn't sort out the problem we'd see them through the courts."

With tensions soaring through the roof it was decided to take a break to cool off. When discussions resumed, BAI said in the interest of goodwill they would write off part of what they were owed, but would take the fire engines.

To which Monaghan retorted: "Hold on a minute. You are taking nothin'. All that equipment belongs to us."

"You did not pay for it," BAI retaliated.

The argument went on but at around 2 am the sides reached an agreement, the terms of which were never made public. The BAI negotiators were heard to remark as they departed Mayo that their opponents on the other side of the table had little to learn when it came to fighting dirty!

*   *   *

1988 had opened quietly enough after the festive rush, but the new Minister for the Environment, Padraig Flynn, was back on familiar ground early in February for an official duty when he launched an international air courier service for documents and small parcels. Behind the initiative was Skyway Global, an Irish company, which opened a depot at the airport.

Barry Desmond, now in opposition, had no intention of letting up on the Airport, though, and in the *Irish Press* on February 24 he accused the company of not paying its State bills. Minister John Wilson told him the amount due to the end of 1987 now stood at

£192,500 and said the Department was pressing the company for payment. Desmond further observed that air traffic control services were costing the airport £36,000 a month.

In April 44 year-old Commandant Michael McGrath was appointed by the Board to succeed BAI's Maurice Buckby as manager. The Army man was looking for a new challenge . . . and he was to get one! Born in Dublin, he had followed his father into the Army and so began a life in aviation. He had been sent out as observer to Golan in 1980, and was quickly appointed Chief Airstaff Officer in Jerusalem for a period of 18 months. On returning to Casement Aerodrome, his main role in the Air Corps was in Air Traffic Control/Air Operations, dealing with air ambulance and air sea rescue.

"I sure got my challenge when I took over the Knock post," he concedes. His appointment was to last for fifteen years, until 2003. Very much taken by the aspirations of Monsignor Horan, he recalls that on taking up his appointment he wrote to the Board and said he hoped to meet with the ideals and wishes of the late Monsignor and to assist in delivering those wishes. "I was quickly reminded that the Monsignor was dead and that the show was moving on," he said.

He took over with a young, enthusiastic staff which had to be trained, and a Board working to make the Airport a viable proposition.

At long last, in May came the official announcement that Horan International was finally to get some EEC money. On a visit to the Airport Peter Schmidhuber, Regional Policy Commissioner, brought the happy tidings that a grant of £1.33 million had been sanctioned. It had proved a long and difficult campaign, but the money was nevertheless welcomed with open arms.

Another breakthrough was to follow. After Michael McGrath took up duty he got a call from one of the secretaries of the Dáil's Public Accounts Committee to arrange a visit for members of that body. The Committee included some of the harshest critics of the Airport – including Barry Desmond and Mary Harney – and they wanted to see for themselves where the Exchequer's £9.858m for the years 1981-85 had gone.

Strangely enough, Barry Desmond decided not to travel, allegedly because Ryanair was not unionised, but, unbowed, he told Damian McHugh of the *Irish Press* of July 26 his criticism of the Airport project stood unrefuted. Board member Ulick McEvaddy had offered Desmond a seat in a private plane to overcome his Ryanair reservations but the offer was not accepted.

Looking back to that Public Accounts Committee (PAC) visit, Desmond said he felt at the time the committee was entitled to hold the review without him going along and getting into a controversy.

And still sticking rigidly to his core views on the Airport as he was, another raging controversy would have seemed inevitable!

Interviewed in 2006, he said there was no way he would have built the airport at Knock. He would have preferred Castlebar where a proper rail service was available. And he said he would have argued with the Monsignor that the money spent on a big runway could have been better spent on a socio-economic cost-benefit basis for the community.

"Horan personally had no money but was very keen to get money to spend on his pet project. There was a degree of, and it is still prevalent in Ireland, where one individual becomes obsessional about their pet project, projected onto their personality, projected onto their sense of community worth, their sense of community standing. People have a huge reluctance in Ireland to join with five or six other people and say, 'Well, it's not my project. Let's make it a community, local or regional project and I'll stand back.' People are not like that in Ireland: we tend to be very dominant, individualistic people holding total control. And the Monsignor had what I would regard as a personality problem of that kind," says an unrepentant Desmond.

He revealed that he went privately, in 2001, to view the airport. "I put on my cap and walked around the airport and I looked at it," he smiled. "I enjoyed the place, and have every intention of going again. To say that I refused to go with the Public Accounts Committee is incorrect, I didn't refuse, nor did I go to the official opening – I was not invited. It became a Haughey jamboree, a Flynn jamboree and I wasn't interested in that kind of *ruaille buaille* (commotion)," he says.

However, as far as the Public Accounts Committee was concerned, instead of coming to bury Caesar – as observers in the West had feared – the Dáil committee ended up praising him! "As a non-believer I am quite impressed," Deputy Brendan McGahon (FG) told the media which had probably anticipated another critical outburst.

But, according to the *Irish Press*, the greatest tribute of all was paid by Progressive Democrats' deputy Mary Harney, a self-proclaimed cynic, who said afterwards, "I admit I was wrong." She said she was delighted the Airport did turn out to be successful but was not prepared to admit she was totally wrong. She claimed the Airport's success was due to Ryanair's low-fare policy and "astronomically high levels of emigration". To the emigration observation, Monsignor Horan probably would have replied, "You have more control over that than I do" as he had said about Barry Desmond and rising inflation some years earlier!

The Chairman of the Committee, Deputy Gay Mitchell, brother

of Jim Mitchell, told the promoters they had done a great job and were to be complimented.

He had proposed the visit. Mitchell recalls: "We 'signed off' on Knock in positive terms. The then Chairman of Knock Airport Seamus Monaghan was so pleased he sent me an unsolicited donation for Our Lady's Hospital for Sick Children in Crumlin of which I was then a Committee of Management member."

The *Irish Press,* in a leading article, had this to say: "As someone remarked on radio yesterday, Mgr Horan must have been wearing his broadest smile. The spectacle of some of his harshest critics publicly recanting after seeing the miracle his courage, imagination and determination created at Knock must have sent that hearty chuckle echoing across the heavens.

"Full marks to the PDs' Mary Harney for admitting that she has been wrong about the airport. No marks at all to Barry Desmond who chickened out on a trip that would have taxed even his formidable talents for talking his way out of political embarrassment. And congratulations yet again to the people of the West, who backed their priest and his vision against the dismal economics of the so-called experts."

*   *   *

By November, the Airport was set for a bumper Christmas/New Year trade with Ryanair announcing it planned to operate 75 flights with 10,000 passengers on board. By then it was hoped to have the extension to the terminal building completed. Already, the facilities were being overtaxed.

Extending the terminal building could have been a costly business, but the Board was keen to keep costs to the minimum. It really had no other choice. Board member John Mahon came up with the idea of asking Sher Rafique of Halal Meat Packers in Ballyhaunis to help out by providing some materials.

A great friend and supporter of the late Monsignor Horan, Rafique took a keen interest in the development of the Airport and willingly rowed in by providing the steel for the extension. John Mahon, John Dillon and Cathal Duffy, all Board members at the time, paid tribute to Rafique for his generosity, estimated to be worth well over £100,000 at the time.

John Dillon recalled that in return for his generous gesture, the only thing Rafique asked for was the use of a small office in the terminal building where he and his wife could wait for their flights. In fact, they used the facility very rarely.

Interviewed, Sher Rafique said he and his wife were very pleased to help. "We were very proud to be living next door to the airport. It is only two hours from Knock to my home in London. We were delighted at what was happening and proud to be part of its development," he said.

Today, a plaque on the terminal wall near the main entrance bears testament to the generosity of Sher and Kauser Rafique. Inside, the small office they sometimes used as a waiting room has been turned into a multi-denominational oratory, complete with a prayer mat facing towards Mecca!

Before 1988 ended there was a nice surprise for Ann McGreal, a physiotherapist from Westport, who won £1,000 as Ryanair's 100,000th passenger through the Airport that year. An employee with Western Care, she was on her way to visit friends in London when Sligoman P. J. McGoldrick of Ryanair presented her with her cheque. Her flight had been delayed the day before!

McGoldrick also revised upwards to 13,000 the number who would be using Ryanair on the Knock route over the festive period.

But the year ahead was going to be far from trouble-free: a high profile director was to be unceremoniously 'sacked' in a highly controversial political putsch and attempts at another's removal almost became an international political incident!

CHAPTER SIXTEEN

*1989: Row over 'sacking' of Ulick McEvaddy - Dáil debate over
dismissal - Car rental controversy - Mayo in All-Ireland football
final - Airport champion Michael O'Malley dies - Ryanair and
Knock 'saved' - Exiles' remittances*

Row as director 'sacked', sadness as another dies

1989 was, like all years, to contain its share of ups and downs around
the world. It was to bring the Hillsborough Stadium disaster which
claimed 96 lives, and while the Berlin Wall was to come down after 28
years, in Tiananmen Square in Beijing the Communist regime was to
brutally crush a student protest. There was to be better news for the
Guildford Four who are freed after 14 years in prison.

In sport Ireland qualify for the World Cup Finals for the first time
ever under manager Jack Charlton, and Mayo are to play in their first
senior All-Ireland football final since 1951.

And Van Morrison was about to have a hit with 'Have I Told You
Lately' but the tones were not to be as soothing back at the Airport. A
high profile director was to be 'sacked' by the Government in highly
controversial circumstances, another was to be saved by events in far-off
Japan. There was to be a row over restrictions on car-rental facilities. And
it was to be a year of real sadness, too, for one of the great champions of
the Airport was to die.

The year opened quietly but hopefully with news that
representations to government to ease the Shannon stopover
restriction on inward charter flights appeared to be paying off. Gerry
O'Hare, writing in the *Irish Press* on January 27, reported the
government was favourably disposed to granting an application for US
charter flights to stop off at Iceland and so get around the Shannon
cost impediment.

Ed O'Brien of the Knock Shrine Association in the US had
negotiated charters with Iceland Air, starting on March 10. He had
already been thwarted from operating a direct commercial charter
because he had to pay a prohibitive $10,000 dollars landing fee/extra
fuel bill at Shannon.

He pointed out that there was considerable potential for pilgrimage flights from the US to Knock, and revealed that the year before over 100,000 had flown from Florida to Medjugorje. He had threatened to take the Government to the European Court if the 1946 rule that insisted that all American flights into Ireland must first land at Shannon was not removed.

Within days, O'Brien told the *Western People* that following intense negotiations with the Government he was hopeful of bringing in between 15,000 and 20,000 pilgrims once the service started. There were still to be slips between cup and lip, though.

However, that story was quickly relegated when it became known that Director Ulick McEvaddy had been removed from the Airport Board by the Fianna Fáil Government, and that an attempt had been made to get Michael Honan, Managing Director of the big Asahi Japanese textile plant at Killala, to step down. Both had been Fine Gael nominees.

Swinford-born McEvaddy's company had been involved in the installation of the vital fuel farm at the Airport. The installation was thought to have cost him in the region of £150,000, with repayment understood to be based on a rental charge.

McEvaddy, when interviewed for this book, said he had been asked by Monsignor Horan to help in the provision of a fuel farm several years before he was nominated to the Board by Jim Mitchell. "The Monsignor had asked me and I had tried to get others interested but did not succeed. I rang him to inform him and he told me to call over to see him. He threw the plans out on the table and said it would cost £65,000 to build it. He said he had the man to do it and that it had to be done if the Airport was to get off the ground. 'You are the man,' he said, and he wouldn't take no for an answer."

The aviation mogul's recall is that the fuel farm actually cost three times the predicted £65,000 when safety aspects, etc. were taken into consideration.

Calling for a judicial inquiry into the circumstances of the Omega Air director's removal, Deputy Jim Higgins told Denis Daly (*Western People*, February 1) that the multinational aviation sales and leasing magnate's removal was an act of 'political hooliganism'.

McEvaddy informed the paper his plans to set up a maintenance company employing more than 100 at the airport were now in jeopardy. He said he had been pushing very strongly to have the jet engine overhaul project located in the free port area adjacent to the airport, and his consortium of investors was almost the same as the group responsible for the provision of the fuel farm.

"A number of the investors want to locate the facility for overhauling jet engines on mainland Europe, and now that I have been removed from the Airport Board my negotiating position has been considerably weakened," he revealed.

At the time there was a major argument over the issue of flying old and noisy Stage 1 aircraft in and out of Irish airports, with the Department of Transport voicing its opposition and holding the environmental line. In the ensuing war of words, say sources, McEvaddy was removed from the Board by the Government.

As the row over the sacking escalated, Charlestown's James O'Donohue, Chairman of the Airport fund-raising campaign, joined with McEvaddy in calling for the establishment of a non-political Trust to hold the State's investment in the Airport project, and to oversee its proper management and development in the future.

The 'sacking' got an airing on the Pat Kenny radio show on RTÉ. It was a 'dogfight' according to John Healy who was highly critical of his home place for breaking ranks in the face of an outside threat when others would have closed ranks. Such behaviour had always saddened him, he wrote in *The Connaught Telegraph*.

The row hit the floor of the Dáil on February 23 when Ted Nealon and Jim Higgins (both FG) placed questions for the Minister for Tourism and Transport, John Wilson, asking if it was his intention to replace any other member of the Airport Board. They also asked what was the position in relation to setting up the Trust to deal with the ownership issue.

The questions were fielded by Minister of State Lyons who said under the provisions of the memorandum and articles of association of Connaught Airport Development Company Limited, the Ministers for Finance and for Tourism and Transport had the right to nominate a total of three directors to the Board of the Company. It would not be appropriate to speculate on any changes in their nominees to the Board of the Airport Company which the Ministers might decide to make in the future, in the exercise of their rights in that regard, he stated.

He confirmed that the establishment of a Trust in favour of the people of the West, and of County Mayo in particular, for the ownership and control of the Airport was at an advanced stage and would be in place 'in the near future'.

Mr. Nealon: Is the Minister aware that ownership of Horan International Airport, with more than £10 million Government money, is now vested in the Directors who each have a £1 share in the Airport? Irrespective of the merits of the Board of Directors, would the Minister not agree that it is a shame that the Trust has not already been put in place? Can he give the House an explanation for the delay occasioned over the past three or four years in implementing the terms of the deed of trust originally drawn up, supported by the late Monsignor Horan and the former and present Archbishops? Can he explain why the terms of the Trust are not operational other than in the fact that it would appear to be the wish of the Government to maintain the Airport within the control of the present Board of Directors?

Mr. Lyons: As I said at the outset, Fianna Fáil commitment to the airport is well established.

Mr. Nealon: They did not allocate any money to it.

Mr. Lyons: This Government will continue to assist in ensuring its continued success. As the Deputy is probably aware, a deed of trust has been agreed in principle with the company whose purpose will be to ensure that the Airport is developed for the benefit of the west and of County Mayo in particular. Counsel appointed by the Attorney General's office have raised a number of technical queries on the draft deed of trust which are being considered by the Chief State Solicitor's office and the Attorney General's office.

Mr. Nealon: Can the Minister explain why it has taken the Attorney General's office and the Chief State Solicitor's office more than three years to implement its provisions since it was originally drawn up in a very thorough manner?

Mr. Lyons: All I can say is that the legal aspects of this deed of trust are being considered by the Attorney General's office and the Chief State Solicitor's office. Naturally it would be our wish, as it is the Deputy's, that the deed of trust be put in place. I hope that the legal technical difficulties will be cleared up soon.

Mr. Jim Higgins: Will the Minister of State acknowledge that as well as the recent sacking of Ulick McEvaddy from the Board of the Airport Company . . .

An Ceann Comhairle Seán Treacy: I would prefer if the Deputy did not refer to personalities outside the House.

Mr. Higgins: I shall refrain from naming any personalities. Will the Minister of State confirm that a decision was made at Government level to discharge from the Board the managing director of a Japanese synthetic firm in County Mayo and that had it not been for the unfortunate but timely death of Emperor Hirohito the said person would no longer be a member of the Board of Horan International Airport?

Mr. Lyons: I am not sure that the Deputy has put a question to me. I have replied to the questions raised earlier by the Deputy and Deputy Nealon. If the Deputy has a question to put to me I should like him to do so.

Mr. Higgins: By way of further elaboration I should like to ask the Minister of State if a Government decision was taken to discharge a member of the Board, namely, the managing director of a multi-national firm in County Mayo.

Mr. Jim Mitchell: Will the Minister confirm that a deed of trust, taking out of the ownership of the ten directors who paid £1 for that ownership, was ready three years ago, that at that time no further questions remained to be answered and that some Directors of the Board persist in their claim that the Airport is their property for their £1 investment and not the property of the State or the public? Will the Minister of State explain why one member of the Board, who is not a member of Fianna Fáil, has been sacked and why an attempt has been made in recent weeks to sack another member of the Board who is not a member of Fianna Fáil?

Mr. Lyons: As I indicated, it is the prerogative of the Ministers for Finance and Tourism and Transport to appoint nominees to the board. I have outlined the position in regard to the deed of trust.

Airport Board chairman Seamus Monaghan, looking back on the event, said he was in America on business when McEvaddy was sacked. He acknowledged that there had been personality clashes between some Board members and politicians but he was completely against any moves to get rid of him. "I always thought McEvaddy was a decent enough fellow. While I was in America I got a call from him to say he had been sacked. I was awfully annoyed that this could be done when I was out of the country. There was never any reason to sack him, and it shouldn't have happened." He agreed with Enda Kenny's pronouncement at the time that it was a case of 'internal jealousy and spite'.

Monsignor Grealy, a former Chairman of the Board, and later Director, also felt the removal of McEvaddy was a big loss to the fledgling, inexperienced company.

Former Minister Paddy O'Toole says the appointment of McEvaddy to the Board was seen as a step in the right direction as he was the member with an aviation background and had experience that could be used for the future development of the Airport. "His dropping by the FF Government was seen as purely political with scant regard for the future of the Airport and a further example of the politicisation of the project."

Michael Honan recalled that there were fraught Board meetings, with rows over catering and other issues. "It got to a point where certain Fianna Fáil vested interests wanted McEvaddy out. He was a marvellous asset to the airport with his aviation background. When you think of what was left on the Board, a guy of his calibre, unceremoniously kicked off it, was a Fianna Fáil versus Fine Gael kind of thing. McEvaddy was an outright Fine Gael person, a good friend of Jim Mitchell, and was very outspoken, too, like Monaghan and myself."

The putsch extended to Honan, who conceded he had also been seen as a 'Blueshirt interloper' because he was a Fine Gael nominee, but the move against him was 'the rock they perished on and it brought the roof down around them'. Asahi was then a flagship Japanese company, employing over 500, and had encouraged other nationalities to invest here. "Now here was the guy that had helped keep Asahi in business being shafted by the parish pump politicians," says Honan. But the timing was all wrong. Hirohito, the Japanese emperor, died, and the attempt to remove Honan was highlighted in Dáil Eireann. Behind the scenes there were fears that removing the MD of a large Japanese plant in Ireland would send out the wrong signal in terms of badly needed inward investment.

"They backed away so quickly they nearly fell over each other. Seamus Monaghan was instrumental in telling Ray MacSharry that under no circumstances was I to be touched. He was horrified. Monaghan would have regretted the removal of McEvaddy also," said Honan.

Speaking in 2006, McEvaddy, who said he had enormous admiration for Horan and what he had achieved, said when he joined the Board after the Monsignor's death in 1986 he planned to create jobs at the Airport for jet engine maintenance.

"Unfortunately, the vested interests of some of the members led to friction," he said. He was dropped from the Board and subsequently created 25 specialist jet engine maintenance jobs in Dublin which are still operational. "We overhaul engines for airlines worldwide, for the Australian air force, the Italian air force; we specialise in overhauling military tanker aircraft. It was my intention to set up those jobs in Knock," he says.

John Healy gave another perspective on the McEvaddy controversy in his Strictly Healy column in *The Connaught Telegraph* of March 1 when he observed: "The former director (McEvaddy) of Knock Airport must be somewhat embarrassed by his friends who keep on assuring the public that his reinstatement on the Board would result in a hundred new jobs he could provide reconditioning Aeros engines for Boeing: Ulick, in his turn, appears not to want to wrongfoot them in public by stating the correct position.

"It was his intention to have a reconditioning plant at Knock to employ 100 people but sometime last October, while still a member of the Board, he announced, as I understand it, that he was moving the operation to the Continent.

"The Board accepted the news with regret: in commercial life these things happen and there are always centres competing for hi-tech work of this nature," wrote Healy.

Airport Company chairman Seamus Monaghan announced in March he was seeking the nomination for the Sligo-Leitrim by-election following the appointment of Ray MacSharry as EC Commissioner in 1988. He did not pursue his bid, however: the by-election was actually subsumed into a full-blown General Election in June.

In the run-up to the General Election, the McEvaddy issue reared its head again when Enda Kenny of FG termed his dismissal 'unjust and disgraceful' and again repeating it was responsible for Knock losing 100 jobs to Shannon.

Monaghan hit back, telling Fine Gael to stop playing politics with the Airport. He revealed that two Board members had offered to resign from the Company in favour of McEvaddy if he could guarantee the 100 jobs. "I also informed him that I personally would resign and be replaced by him if he could even get fifty jobs for Knock," he stated.

Michael Honan, however, maintains McEvaddy was serious about setting up the maintenance plant. "Actually, he asked me to get involved with him. It wasn't wishful thinking on his part. And even if he did not deliver 100 jobs, in business you accept that and look to the next opportunity; there'd always be the next start-up. Why had it to come to a confrontation? McEvaddy would have delivered if he could have; some things work; some things don't. It should not turn into a case of put up or shut up. I'd much rather have had him on the Board. He had the Airport at heart. The Monsignor, as far as I knew, thought the world of McEvaddy though he did not join the Board until after Horan's death," he says.

Two days before the General Election, the *Irish Press* revealed that the Omega Air Company's reconditioning plant would now be locating at Shannon. Mr Charles Kelly, a spokesman for Omega Air, told the paper that £2m was being invested in the Shannon start-up, and claimed that McEvaddy had been removed from the Board by the Government after 'in-fighting over a car-leasing contract'. He added that the removal showed 'a pattern of Airport Board decisions being made for personal rather than business reasons'.

Despite all the bickering, the internal rows and the political biases, Honan said he retained no bitterness or rancour. "In the circumstances, everyone tried to do their best, and I am still very friendly with all the directors who served with me at the time," he says.

*　　　*　　　*

Meanwhile, the Airport Board was spreading its wings in other directions. It joined a consortium bidding for a local radio station licence for Mayo. In March, after public hearings in Galway, the consortium received news that its application had been successful. The promoters consisted of Connaught Regional Airport, North Connacht Farmers Co-op, The Federation of Western Churches, the *Western People* and *The Connaught Telegraph,* and Chris Carroll and Paul Claffey who had been part of the old pirate radio station. The station, which would go on air in May, was to be called Mid West Radio. The Airport Board's interests were represented at the radio station's table by Cathal Duffy and Jim Ryan.

Aer Lingus finally got a foothold in Knock in April when it inaugurated its service to Dublin. Minister for Tourism and Transport John Wilson was among 70 dignitaries who flew in to launch the daily Shorts 360 aircraft schedule. The cost of the round trip Knock to Dublin would be £39.

The General Election was held on Friday, June 15, three weeks after the dissolution of the Dáil. Opinion polls had shown that Fianna

Fáil had gained in popularity and that an overall majority was a distinct possibility. The party actually lost seats. Fine Gael made a small gain, but nothing substantial. The Progressive Democrats also did badly, losing over half their deputies. The Labour Party and the Workers' Party gained working-class votes from Fianna Fáil, but failed to make the big breakthrough. In Mayo, Denis Gallagher had retired and his seat was retained by long-serving Fianna Fáil county councillor, Martin J. O'Toole. Again, Fianna Fáil took four of the six Mayo seats. In Sligo/Leitrim Gerry Reynolds of Fine Gael headed the poll. There were seats, too, for his party colleague Ted Nealon and for Fianna Fáil's Mattie Brennan and John Ellis.

The prospect of forming a government seemed remote, so much so that Charles Haughey was forced to formally resign as Taoiseach. For the first time in Irish history a Taoiseach and a government had not been appointed when the new Dáil met. However, twenty-seven days after the general election Fianna Fáil entered into coalition government for the first time ever with the Progressive Democrats when a deal was struck. Padraig Flynn was appointed Minister for Environment, with Albert Reynolds as Minister for Finance, and Seamus Brennan as Minister for Tourism and Transport.

Meanwhile, back in Mayo a vexatious Airport issue was being aired in public. The car-leasing arrangements at Knock had been bubbling under the surface, with the facility confined exclusively to Diplomat Car Hire, a company owned by Iarla Duffy, son of Airport Director Cathal Duffy. In September the simmering discontent became public knowledge when the Car Rental Council of Ireland issued a statement revealing that it had submitted a tender on May 25 for £10,000 for pre-booked facilities on behalf of eight members. On May 30 the Car Rental Council was informed its tender was unsuccessful and the cheque was returned.

The Car Council revealed it had sought a meeting with the Airport Company through Bord Fáilte. A local car-leasing firm told the *Western People* on 6 September that its operatives had to remain outside the gates of the Airport and that this created difficulties for people who hired cars from them. He described restrictions on the pre-booked desks in the Airport as 'severe'.

New York tour operator Brendan Ward joined in the criticism, telling the paper it was wrong that one company should have exclusive rights. However, Airport secretary Jim Ryan rejected any criticism. He accused 'cowboy' car-hire firms of wanting the facilities without paying for the right to use them, and said those car-hire companies were free to operate outside the gate which was only 80 yards from the terminal building. He put it on record that the Airport had advertised for car-rental tenders in the papers but only one company had met the conditions.

Looking back on the rumpus, Seamus Monaghan remembers a time when not another person in the country was prepared to put cars at Knock. "To be fair to Cathal Duffy, he invested when others did not want to know. Not one of them. But within 12 months they were all trying to get in. Cathal took the risk and he put it there and the Monsignor appreciated it."

Michael McGrath, who was Airport Manager at the time, recalls there was huge controversy over the methodology of the car-hire business at Knock. "Diplomat Cars received the sole concession for ten years at the airport from Monsignor Horan shortly before his death. Subsequently, other car-hire firms wanted to get in but were not allowed and it created great friction and major difficulties. Car-hire companies were all outside the gate," he says.

The issue ended up in the Airport Company taking the car-hire companies to the High Court in an attempt to get a restraining injunction. Eventually the matter was resolved and today all the leading car rental companies operate out of the Airport terminal.

While all this was going on football fever was gripping Mayo as the senior team made its way out of Connaught after a dramatic replay against Roscommon. Tyrone were overcome in the All-Ireland semi-final to ensure a place in the final for the first time since 1951. Green-and-red colours bedecked town and village. The atmosphere was electric, full of hope. Only Cork now stood in the way.

Ryanair flew the Mayo team from Knock for the final. Chief Executive Cathal Ryan had likened Mayo's efforts to get to the top of the football world with Ryanair's battle against some of the heavy hitters in aviation.

Unfortunately, John O'Mahony's charges fell just short of taking out Cork, but an estimated 10,000 fans gathered at the Airport again on Monday to welcome the team home. Cheering fans, waving the county colours, were everywhere. Captain Jimmy Browne was almost lost for words. "We expected a turnout, but this we hadn't planned on receiving. Imagine what it would be like if we had won," he said as he looked around the massed support of chanting fans. Director Honan said it was one of those very special occasion at the airport. He described it as 'a day and a half of great memories'.

*   *   *

While Mayo players had been fighting for their pride in Croke Park, elsewhere Ryanair had been fighting for its very life. Aer Lingus, backed by the taxpayers' money, now really took the gloves off to bury its upstart competitor. It slashed fares on the London-Stansted route and offered greater choice. The squeeze was hurting Ryanair badly. So badly in fact that, according to Siobhan Creaton in her book, *Ryanair*, the future Chief Executive of the company, Michael O'Leary told his boss Tony Ryan to close the airline. The losses were reported to be staggering. Six hundred jobs were on the line.

Minister for Transport Seamus Brennan met a deputation from Ryanair who pleaded with him to give the company exclusive rights to fly to Stansted as a solution to their woes. Convinced by their argument and desirous of freeing up the market, he took a set of proposals to Cabinet to save the company which would have otherwise folded, and in the process could have cost the exchequer £18m if alternative jobs could not be found for the staff.

The big fear was that Aer Lingus would fall back on its monopolistic ways and jack up fares again once its competitor was out of the way. And the compliant taxpayers would foot the bill. Of course.

In September the Government agreed to give Ryanair exclusive rights to fly into Luton and Stansted. Aer Lingus was also ordered to surrender its Liverpool and Munich routes to Ryanair for three years, with Aer Lingus in turn given exclusive rights to fly into Manchester and Paris. The bold decision saved Ryanair.

And it almost certainly saved Horan International Airport which was able to report early in October that profits in the year to June had increased from £50,000 to £157,000, with passenger numbers up 46%. And by December the Board predicted its passenger throughput would hit 180,000.

Another valuable profit stream was opening up, with the *Western People* reporting that duty-free sales had increased by 54%, and a new observation lounge with bar and restaurant facilities, extended and upgraded arrivals hall and check-in facilities had been completed. It was also announced that an £800,000 freight taxiway was next on the 'to-do' list. (See Chapter 18 for more on duty-free shop.)

But the run of good news ended abruptly when Mayo County Manager Michael O'Malley, who had been there to welcome the Mayo team home just a few weeks earlier, died suddenly on October 11. He had been one of Monsignor Horan's greatest supporters, a founding director, and had carried on the fight for the Airport in the three years since Horan's death.

News of his passing spread like wildfire. Everyone knew that the county – and the Airport – had lost a supreme champion. He had stood shoulder to shoulder with Horan as they first transformed Knock village and then built the Airport.

John Healy, in a tribute, said O'Malley had a lot of the temperament of his great hero, Donogh O'Malley, the man who introduced free school transport to Ireland. "Like dead Donogh, he was a doer. Once he was satisfied the action was right, the course of the action right, he gave the order to go to it. He'd be 'responsible'. That meant he hadn't the money in the kitty but that never stopped O'Malley as long as what they were doing was right and for the community's good. Was he a good one? He was – the best."

He was right, of course. Michael O'Malley from Tourmakeady was more than a public servant. He put the jizz back into his native county when appointed County Manager, pushing projects through, encouraging enterprise, motivating people. He and County Development Officer Seán Smyth cut a swathe through the long grass of inaction, and guided a willing Monsignor Horan to take on a most extraordinary challenge. Both were also behind many other confidence-building initiatives of that time.

*   *   *

That Christmas, business at Knock set new records. Jim Ryan revealed that 17,130 passengers were expected, with Ryanair, Aer Lingus and Celtic Airways all reporting heavy bookings. In addition, two international charters were coming in from the US. "In a way," said Ryan, "the numbers coming are a sad reflection because they are mostly emigrants coming back to visit their loved ones."

The pangs felt by emigration were prevalent across the West of Ireland. Duty Officer Matt Macken remembers going to Christmas Mass in South Mayo in the '50s and when he came home the query always was, 'Who's home?' "You would see them all at Mass and after Mass they'd meet the neighbours, and in the pubs they'd meet up again. They had to emigrate. There was nothing else for them to do."

His father and his father before him had left to work on the big farms in Lancashire, getting the train in Claremorris to Broadstone in Dublin, and then the boat. "You could imagine the journey, and the pain of separation. They'd be gone for six months at a time and the women would have to look after their families and the small farms. They were great women," attests Macken who says remittances sent home kept the country afloat over decades.

Bearing this out, Peter Sutherland, former Irish EU Commissioner, told the *Irish Post* in London in March 2006 that estimates put the amount of money sent back to Ireland from emigrants in Britain at anything up to £4.5b sterling. Former Mayo Person of the Year, Professor Seamus Caulfield, who carried out a study of such remittances, estimates the return to have been even higher. And then, of course, there were also the remittances from exiles in the US and elsewhere.

In his book *The Men who Built Britain – A history of the Irish Navvy* (Wolfhound Press, 2001) historian Ultan Cowley estimated £2.2 billion sterling in cheques and money orders alone came from the Irish in Britain between 1939 and 1969. "It wasn't for nothing that a railway porter in the Irish midlands used to call out, 'Connaughtmen, and horned cattle, to the far platform, please!' in the early 1900s," he wrote.

He added that the State's education budget in 1960 was £16 million. Emigrants' remittances that same year totalled £15.5 million sterling! Yet 82% of emigrants to Britain in 1960 had left school by the age of fifteen. And two hundred thousand Irishmen worked in British construction in the 1960s.

Minister for Community, Rural and Gaeltacht Affairs, Éamon Ó Cuiv, was reported in the *Mayo News* (April 2003) as saying some £2 billion sterling had been sent back to the homeland by Irish emigrants between 1975 and 1995.

With increased passenger numbers came the need for greater security vigilance at the Airport, and this led to some lighter moments. Matt Macken remembers an instance when a briefcase containing important documents was left unattended by a businessman.

"It had to be taken away and exploded to ensure it was not a bomb," he said. "You cannot treat such incidents lightly, even if it was a bit inconvenient for the businessman," he conceded.

CHAPTER SEVENTEEN

1990/91: Saddam Hussein strikes – Shannon stopover issue raised –
Emigration hits GAA – Mary Robinson elected president –
Airport advocate John Healy dies – Trust Fund issue resolved –
US equity sought – Vested interest query raised

Saddam Hussein's invasion sends aviation into a spin

ANOTHER year dawns quietly but gathers momentum. It is to be the year that Mary Robinson is elected first woman President of Ireland and, after 1,597 days as a hostage in Beirut, Brian Keenan is to be freed, as is Nelson Mandela in South Africa after twenty-six years in jail.

By August Saddam Hussein will invade and annex Kuwait and take Western hostages as 'human shields'.

And in Galway, The Saw Doctors produce another hit, 'I Useta Lover.'

The year at Knock started off on a by now familiar note – the mandatory Shannon stopover was still impacting adversely on transatlantic ambitions. The problem had not been fixed, and one of the more persistent operators who attempted to get the cross-Atlantic trip up and running found he had to fork out up to 10,000 dollars for the privilege of bringing tourists to the West of Ireland. It was killing business before it even began.

Ed O'Brien thought he had received clearance from Tourism Minister John Wilson to fly from New York to Knock with a charter-load of pilgrims over the Christmas period. He was given to understand that the Iceland touchdown on inward flights would meet requirements.

But there were last-minute problems. The issue was not to be as clear-cut as that, after all. The passengers turned up at Kennedy on December 21 and took their seats, anticipating the direct flight to Knock in time for the Christmas festivities. But the plane sat on the tarmac for four hours before being cleared on the instruction that it could by all means touch down in Reykjavik in Iceland but would also have to stop over at Shannon! It did just that, and a furious O'Brien had to stump up the requisite number of dollars per head before the plane could be sent again on its short final leg from Co. Clare to Knock.

O'Brien got an itemised bill: landing fee at Shannon £911 plus £3,600 for fuel eaten up on landing and take-off, making the total an unnecessary £4,600 for the stopover. He complained about the cost and the additional flight-time expended, and said it would make sense to pay Shannon the landing fee and allow direct flights in and out of Knock. The delays had added six hours to the flight and dampened the ardour of exiles in their desire to spend Christmas on the old sod. Meanwhile Bord Fáilte was spending millions trying to attract American tourists to Ireland!

O'Brien was supported in his fight by two senior Fianna Fáil politicians from Roscommon, Minister of State Terry Leyden and the Cathaoirleach of the Seanad, Seán Doherty, who attended a press conference at the Airport on January 2 before the flight returned to the States.

Doherty lashed what he called a 'ludicrous concept' which accorded Shannon special privileges. And there was support too from the Irish Countrywomen's Association vice-president, Nancy Smyth, who warned that Ireland was cutting itself off from its share of the 200,000 American Marian Shrine pilgrimage business.

John Healy rounded on the Shannon lobby and Willie O'Dea in his weekly offering in *The Connaught Telegraph*. He said Shannon had grown fat as a stall-fed dog in a fatter manger: the taxman had carried it for a long, long time. In one breath Shannon was doing a bomb; in another to be deprived of the £900 landing fee was to bring disaster to Shannon and the mid-West, he chided.

By the time the Christmas visitors to Knock were back in a freezing New York, Horan International was looking to the sun for its next opportunity. On January 8 a pioneering sun charter service linking Knock and Palma in Majorca was announced at a press reception at the Airport. It was a new outlet and was warmly greeted. Gillian Bowler, MD of Budget Travel, and Sligo-born P. J. McGoldrick, Chief Executive of Ryanair, announced that the new service would operate fortnightly from May 26 to September 29. It was to be the first holiday destination to be sold from Knock.

However, within two months, and before the service began, Budget Travel announced they were scrapping the planned operation because of lack of support. The President of the Connaught Branch of the Irish Travel Agents, Fergus Kilkelly, laid the blame at the door of West of Ireland travel agents who, he railed, hadn't pushed the promotion hard enough. He particularly blamed Galway travel agents for lack of enthusiasm. A wonderful opportunity had been lost, said the Castlebar man.

Ms Bowler indicated that the take-up had been less than 10%. "People from the region seem to prefer to book flights out of Dublin when going on holidays," she said. If that was the preference then – and the sole reason for the cancellation – it was to change radically within a few years when sun holiday destinations from Knock really took off.

There were better hopes for direct flights from the US in March when economic consultants Davy Kelleher McCarthy Ltd reported findings which indicated the compulsory stopover in County Clare for transatlantic traffic was inhibiting the expansion of the North American tourist capacity into Ireland. The report's bottom line was that the regulation was preventing the development of Irish long-haul aviation and was driving Irish traffic into the hands of British and foreign airlines. Ed O'Brien welcomed the findings, saying he had been vindicated in maintaining Shannon interests were exaggerating the damage that the abolition of the stopover would have on the mid-west region.

There was another chink in the Shannon armour in April when Transport and Tourism Minister Seamus Brennan drew a distinction between transatlantic charters and scheduled services. He was speaking at the Fianna Fáil Ard Fheis in Dublin. A minister had finally mustered the courage to bite on the bullet and introduce some form of liberalisation, even if credibility in the Knock service was taking a battering.

Clearance for direct charters to Knock from America was given by the Government on April 17, and Seamus Brennan flew down to Knock to make the announcement. He said he looked forward to the Board developing the business in a systematic way. Brennan had always been a keen Knock supporter and was a no-nonsense Minister when it came to liberalising the sector. Predictably, however, Shannon did not like the decision, one Fianna Fáil politician from the Shannon region branding the Minister's reasons as 'just muck'.

The US charter service depended to an extent on emigration, and even with visa laws being tightened all the time the drift to America continued. Emigration was very much in evidence throughout the West, a point illustrated by a Mayo GAA study which looked into the declining playing numbers in its 52 clubs over the previous two years. It found that 600 players had emigrated from the county in that period, with 85% going to the UK and 10% to the US. 70% were adult footballers, and 30% under-age players.

Commenting on the findings, County Board Officer Paddy Muldoon said they had come across a sad case of a former Mayo Under-21 County player sleeping in a cardboard box in London, and he appealed that every effort be made to engage the IDA and the County Development Team in creating jobs at home.

To compound matters, findings carried out by the Western Branch of the National Conference of the Priests of Ireland under the chairmanship of Kilmovee PP, Fr. Greg Hannon, showed that communities throughout the West had been virtually wiped out by emigration with a decrease in overall population levels of the order of 10%.

Twelve communities had been randomly selected, and all but one showed declining populations. A survey of 667 people who left school in the period 1978-80 showed 69% had departed their home parishes. In one County Leitrim community, townlands which had supported up to fifteen families thirty years previously now had one person—or nobody!

The first of the recently approved direct flights from the US to Knock landed towards the end of July, dropping off 250 passengers before journeying on to Belfast. Another four direct flights were scheduled for the remainder of the year, the *Western People* reported.

There were signs, too, of greater goodwill within political circles in the West when sixty councillors from the five Connaught counties met to discuss plans for a better deal for the Airport and the region in general. P. J. Morley, chairman of Mayo County Council, said he was happy that parochial issues had been set aside.

A few weeks later Taoiseach Charles J. Haughey helicoptered into North Mayo to give his backing to a Stone Age Visitor Interpretative Centre at Céide, near Ballycastle. "It ranks," he said, "as one of the greatest wonders of the ancient world. I am personally attracted to the development – it's the engine of recovery for this region and I want to see it happen."

The project had been mooted for years without getting anywhere, and there are those who believe the tourism/educational potential of Céide would have lain under its blanket of bog had not Haughey's interest been aroused.

Minister of State Seán Calleary was there when Haughey plunged an iron rod into the peat and struck a field boundary rock untouched by human contact for over 5,000 years. "I once heard Charlie Haughey described by a man as someone able to look at a thing, cut out the red tape and all nonsense, and get something done. Knock and Céide were cases in point. He saw the Céide potential and he called me into his office one day and said it was a fine project and I was to keep my eye on it. I knew he wanted action," said Calleary.

Promoters of the Céide Fields project had been hitting a stone wall of official resistance for years in their efforts to release the tourism potential of a discovery as old as the pyramids of Egypt. As at Knock, Haughey broke through the red tape.

In mid-August another charter arrived from the US with 270 passengers on board, but events in the Middle East were unfolding which would cause a crisis for aviation around the world. Saddam Hussein marched into Kuwait and tensions rose in the oil-rich region. The Gulf War was to follow the next year and that would put the industry into a tailspin. Knock was not to be immune.

Meanwhile, though, the West was crying out for jobs, and was haemorrhaging people in the catharsis. Monsignor Horan had hoped that the Airport could be the catalyst, if granted tax-free status. The first breakthrough came with the cutting of the sod for the first factory adjacent to the Airport by Environment Minister Padraig Flynn on October 15. Westech Developments Ltd and Crisham Industrial Properties Ltd were behind an electronics factory which promised 30 jobs initially. Unfortunately, Westech, which had IDA approval, never got off the ground, its English parent company running into difficulties. (See Chapter 21.)

In November, distinguished constitutional lawyer Mary Robinson was elected first woman President of Ireland. The 46 year-old mother of three was given an enthusiastic reception by an attendance of about

7,000 when she returned to the place of her birth, Ballina, after the election.

She had fought an extended campaign over seven months and beaten off the challenge of Fianna Fáil's Brian Lenihan. In her address, she spoke of lighting a candle in Áras an Uachtaráin for the people of Ireland and especially for the Irish diaspora. She was installed as President on December 3.

One of those to congratulate her was Environment Minister Flynn who told *The Connaught Telegraph* it had never been his intention to cause any hurt to the President-elect or her family by his pre-election remarks on Radio Éireann for which he had already apologised. The media and opposition politicians had criticised the Minister for his personal attack, and it marked one of the turning-points in the campaign.

Also under attack was the aviation industry. With fears rising over the Middle East conflict and fuel prices spiralling, Ryanair and Aer Lingus indicated they would be reducing services through Knock in the New Year. Aer Lingus was in the process of radical restructuring to avail of rescue subsidies from the Government after seeing its holiday company collapse. The picture was far from cheerful.

To overcome curtailed services by Ryanair and Aer Lingus, the Airport Company disclosed it was in negotiations with two British carriers to operate flights to fill the anticipated void on the Manchester and London routes. Seamus Monaghan, Company Chairman, said between December 15 and January 8, 102 flights would come into Knock. And he reported a positive response from a promotional visit to New York, Boston, Philadelphia and Chicago by Monsignor Grealy and himself. However, the valleys were going to outnumber the peaks as the industry fought for stability.

Perhaps indicative of the lack of confidence in the hospitality business here, Ed O'Brien of Knock Charters in the US, found a lukewarm response to his campaign to get people in the accommodation sector in Connaught/Donegal to take £50 shares in a marketing company he planned to set up to promote the region in America. Only 2% of the sector had so far taken shares, he indicated.

In the background, the matter of setting up a Trust to hold ownership of the Airport was still being debated. Transport and Tourism Minister Seamus Brennan confirmed he had been asked to consider having a member of the family of the late Monsignor Horan on the new body. Nancy Horan, the late Monsignor's sister and close confidante, was being mooted as a director to ensure her brother's ambitions were carried out.

Just before Christmas Aer Lingus bowed to political and business pressure and announced it would retain its Knock-Dublin service. It had fought to get in, now it was being forced to stay. And Airport Secretary Jim Ryan set the tone for a busy Christmas when he announced that close on 19,000 passengers would pass through the facility during the festive period, up 1,000 on the corresponding 1989 figure.

*   *   *

1991: The New Year came in with a bang. A very sad bang. On the morning of January 6, the great defender of Knock Airport, John Healy, died suddenly. The colourful tell-it-as-it-was reporter from Charlestown was only 60.

In the many tributes that followed, the *Western People* headlined its front page with 'John Healy – Giant of modern Irish journalism.' It traced his formative years in journalism, from 1947 when he cycled all the way from Charlestown to Ballina to ask the paper's editor Fred Devere for a job, to his departure for Dublin in 1950, after he had seen Mayo regain the All-Ireland senior football title they last held in 1936. Healy was an avid Mayo and Charlestown GAA fan, and also loved his handball. Danno Regan of the all-conquering Mayo team of the 1930s was his great hero.

Healy first edited the *Gaelic Sportsman* in Dublin, departing a couple of months later for the *Irish Newsagency* which had been set up by the government to promote Ireland's media interests abroad.

Moving on to the *Irish Press,* he had subsequently become Editor of the ground-breaking tabloid *Sunday Review* where his penchant for taking the mystique out of politics was first seen to stunning effect in his Backbencher column, a pioneering feature at that time.

Healy continued to write a highly popular weekly column for the *Western People* from the mid-60s through to the mid-70s. His acerbic and earthy insights into politics made for *de rigueur* reading, and his trenchant campaign for a better deal for the region was unquenchable. He had seen emigration trains depart from Charlestown, and fires go out in houses around the adjoining townlands. Through his typewriter, he was to rattle off millions of stinging words at the neglect of the West.

When he moved to *The Irish Times,* he took his Backbencher column with him, and from the late '60s to the late '80s he was a constant contributor to that paper. He wrote two stirring books, *The Death of an Irish Town,* and *Nineteen Acres,* and he presented *The Hurler on the Ditch* and *Headlines and Deadlines* on RTÉ. He won a Jacobs media award in 1967, the same year as he was proclaimed Mayoman of the Year for his 'witty, earthy, sardonic and iconoclastic' Backbencher column.

He had a great interest in the environment, and was the man behind the O'Dwyer Cheshire Home (Bohola) Trust Forests in Carracastle, near Charlestown, and other locations in the West. And next to Charlestown in his heart was Achill Island where he had a holiday home and where he wrote and painted over the years.

In 1977 he was co-founder of the *Western Journal* which had its head office in Ballina and produced Sligo and Mayo editions under founding editor Jim McGuire. In 1989 the National Council for Education conferred an honorary Doctorate in Law on Healy.

A committed European, he had written incisively about the emerging community and Ireland's place within it, and he had worked as Information Officer – at the request of Taoiseach Charlie Haughey –

during Ireland's highly successful presidency of the EEC in 1990. One of the great memories of that period was Healy in the EEC media tent in Dublin crying with pride on camera as the Republic of Ireland soccer team performed with great gusto in the World Championships in Italy.

At the time of his death he had been revising his latest book on the Three Musketeers, Haughey, Donogh O'Malley and Brian Lenihan, and had written an account of the first thirty years of his life in journalism. "It was," according to his great friend and former *Irish Times* editor Douglas Gageby, "hilarious and gutsy and also instructive and basically serious."

Charlie Haughey, who first heard of Knock Airport from Healy, described him as a brilliant journalist, writer and commentator with his own inimitable style. "He had a great love for the people of his native Mayo and the West of Ireland, whose best interests were his passionate concern." Healy had taken Haughey west in 1964 to visit the 'snipegrass' on the TD's elevation as Minister for Agriculture.

Archbishop Joseph Cassidy said he knew Healy when they were both growing up together in Charlestown. "He had a strong sense of mission even then. It was something he would live out later as a celebrated political journalist, an advocate of Western causes, a powerful evocative writer, more especially in *Nineteen Acres.*

"There was nothing anaemic about Healy. He was a red-blooded writer all the way. Indeed he had such a grip on life and wrote about it at all times, with such lyrical beauty that it's hard to believe he is dead," said Cassidy in his tribute.

Michael Commins, writing a tribute in *The Connaught Telegraph* of January 16 1991, said Healy's role in influencing decision-makers could not be over-estimated: ". . . how influential was Healy in talking O'Malley into providing the free education and buses . . . and on a more local level, what part did he play in forcing Charlie Haughey's hand on Knock Airport? Next to Msgr. Horan, I would venture to say that Healy had far more influence in that decision than any Minister or TD West of the Shannon.

"To my way of thinking, Healy was the real 'Backbencher' whose role in securing an International Airport for Barnacuige, Charlestown, has never been understood – but who 'delivered' more than any elected representative ever could. And when you realise this, you begin to understand why John Healy stood by Charlie and why Jim Mitchell's 'foggy boggy mountain top' remark drew his fire in abundance," wrote Commins.

How would Healy have reacted to the later revelations about Haughey and his lavish lifestyle supported by generous benefactors? Former *Irish Times* correspondent and Healy friend, Michael Finlan, has no doubts. "Healy would not have been afraid to criticise and criticise severely this man who let down the whole nation. Healy was fond of saying it's easy to criticise your enemies but the real test is to be able to criticise your friends. Whatever Healy would have written of Haughey it would never be set down in malice," he said.

*   *   *

Direct Knock-New York flights were given a boost when NY tour operator Brendan Ward, a director of Sceptre Charters, announced that weekly flights had been lined up from June 28 to September 7. Tickets would be sold on both legs and the potential traffic was 3,000, he estimated. Early-bird fares were pitched at £289. He also spoke of the possibility of a NY/Knock link up-with Medjugorje.

In all, Ward estimated he organised close on 50 flights from New York to Knock over a ten-year period, dating back to July 1986. He was in a good position to analyse that market and in an interview for this book he poured cold water on the notion that the Shannon stopover was the main reason why the flights were ultimately abandoned.

"You must remember the stopover regulation for transatlantic charters had ended in 1991 and I had little difficulty in filling aircraft coming from New York. The problem was there was no support on the Irish side, with very few from the western region taking up the option to fly on the outward leg. On one occasion, the most we could get for the return leg was fifteen people from the West," he recalls.

There were a few reasons for that in his view: the Irish economy had not picked up, but more to the point, he felt travel agents were more inclined to sell seats on regular Aer Lingus flights rather than on charters because their commission was higher. He conceded it was hard to blame them for that.

Ward, a native of Foxford who emigrated to the US in 1955, still recalls how excited Monsignor Horan was when the first aircraft landed from New York in late July 1986. "He was thrilled, but only a few days later I was flying back to Ireland again for his funeral," he recalls.

Describing Horan as an 'incredible man', he remembers his visits to New York to create awareness of the Airport. "He stayed with us and was the same man in New York as he was in Knock, without airs or pretensions," he says.

*   *   *

Horan International, although it had recorded a profit of £200,000 for 1990 according to Chairman Monaghan, was strapped for cash to develop the facility further in terms of better lighting, radar and modern fire-fighting equipment. He told the *Western People* of January 23 he would like to see the Airport go public in a bid to raise £3m to £4m.

It seemed to him, he said, that it was the only possibility to succeed, but indicated that the Board would be holding a controlling 51% of the shares. The Board had an American suitor, badly needed the money but could not proceed in selling a stake in the Company until the Deed of Trust was completed, he indicated.

In early February Ryanair dismissed rumours it was going to be gobbled up by Aer Lingus, with Chief Executive PJ McGoldrick announcing that the company had enjoyed its best year to date, carrying

750,000 passengers on all its routes with an average load factor of 71%. He also announced that it was adding Stansted to its Knock routes, in addition to maintaining the Luton link. Loganair also announced it was to operate four flights a week on the Knock-Manchester route from 1 April.

However, the additional routes could not prevent further cutbacks at the Airport, with 20 of the 30 permanent staff finding their hours cut in half as the company struggled to ride out the Gulf War disruption and a British recession.

Some relief came Knock's way in late March when Minister Brennan announced an allocation of £425,000 from ERDF funding in aid of proposed works.

The increasing cost of airfares caught the headlines in May when Tom Beisty, founder of the Safe Start Foundation in London – set up to give Irish emigrants to the London area training and an accommodation base – warned that rising charges on Ryanair's Knock to Luton route would kill regional airports. He pointed out that fares had started out at £84 return but in some cases were now as high as £264. There was a growing feeling at the time that Ryanair's monopoly of the route was leading to higher fares than operated on other routes out of Ireland.

The reality was that Ryanair were still encountering financial difficulties and the April 11 edition of *Business and Finance* put the deficit as high as £22m, and said the airline had initiated cutbacks including reduced landing fees at regional airports. At this stage it was estimated that Ryanair was losing £2.5m a year on its Kerry, Galway and Waterford services which were using the more costly ATRs aircraft. Galway was the biggest loss-maker for Ryanair, dropping £623,000, followed by Kerry on £508,000. Knock was by then a profitable route for Ryanair.

The picture continued to look bleak for the aviation industry, and there seemed no light at the end of the tunnel. Economist Seán Barrett told *Business and Finance* the industry had been stagnant between 1978 and 1985 with just Aer Lingus controlling the market. Then the market became competitive but nosedived at the end of 1990. Barrett was critical of the Knock Airport management, saying there was no marketing strategy in place, and that European routes should have been developed. The Board knew this, but interested carriers, keen to preserve their core business, were thin on the ground.

The magazine also referred to a row over catering contracts at the Airport, saying it understood Gay Nevin, the president of the Irish Vintners' Association, was planning a High Court action against the Board for alleged failure to keep agreements. Airport Chairman Monaghan told *Business and Finance* the catering problem started with the Gulf crisis when passenger numbers started to drop off. Dublin Airport caterers had taken a drop of between 40% and 45%, he said.

In a wide-ranging interview, Monaghan again denied directors were profiting from their Airport connections. He said his company's tender for lighting was the lowest. And on the issue of car rentals, he said that Avis and Hertz had originally turned down the offer to provide a service and Cathal Duffy had provided about ten cars at a cost of £60,000 to get the service up and running after signing a contract with Monsignor Horan. But when the Car Rental Association saw the potential they threatened legal action against the Board if they were refused self-drive pick-up facilities inside the gate. He revealed that car rentals under the new liberalised agreements were worth £22,000 a year to the Airport in 1991.

Great sadness descended on the Airport around this time when a popular employee in his early '20s was killed in a car accident within the complex. "It was a terrible tragedy," said Chairman Seamus Monaghan.

*   *   *

Meanwhile, the drawn-out Trust ownership wrangle had been bubbling just under the surface and erupted again to claim the column inches in the local and national press in March when the issue was raised in the Dáil. Liam Horan, writing in the *Western People*, outlined that the Horan family were not happy with the details of the Trust. In their opinion, Monsignor Horan had always expressed the hope that such a Trust would leave the Airport in the hands of the people of Connaught, with any profits accruing to be re-invested in different types of industry.

And the family were not happy about the exact number of acres which would be transferred, stating of 545 acres only 93 had been included in the holding being put into Trust for the people of Connaught. Another 100 acres could be accounted for in the industrial estate, but they wanted to know where the remaining 352 acres were going.

Deputy Emmett Stagg, who had tabled the Dáil question, said the family believed the Airport was not being run in accordance with the spirit in which it had been built by Horan. "People who didn't make substantial financial investments are now, in effect, paper millionaires thanks to their position as shareholders. The family are extremely disturbed," he said.

With rumours running wild suggesting some directors wished to retain a personal ownership in the company and about land being sold off, the Airport Company, through its chairman Seamus Monaghan, issued a blunt statement which set out to rectify 'the many false rumours which are once again circulating about Horan Airport, and false accusations against some of the Directors regarding the Deed of Trust, and regarding the sale of land, etc.'

He outlined that:
• The Board had been pressing the Department for five years to have a Deed set up whereby ownership of the Airport would be placed in trust for the people of the West.
• On June 25, 1990, the Department had requested the Board to arrange to have Monsignor Horan's share transferred by his sister to Monsignor Grealy, and to have Ulick McEvaddy's share transferred to Peter Hanley (a new director).

- On July 9 1990, all the Directors had signed an agreement to transfer their shares over to the Trust.
- On July 9 Monaghan and John Dillon, Directors, on the Board's direction, called on Monsignor Horan's sister (Nancy) to inform her of the Department's instructions. She refused to sign over her brother's share.
- Since then the Board had been informed by the Department that it was considering other structures rather than a Deed of Trust.
- For ten years no director had received one penny from the Airport, 'even though some of us have sacrificed up to two days per week at times from our businesses which have suffered as a consequence'. Trips to Dublin and London had on several occasions been made by the Directors at their own expense, he added.
- No land or property owned by the Airport Company had been sold by the Directors, or by anybody else.

Directors listed at the time were Archbishop Joseph Cassidy, Michael Honan, Peter Hanley, John Mahon, Des Mahon, James Ryan, Seamus Monaghan (chairman), John Dillon and Cathal Duffy. Hanley was a Rooskey, Co. Roscommon-based meat-plant owner who had been a director of Aer Rianta.

Some weeks later, sources close to deposed director Ulick McEvaddy indicated to *Business and Finance* that, like Nancy Horan, he was concerned lest the Directors benefited personally from the Trust. As the proposal stood, he would not sign, he told the publication. And a defiant Nancy Horan steadfastly maintained she would not be signing until outstanding issues were cleared up. "Why should I sign over my share which in theory could be worth £330,000 when you add the Government grant of £10m and the Church contribution of over £3m?" she asked. The 'Church contribution' comment was in reference to the fund-raising efforts of her brother and Monsignor Grealy as parish priests of Knock and Board Chairmen.

By October James Morrissey, writing in the *Sunday Business Post*, reported that the Trust row was still alive and kicking. He wrote that the Minister for Energy Bobby Molloy was opposed to the Trust as long as Nancy Horan was unhappy that her brother's wishes were not being followed. Molloy said he was eager that the matter be resolved amicably. Morrissey also indicated that the financial outturn for 1991 was likely to result in major refinancing, and revealed that in August the company had written to Minister Brennan warning that it would be placed in receivership if a Trust enabling the raising of fresh finance was not quickly established.

Finally, on November 3 the Trust row was settled. Minister Brennan announced the setting up of the Horan International Airport Trust, with eight Trustees, three of whom, by virtue of their office, were to be permanent. They were the Archbishop, the County Manager and the Chairman of the Board. Nancy Horan was one of the Trustees. All shares were signed into the Deed of Trust. The Trust was to 'benefit the residents of Connaught in general and the County of Mayo in particular', and was to promote new private-sector investment and new airlines, and to encourage and promote the tourism, cultural, commercial and industrial interests of the residents of the area.

Under the new ownership agreement, the Trustees could authorise the Board of the Company to enter into arrangements with other persons or bodies and could cause the Company to allot shares to any person or body wishing to invest in the company provided that the Trustees held at least 51% of the voting shares of the Company.

Minister Brennan also wrote off the Government grant of £9.8m given when the airport was set up. And he made three specific requests of the Board. He advocated an immediate injection of fresh investment, through, perhaps, selling 49% of the shares; the acquisition of expertise in various areas; and the provision of a ambitious marketing plan 'as the airport needs added business and needs it urgently'.

Ulick McEvaddy, though his solicitor Charles Kelly, said if the Trust was meaningful and safeguarded the Public Funds expended at Knock, he would have no objection and would, indeed, welcome the Trust in the public interest.

Kelly added that McEvaddy had not, despite requests to the Minister, received a copy of the Trust document.

Chairman Monaghan said the Board would now endeavour to attract new investment – as had been advised by Minister Brennan – and had particular investors in mind who might be interested in coming on board. (See Chapter 21.)

The first meeting of the Trustees was held at the Airport on November 18 1991. Another long and tortuous wrangle had been settled. And the Horan name had been restored to the Boardroom. Manager Michael McGrath saw Nancy Horan's arrival on the scene as a very good thing for the airport. "She was quite an intelligent lady, and she was very conscious of what her brother wanted for the airport. She had been very close to him and knew the difficulties which existed within the Board. She had had a long and bitter fight with people on the Board before she became a Director at all. She fought long and hard to get on the Board. It was a pity she had to fight because her value and her worth should have been recognised.

"Once on the Board she was a highly respected member; she questioned issues and would delve into areas and make sure she understood all the complexities. She brought hope to the staff. She told me how the Monsignor used to be physically ill before attending Board meetings. He was not as hard as people thought. As far as the Monsignor was concerned, she told me everything was for the people, for the Airport, for the Shrine. He did not have £10 when he died," said McGrath.

CHAPTER EIGHTEEN

*1992-2002: Albert Reynolds becomes Taoiseach -Padraig Flynn goes to
EU - Cathal Duffy new chairman - Genial Jim Ryan dies - First air
crash - 10th anniversary celebrations - Ross Perot Jnr company plans –
Duty-free shop - Ryanair threatens pull-out -Twin Towers attack*

Ryanair threatens to pull plug

IN the six years that had elapsed since Monsignor Horan's death in
1986 not a lot had happened improvement-wise in the West. In fact if
he had been still around he would have been rattling at cages and
vigorously demanding a fair deal for the region.

The very fabric of rural life was breaking down in rural areas as the
drift to urban centres gained momentum. The chronic disintegration of
the population base was highlighted at the Bishops' Developing The
West Together seminar in Ballina in February 1992. Garda stations,
schools, banks and post offices were being closed down as the drift from
the land continued. Worse still, some communities had gone past the
point of being able to renew themselves. Deaths were outpacing births,
delegates were told.

The conference heard that between 1921 and 1991 Connaught's
decline in population was 24%, while the population of Leinster had
grown by a massive 62%. The Western province had lost 2% of its
population in the five years between 1986 and 1991, with Mayo's loss
being twice that figure.

Delegates further heard that:
• Per capita income in the West Region was 55% of the national
average.
• The average farm income in the West was £4,277 pa. compared
to £12,000 in the South East and £10,000 in the South West.
• Over 50% of farmers in the West had an income of £50 per
week or less from their 1989 farm enterprises.
• EC structural funds intended to assist regions on the periphery,
like the West, were being used to widen the disadvantage. Of funds
made available for 1989-93, £425m had been voted for the
roads/rail access network heading for Dublin City and County,
while the Galway/Mayo/ Roscommon region got £85.5m.

Albert Reynolds had just taken over as Taoiseach from Charlie Haughey who officially retired on January 30 after a series of heaves. The final straw had been Seán Doherty's revelation on a *Nighthawks* RTÉ programme, coming from Castlerea, that Haughey had personal knowledge of the illegal tapping of journalists' telephones some years earlier.

Padraig Flynn, who, like Reynolds, had been sacked the previous November after a move against Haughey, was restored to the Cabinet by Reynolds as Minister for Justice, but Minister of State Seán Calleary was dropped. His support for Reynolds in the challenge against Haughey was seen as lukewarm at best. A year later Flynn was to be rewarded by Reynolds for his support in what had been termed a 'country and western' campaign to take out Haughey. The Castlebar man took over as EU Commissioner with responsibility for social affairs and employment, immigration, home affairs and justice.

When Seamus Monaghan stepped down as Airport chairman in 1992 he was succeeded by Cathal Duffy who had also been on the Board from the very beginning. Indeed he had been a member of the original ad hoc committee, and had enjoyed a long and close relationship with Haughey. It was well known that the Castlebar businessman had put in a spoke for Flynn when he got his first ministerial appointment in 1980, but after Flynn deserted the Haughey camp locals discerned a cooling in relationships between the two Castlebar men.

Times were still challenging at Knock Airport, and were pushed to the very edge when the Guinness Peat Aviation flotation failed to take off and threatened Ryanair's future. GPA was headed up by Tony Ryan as was Ryanair, and when the flotation of the highly-successful GPA had to be aborted in June 1992, Ryan lost over 300m dollars within hours. His Ryanair company now carried all his hopes.

With the aviation industry going through such a turbulent time one would have thought there would be little interest in setting up further airports in this country. However, in beautiful Clifden in County Galway there were no such misgivings. Local hoteliers, in an effort to boost tourism, aired plans to build their own airport so that they could fly in customers before they were sidetracked elsewhere by competing forces.

Clifden is, of course, linked with the first non-stop flight across the Atlantic Ocean in 1919 by British aviators Captain John Alcock and Lieutenant Arthur Whitten Brown. Flying a modified Vickers Vimy IV twin-engined bomber, they took off from Lester's Field, Newfoundland, in the late afternoon of June 14, 1919 and crashlanded in a bog near Clifden in Connemara, at 8.40am on June 15, 1919, crossing the coast at 4.28pm. They flew 1890 miles in 15 hours 57 minutes, at an average speed of 118 mph. Their aircraft was powered by two Rolls-Royce Eagle engines.

The Clifden campaign was shot down, mainly by environmentalists, including David Bellamy, who pointed out that the site was environmentally precious. No doubt the Department of Tourism and Transport breathed a sigh of relief. The same department released figures published by *The Irish Times* on September 15 1992 which showed what the Exchequer had paid out in grants to regional airports: Knock £9.858m; Carrickfin (Donegal) £375,000; Galway £1,187,500; Sligo £374,250; Kerry £1,319,979; Waterford £1,082,500.

In addition, Jim Dunne reported that the six airports were in receipt of financial assistance on a pound-for-pound basis from the European Regional Development Fund (ERDF) for approved development works to be completed by the end of 1993. The amounts approved for each individual airport under the £18.8 million package were: Knock £900,000; Carrickfin £2m; Galway £1.2m; Sligo £900,000, Waterford £3m, and Kerry a whopping £10.6 million mainly to build a new runway to take jet aircraft.

Totted up, the grants made for interesting reading: Kerry-£11,920m; Knock, £10.758m; Waterford, £4.082m; Galway, £2.387m; Carrickfin, £2.375m, and Sligo, £1.274m. People wondered what Healy would have written following that disclosure! Kerry had, nicely and quietly, been approved for as much aid as Knock had received!

However, that was not to be the full story, for three years later, in 1996, when the Dáil Public Accounts Committee were considering the Comptroller and Auditor-General's report, they found that in the period 1989-93, the Co. Kerry airport actually received £12.62m, more than half of the £20.85m allocated to the six regional airports. By comparison with the £12.62m spent on Farranfore during that period, Connaught Airport got only £43,000, Sligo £40,000, Carnmore in Galway, £1.18m, Waterford, £2.80m and Carrickfin in Donegal, £3.42m, wrote Joseph Power in the *Irish Independent* of June 14 1996.

1993: By the end of 1992 Ryanair was at last on an upward graph. It carried almost 2.5 million passengers and profits were reckoned to be between £1 million and £3.5 million. In 1993 Ray MacSharry, having served his term as EU Commissioner, was enticed by the Ryans to join their airline as Chairman. He accepted the offer, despite also being courted by Aer Lingus.

Shortly afterwards Aer Lingus attempted to buy out Ryanair and negotiations reached £25m before the talks were called off. Michael O'Leary had now become Chief Executive of Ryanair and the company was well and truly in profit, with cash reserves said to be approaching £12m and an annual profit figure of, some analysts suggested, £10m.

Ironically, Aer Lingus was at the very same time on the verge of going bust itself. The good old taxpayer, who would have had to cough up the funds for the Ryanair takeover had it succeeded, now had to pump in many millions to keep the national airline afloat. The State-bankrolled Aer Lingus had the best of all worlds, it seemed. The taxpayer paid up, the passenger was fleeced and in that cosseted environment, there had been very little desire to grow traffic numbers into the country. Many laid the blame at the door of Aer Lingus: in reality the

Government held the reins and lacked the enterprise to deregulate its hamstrung aviation policy.

Around this time there was great consternation when Ryanair announced it would no longer carry coffins into Knock because of handling difficulties. Knock had been a godsend for families returning home for funerals or flying in the remains of their loved ones. Achill-born Terry Gallagher, Chairman of the Mayo Association in London, says people cannot imagine how reassuring it is to be able to use the service at such times. "You feel you are at home amongst friends from the moment you arrive, and when the transportation of coffins was threatened the then chairman of the Association in London, Tom Beisty, began a one-man campaign to have the invaluable service restored. Michael O'Leary of Ryanair said if Beisty could find someone to handle the coffins at the UK airports the service would be resumed. To the great relief of grieving families, Tom found a company and Ryanair stuck by its word," he says.

1994: There was a noticeable lull in national media interest in Knock after the Trust ownership issue had been put to bed and Cathal Duffy had taken over as Chairman. The Castlebar businessman took a tighter grip on feeds to the press, though he enjoyed a good working relationship with the local media.

Tom Shiel, writing in the *Irish Independent* in March 1994, paid tribute to Duffy: "When asked to explain how a small airport in a declining corner of Europe has defied the prophets of gloom, some will point to the no-nonsense tactics of the Board, now chaired by Cathal Duffy, one of the bigger names in the West of Ireland garage business."

Director John Dillon knew a lot of the success being enjoyed was down to Ryanair. "They put their faith in us when others were reluctant. They also made a marvellous contribution to reducing fares. This has been vital to the survival of the Airport," he affirmed.

Knock was hopeful, too, of developing the US charter business, having welcomed flights from New York and Boston in 1993, and was looking forward to Philadelphia being added to the departure points.

*   *   *

It was now possible to see celebrities passing through the airport, with Ashford Castle and other top hotels in the region drawing them in. English cricket star Ian Botham, film stars Woody Allen and Mia Farrow (before their divorce), Bishop Desmond Tutu (on his way to take part in the AFRI Famine Walk in Louisburgh), Bob Hope, Vanessa Redgrave and John Major were amongst those who had come through the airport by 1994. Others were to follow, including Robin Williams, Hugh Grant, Minnie Driver, Prince Charles and Prince Edward, rock stars Eric Clapton, and Liam and Noel Gallagher of Oasis whose grandmother hailed from Charlestown; soccer stars George Best and an English captain Bryan Robson, British Prime Minister Tony Blair, and the remarkably charismatic Mother Teresa of Calcutta *en route* to a visit to Knock Shrine.

250

There to greet the big names as well as the man and woman in the street were, likely as not Michael McGrath and Jim Ryan. Knock had always made a point of looking after visitors, and that continues to this day.

Security Officer at the Airport, Matt Macken, underlines that commitment to service. "Every customer is important to us, and over a period of time people have become familiar to us and we can address them by their first names in many instances. The personal touch is very important to us here, and we are on the same mission that Monsignor Horan started," he said.

Sadly, in June 1994 Company Secretary/Director Jim Ryan, the man who had shaken so many passengers' hands, died. He had been there from the beginning of Monsignor Horan's crusade to build an airport; in fact it was he who brought Horan up to speed on aircraft and runways, and it was he, too, who had won over the landowners to sell their plots in the interest of developing the region.

His ready smile and great sense of decency and sincerity always shone through, and he was the ideal public relations man as the Airport struggled to its feet. A member of a well-known Westport family, his interests included horses and boating, and for many years he was a familiar figure as 'call in' steward at the Westport Horse Show on the lawn of Westport House. But most of his time over the previous fourteen years had been devoted to the airport.

Chairman Cathal Duffy in a tribute, said Ryan's loss would be greatly felt by all, directors, staff and passengers who had many fond memories of his warm welcomes.

*   *   *

The first recorded air crash at the Airport occurred on August 19 1994 when a six-seater Cessna plane, with two on board, hit a wall on its approach to the runway. They were on a training flight from Dublin when the plane developed engine trouble. Both were taken to hospital with serious injuries. Airport staff and the emergency services were praised for their speedy and efficient response.

The new Arrivals Hall and Met Station at the Airport were opened by Minister for Energy Noel Treacy on October 7. It had responsibility for providing weather data to the aviation industry and also to Met Éireann HQ. Six staff now work over a 24-hour roster at the airport.

The pick-up in business was now evident and the Minister said Knock's throughput in 1993 of 107,000 passengers was likely to be surpassed by 40,000 by the end of 1994. Business to July was already up 42%, he disclosed.

Profits for the year, up to the end of June, 1994, were £334,125, the best results ever achieved, according to Chairman Duffy. At that time Aer Lingus were flying the Dublin route, Ryanair was on Stansted, Manx Airlines were servicing the Manchester route daily in summer and four times weekly in winter, and Loganair was operating a three-day-per-week schedule to Glasgow from June to September.

A potential lucrative operation ran into difficulties when attempts by a northern businessman Sam Smyth to export livestock through the Airport to Europe came to a halt in October after the Department of Agriculture 'dragged its feet' in issuing a licence. An earlier shipment had been approved, but when the second application was delayed the exporter moved his business to Belfast Airport.

Livestock exports through Knock were to recommence in March 1995, but were eventually ended, partly because an Animal Rights group, Compassion in World Farming, staged a series of protests and expressed concern with the treatment of calves on the continent, especially those destined for white veal productions systems there. The Irish organiser for Compassion in World Farming, Mary Ann Bartlett, from Cork, handed in an open letter of protest to the Airport Company. The protests were part of a series mounted at ferry ports, including Cork and Dublin at that time.

Connaught IFA vice-president Pat Donnellan told the media the protest had little support in the area, and he argued it was not in the interests of local farmers and the economy of the region that the campaign continued.

1995: Indicative of the growing numbers by then using Knock, Chairman Duffy welcoming Ryanair's 10th anniversary in May, said the airport was targeting a passenger throughput of 180,000 by the end of the year and 250,000 by 1997. "It took Cork Airport 17 years to reach a throughput of 140,000, but Knock International Airport passed this benchmark in its 4th year of operation," he announced proudly.

In May also, Crossair, a Swiss company, inaugurated weekly charter flights which brought in touring parties from Hamburg, Berlin and Switzerland over a five-month summer period. The big attraction was boating on the Ballyconnell/Shannon/Erne waterway.

In June the one millionth passenger passed through the Airport. It was a landmark reached well in advance of the predictions of the nay-sayers back in the early 1980s.

1996: With funding scarce, marketing budgets at the Airport had always been very lean, but a major marketing initiative was unveiled in January 1996 when Minister Michael Lowry allocated £67,000 to the Airport for promotional work. The aim of the blueprint was to establish Knock as the jet airport for a 69-mile radius covering counties Galway, Mayo, Sligo, Roscommon, Leitrim, Donegal, Monaghan and Longford.

Working with Tourism Minister Enda Kenny and tour operator DER and Cosmos ICS Tours from Zurich and Basle, the Board planned to attract 15,000 visitors to the region between March and September. Confidence was now growing, with the Board reporting a profit of £772,000 for the previous three years, while the outcome for 1996 was likely to be in the region of £400,000 profit, with traffic growing at the rate of 18% per year. French and Spanish charters were also beginning to materialise.

*   *   *

May 30 marked the tenth anniversary of the Airport opening and Charles Haughey, now retired from politics, was on hand to unveil a bronze bust of the late Monsignor Horan in the main concourse. Sculpted by Robin Buick, it was of a 'builder with vision'.

Paying tribute to Horan, the former Taoiseach said the Monsignor saw that there would be no real progress without a major and dramatic improvement in access transport for the Western region. The Monsignor could also see that merely improving the existing land-based transport facilities would not be enough and, showing that clear insight which distinguished leadership, he identified a regional airport as the key to the future. "His persistence, shrewdness and determination overcame inertia, bureaucratic resistance and surprisingly widespread opposition," said Haughey.

He went on: "This monument will remind us of many things: the power of an idea, the value of imagination and vision, the need at every level of our nation's affairs for courageous leadership and the great inherent strength that resides in every community waiting to be harnessed.

"Monsignor Horan was unique. Though one could, in one sense, say that we shall not see his like again, I would prefer to hope that we shall see many more like him in the future because there are still mountains to be climbed, and room for imaginative projects to be conceived and achieved.

"Perhaps his greatest legacy to his beloved Connaught and to Ireland will be to serve as an inspiration to many others who will follow him in creating new opportunities in the very exciting but equally challenging era now opening up for the Irish people," he said.

Chairman Duffy described Horan as 'one of the greatest Mayomen of the 20th century', who had been born in Partry, a mere six miles from where Haughey first saw the light of day. By authorising the project, he said Haughey had done more for the people of Connaught than any politician in the last hundred years.

Earlier that day, at lunch in Breaffy House Hotel in Castlebar, Haughey related a story told by a local barman that summed up Monsignor Horan's infectious enthusiasm as well as the faith he inspired in others:

"You know," said the barman, "the Monsignor fancied himself on the accordion. One night he took it out at a concert beyond. He played 'The Coolin'. Now do you know anything about Irish music? Well, 'The Coolin' is a real difficult tune to play, even if you're good. Oh, now this was good all right. There was an oul fella there that was a real traditional musician himself.

"You could see he was in agony. He just pulled down the cap over his face and took a suck out of his pipe. But, you know, when the Monsignor was finished, the oul fella sure clapped like everyone else."

On the following day, at Knock Shrine, after a commemorative Mass, EU Commissioner Padraig Flynn laid a wreath at Monsignor Horan's tomb.

And Minister Enda Kenny launched the Monsignor Horan International Air Rally, with forty aircraft from flying clubs in Ireland, England and Scotland participating. He announced that the Government had approved a £2m package to fund a runway lighting system that would eliminate 95% of diversions. The airport had been experiencing an average of 40 diversions each year up to then, he said. (See Appendix for up-to-date diversion rates.)

Duffy and his Board enjoyed a very good working relationship with Kenny, and Duffy commented that, as Minister for Tourism and Trade, the Castlebar man was very helpful. "He organised five inward flights from Germany, Switzerland and Holland to our Airport, bringing some 15,000 visitors to our region. Unfortunately those flights are no longer available," he says.

On December 16, the local media was invited to fly to Stansted to mark the tenth year of Ryanair operating out of Knock. At a reception in London, a smiling Duffy described CEO Michael O'Leary as, "Young, dynamic, commercial, aggressive, ruthless and, at times, overbearing but he is a huge success – not just in Ireland, and has no peer for this type of operation anywhere in the world. Both Ryanair and Knock are geared to reach heights of achievements yet undreamed of," he predicted.

O'Leary said Knock was the country's most successful non-government owned airport. A few days earlier he had written that during the difficult years of financial crisis which was faced by Ryanair in the late 1980s and early '90s, it was no secret that Ryanair would not have survived at Knock without the help and support of the Airport Board, who introduced a joint programme of lower costs in return for lower air fares and more traffic from Ryanair. "Knock and Ryanair have delivered Monsignor Horan's dream," he said.

The dynamic 32-year-old executive could afford to smile for in 1997 he was to be paid a £9.8 million bonus and would own 18 per cent of the airline in advance of its going public. When it was floated, O'Leary's shares were valued at £71 million, and staff investments doubled in worth from £5,000 to £10,000.

The growing prosperity of Ryanair was enthusiastically greeted back at Knock: the airline they had attached their star to in very precarious times was beginning to soar, and the future beckoned promisingly. But, as inevitably happens in business, there would be tension between the two companies up the road.

1997/1998: Knock had continued to search for opportunities to get its industrial park up and running. Despite efforts, it had singularly failed to do so. But prospects behind the scenes had been developing over 1996 and were now beginning to look promising. US billionaire Ross Perot was, it was whispered, interested in creating an EU headquarters for a freight-forwarding operation from the East Mayo base, at an estimated cost of £30m. Perot had stood for the US Presidential election some years earlier. (See Chapter 21 for Industrial Zone developments.)

In the General Election of June 1997 the Rainbow Coalition was defeated and Fianna Fáil and the PDs formed the new Government with Bertie Ahern as Taoiseach. And in October Mary McAleese succeeded Mary Robinson (who served one term) as President of Ireland.

Moves to pick up the pieces and move ahead in search of new investment continued at the Airport. The whole area was desperate for jobs. At the time, Coca-Cola advertised a recruitment campaign for 60 specialist jobs for their start-up in Ballina, and were astounded to receive 3,500 applications. Queues formed on the streets around the interview centre on the banks of the River Moy. An IDA executive commented that the people with the necessary skills were already living in the vicinity or wanted to come home.

"There is no problem with labour or skills, we have checked, and a lot of the reasons for not attracting new start-ups is down to access," the IDA spokesman told *Business and Finance*. That was precisely the point Monsignor Horan had been hammering out almost twenty years earlier.

*   *   *

1999: A very substantial threat to revenue streams at the airport had been looming for some time. Around that period the EU had been moving to close down intra-EU duty-free shopping and, while, there had been stern resistance from airports, the resolution became law at the end of June 1999. A drop in its meagre profits seemed inevitable for Knock.

The Duty-Free shop had been set up in 1987 under Monsignor Grealy's chairmanship when a number of commercial options was being examined. Airport director and Spar supermarket owner in nearby Charlestown, John Mahon, recalls that the proposal for the duty-free shop was going out to tender when he went to Monsignor Grealy and advised him to keep it in-house. "I felt we could run it ourselves within the Company, and I managed it for the first year, free of charge, to get it up and running. In the first six months it made £80,000," he said.

The shop prospered still further and Mahon says it was the vehicle that paid the staff wages because there were not enough passengers coming through in the early years to meet costs from flights alone. Mahon also did a sponsored slimathon to raise £5,000 for fitting out the shop.

When the duty-free shop status was abolished in 1999, the Airport Board was without a lifeline. The projected loss was £600,000 per year, and the annual wage bill was running at £660,000. It was then that the £6 levy on outward passengers was introduced.

"The airport could not have survived without the levy," asserts Mahon. It was a point fully concurred with by Michael McGrath:

"Without the duty-free sales we had nothing and had to secure alternative revenue. It was a real crisis and we had to introduce it," he recalls.

The move led to an immediate confrontation with Ryanair, Michael O'Leary threatening to pull his planes from the airport if the decision was not rescinded. He argued it cut against the thrust of low-cost fares. Around the same time, Kerry Airport was imposing a £5 departure charge to fund on-going development, and, in retaliation, Ryanair threatened to cut services there also.

The Knock-Ryanair row was raised in the Dáil by the Mayo deputies in January 1999, Deputy Jim Higgins calling Ryanair's threat nothing other than 'sheer blackmail'. He said Ryanair knew it had Knock literally over a barrel. Ryanair accounted for 90% of Knock air traffic business. Michael O'Leary and Ryanair knew well that by pulling out of Knock, they would not just cripple Knock Airport, they would close it, said Higgins.

"Ryanair," he said, "would like to have Knock Airport understand that they have always done Knock Airport a service or a favour. It was a service or a favour that paid Ryanair rich dividends. When Ryanair was a struggling company, the people of the West rallied and supported it. They paid, and still pay way above the going rate. While Ryanair offered cut-price fares of £19.99 from Dublin to UK destinations, passengers to and from Knock paid an additional £120 or £130 to and from the same destinations. People paid this out of a sense of service and loyalty to Knock and Ryanair."

Higgins argued that without duty-free sales, there was literally nowhere to go and he appealed to the Minister (Mary O'Rourke) to approve a subvention of £1 million for Knock to ensure that the vision of Monsignor Horan was not extinguished. It was a small price to pay to retain a service that linked the remotest corner of rural Ireland with the capital of the United Kingdom in less than one hour. "It links fathers working in Kilburn with their families in Kiltimagh and young people working in Glasgow with their families in Geesala. There is a social and economic dimension to this," he said.

Deputy Kenny said he disagreed with Michael O'Leary's decision. Knock was being used as a pawn. "I am well aware of the ruthlessness of this cut-throat business. He has a duty and, as the manager Michael McGrath has pointed out, it is a question of survival, but the Government has a duty to ensure that the infrastructure of this region is developed."

Deputy Beverley Cooper-Flynn disclosed that in 1992 Ryanair was paying a landing fee of £7 per passenger. Now it paid £2.50 for the first 60,000 passengers and nothing for passengers in excess of 60,000. That worked out at an average rate per passenger of £1.80, she said.

"One would not get from Swords into the city centre on a bus for that amount of money. Ground-handling fees are provided free of charge because the job is done by the staff of the Airport," she said.

Minister of State at the Department of Health and Children Dr. Tom Moffatt and Deputy Michael Ring also called for the Ryanair threat to be removed. Ring called on the Minister to meet the Board as a matter of urgency to see how she could help in solving the difficulties at Knock Airport. "The Board together with Ryanair must take much of the blame. Both have acted very badly in this matter," he said.

Minister for Public Enterprise Mary O'Rourke, who was a constant publicity target for Michael O'Leary's full-page advertisements critical of government transport aviation policy, was in trenchant mood.

"This is blackmail. Michael O'Leary is doing very well out of Knock Airport. I am extremely angry at the way he is using a people, a region and an airport. This is a disgraceful act; a company making good money from a route is capriciously saying that that is the end and it is pulling out," she said in horror.

Airport Manager Michael McGrath was delegated to negotiate with O'Leary. "We stuck to our guns. I presented our case. Our point of view prevailed and there was mutual respect for each other's positions after that," he said. Ryanair recognise Knock as a special case. The levy remained and was later to be rounded off at 10 euro, applied on all departures from the airport. Over the years it has been a bone of contention with some travellers, many in the UK writing to the *Irish Post* and Mayo papers to express their opposition. The Development Fee issue is addressed in Chapter 20.

*   *   *

2000: The Board made submission to the Department of Public Enterprise in January 2000 for the provision of daily Knock-Dublin return flights under the Public Service Obligation (PSO) grant scheme. This allowed Knock passengers access to other destinations through Dublin Airport.

Acting on a development plan drawn up by Murray O Laoire Stanley, who were involved in the development of the new Manchester Airport, the Board made an application for upgrading of the airport facilities under the National Development Plan 2000 - 2006 and submitted ten projects for funding. Planning permission was sought and obtained for all the developments.

But, in January 2000, with short-time working again introduced as passenger numbers remained stubbornly turgid, staff expressed concerns about the future of the Airport in local newspapers.

"We are genuinely nervous about our future," the staff wrote in a letter to all Board members. While making the point that they acknowledged the good work by past and present Board members, they raised the possibility of a Task Force made up of Board members and 'influential people from industry, tourism, regional development and the aviation sectors to boost business'.

257

They further stated that the average wages of staff were then 20/30 per cent below the average industrial wage and that the specialist training required of airport staff was being wasted because of the high turnover of people leaving the Company. The letter also called for the appointment of a staff representative to the Board as a first step in a change to a more consultative and partnership-based approach.

2001: During the year the UK experienced its largest recorded outbreak of foot-and-mouth disease. The first case was identified on February 19. Ireland took strict precautions. The outbreak had an adverse impact on travel around that period, as did the horrendous attack on the Twin Towers in New York on September 11.

2002: On January 1 2002 Ireland, along with eleven other EU countries, replaced its bank notes and coins with the euro. The currency was not the only thing to change: having given 21 years' voluntary service to the airport, Cathal Duffy advised his co-Directors of his intention of stepping down within a year. "This was to give them an opportunity to select new Board members (preferably equity-investing directors) to carry on and build on the success that was already there," said Duffy as he stepped down on 15 May, 2002.

"I handed over the airport to my successor with a clean balance sheet, a successful developing business and borrowings of £192,000," says the Castlebar man.

While Duffy's autocratic style of leadership would have inevitably raised hackles, even his staunchest critics credited him with holding the company together at a really difficult time. Michael McGrath, who served as Manager for fifteen years and would have liked to have seen a more progressive approach to the business, nevertheless praised the commitment of the Directors during that period. "If they hadn't stuck with it at the time it would not have happened and I take my hat off to them, including Jim Ryan, Cathal Duffy, Seamus Monaghan and others. Now we are seeing the efforts of all of the people who have gone before bearing fruit," he said when interviewed.

And engineer John Balfe acknowledges Duffy's contribution, first on the steering committee and later on the Board: "He was genuinely there for the good of the West, and as Chairman he kept it tight when it had to be kept tight, at a time when fingers would have been pointed if things started to go wrong."

Jim Mitchell, the man who had a turbulent relationship with Monsignor Horan, died in December 2002 after a three-year fight with cancer. He was 56. He will be best remembered in the region for his 'foggy, boggy' remark but nationally he will be remembered for his outstanding performance as Chairman of the Public Accounts sub-committee that investigated the DIRT tax evasion scam in 1999 which netted £400m in back taxes. It was the first time a Dáil sub-committee had taken on an investigative role and Mitchell determined that this type of inquiry would be seen as a viable alternative to expensive and bureaucratic tribunals.

CHAPTER NINETEEN

2002– 2006 New chairman and management – 3 millionth passenger –
Airport wins awards – More carriers on route – Charter holiday
business expands – Defence Forces fly in – Plans for new hotel –
Decentralisation move sanctioned – Charles J. Haughey dies

Celtic Tiger and new vision reap dividends and awards

WHEN Cathal Duffy stepped down as Chairman of the Board in 2002 he was succeeded by well-known businessman in the UK, Patrick Joseph Kennedy, who brought with him a strong business acumen and high level business and investment contacts.

Kennedy, who is a native of Doocastle in Mayo, is one of the most successful Irish business people in the UK. Leaving school at 14 and emigrating to England to find work at 15, he was employed for a period in the construction industry in Britain before establishing his own construction and cable-laying company which he grew to become a multi-million enterprise. He also established the Kennedy Charitable Foundation through which he has supported hundreds of causes with generous donations both in Ireland and the UK, including peacemaking in Northern Ireland. He now chairs PJK Investments which specialises in major shopping centre developments in the UK and which is run by his son, John.

Early in 2002 he was asked to join the Airport Board as Director with other new bloods, Sean Noone from Belmullet and Brian McEniff from Donegal, and his experience and clinical analysis of the situation made him an automatic choice as Chairman when Cathal Duffy stepped down in May.

Passenger numbers were then just short of 200,000 for the full year. Kennedy quickly set about building up a strong and creative management team to explore and tackle opportunities. Marketing was addressed, new contacts within the business established and new facilities were provided at the Airport. And it helped that the economy, in the shape of the Celtic Tiger, was very much picking up.

Kennedy brought on board Leitrim-born Liam Scollan as Chief Executive in 2002. Scollan has worked extensively in regional development in Ireland and the UK. He was previously Chief Executive of the Western Development Commission where he built the organisation from scratch and championed a wide range of regional development policies, many of which have since been adopted by Government. In the 1980s he played a leading role in urban and regional development in both County and Regional Authorities in the UK East Midlands where his work led to significant job creation and regeneration in towns. The Chairman and his CEO immediately hit it off and they brought new dynamism to the task.

Since then the Airport has experienced record-breaking passenger numbers and business growth. "In facing the challenge of developing the Airport, priorities were terribly important and one thing was certain – there was nothing to talk about without more airlines and more routes and more passengers at the Airport. That was where the focus was," recalls Scollan.

The Board led by Chairman Kennedy allowed the management at the Airport to play an aggressive, expansionary role. "There has been trust all round, trust in the Chairman, trust in the Board and between Board members, trust in the management, and trust and commitment among the staff. I have never worked anywhere where I have seen such commitment from people at all levels as I have seen here since arriving in 2002," says Scollan.

Capitalising on a time when people now had more money to fly, the priority was to go to all the airlines and show what the airport had to offer. Ryanair, Aer Arann, Aer Lingus, bmibaby, MyTravelLite, easyJet, Jet 2, British Airways and many more smaller airlines and airports in the UK, and, crucially, all the tour operators, were visited.

"We were armed with great information. We are able to tell airlines that more than three quarters of the people in the region wanted to fly from Ireland West Airport and that people in the UK were frustrated with the absence of sufficient flights through the airport. We decided to offer good but fair commercial deals and we just kept trying. Most of all though we were armed with great people with great commitment. The airlines and the routes and the passengers came," he says.

2003: In June hundreds of people gathered at Knock International Airport to see a Boeing 747 land with 500 pilgrims returning from Lourdes. The aircraft stood almost as high as the Airport's Air Traffic Control tower. It was only the second of its type to land since the Airport's establishment.

On 30 March, MyTraveLite started a daily service to Birmingham which in year one carried over 80,000 passengers: Joe Kennedy's legendary network of connections produced almost instant results here. It just happened that one of the Kennedy directors for over 30 years, Robert Hough, a lawyer by profession, also happened to be chairman of Liverpool Airport. "It was unbelievable, two chairmen of two airports from the Kennedy company," says Joe Kennedy. "We wanted someone to put on a flight from Birmingham because we knew for years of the need for it. Robert put me in touch with Tim Jeans who used to be with Ryanair, and was now with MyTraveLite, and within three months we had a scheduled service on the Birmingham route," he says.

The Airport achieved 250,000 passengers for the full year. By now employment stood at 60 people.

2004: Passenger numbers grew to 375,000 for the full year. Charter passenger numbers reached 58,000. New arrival and departure facilities, check-in and baggage-handling systems were completed. Employment rose to over 120 people.

The Airport won 'Best Regional Airport' accolade at the annual Airline of the Year Awards ceremony presented by the Air Transport Users Council of the Chambers of Commerce of Ireland. The Airport was the first winner in the category. And making it two successes in three years Ireland West Airport Knock was again to be named 'Best Regional Airport of the Year' at a ceremony in Dublin in 2006.

2005: Between these successes, in 2005, the customer service staff at the Airport was voted as the very best in the business by easyJet airline. easyJet's customers voted the Airport as having the best Check-In process across its entire network of 68 European airports. The airport also achieved second place in the category of Best Sales Desk in Europe. easyJet have been operating a daily flight service from Knock to London Gatwick since January 2005. And the Airport was ranked in the Top 10 on punctuality in Ryanair's network of 107 airports.

Another notable landmark was achieved on 18 January 2005 when Mrs Margaret Mary Hawksworth from Wilmslow, Cheshire, became the 3 millionth passenger to have used the airport since it opened in 1986. She arrived on the bmiBaby daily flight from Manchester which had been inaugurated the previous year. Née O'Shaughnessy, she is a native of Ballintubber, Co. Roscommon.

In April of the same year the Defence Forces 29th Infantry Group, who deployed to Kosovo in October 2004, returned to Ireland, with the Ist Chalk of the 213-strong contingent flying into Knock. The airport had campaigned for the business, and it marked the first time troops returning from overseas duty flew in through Mayo. The Deputy Chief of Staff (Support) Major-General Dermot Earley and the General Officer Commanding the 4th Western Brigade, Brigadier General Fred Swords, met the group on arrival, with the Mayor of Mayo, Eddie Staunton, in attendance. Staff at the Airport have fond memories of the carnival atmosphere which pertained as loved ones were reunited.

In July the Minister for Community, Rural and Gaeltacht Affairs, Éamon Ó Cuiv and the Minister of State with responsibility for the Office of Public Works, Tom Parlon, visited the site adjacent to the

Airport chosen for the new HQ for the Department of Community, Rural and Gaeltacht Affairs. The move had been announced earlier but here now were the two Ministers directly involved photographed under an OPW sign proclaiming 'Reserved for Government Decentralisation'.

The six-acre site has been designated to house 160 civil servants as part of the government's major decentralisation programme. Minister Ó Cuiv indicated that building would start in 2006 and would be completed in 2007 when staff would start to move in. He said that despite what the sceptics were saying and despite all the doom and gloom in some of the Dublin newspapers about the Government's decentralisation plans, "You can take it from me that when the building goes up here, it will be the HQ of the Department of Community, Rural and Gaeltacht Affairs," he pledged.

The Airport had another great year in 2005 with passenger numbers reaching 530,000, an increase of 42% on the previous year's figures. The Airport's scheduled routes business increased by 34% as a result of a number of new daily services operated by a choice of international airline brands whilst the holiday charter business had almost trebled since 2002 to more than 55,000 passengers carried in 2005.

First to pioneer the sun charter service was Paul Claffey, MD of Mid West Radio, who started music trips to the Caribbean, Spain, Portugal and South Africa direct from Knock. "The torturous days of having to drive for up to three hours to Dublin in order to get a flight are well and truly over," said Claffey who established his own company Paul Claffey Tours. He identified a niche in the market and has seen it rapidly grow. His market is the over-40s who are interested in flying direct from Knock to sun destinations with accommodation, music, fun and craic all part of the package.

He recalls that he filled his first music trip to Spain in 1997 within three days, and had done between 25 and 30 trips from Knock to that particular destination by 2006. "The success of the first charter showed me there was terrific potential in Knock despite being told that a travel company had done a survey which indicated people did not want to travel from Knock because they did not want their neighbours to know where they were going on holidays."

After opening up Spain and Portugal he tried a holiday package to the Caribbean, again direct from Mayo. "I had visions of what Monsignor Horan might think: have your breakfast at Knock and your evening meal in the Caribbean and that whole kind of buzz got me going. All of the 325 seats were booked in the first few days, and we ended up with five trips to the Caribbean. You'd have to admire the foresight of the Monsignor. His idea was probably to bring them in to the Basilica in Knock, but, when you look at the bigger picture now, he must be delighted people are going both ways," he adds.

He believes transatlantic flights to Knock would work on a weekly basis during certain times of the year. "I don't see why we cannot do music holidays into the West also, from Germany and from America, especially with some aircraft coming in to Ireland empty," reasons Claffey who operates his tour programme in association with Joe Walsh Tours.

Other tour companies introduced a range of new holiday packages to European sun, winter ski and pilgrim destinations in 2004. Operators include Stein Travel, Falcon JWT, Slattery's Sun, Joe Walsh Tours, Concorde Travel and newcomers Mayo Travel and ski experts Topflight. Tour operators Sunworld and Sunway now also offer holiday packages from Knock. In 2005, a total of 45 daily scheduled flights each week, connecting to 574 world-wide destinations, were operated by airlines bmibaby, easyJet, Ryanair, and British Airways' franchise, Loganair.

The additional services put in place included new Ryanair routes to London Gatwick and Luton airports to complement its busy London Stansted route. Following the success of its Manchester route, bmibaby also launched a new Birmingham City route which was set to increase to twice daily rotations for the Summer 2006 season as well as an extra Saturday service from March '06. British low-cost carrier easyJet was also introduced as a new airline operator with the launch of its London -Gatwick service. In July 2005, British Airways partner Loganair commenced its daily service to Dublin following its award of the PSO (Public Service Obligation) contract.

In December 2005, the Western Development Commission (WDC), a statutory body for the region, announced it would fund expansion of the Airport's car parking, catering and retail facilities in a €1 million investment programme. The Commission believed the improvements were necessary to cope with a predicted doubling in passenger numbers over the next five years.

Support was also provided by Minister Éamon Ó Cuiv under the Clar initiative, through the provision of €1.3m over a three-year period, and Transport Minister Martin Cullen contributed an additional €2.35m. The Clar contribution allowed two of three new fire tenders to be purchased, enabling the elevation of the airport to Category Nine emergency services cover and boosting the range of routes offered. The new 6x6 Titan tenders, costing €550,000 each, can carry up to 11,000 litres of water and 1,500 litres of foam which can be projected up to a distance of 80 metres. The staff of over 20 fire-fighting personnel under-went a rigorous training programme on the newest fire-fighting equip-ment in the country.

Minister Cullen said the Government was 'ready, willing and able' to invest in the airport, and was working closely with management to ascertain the precise scope of the infrastructure required to allow the Airport to conform with all relevant safety standards as it developed into the future. Mayo County Council also presented €100,000 in 2005 to enhance the landing facilities at the airport.

In keeping with its community ethos, staff at Ireland West Airport Knock engaged in its third major fund-raising drive to raise money for charities in the West of Ireland in 2005. Donations totalling €41,000 were given to three charities, Western Care's Highland Lodge in Kilkelly, the Mayo Roscommon Hospice and Hope House in Foxford.

The money was raised by organising a 25-Drive Card Game which took place in the Airport on 19 October 2005 as well as a very well attended Annual Gala Night which took place in the Belmont Hotel, Knock, on November 11 2005.

Scollan says the contribution which the Airport makes to the West and North West of Ireland is mostly felt in the tourism industry. "Our Airport's success is very much linked to the region's success and most especially to our €1.34 billion tourism industry. In 2005, the Airport, in partnership with our airlines and the tourism agencies, was responsible for bringing an estimated 310,000 overseas tourists into the region. In broad terms, this represents a quarter of all the overseas tourists who visited the Western region, or 61% of overseas visitors to the North West region."

In November 2005 a planning application was lodged, and subsequently granted, for a 103-bedroom hotel close to the Airport. Plans included a swimming pool, fitness centre, health spa, conference centre and parking space for 200 cars. The application was in the names of JP and Y Duffy.

One of the pleasing aspects about Ireland West Airport Knock is the pride staff take in the facility and their willingness to go the extra mile to help and assist passengers. It was therefore appropriate that longest-serving staff members were named and their loyal service marked at the 2020 Vision launch in 2005. They were Michael Grealy, Paul Morris, Ann Marie Murphy, Majella Walsh, Jim Corry, Pearse Concannon, Jimmy McNicholas, Elaine Harrison-Grealy, Gabriel Johnson, Aidan Horkan and Matt Macken.

*   *   *

2006: In March 2006 the first service from the West of Ireland to North East England became operational on the new bmibaby route to Durham Tees Valley Airport. The service, to operate four times weekly, was expected to provide direct access to the city hubs of Durham, Newcastle, Middlesborough, Sunderland and York. It was announced at the launch of the service that an additional 50,000 bed nights would result in a €4 million tourism spend by passengers. Destinations in 2006 included Cadiz, Crete, Lisbon, Salou, Salzburg, Split, Faro, Gran Canaria, Lanzarote, Malaga, Palma (Majorca) and city breaks. And Aer Arann commenced Leeds Bradford, Glasgow and Isle of Man routes.

Hundreds of invited guests packed into the Airport terminal on May 30 (2006) to mark the 20th anniversary of the official opening. They included former Taoiseach Albert Reynolds, former Minister and EU Commissioner Padraig Flynn, Minister for Finance Brian Cowen, former Chairman Seamus Monaghan and former Directors Ulick McEvaddy and John Mahon, and former Manager Michael McGrath.

Minister Cowen gave a powerful endorsement of the Airport's worth to the region. Referring to the Company's €30m expansion plans, he said he was present 'to ensure your proposals are heard in the inner circles of power in Dublin'. He hoped to have the €100m announced for regional airports in the 2005 Budget allocated by the end of 2006.

He acknowledged the building of Knock Airport as a major infrastructure project in its own right, providing not only an economic boost, but a timely psychological fillip which imbued an optimism in people about their future prospects at the time. He said the capacity of leadership to deliver was exhibited, creating jobs against all the odds and a motivation sincere in purpose to rally people around the idea that they could initiate change and shape their own future with the help of Government, rather than be passive observers on the sideline.

"It's very easy to forget exactly how bleak the picture appeared to be for this region and our country in the mid-1980s. In the year this airport opened we had the highest debt per capita in the world and a new record was set for levels of emigration. Our airwaves were full of programmes talking about the supposed end of rural Ireland and of the collapse of the West. It was in this landscape of despair that Monsignor James Horan's project stood out as a rare but bright symbol of hope."

He said the Airport represented all that was best about the West in terms of resilience, determination and optimism. Monsignor Horan had the vision to see that things could get better. He also recognised that it was important to put in place an infrastructure to provide the foundation for development. His dream was shared by the thousands of people who played their part in planning and building the airport. More importantly, the reality was that the Airport was making a major contribution to the performance and prospects of the West.

Pointing out that in the last five years €5 million in capital and current grants had been provided to the Airport, he said since becoming Minister for Finance he had met with the Management and Chairman of the Airport and they had outlined their plans for its future development. "Following reflections on these and other discussions, I am glad to say that the Government have included in our transport investment programme, Transport 21, an allocation of €100 million for capital investment in regional airports."

Minister Cowen said in response to the increased allocation, the Department of Transport had revised its investment scheme for regional airports. Under EU rules the revised scheme required EU State Aid approval which the Department of Transport was pursuing. He was hopeful that EU Commission approval would be given to the revised scheme during the course of 2006 and he was confident that the committed management team at the Airport would submit proposals under the then approved scheme that would provide every prospect of further Exchequer support for the Airport in the future and help ensure that the development plan could be assisted and made a reality.

Chairman Joe Kennedy thanked Minister Cowen for his great interest and said the prescription he dished out within the near future could cure any remaining ailments at the Airport! He paid tribute to all who had supported the Airport project over the years, including the Church which had continued to play a crucial role in its running and development. The late Monsignor Dominick Grealy took up the gauntlet following the death of Monsignor Horan, and today, Archbishop Michael Neary of Tuam and Monsignor Joseph Quinn, Parish Priest of Knock and Administrator of the Shrine were on the Board, he pointed out.

He also paid tribute to other former Chairmen, Seamus Monaghan and Cathal Duffy, and to the fund-raisers and 27 landowners who sold their land so that the project could be undertaken.

Managing Director Liam Scollan said the Company's vision was to have the region recognised as a premier tourist destination for people from all over the world, especially the United States. "So we will continue to build an airport that connects this region to at least 12 places in the UK, not just the current six; to at least half a dozen European destinations; to the United States on a continuous basis," he said.

He said in 2006 the Airport would support one million bed nights and tourists coming through the Airport would spend €76m in the region. By 2009 the Airport would be handling one million passengers and tourists coming through would spend over €120m a year and support an additional 1,600 tourism jobs in this region. Today 175 people worked around the site at Ireland West Airport Knock, he pointed out.

He praised Chairman Joe Kennedy, the management and staff for their commitment. "This Airport wants to be world class in its services. You have heard how our staff have attained that standard. However, we do not have Europe's best landing systems. We need Category 11 or 111a landing facilities; we have an aircraft taxiing area that is no longer large enough for the number of aircraft that want to land here and a terminal building that strained under the 3,000 people who passed through it in a few hours last Saturday. By 2015 this terminal building will need to be three times its current size.

"We not only need government funding – this airport deserves government funding. This year we will provide directly and indirectly €12m in tax and PRSI to the Government. Over the next 10 years, even with no further growth, contributions to the Exchequer will be €120m, not to mention other benefits to the region," he added.

He said Minister Cowen had already earned himself a chapter in the story of governmental support for the Airport when he committed €100m to the regional airports in his budget speech in 2005, an increase from 8.5m So too had Minister Ó Cuiv.

"I can certainly turn to the Government tonight and say we are supporting national tourism, national jobs and inward investment, national aviation and transport access and we are providing revenue back for the Government in large measures. Minister Cowen, equally this Airport needs the Government. As Monsignor Horan might have said, we need you to give a biteen of a push to release the money you provided and to address some key road and rail investments in the next national development plan," said Scollan.

Monsignor Joseph Quinn, parish priest of Knock and a member of the Airport Board, pointed to a bright future for religious tourism through Ireland West Airport. He indicated that all the heads of twenty major Marian Shrines throughout Europe would, on September 30, 2006, be flying in through the Airport to visit the Mayo Shrine, and that joint initiatives between the Airport and the Shrine would be developed to realise the potential that existed to grow foreign pilgrimages into Knock. (The link between Knock Shrine and the Airport is still very evident to those who use the Airport: the blue Knock Shrine kiosk sits close to the entrance, and sells Mass cards, rosary beads, religious books, holy water fonts, and Mass enrolment certificates. It has been operated by Marian Bones since the day the Airport opened.)

In a tribute to the many who helped Monsignor Horan and Monsignor Grealy raise over £4 million to complete the Airport, Knock Shrine Chief Steward Tom Neary regaled the attendance with anecdotes of fund-raising heroics, letters of appeal, Jumbo Quizzes, and the Monsignor Horan Roadshow! (See Chapter 10.)

And Aidan Horkan, one of the longest serving staff members, traced the development of the Airport, the commitment of the staff and the confidence there was in the future of the Airport, while Achill-born Terry Gallagher, Chairman of the Mayo Association in London, underlined the social role the Airport had played, easing the way for exiles who once had to endure 18 hours of continuous and uncomfortable travel by ferry and train before reaching their destinations.

Ryanair's Head of Communications Peter Sherrard announced his company would mark the 20th anniversary of the Airport by allocating 20,000 seats costing only 20 cent each to people travelling through Knock. He predicted that Ryanair would, within two years, be the largest airline in Europe. Referring to the success of Ryanair and Knock Airport, which both started out around the same time, he said they had 'proved the defeatists wrong, astoundingly so'.

Minister Cowen unveiled a specially commissioned bog oak sculpture *Art of the Possible,* by artist Ronnie Graham, as a tribute to the many people who played a role in making the Airport the beacon of regional development and success it is today.

In a special *Western People* supplement to mark the occasion, Taoiseach Bertie Ahern said the Airport stood out as a bright symbol of hope. "The Airport has an important role to play today as a central focus and as a hub for transport in the West. It continues therefore to have an important part to play in enabling the communities of the West and the broader Border Midland and Western Region to capitalise on their potential," he wrote, adding the Government recognised the Airport's 'unique role in promoting balanced regional development'.

Also coinciding with the landmark occasion, a small multi-denominational oratory on the upper floor of the main building adjacent to the main restaurant became operational, complete with specially commissioned altar, tabernacle, seating, stained glass windows and prayer mat. A discreet contemplative haven in a busy world.

*   *   *

Throughout the night of the 20th anniversary celebrations the name of Charles J. Haughey was mentioned often, from the podium by speakers and in animated conversation afterwards. He had been, after all, the politician who had given Monsignor Horan's dream the green light for take-off, and had stood steadfast behind the project when the going got tough.

He had opened the airport in 1986 and ten years later, had unveiled the bust of Monsignor Horan at the Airport. He was too unwell to accept the invitation to attend the 20th birthday celebrations. But the invitation delighted him. "Do people really want me to attend?" he had asked when he personally contacted MD Liam Scollan a few days before the event. When assured that that was the case, he said he'd have loved nothing better, but his doctors had advised against the trip West. "He was really chuffed to know that he would be so welcome," said Scollan, who added that Haughey had commented that the Airport had probably lost him an election!

On June 13 2006, just two weeks after the celebrations, Charles J. Haughey died at his Kinsealy home, at the age of 80. He had been fighting a battle against prostate cancer for the previous six years.

At his funeral Mass in Dublin, Haughey's Mayo roots were not forgotten. Kerry poet Brendan Kennelly told of Haughey's fondness for the poems of Raifteiri[9] and he quoted passages from *Cill Aodain:*

Anois teacht an earraigh, beidh an lá dul chun síneadh,
'Is tár éis ná Féil' Bríde ardóidh mé mo sheol,

---

9   Kiltimagh-born Antoine Ó Raifteiri (Anthony Raftery) (1784 - 1835) was an Irish language poet, one of the last of the wandering bards.

'O chuir mé im cheann é ní stopfaidh mé choíche
Go seasfa' mé thíos i lár Chontae Mhaigh Eo.
I gClár Chlainne Mhuiris a bheas mé an chéad oíche
'S i mBalla taobh thíos de 'thosós mé ag ól,
Go Coillte Mach rachad go ndéanfad cuirt mhíosa ann
I bhfogas dhá mhíle do Bhéal an Áth' Mhóir.

Concelebrants at the Requiem Mass were Haughey's brother Fr Eoghan, the Archbishop of Dublin Dr Diarmuid Martin and Monsignor Joseph Quinn, parish priest of Knock and a Board member of the Airport. Quinn's father, Paddy, a member of the Mayo 1936 All-Ireland winning side, had been a loyal supporter and friend of Haughey, and the Quinn household on New Antrim Street in Castlebar was an obligatory stop whenever the Fianna Fáil leader was in town.

Ireland West Airport, Mayo and the West of Ireland were well represented at the funeral. A Book of Condolence was opened at the Airport, on a table in front of the bust of Monsignor Horan, and thousands signed. Some were seen to bless themselves before signing.

*   *   *

Mary Croghan from Castlerea, Co. Roscommon, travelling on Mayo Travel's charter to Crete on 5 July 2006 became the Airport's four millionth passenger. The three-millionth-passenger landmark had been achieved on January 18, 2005.

*   *   *

With the team approach now very evident around the Airport – and recognised in awards won – management and staff speak with great pride of the memorable events, big and small, which have helped bond their growing numbers.

They point to events like the great annual staff-led fund-raising celebrations with music and fun late into the mornings when the whole local community seems to converge on the Airport and truly reveal it as the airport of the people.

Or the celebrating of new routes with music played and songs sung by Airport staff, or the Christmas parties, the Christmas Board dinners, or meetings with the Irish community in the UK and hearing their stories about what the Airport means to them and knowing how important those stories are.

MD Scollan recalls special moments like Gareth Edwards and the Welsh rugby legends arriving at the Airport and getting a special 'Knock' reception that almost swept them off their feet, or learning from businesses like the members of Mayo Industries Group just how vital the Airport is for them.

"Everyone here takes great pride from seeing the Airport emerge as a regional force for good, taking its place alongside other bodies with the region at their heart, notably the Government's Western Development Commission or the voluntary Council for the West," says Scollan.

But most of all, one suspects, seeing the cynicism and the 'bog image' being replaced with respect from around the country, respect won by genuine effort, efficiency, professionalism and goodwill of people.

Scollan wholeheartedly acknowledges the support the Airport commands around the region. "It is something I have seen only in sport. It is like a provincial team but with the ferocious commitment that we witness every summer when people support their county GAA team. The sense of pride which people have in the Airport is heartfelt and I can see it every time there is another milestone achieved, another route abroad, another building project, another award. We know that everything Ireland West Airport does means so much to so many in the region and abroad. Long may we remain an Airport close to people. While that is the case we can all be assured of many more milestones to come," he vows.

Directors of Ireland West Airport Knock since incorporation in 1981: Monsignor James Horan, Chairman 1981-86; Archbishop Joseph Cunnane, 1981-87; Patrick J. Casey, 1981-87; Cathal Duffy, 1981-2002; Seamus Monaghan, 1981-1992; Michael O'Malley, 1981-89; James Ryan, 1981-94; Michael Buckley, 1981-82; James Feehan, 1981-86; Patrick Ryan, 1981-1986; Stephen O'Neill, 1981; Robert Whitty, 1982-83; Raymond Byrne, 1983-84; Dominick Grealy, 1986-2005;

Michael Honan, 1986 -1992; John Mahon, 1986-2005; Ulick McEvaddy, 1986-1989; Archbishop Joseph Cassidy, 1987-1994; Peter Hanley, 1989-1992; Nancy Horan, 1994-1999; John Dillon, 1981-; Des Mahon, 1990-; Archbishop Michael Neary, 1997-; Joseph Kennedy (Chairman), 2002-; Brian McEniff, 2002-; Sean Noone, 2002-; Martin Gillen, 2002-; Liam Scollan, 2005-; John Travers, 2005-; Monsignor Joseph Quinn, 2006-.

CHAPTER TWENTY

Airport gets new name in marketing drive –
Monsignor Horan's thoughts on 'Knock' name –
Development fee and costs explained – Diversion rates set to lessen

Name change, development fee and diversion issues

WHEN the Airport was being planned and built, Monsignor James Horan was adamant that it was a facility for the whole region of Connaught and he insisted on its being known as Connaught Regional Airport. He also ensured the company was incorporated as Connaught Airport Development Company Ltd.

In his very first press release on the proposed airport on June 26 1980 he called it Connaught Regional Airport and said it would be located in the general area of Charlestown. The site chosen was less than four miles from Charlestown and 10 miles from Knock village.

He was at pains to point out to the media that it was not to be known as 'Knock' Airport, indeed wondered why they insisted on calling it 'Knock,' and one of his trademark 'branding' poses for photographers was a Connaught Regional Airport travel bag held aloft. The bags, incidentally, were manufactured in Kilkelly by Martin Nyland, upholsterer and leather goods specialist, and went on sale at £5 each in the summer of 1984.

Shortly before he died in 1986, the Monsignor attended a fund-raising function in Knock and declared that henceforth the airport would be known as Knock Airport, but it is clear that he was only playing to his local audience, for around the same time he told Tuam journalist Tom Gilmore in an interview for the *Pioneer Magazine* that he was always careful to call it Connaught Regional Airport. He called it Connaught because he had always maintained it was an airport for the region and the province's catchment area was obviously strategically important in the battle to win wider support.

In fact Horan so wanted to ensure that it was recognised as an airport for Connaught that he issued another press release in 1982 in which he said: "This Airport is not at Knock and was never meant for Knock any more than for any other village in Connaught. It is actually situated in the Charlestown-Kilkelly area, at a distance of ten miles from

Knock, and at a convenient distance from many of the surrounding towns. It will be of great benefit for people in Connaught who are actually up to 220 miles from any airport."

He continued: "It is very funny to note that since this controversy (over the building of the airport) started, thousands of people have been coming to Knock Shrine and were disappointed when they could not find the Airport on the spot. I am afraid that a deliberate attempt was made to make it a thoroughly and truly religious airport and thus a much more convenient 'cockshot' for the mavericks in our society. It is clear that the same elements in our society that sent us 'to hell or to Connaught' are now trying to keep us in the same backward conditions. It is hard to believe that their lead is slavishly followed by some politicians in this region who should have the interests of Connaught at heart."

Horan was right in his assessment that the ecclesiastical peg was a convenient one for some sections of the media to hoist the Airport on, and the adoption of the Knock location suited that 'knocking' agenda. It was, of course, also a location known to most people who sought to fix the place geographically in their mind.

That was one of the reasons he was a stickler for referring to the Airport as 'Connaught Regional' in television and radio interviews; he was worried that the slings and arrows being fired at the Airport would damage the Shrine's reputation. He had good reason to: he remembered the description by the *Sunday Tribune* of November 6, 1983: 'the airport that gave shrines a bad name'. It hurt.

Horan knew how to brand his product for the market though and when he launched a major newspaper campaign in September 1985 for funds he did so in a letter under 'Our Lady's Shrine, Knock' and headed the appeal KNOCK AIRPORT in bold lettering. Mind you, in the body of the text he used the Connaught Regional Airport title!

Former Minister and EU Commissioner Padraig Flynn revealed that one time in a conversation with Monsignor Horan, he kept calling it Knock Airport. "But the Monsignor would correct me and say it was Connaught Regional Airport! I'd reply it would always be known as Knock Airport. It had a ring to it and it was already known internationally through the connection with the Shrine. Mind you, some were calling it the Blessed Virgin Airport," he recollects with a smile.

When Horan died on August 1 1986 the Board of the Airport immediately indicated that henceforth it would be known as Horan International Airport and it was so renamed. However, the Knock name stuck in the public consciousness. The connections between Horan and Knock (of which he was Parish Priest) and the Pope/Horan/ Knock/ Airport linkage proved too strong to be supplanted in the minds of supporters who had been fed on the media's constant 'Knock' diet over a prolonged period.

In October 2005, the Airport was to get a new official name, and yet again it was to prove controversial. Now it would be known as Ireland West Airport Knock. The re-branding set out to assert the

Airport's positioning as the international air access hub serving the West and North West of Ireland whilst facilitating an increased awareness of the Airport in the overseas non-VFR (Visiting Friends & Relatives) tourist markets.

The Airport's then Director of Development, Kevin Heery, said the renaming and rebranding was the first step towards achieving long-term business goals. "Our research has shown us that we are consistently the leading airport associated with the West of Ireland and we hope our new name and logo tells our target markets what we are, where we're located and where we grew from. In deciding the name, we have built on the high recognition and strong affiliations there are with 'Knock Airport' whilst repositioning our business as main access hub of the West of Ireland. Our name and image say that we are proud of our past and confident of our future."

 Ireland West Airport Knock

According to the creative interpretation of the new logo, it symbolises a dove in flight, uniquely styled, silhouetted against a sphere or the earth's globe. The bird is breaking free, reaching out and rising to new horizons – an apt metaphor for global travel and the Airport's future strategic development. The wings' edges and tail feathers depict the rugged west of Ireland coastline and denote the Airport's geographic location and catchment area.

However, what was perceived as the 'downgrading' of the Knock connection led to calls for a rethink on the new name. The Claremorris Electoral area meeting of Mayo County Council members unanimously proposed, at a meeting in April 2006, that the word Knock should be restored to the front of the new title.

Cllr John Cribbin said they were proud of Knock Airport and its role in the life of the region. "Msgr Horan would turn in his grave if he thought Knock was being pushed to the rear as it clearly is with the new name," he said. Little did he realise how hard Horan had worked to have it known as 'Connaught Regional' all those years before!

A whole programme on RTÉ's Joe Duffy's popular *Liveline* programme was devoted to the issue on April 21 2006, with the majority of views supporting the retention of the Knock name in a more prominent format. However, Ballyhaunis Chamber of Commerce and others expressed satisfaction that the new name positioned the Airport in the correct marketing category and field of international identification.

Chief Executive Liam Scollan remembers that when he joined the Airport in 2002 he visited British Airways in Heathrow. When he told the receptionist, an English lady, that he was from 'Knock Airport' she enquired where in the Middle East this airport was!

Said Scollan: "Many English people, not to mention mainland Europeans, have no idea where Knock is. We had a passenger arrive last year at our airport believing he was in Belgium. When an airport expands to the international level it is advisable that people should recognise what country it is in and where about in the country it is. Connaught Regional Airport did signify that it was a province in Ireland but then most non-Irish would not know what 'Connaught' was. As someone from Connaught and having lived in England for 10 years I was very aware of just how little is known of our provincial names. The later name of 'Knock' had a similar difficulty. Eventually, it was decided to call it something that had 'Ireland' in it, showing that it was in the 'West' of Ireland and also that it retained that all important link with its spiritual route – Knock."

The new name basically was a return to the original idea that the Airport was built to serve Connaught and was connected to the Shrine in a special way also. It was also a name that was more easily recognisable for marketing throughout the world and that could only help more tourists find their way directly to the West of Ireland. The name 'Knock' would of course be retained and highlighted. Furthermore, a symbol had been developed that reflected for the first time the spiritual connection which the Airport had, he said.

Scollan was very taken by the words of a Donegal woman, Annette O'Donnell of Inver, who wrote to the Airport explaining the symbol in a beautiful way:

"As one who has used Knock Airport several times during the past year I have always found such a welcome from all your staff. Delighted with the new name. We on the West coast have for so long been forgotten by the powers-that-be, and what a fab logo. For me I see the West coast, see the Dove of Peace, I see world horizons, I see the voice of the west announcing a new future for you all. I hope as your numbers continue to grow that you will not lose what is so special about your airport and that is your Cead Mile Fáilte that awaits all who travel through your airport."

Airport Company Chairman Joe Kennedy says it should be remembered that 60m people live in Britain and 95% of those didn't know where Knock was. "We have to let people know where we are, where Knock is – it is our duty to provide a signpost for those 55m people living beside us. It is commonsense. We do not want to hurt anyone. It's just good business to let people know where we are.

"Everyone around Mayo and the West of Ireland know where Knock is, of course, and here it will never change: it will always be Knock, Knock Airport, Knock Shrine, it will never go away, nor should it. I used to refer to Shannon as Rineanna, and still do at times; when I was growing up it was Rineanna. It takes generations to change a name," he says pragmatically.

Scollan says the big challenge facing the Airport in the first decade of the 21st century is to build more routes into Europe, to the USA and the world and to attract people, including tourists who are very unfamiliar with Ireland. "We faced difficult choices in the past 20 years to get the airport built, to get it to survive and more recently to thrive. The new name and the very special logo was created in the face of the even tougher challenge ahead of attracting people from around the world to the West of Ireland and at the same time standing clearly for the fact that there is also a spiritual dimension to coming to this part of the world too."

There is a lot in a name of course. Many people grew up with the 'Knock' name, and it is near and dear to them: they identify with it and the battles won. They will always remember it as Knock. Others will be quite happy with Ireland West Airport Knock. And in the future, as the challenges shift and change, a new name will undoubtedly be found.

Monsignor Horan, the target of so many media slings and arrows, once observed he had fared well with the media and the ensuing publicity had been beneficial to his work in so many ways. He would surely have smiled over the 'new name' debate, recognising that while people were talking about his Airport it was on a winner.

Rationale behind Development Fee

ANOTHER issue which constantly raises its head is the development charge of €10 imposed on passengers over 12 years of age departing from the Airport. It was initially introduced when the Duty-Free shops concession was ended by the EU in the late '90s. The new charge led to an immediate dispute with Ryanair which, as a low-cost airline, did not agree with levy charges being imposed or people being asked to pay a separate charge.

Views vary on the charge. A Mayoman living in London N9 for 20 years, Ray Gallagher, complained to the *Irish Post* in '06 that he travelled regularly to Knock with his family of four and said the fee of 40 euro for each departure was 'wholly unacceptable'.

An Achill man flying to London told *The Irish Times* nobody was happy with the fee.

Another user of the airport, Mark McSweeney, visiting Leitrim with his family, was annoyed that on the way back to the UK they would be hit by the fee. "It's about supporting the area, isn't it?" he asked. "It's not fair on tourists."

Christy Moran, chairman of Westport's Liverpool Supporters' Club, heading off with colleagues on a flight to Manchester to see Liverpool play West Ham, said he didn't have a problem with the development fee. "I was discussing it here with the boys travelling with me and they didn't realise they had to pay it, but I don't think it is a problem, I don't begrudge it to them (Company). If you had to drive to Dublin and stopped on the way for a bit of food it would cost that at least, and you'd have to leave at 5 or 6 in the morning. We left Westport to come here less than an hour ago. It's wonderful. We'll have time to sit down and relax before going on the flight; what more do you want?"

Joe, from Tuam, who lives in Manchester, gave his view: "My wife and I were giving out about paying the €10 fee. It hasn't been properly explained, but my wife was saying if it goes towards the airport and keeps it open that is fair enough really . . . if not we'd have to go to Shannon or Dublin. It's much more convenient to come home directly to visit with the baby, much more convenient than four hours on the road to and from Dublin."

Said another, Tom, from Sligo: "Nobody likes paying fees, but they apply at many airports around the world. And what people forget is that if they fly out through Dublin they incur a whole rake of charges, including road toll charges, meal charges, petrol charges and much higher charges at a nightmarish car park. Put against that, €10 is nothing."

A woman from Irishtown, Co. Mayo, flying back with her daughter to Manchester, said she never really agreed with the €10 fee. "When you are born and bred over here you don't expect to pay. I asked once what it was for, but I don't really remember the explanation I got."

A Mayo man, seeing his daughter and granddaughter off, has great loyalty to the memory of the Monsignor and his Airport. "I have four daughters in the UK, and I don't see the levy as any big deal, given the convenience we have here," he said.

A couple from West Mayo said they'd prefer not to have to pay the fee, "But we know it is there." However, they observed there should be more information about the charge.

Originally vehemently opposed to the levy, the Chief Executive of Ryanair, Michael O'Leary, said his company was against additional charges but recognised Knock was a special case. He conceded costs for carriers were low at Knock and that enabled new routes to be developed. "One of the problems in aviation is having this huge public service obligation (PSO) subsidy. The money should be given to the airports, for marketing, etc. It's not doing anything for developing traffic to Knock or the West of Ireland," he said.

While views may differ, there was almost complete unanimity that much could be done at the Airport to more fully explain the charge. Many passengers complained there was no notice satisfactorily explaining what the money is used for.

It is a point readily acknowledged by Airport MD Scollan who said the Company was doing everything it could to make sure people were more informed. "We have written to all the airlines and scores of tour operators asking them to display our Development Fee to people purchasing seats. The problem here is that people do not have to contact Ireland West Airport before making a booking so we are reliant on others to ensure people are informed. We now have better displays around the Airport explaining the facts," he said.

He said Ireland West Airport Knock like all other airports charged for its services and facilities. Other airports charged service fees and collected them through the airlines. "Most include them in the taxes, fees and charges you see at the time of booking your airline ticket. You pay for it when you are paying for your ticket. Here the difference is that most of our regular charges are shown directly to the passenger," he says.

"Ireland West Airport Knock's aviation fees are lower than most of the large airports to which we fly. People think that they are being charged extra. This is not the case. In fact the total charges at Ireland West Airport, including the Development Fee, are likely to be over 20% less than what you pay for going through Dublin Airport or other UK airports. Normally, smaller businesses have to charge higher fees but in our case we are managing to be more competitive than most of the larger airports. We are also more competitive than most of the smaller regional airports in Ireland for international flights."

He concedes Ireland West Airport might be more expensive in some instances and said there were airports in Europe, many of them loss-making, which charged less but he could assure passengers that the Airport was charging as little as it possibly could. "We recognise there is a level of service to be provided and we try to improve our standards rather than lower them," he says.

The Airport MD said when one considered that they did not charge the Development Fee for children under 12 years one could see that the real charges for families using the airport – a non-state facility – were even more competitive than the larger airports.

And he pointed out that car parking charges were much less than at other airports, at just €22 for one week's car parking. The weekly rate charged by Dublin Airport is €55.50 for long-term and €210 for the short-term park. "In fact our weekly car parking rate is between €13 and €37 less than the other international airports near to us. We are also cheaper for daily, monthly and all other rates," said Scollan.

Ryanair Chief Executive Michael O'Leary acknowledges Knock's low operating costs and says that provides a basis on which to expand. "We'd be looking at putting in more routes there as opportunities arise," he predicts.

Former Director John Mahon has no doubts about the development fee: "Without it the Airport could not have survived through difficult days and now be in such a strong position to move forward," he says.

Diversion rates and what's being done

ONE of the big arguments when the airport site was selected in 1980 was the likelihood of flight diversions given that the runway is located on top of a high plateau of 210m, or over 600 ft, which opens up the possibility of low cloud cover.

Diversions have never proved to be a major problem but, of course, if you happen to be on a flight that's been diverted you probably won't share that view!

Modern technology is bringing down diversion rates at airports throughout the world and Ireland West Airport has worked hard over the years to keep up with developments in this regard. So what is the position now?

Over 80% of landings at Ireland West Airport Knock are on Runway 27, the eastern end of the runway nearest to the terminal building. Operations on Runway 27 are assisted by what is known as Category I Instrumentation Landing Systems which basically enable aircraft to land, provided the pilot can see the runway from 200ft above and there is runway visibility of 800m.

Diversion Rates

- In 2004 there were 7,589 total aircraft movements at Ireland West airport; 4,391 of these were commercial passenger aircraft; 29 of these commercial flights or (0.66%) were diverted.

- In 2005 there were 8,636 total aircraft movements at Ireland West airport; 5,335 of these were commercial passenger aircraft; 30 of these commercial flights (or 0.56%) were diverted.

The implementation of Category II precision approach facilities on Runway 27 will permit aircraft to land when the altitudinal visibility is 100ft and where there is visibility ahead of 350m. This would be a considerable improvement on the existing distances minima of 200ft and 800m.

These improved facilities will enable operators to build up a high level of confidence of continued operations in low-visibility conditions which is essential for the retention of existing routes in a very competitive marketplace.

The airport is 210m. above sea level giving rise to a slightly higher frequency of low-cloud conditions which leads to aircraft pilots not having the necessary levels of visibility to effect a landing when such conditions are severe. A recent meteorological study indicates that poor weather conditions at the Airport tend to occur in the early mornings and late at night with a general improvement during the day.

The implementation of Cat II or possibly CAT IIIa precision approach facilities for Runway 27 would reduce diversions to fall in line with norms for international airports.

The Airport has identified CAT II investment and the general improvement of landing systems as a major priority. It has prepared a roadmap for the upgrade and implementation of improvements to its landing systems. The first two phases of this involve the implementation of Category I Instrumentation Landing Systems on Runway 09 (the end of the runway on the western or Kilkelly side) and the installation of a perimeter fence to protect the airfield from intrusion, part of which commenced in 2005.

CHAPTER TWENTY-ONE

*Many false dawns – Unfulfilled promises – Healy clashes with
Monsignor – Ways to attract investors – Hopes of thousands of jobs*

Business Park the next big leap

ONE of the great unrealised ambitions for the Airport must surely be the huge untapped potential that lies within the industrial zone. In 2006 – and twenty years after the official opening – less than 100 people work in the Industrial and Business Park while 125 work within the actual airport.

Yet, given the right tax conditions the widely held belief is that a Business and Technology Park at Ireland West Airport could create up to 2,000 jobs within a five-year period. That's would constitute a massive leap forward for the area in terms of jobs.

Not many people realise that the whole of the Airport complex comprises well over 500 acres. In fact, when he was setting out to acquire the land for the Airport in 1980 Monsignor Horan bought up circa 520 acres. For a runway of even 10,000 ft – which was what he wanted – a terminal building, car parks and ancillary services, that constituted a lot of land.

Of course, he was not just thinking about a long runway. His ambitions did not end there: he knew the Airport would make a significant contribution to the industrial development of the region. He knew people did not have jobs and had to emigrate. He constantly talked about a 49% unemployment level in the Black Triangle of East Mayo and the need to create jobs.

And remember that on his Steering Committee in early 1980 were two men highly committed to attracting jobs to Mayo: County Development Secretary Seán Smyth and County Manager Michael O'Malley. These two had already achieved considerable success in bringing some major investment into the county, Asahi Chemicals near Killala, Travenol Laboratories in Castlebar, Hollister in Ballina and Allergan Pharmaceuticals in Westport to name a few. So hopes were high that at last, the County could achieve industrial lift-off. In the early 1980s, 6,000 people were employed in manufacturing in the County.

Smyth and O'Malley shared a similar passion with Horan: all three admired what Shannon Free Airport Development Company had achieved for that part of the country in terms of jobs. Horan himself had seen it develop over the years through regular trips to the Co. Clare Airport in which he took such a keen interest. So when it came to planning the airport Horan would have needed very little prompting from Smyth and O'Malley to acquire plenty of land. Smyth, particularly, was a forward thinker. He realised that tax incentives could turn the industrial zone into a real magnet for investors and could help transform the region at a stroke.

Taoiseach Charlie Haughey was also taken by the idea and more than once over the following years spoke of the benefits tax-free status could confer on the industrial park. However, the park has yet to be developed; almost all the attention had to be diverted to getting the Airport itself up and running.

*   *   *

The first public mention of investment in the Airport hit the national media while Monsignor Horan was still in Australia in 1984. Connaught/Ulster MEP Seán Flanagan claimed the headlines in the *Irish Press* of March 29 and April 4 with a story suggesting that $40 million was heading for the West within days, and a large chunk of that was for the Airport!

The advance cash, the paper claimed, was part of a $500m investment deal announced the previous week by Flanagan in Strasbourg. It appeared the projects were being fronted by a company called AGM Holdings of Maryland and investments would be made in peat and seaweed processing plants, with 'a huge investment in Knock Airport' of £20m to develop it to international standards. An incredible 225m dollars was also earmarked for a pelletised peat production plant in Mayo which 'would create hundreds of jobs over the next ten years'.

Subsequent press reports indicated that the Chairman of the Board of AGM was Dr Sandor Mihaly, who had offices in Cannes, France, and in Monte Carlo. AGM's Irish agent was a Mr John Duff who was associated with a firm called Gaelic Milled Peat in Milltownpass, Co. Westmeath, which had subsequently gone into liquidation.

Duff told the *Irish Press* he was introduced to AGM while he was in Saudi Arabia trying to sell liquid peat. A new Irish company was being formed called Irish Diversified Industries Ltd and the directors would be himself, Dr Mihaly and Mr Marar, a Jordanian Arab based in Saudi

Arabia. He revealed the projects identified for investment included peat briquette factories in Roscommon and Mountmellick (12m dollars); peat moss production, Dalystown, Mullingar (12m dollars); peat-derived fuel, Co. Mayo (225m dollars); peat moss to Saudi Arabia from Limerick (10m dollars); biocompatible farming (39m dollars); biocompatible pest control (17m dollars); composting (3m dollars); fishing and fish processing (7m dollars); pharmaceuticals (29m dollars); seaweed factory (5m dollars), and marketing (7m dollars).

He further revealed that Mr Haughey had been shown a copy of the contract for the package and was 'very enthusiastic'. Just a few days earlier, Duff had told the *Irish Press* Flanagan's announcement was premature and had sent bogland worth £300 an acre rocketing to an asking price of over £1,000 after the story broke. He said the company had options on 5,000 acres of land in Mayo. But MEP Flanagan maintained the land had already been bought.

Efforts by the *Irish Press* to trace the company in France and the US proved frustrating, though it named an American broker Joseph Leary, Executive Vice-President for Special Operations with the K-Chuga Corporation, who claimed the first lodgement of 40m dollars would be deposited in a Dublin bank within a matter of days.

Leary told the *Irish Press* he had been in Ireland for three months, and was also operating on behalf of another group of investors who were interested in a peat-processing industry in the midlands. No further details as to the origins of the latter group were given, but it was understood that that consortia was British. The potential for liquid peat/peat pellet processing in the 1980s was very much in the news, with Erris seen as a prime location for development, and Ballina port was mentioned as a possible point of export. Liquid peat was then as biomass is now, a great buzz word in the energy lexicon.

There was a huge deal of scepticism about the story and the vast sums of money involved. Critics likened it to Ripley's 'Believe it or Not' and Flanagan's political opponents pointed to the proximity of the European elections as the real driver of the story. However, the former Mayo All-Ireland winning captain said he stood over everything he had said, adding, "I don't fly kites." The story ran for a few weeks and then disappeared out of sight.

Though it all sounded fanciful, in fact in early 1982 the Regional Development Organisation and the Minister for Transport John Wilson had met to discuss a proposal to sell liquid peat to the Middle East in giant ocean-going tankers. Martin Finn, chairman of Mayo County Council, was reported in the *Western Journal* of July 23 1982 as saying that the RDO had been approached by a company interested in shipping the peat to the Middle East where it could be used as top soil or fertiliser.

Kiltimagh and Charlestown were mentioned as being locations for the project. Interestingly, the story was penned by Conal Healy, son of John, so his sources would have been reliable.

Though it was the first 'investment interest' story to claim the headlines, it was not in fact the first such expression of interest advanced in the Airport. The first toe-in-the-water in this regard had come in 1982 from a Nottingham firm which had a prominent Mayo connection.

Revealing that contact a few years later, John Healy said that the English firm, already well established running golf courses, had switched from Brussels to Barnacuige (the Airport location), "Where they took an option on 100 acres of land for a major 18-hole golf course with a new 100-bedroom hotel. The contact was Michael Gallagher, the MEP from Nottinghamshire, a man who was born on the perimeter of the Airport, outside Charlestown." He was well known to Healy who was a huge advocate of the European movement.

Healy also revealed the company had sought and been given EEC funding in 1981/82 for a feasibility study for a development which would cater not only for weekend golfers from Britain but also Monday-to-Friday British anglers. The Airport, Healy pointed out, was 45 minutes from Europe's most prolific sea-angling waters in Clew Bay, an hour from Blacksod and Ballysodare Bays and had, in the Moy, one of Europe's last free fishing salmon rivers.

As we have seen above, American broker Joseph Leary had claimed he was also operating for a British consortium interested in peat processing. Perhaps he was referring to the Nottingham group: around that period Gallagher had a huge interest in liquid peat and in developing a special coal briquette of mixed imported coal and local peat which he hoped to produce in Ballina.

*   *   *

The jobs/investment trail went cold again, at least publicly, until September 9 1985 when John Healy, in *The Irish Times*, caused something of a furore when he penned a highly critical article under the intriguing headline: 'Why Mayo is puzzled by the Monsignor'.

He referred to a press statement issued by the Monsignor some weeks beforehand. In an appeal for funds, Horan had alluded to a US consortium offer to buy equity, saying: "There has been much misunderstanding about recent statements in the press and radio about a proposal by an American consortium to give some millions of pounds for the completion of the Airport. While such a proposal was made it is not acceptable to the Minister and to the Department owing to the conditions attached. I must state that the only hope of completing the

Airport is through the subscriptions that we have received and are receiving from our friends in Ireland and overseas."

The tenet of Healy's article in response was that Horan had lost sight of offers from American and British consortia to create jobs at the airport in a flurry of public relations building up to a flight in October, from an incomplete airport to Rome. Whether or not that flight materialised, questions remained as to why there had not been a thorough investigation of the American offer to finance the completion and the initial running of the airport, said Healy. (It should be pointed out that while the British consortium was still the same, the American group now being referred to was different from the one mentioned by Seán Flanagan some years earlier, and already dealt with in this chapter. The latest American consortium was thought to represent aviation interests in Chicago.)

It was highly unusual for Healy to raise any negative vibes about the Airport in his writings, but now he was clearly peeved at what was happening – or to be more accurate – not happening, within the Boardroom.

He placed it on the record that the US consortium had offered not alone to complete the Airport, but to move in and set up an industrial warehouse complex with jobs for 400. And the British group had offered to build an 18-hole championship golf course with a 100-bedroom hotel, providing a further 60 to 100 jobs, he further stated.

Healy said the Monsignor first denied, in an interview, that he knew anything of the British plans, but that later, in a local newspaper, he agreed he did indeed have knowledge of the plan. (Author's note: In fact Seán Smyth, Michael O'Malley and Cathal Duffy travelled to Nottingham in 1982 to meet up with Gallagher and his business partners and they were joined in discussions by Seán Flanagan.)

Warming to his theme, Healy declared he was the person who met the British directors at the ferry, brought them to Knock and later showed them around the area. "The British directors were promised a contract giving them an option on the land for a golf course and a hotel. It is over two years ago since this was agreed yet the Board has not forwarded the documentation. The Taoiseach of the day, Charles J. Haughey, met the directors and discussed the project with them and was satisfied to the extent that he appointed a senior civil servant to liaise with the group on the development," he wrote.

Moving on to the US proposal, *The Irish Times* columnist said the Americans were prepared to finish the Airport, had offered airport management experience and in fact specialised in air-freight, which he described as the fastest-growing segment of the airline industry at the time.

"The package envisaged joint control by an Irish-American company to run the airport but one Irish director believes that if the Government was really interested, the American promoters would settle for a smaller percentage."

Healy said the Monsignor in a later statement claimed the plan had been opposed by the Minister (Jim Mitchell) and was withdrawn. However, he went on, two civil servants on the Board had written to the papers saying that was not so, the Minister had not rejected it. (In fact the Minister wrote a letter to the local papers to refute Horan's claim: it appeared in the *Western People* of October 9, 1985, and Mitchell said he had only the vaguest details of the offer, did not have any names of individuals or the organisation behind them, nor were the terms of the offer declared to him. He said he had no hand, act or part in discouraging the offer.)

Healy went on to decry the lack of urgency on the part of the Board to pursue either project, and seemed to pour cold water on the Monsignor's efforts to raise funds by merely running 'another raffle.' The Airport could not be financed by annual raffles, he said. He was also critical of the 'spectacle of cars being charged £2 a visit, motorists who, as taxpayers, had already paid once for the airport without being dunned a second time. The charge is now gone'. He was referring to Sunday drivers who took their cars out on the runway with the money raised going to the fund-raising drive.

Rounding off his highly charged column, Healy wrote: "What puzzles Mayo is the sight of the miracle-working Monsignor not being able to capitalise on American private enterprise and the stroke of providing 400 jobs and a secure future in air-freighting traffic for the white elephant airport. Too many pieces aren't adding up." Healy was among a few close to the project who felt that the Monsignor was not interested in the proposals because the approaches had not come directly to him in the first instance.

After reading what his old friend Healy had written, the Monsignor wryly remarked, "I wonder what that Healy is up to?" And in relation to the British offer to acquire a site for a golf course and hotel, Horan was against it. "We won't waste that land on a golf course. We will put in an industry there," he had argued at the Board table. So ended the British proposal.

Paddy O'Toole, who was a Government Minister at the time, recollects the question of US investment being raised by the Airport Board, and the outcome. "An investment of 2.5m dollars," he said, "was being proposed by a group who, in return for their investment, sought 40% of the company.

"Minister Mitchell responded to the Company stating that he had no objection in principle to the proposal but questioned the wisdom of handing over 40% of a company valued at £14.9m for the sum of 2.5m dollars, He suggested that 20% might be more appropriate or 30% if they insisted," said O'Toole.

There the American offer rested until Seamus Monaghan took over as chairman and had sorted out the Trust ownership issue in 1990. Now, he said, he would endeavour to attract new investment – as had been advised by Minister Seamus Brennan. He indicated he had particular investors in mind who might be interested in coming aboard. Apparently they were the same investors as had been involved five years earlier.

Monaghan later recalled that the American investors were very interested. Several meetings were held. "We were all on for the invest-ment, as it was a particularly bad time for the industry. But then when we considered all the angles we backed away from it. It never became anything," he said.

Director in the late 1980s/early 1990s, Michael Honan remembers that discussions were held and some propositions were indeed made. "If we had a worthwhile offer for 49% of the company then we would have taken it because the Airport badly needed the money. Obviously the suitors were not taken by what they heard and walked away," was his impression.

The failure to clinch a deal took close observers by surprise, particularly as some members of the Board had been highly critical of Horan for not tying up a deal when offered 2.5m dollars for 40% of the company in the mid-1980s.

"Everything had looked positive, negotiations appeared to be going well with the American negotiators and then all of a sudden it just mysteriously died," recalled a source.

In the late 1980s there was also the proposal by Ulick McEvaddy to set up an engine-maintenance plant at the Airport but this came to naught in controversial circumstances as detailed in Chapter 16.

*   *   *

The next big window of opportunity for the industrial park opened up in 1996 when a company within the Ross Perot Group, Alliance International, was seeking to create an EU headquarters for a freight-forwarding operation from the East Mayo base. Ross Perot snr had stood for the US Presidential election some years earlier. The development had an estimated cost of £30m.

In the autumn of 1996, in a bid to swing the deal, Government Minister Enda Kenny had flown to Texas with Airport Chairman Duffy and Directors Monsignor Dominick Grealy and County Manager Des Mahon to meet Perot jnr, and there was a fair deal of optimism that the deal could be pulled off.

Alliance indicated it wanted to build air-freight 'bulk heads' in Europe, one in Amsterdam and the other in Knock. The plan was based on the air freight idea developed by Alliance at Fort Worth in Texas where 20,000 jobs had been created over five years.

Special tax reliefs were essential to progress the deal and on April 29 1997 Finance Minister Ruairi Quinn took a proposal for Knock and other locations before the Cabinet. The deal was approved. Tourism Minister Kenny, who had pushed Knock's case strenuously behind the scenes, announced that reliefs would apply to the area immediately surrounding the Airport. It was seen as a deal clincher. 200 acres would be covered by the designation with an extension of the 10 per cent corporation tax to specified sectors. Hailing the initiative, Kenny said the decision would prove to be one of the most significant in the development of the area and would 'mark Mayo's coming of age as a major employment centre'.

John Flannery (FG) of Charlestown, who was Chairman of the County Council at the time and was therefore party to talks with Alliance, said, prematurely as it turned out, that it was a wonderful day for Mayo. "We have the potential to be a gateway into Europe," he said.

In the General Election of June 1997 the Rainbow Coalition was defeated and Fianna Fáil and the PDs formed the new Government with Bertie Ahern as Taoiseach. And in October Mary McAleese succeeded Mary Robinson (who served one term) as President.

A planning application for the Ross Perot project was lodged for a 30,000 sq. ft development in December 1997. At that time there were reports to the effect that the development could lead to the creation of as many as 2,000 jobs in the area.

Unfortunately, the maxim of 'many a slip between cup and lip' was again to be proved correct. The deal fell through. Instead, in August 1998, Tanaiste Mary Harney announced that the Perot group was to establish a joint venture project with Bank of Ireland in Dublin creating 250 jobs initially and expanding to 500. The press conference was attended by Ross Perot (snr.), but while the same company was involved the nature of the Dublin investment was different from what had been proposed for Mayo.

Mayo Dáil deputy Michael Ring (FG) remarked at the time that he was sure everyone in Mayo was asking the question that was on his mind: how come Dublin could get these jobs while Knock was still waiting and wondering?

Looking back on events, Enda Kenny said the Ross Perot analysis of Knock Airport's potential was based upon a tax-free designation being granted to the Airport and its surrounding lands. "I travelled to Dallas to see the Perot operation. Subsequently I had the Government approve tax-designated status for Knock. Once tax designation was approved the question of investment lay with promoting the idea and having investment take place. This did not happen in the way envisaged."

Asked was an opportunity lost by the Airport Company to maximise the special designation, Kenny firmly replied: "Yes."

Senator Jim Higgins was more forthcoming: he saw the tax concession as a missed opportunity which the Airport Board let slip through its fingers. "Enda Kenny and myself were pressing for the tax-free designation and the Government agreed to give it, providing a two-year window. That should have been the trigger for major development, but the management at the time did not have the entrepreneurial know-how or the will to go out and attract industry on a major basis like they had done in Shannon. It's very doubtful that they will ever get that chance again," he said.

A source close to the scene at the time claimed the US company got cold feet and pulled out after the issue became politicised in the lead-up to the General Election when talks of 'phantom jobs' hit the headlines. Local politicians have dismissed that notion as a piece of nonsense!

In the late 1990s, the Airport Company invited developers headed by Jed Pierse, who had developed East Point Industrial Estate in Dublin, to invest in the Airport's 140 acre Industrial Estate. The response was positive but again hopes were dashed. According to Cathal Duffy, the group decided to purchase 24 acres in the estate and they were prepared to invest £70m in new buildings provided the Government would grant tax concessions, i.e., capital allowance on buildings in the upcoming Budget. "Undertakings were given, political promises were made, but Finance Minister Charlie McCreevy failed to deliver tax designation to Knock Airport Industrial Park," he added.

"We were promised again that the Minister would grant tax designation in the 2001 Budget but the guys with the long coats in the Department of Finance opposed it even though it would create 2,000 industrial jobs. As far as the officials in Finance were concerned, Knock Airport was a big mistake, it should not be there and thus the same policy seems to continue to this day," said the former Chairman.

*   *   *

What looked like a breakthrough came in a modest way with the cutting of the sod for the first factory by Environment Minister Padraig Flynn on October 15 1990. Westech Developments Ltd announced they were setting up an electronics factory which promised 30 jobs initially. Mayo development company Crisham Industrial Properties Ltd were building the unit.

Unfortunately, Westech, which had IDA approval, never got off the ground, its English parent company running into difficulties. But Swinford-born Tony Pidgeon and his company, Crisham Development Ltd., have continued to develop the Business Park on a 20-acre site. It now has 13 units totalling 120,000 sq ft with a mix of businesses, and employment was expected to reach 100 by the end of 2006. The mix included warehousing, freight-forwarding, logistics and computer hardware.

"We are working very closely with the Airport Management and the outlook is very positive. The site is fully serviced, with main sewerage scheme and water, and existing satellite broadband will shortly be switched to cable form," said Pidgeon in early 2006.

Western Development Commission Chief Executive Lisa McAllister sees considerable potential in an industrial hub around the Airport. "A top-class international airport at Knock is vital to attract outside investment here. Access is an essential component in keeping the businesses and jobs we have in the West competitive. There is potential for the development of a significant industrial hub around the Airport. Not only in the Airport itself but the availability of international air access could also be harnessed to promote and develop the attractiveness of the smaller towns in the catchment area as business locations. The feasibility of developing a cluster zone of smaller towns in a region in the catchment of a significant international airport could be an interesting and relevant model of development for the Western region which is predominantly rural in nature made up of a large number of smaller towns rather than dominant cities," says Ms McAllister. (The Western Development Commission is the statutory body promoting the economic and social development of the Western Region – the five Connaught counties, plus Donegal and Clare.)

Airport Board Chairman Joe Kennedy is also excited about the potential of the Business Park: "I see great developments coming. There are great possibilities, offices, warehouses, hangarage for private and commercial aircraft and parking. We continue to talk to Government in pursuit of opportunities and we looking forward to the decentralisation of the Department of Community, Rural and Gaeltacht Affairs as a very positive step," he said.

Airport Trust Chairman Des Mahon, Mayo County Council Manager, says industrial expansion at Knock along the lines of what has taken place at Shannon would lead to employment growth and enormously help the surrounding towns of Charlestown, Swinford, Ballyhaunis, Ballina and Castlebar. "Such industrial expansion may need the support of Airport lands being designated as a Strategic Development Zone, thereby fast-tracking planning of suitable developments.

Maybe Ireland West Airport Knock as an Aviation Training Centre can give the Airport a niche market with commercial benefit," he says.

Seán Hannick, Chairman of the Council for the West, a voluntary non-political lobby group for the region, sees the next milestone being tax designation for the Business and Technology Park. He says he is confident that this development could help create thousands of jobs within five years and says the Council for the West will continue to campaign for such designation.

"Hopefully, the Government will see the merits in the case being made by the Airport Board and thereby help transform what was once known as the Black Triangle into the Golden Triangle of the future. With accelerated capital allowances we could get the necessary investors for the buildings and the employment projects to go into those buildings." He says 'back office work' by financial institutions, insurance business, etc., etc., could be done at Knock and people could live in local towns within a 30-mile radius of their work, housed at half the cost, free of traffic gridlocks, and with good adjacent schools and amenities and lovely natural landscapes.

Airport Managing Director Liam Scollan believes the Business Park can indeed be the location for many jobs. He said that to be competitive in business one needed to be in a good location, have the right services, access to quality workers, air access, broadband, affordable property, social and educational services, be located around other employers and most importantly, be an attractive place in which to live. "Ireland West Airport simply provides all of these advantages and therefore a huge opportunity exists to attract employers from around the world," he said.

He said modern business wanted to move its people around the world fast and distribute information and light, high value goods easily with overheads as low as possible. "Over 125,000 people in 40,000 households live within a 45-minute drive of Ireland West Airport. They are highly skilled with 27% in managerial/professional occupations and 37% being skilled manual or in supervisory/junior manager positions," he said.

He said the type of employment that may well be found around the Airport in the next 20 years may be airport-related activities like freight-forwarding and distribution, aircraft servicing and maintenance and the sort of retail and service businesses to be found around any modern Airport. "However we also aim to attract a wider range of businesses such as those in the high-technology manufacturing (office equipment, computer hardware, consumer electronics, medical devices, and pharmaceuticals), internationally traded services and headquarters of businesses or organisations where travel is important," he added.

Pointing out that the Airport itself was an airport of the people, built by people's own will and was successful because local people and those who emigrated love it. "It has served to bring our people home. Wouldn't it be wonderful if the Airport was able to attract back the people who left here generations ago and who have now set up successful companies abroad? It is of huge importance that Minister Ó Cuiv and the Government decided to relocate a Government Department to the area. However, rather than relying on the State alone to bring in the jobs, wouldn't it be great to see those with cunning, enterprise and resourcefulness bring it back home and build the best of all business centres, again in the bog?" he added.

Calling for the extension of natural gas supplies to the Business Park which he said would be a great boon and would be of major assistance in accelerating job growth, he underlined that if the airport vision was to really take off in the future it would be because many people joined in, decided to make the vision their own and bring their own project to bear on the area. "Please God that will happen," Scollan said.

If it does it will see the realisation of Monsignor Horan's great dream of people finding work where jobs were once as scarce as hen's teeth.

CHAPTER TWENTY-TWO

MD Liam Scollan looks to the future – Ryanair Chief Michael O'Leary sees great prospects – Western Development Chief says Airport major catalyst for regional development – Chairman's hopes for 'religious-tourism' charters

Looking to the future . . .

THERE was a time when some politicians and civil servants feared that the building of Knock Airport was, almost single-handedly, going to plunge the economy of the country into a disastrous tailspin. We'd all be ruined, they wailed. They railed at the prolificacy of madmen coming out of the West and daring to build a decent airport of all things, and accused those supporters at the levers of power of being mendacious. The white elephant would graze on the grass growing on the runway, and the bog on which it was built would absorb the stretch of tarmac and bury that audacious piece of madness, they warned.

You get the drift, as John Healy might have said.

Now get this. Just twenty years after the opening, Ireland West Airport Knock is on target to register 650,00 passengers in 2006. By 2020 it will be servicing 50 destinations worldwide and carrying at least two million passengers.

In 2005 the airport employed 122 people and supported almost 780 jobs in the region. So what about the good old pounds, shillings and pence the economists saw gushing down a bog hole in East Mayo back in the mid-1980s? Well, total spending by inbound tourists was estimated at €78m for 2006 with close on €10m being paid to the national Exchequer in income tax and PRSI.

And not content just to put bums on aircraft seats and push tourism along, the Airport Board plans to build a Business Park creating at least 2,000 jobs within the next ten years. The Black Triangle, as Monsignor Horan had hoped, stands on the verge of being transformed utterly.

Managing Director Liam Scollan sees the progress as simply continuing in the spirit of the original dream. "Today, more than ever, airports, and ours in particular, are critical to economic success," he says as the Airport moves on to embrace the 'art of the possible'.

Looking forward to what the future holds for the Airport, Scollan is very optimistic. "Samuel Johnson once said, 'Nothing will ever be attempted if all possible objections must be first overcome'. When the Airport was launched in 1986 the aim was that it would connect the West of Ireland to the UK and other places to which the Irish had emigrated overseas; that it would help the region of Connaught by bringing jobs and industries and finally that it would be a link to the Marian Shrine and religious tourism. As we now enter the next 20 years of the Airport's life it is timely to see how that vision continues to be realised. Twenty years ago they said it couldn't be done; half a million passengers in 2005 and 25 overseas destinations show that it can," he says.

He said though he had been around the Airport only for the past four years he could testify to the fact that there had always been a spirit of adventure at the Airport, the spirit to try things, the acceptance that some of it would go wrong and more of it would go right. "You might say none of us here ever took W.C. Fields' words to heart: 'If at first you don't succeed, try again. If you still don't succeed, quit. There's no point in making a damn fool of yourself'. Sometimes, when you work against the odds, W.C. Fields' advice is tempting," he said. However, people who were close to the 'Knock' story had never any doubt that the vision was and is the right one. "So here's to those who try and try again for something they believe in and are not afraid to risk making fools of themselves," he added.

Trying to predict with accuracy the future of world aviation was difficult, he said. "Two outcomes though are very likely: more people will be flying and they will be flying on low-cost carriers. It is for instance estimated by the manufacturer Airbus that passenger numbers worldwide will have more than doubled between 2000 and 2020."

He said low-cost carriers such as South West Airlines in the US and Ryanair and easyJet in Europe had attracted a huge growth in numbers, especially across the shorter journey times. In 1991 low-cost carriers carried 500,000 passengers per week. By 2004 this had risen to 7.5m, 15 times higher. The trend was set to grow. "Now almost 20% of air passengers in Europe fly using low-cost carriers. By 2010 half of all passengers in Europe will be using low-cost carriers," he said.

"So, when we work to grow Ireland West Airport we are part of a global trend where more and more people will travel, a trend that will make the world smaller and bring people from around the world closer together. What started as an airport that connected the Irish with their loved ones who had emigrated is becoming an airport that is connecting with all nationalities and bringing people into Ireland who never came here before and have no Irish connection at all," he pointed out.

Scollan said the predominant image of the passenger profile using Ireland West Airport in the early days was that they were largely people using it for emigration. That had dramatically changed, a reflection of the changing fortunes of the West of Ireland to see more smiling faces of people going travelling for holidays as distinct from the sad image of parting relatives.

"People who currently fly through Ireland West Airport Knock do so mainly for leisure purposes, secondly because they are visiting friends and relatives, and thirdly for business reasons. In 2005, of the 530,000 who used the airport, 48% was leisure, 45% was visiting friends and relatives and 7% were on business. It is likely that the Airport and the region will become more dependent on tourist or leisure visitors as distinct from people coming to visit friends and relatives in the future," he said.

While currently the Airport flies scheduled services to six UK airports (Stansted, Luton, Gatwick, Birmingham, Manchester and Durham Tees Valley) they estimate demand for at least six other UK destinations including Scotland. They also know there is considerable demand for travel to and from destinations in Europe (Germany, France, Italy and Spain in particular) and also to the United States and Canada.

"Lansdowne Market Surveys questioned people in Connaught, Donegal and Longford in two separate years and consistently found that 75% of people in that region would prefer to use Ireland West Airport. So while we currently fly to about 25 destinations and carried 530,000 passengers in 2005, we predict that by 2020 we will be flying to 50 destinations worldwide and carrying at least two million passengers," he said.

And pointing to the Airport's impact on the wider economy, Scollan said while the area around the Airport had traditionally been a large unemployment black spot, sometimes called the 'black hole of Connaught', there was now not only growing employment there but it was also now driving up employment elsewhere in the region. "It is possible that by 2020 the airport will be contributing €200m annually in tourism spending and supporting between 2,000 and 3,000 jobs," he said.

"Achieving this vision will simply require co-operation. Ireland West Airport Knock will need to attract more UK, transatlantic and European routes and regional development agencies and those with a stake in the region's future will need to sell the region's business potential successfully," he said.

He stressed that building new routes and connections for people from around the world into the West of Ireland had been and would continue to be at the core of the Airport's plans for the future. However, the Airport also planned to use its presence to act as a magnet for other businesses in aviation: services distribution, and the production of high value-added exportable goods and information technology.

Already the momentum was gathering, he said. The relocation of the Department of Community, Rural and Gaeltacht Affairs would bring 148 jobs to the area and the granting of planning permission for a 100 + bedroom hotel were signals of tangible and continued progress.

"With high-speed broadband technology, high-speed jet access and pools of highly skilled labour, there is every reason why we should be developing Ireland West Business Park, a place where people from here and all over the world can work and live in a beautiful region and, connect to anywhere in the world. So much for the 'black hole'," he added.

Pointing out that while tourism was the most significant industry in the West of Ireland, the region faced intense competition from other tourist destinations. "We are not just competing with the Spanish, Greek and traditional sun holiday destinations. We compete with hundreds of destinations in Europe and elsewhere which are now within easy access from here and the UK, the two countries on which we are most dependent for our existing tourism business in the West of Ireland. Irish and non-Irish alike living in the UK can get to over 200 destinations around Europe, to the traditional standards like Faro, Malaga and Paris or newer locations near airports used by low-cost carriers, e.g. Poznan, Leipzig and Graz," he pointed out.

He said the future of new routes into Ireland West Airport was now closely tied to the region's ability to sell itself as a successful tourism destination for scheduled commercial jet traffic all the year round. No longer could our success in tourism be guaranteed because we had beautiful scenery, lakes and other natural attractions, heritage, friendly people and a vibrant culture. Long gone was the 'paddy whackery'.

Successful tourism locations worldwide, he said, were those that managed to interpret the landscape and culture and other natural attractions and create experiences for people not just in summer but throughout the year.

"When, for instance thousands of families with children arrive at Ireland West Airport in the middle of months like January or February, or November and have a variety of exciting choices to occupy them for periods of three days to a week and when that experience can be achieved during any of our four seasons then we will have reached a point where our tourism can compete on a global level. We, as a region, are not there yet."

Scollan recalls once playing with a group of musicians in Killorans' in Tubbercurry for a group of Americans who were stopping in South

Sligo for the night in the middle of a two-week holiday mainly spent in Dublin. "At the end of each night we would often witness some of them come up to us in tears. You might be justified for thinking this was as a consequence of our music. Maybe sometimes! The truth was that the fun, the music and the experience they got on those nights were what they came to Ireland for and they had realised too late that their holiday schedule was all wrong. Over half of all US visitors coming through Dublin Airport visit the West of Ireland but sadly only for a brief stopover. The truth is that the experience they seek in coming to Ireland is best got in the West and the courage to have the vision to respond to that need is one hugely important requirement for the next 20 years," he said.

Success in business depended, he said, not on what you supply but the standard of service you give, its friendliness and efficiency. "The Airport has always had a reputation for friendliness. It gives me great pleasure to read letters from people directly addressed to the Airport: firemen that resuscitated a passenger who had taken ill, the customer services agent who went out of her way to help a woman passenger who had forgotten valuables she had mislaid, or the security person who found jump leads to start a passenger's car. These are typical instances," he added.

The buzz word in business management circles was how to achieve 'corporate citizenship'. He would like to think that such friendliness and dedication, aspired to now in global corporations, came as standard at the Ireland West Airport. But as they moved to greater numbers of employees and passengers, with tougher security measures, the Airport was conscious of having to have a more deliberate policy of encouraging and rewarding friendliness. "We run a customer services survey every month. This is telling us where we are doing well and where we are not. We want to achieve 10 out of 10 for customer services. At present our survey is scoring at 7.3 and each month we work to improve," he said.

But, Scollan conceded, friendliness was not enough. They wanted to be the most efficient airport in the UK and Ireland. They measured efficiency in many different ways. For instance the shorter the time between an aircraft arriving from Manchester and the time it took off mostly determined the speed at which the passenger could get through the Airport. In March 2006 for instance 95% of aircraft were 'turned around' in 25 minutes or under, he pointed out.

Those efficiencies are being recognised. In 2006 the Airport accepted the 'Best Regional Airport Award' from the Air Transport Users' Council of Ireland. It was the Airport's second time winning it in three years. Prior to that, in 2005, the Airport won first for customer services across easyJet's European network of 68 airports. The Airport out-performed every airport in Europe for friendliness and every airport bar one for efficiency of baggage handling.

Looking ahead, Scollan said a 30-year physical master plan had been prepared which would guarantee that there would be the space and forward physical planning to accommodate the vision for the Airport's continued expansion. "By 2015 the current terminal building will have trebled in size to around 15,000 sq. metres and the car-parking provision will have trebled to 3,000 spaces. The 'apron', where passengers disembark from the aircraft, currently can accommodate three Boeing 737 size aircraft. By 2015 it will need to be five times its current size, accommodating 14 aircraft at any one time. We envisage having Category II or possibly IIIa instrument landing systems by 2008, enabling landings in most low-cloud conditions," he said.

And they envisage a business park that was landscaped in keeping with the local environment. The decision by Minister Brian Cowen in 2005 to radically increase the allocations to Ireland's regional airports to €100m was profoundly significant. It could enable Ireland West Airport to complete the urgently needed expansions, provided the Airport succeed in getting its just share of the resources, he added.

"The future of the Airport is also dependent on how quickly local road, rail, and public transportation services are improved. It is vital that the Western Development Commission's proposals to the Government for this region are implemented in the new National Plan for 2007 to 2013. If it is, we will see by 2013 dual carriageways from Sligo to Galway and from Longford to Castlebar and Ballina and better road linkages from outlying towns like Athlone, our islands and coastal areas. We hope to see a Western Rail Corridor which connects to the airport from a station in Kiltimagh and regular public transport connections with Galway, Donegal, Athlone, Longford and Carrick-on-Shannon. We hope to see the expansion of gas and renewable energy networks throughout the region and supplying the business park at the Airport," he said.

Scollan said there were things the Airport had done and would continue to do which did not necessarily have a monetary value. That went back to the fact that the Airport was formed as a Trust, a not-for-profit Trust where all profits were invested back into the business. Likewise, energy was invested in objectives which might not reap money but which reflected a wish to see the Airport Company play a responsible role in society. "The Airport is conscious of its place not just in the region but also of its connectedness with people outside the region and to other countries and continents. This grew out of the reasons the Airport was built in the first place – to connect people who then had been parted through emigration," he said.

How they behaved towards each other as staff, business partners, and how they treated customers and the local environment were all a conscious part of the vision for the future and were grounded as real targets in their strategic plans. They had commitments to achieve better work-life balance for all staff, commitments to reduce CO_2 emissions, commitments to introduce bilingual signage (Bearla agus Gaeilge) and commitments to raise money for charitable causes. "In many ways we see a company in the modern world as having to make similar decisions as individuals," he said.

One of the smallest infrastructure projects the Airport completed in 2006, "But perhaps the largest in terms of the spirit of the place was a small oratory at the Airport. Our oratory is meant to be a space for people of all faiths and none, who want some quiet time for reflection This is underpinned by a wish to have a place of reflections for people, staff or passengers, regardless of what faith they practise," he said.

Setting the bar high, he said: "Looking ahead twenty years the impression a visitor should get, on first approaching Ireland West Airport, should be of a place that is bustling with business and services in a modern but natural environment in the West of Ireland, leading on to an Airport that provides simple easy access to destinations worldwide. We would like the Airport and its environs to reflect what is possible in the West of Ireland, to be able to compete with and trade with the rest of the world without having to live anywhere else but here. In the past Irish people had to leave here to do that.

"The success of the West of Ireland will ultimately be written from the stories of entrepreneurs and people with spirit who dared to do. Ireland West Airport Knock simply mirrors the experience of so many others who have worked against the odds and succeeded in this region or when they emigrated.

"One might ask: can we be certain of achieving our goals for Ireland West Airport and can the region itself succeed? Of course, nothing in this life is for certain. As Voltaire said, 'Doubt is uncomfortable, but certainty is ridiculous'. Nothing has ever been achieved without struggle," said the Airport's Managing Director.

*   *   *

Others are equally excited about the Airport's prospects. Michael O'Leary, Chief Executive of Ryanair, sees a bright future for the Airport as the gateway into the West of Ireland. "We at Ryanair are expanding the number of routes into the Airport. The next challenge for us will be putting the routes in there for Europe. We are working with Liam Scollan and his management team. We have cracked the UK market, now we have to have a look at opening it up as a European base, using Knock as the gateway to the West of Ireland. I'd be certain that can be done. The costs are low at Knock and we'd be looking at putting in more routes there as opportunities arise," he said.

He paid tribute to the wider team at the Airport over the years, to the late Monsignor Grealy, to Cathal Duffy, Liam Scollan, Joe Kennedy, and others. "Knock is very fortunate in having the best management of any of the airports for many years and that is why it has succeeded. Very good people have been involved over the years who have been committed to the Airport," he added.

Lisa McAllister, Chief Executive of the Western Development Commission – a statutory body promoting the economic and social development of the five Connaught counties plus Donegal and Clare, sees the successful development of the Airport as a major catalyst for regional development in the West. "It is a very important regional infrastructure asset," she says.

The WDC has invested over €1.3m. in the Airport through its WDC Investment Fund for an expansion of car parking, catering and retail facilities.

However, Ms McAllister said if the full regional development benefits of the Airport are to be realised, greater priority must be given to improved surface transport links between it and the rest of the region. "Ireland West Airport Knock is very well located at a strategic crossroads between the North-South N17 route (part of the Atlantic Road Corridor) and the East-West N5 route. Both of these roads urgently need to be upgraded. While they are included in the Government's new 10-year transport plan – Transport 21, they need to be completed much sooner than currently planned."

She added that public transport services were also critical. These included improved bus services linking the Airport with the region and beyond, particularly to facilitate tourist access to rural locations across the region. She said the Western Rail Corridor, located close to the Western Rail Corridor at Charlestown, would, when fully re-opened, also provide much improved access from Sligo in the north, to Ennis and beyond in the south.

The WDC CEO said the Airport had another crucial role as the Western Region experienced a sharp decline in some of its more traditional economic sectors. 'Knowledge-based' activities were becoming far more important to development, and access to a well-connected international airport was essential for such businesses. "It is one of the factors taken into account by transnational companies when making their location decisions. Ireland West Airport Knock can underpin the development of the region as a dynamic knowledge-based economy and if the decline in the West's tourism is to be reversed, the Airport must play a pivotal role," she added.

Ms McAllister revealed that, given the international trend for more frequent but shorter breaks, cheap direct access to Dublin had resulted in substantial growth in tourism numbers in the capital, while tourism in the regions had declined. Between 2000 and 2004 overseas visitors to the North West fell by 19% and to the West by 5%. In 2004, 79% of all overseas tourists arriving in Ireland came by air, with the majority of these arriving via Dublin, she said.

Chairman Joe Kennedy sees particular potential in developing religious tourism charter-flight packages into Knock Shrine, one of Monsignor Horan's great dreams. He said research was being carried out and the Shrine and the Airport were working together to tap into that segment of the American market. "We believe this is definitely on. We believe we have the Lakes of Killarney in Knock Shrine. We will need others to put in necessary tourism-support packages, and if that is done we see no reason to believe it won't succeed. It's a niche market. People are flying to Fatima, Lourdes, Medjugorje from all over the world – we have to market what we have to offer in conjunction with Knock Shrine," he said.

Kennedy said everyone at the Airport was very mindful that the Trust had placed the Airport in the ownership of the people of the West. "We are entrusted with its development – it is the jewel in the crown of the whole region; people are travelling from Donegal, Cavan, Meath, Tipperary, Clare, etc. to use Ireland West Airport and it is great to be able to fly in and be home within a few hours. We are custodians for the people of the West and we must deliver the best service for the people and look after the staff and all those using it in a friendly and efficient manner. Monsignor Horan left a great gift to us and we are trying very hard to deliver his wishes," he underlined.

The final surprise . . .

SO how do you categorise Monsignor James Horan? Dreamer? Chancer? Mischievous rogue? Doer of good deeds? Taker of short cuts without weighing up all the consequences? Ruthless? Reckless? Charismatic? Exceptional? Obsessional? A genius? In fact he has been called all of these things.

Former Taoiseach Charles Haughey described him as a unique person. "He showed that clear insight which distinguishes leadership; he identified a regional airport as the key to the future, his persistence, shrewdness and determination overcoming inertia, bureaucratic resistance and surprisingly widespread opposition.

"*Si monumentum requiris, circumspice* – if you seek his memorial look around you," said Haughey, quoting the inscription on the tomb of architect Sir Christopher Wren in St. Paul's, London.

Former Taoiseach Garret FitzGerald, whose government finally ended State funding for the Airport, said there had been concern on two fronts: one, that Monsignor Horan might exceed the provision made by the State in respect of the Airport, and two, the fact that his ambition to attract transatlantic flights led him to construct a runway very much longer than that required for intra-European services.

And on the question of East/West bias, Dr FitzGerald said given there are now five international airports in the BMW region – Donegal, Knock, Shannon, Galway and Kerry, as well as a domestic airport at Sligo, "It would be ludicrous to suggest that the State or its governments have demonstrated any bias against the West in its airport policy! I cannot recall offhand any case elsewhere involving such a concentration of airports near each other in a less developed region of a state."

While refraining from specifically commenting on Monsignor Horan, Dr FitzGerald conceded his government had been politically out-manoeuvred in relation to the building of the Airport.

Michael O'Leary, Chief Executive of Ryanair, is unequivocal. "Monsignor Horan was a genius: to build an airport where he built it without support and with no help for years, the guy was clearly a genius. He should have been running the country. He was revered as a hero by the time we launched Ryanair flights from Mayo and if he could have done that down in Knock, imagine what he could have done had he been running the country. I'd put him in charge of sorting out the health service, and he would have done a much better job on Ireland's transport systems than the politicians. He was a visionary, way ahead of his time."

Ken Holden, aviation expert and main author of the TAI feasibility study and later CEO of the Central Remedial Clinic, has no doubts either. "He was an amazing businessman. He was truly outstanding; charismatic, capable, competent, absolutely one of the great Irish people of the generation. If he had been in business he would have been the head of the biggest corporation in Ireland. He had all the qualities needed. He was also a man of great humanity."

In the other corner, Barry Desmond is still not convinced: "Monsignor Horan had no conception whatsoever of public financial accountability. Zero. None at all. He had a sophisticated appreciation of how to manipulate politicians. And that is understandable. He wasn't the first clergyman in Ireland to manipulate politicians to his own advantage. You can't run a country on that basis. You can't run the Department of Transport on that basis. He immediately saw an opportunity of availing of the temperament of Padraig Flynn, the incapacity of Padraig Flynn to say no to anyone within his remit or constituency, and then there was the mendacious approach of the Taoiseach, Charlie Haughey, who was an alleged son of Mayo and on that basis Horan decided to milk it for whatever it was worth."

Castlebar businessman Frank Durcan, a former county councillor, one-time critic of the Airport but long since converted, described Horan as a typical parish priest of that time, lord of all he surveyed and it was God help anyone who opposed him. "He did not see any problems. He just walked over them, that was his stand, and that is the way to get things done in this region. Nice fellows never get anything. He was ruthless and he had to be, otherwise you wouldn't have got the facilities. He wouldn't have got the Basilica, he wouldn't have got the Pope to Ireland, he wouldn't have got the Airport. He had the courage. There are plenty of people in Ireland like him but within the political system they are not allowed to operate. The red tape is there to restrain them: unless you are very wealthy and have the stamina and courage to take on the establishment – the faceless mandarins in the civil service rule the country, the bureaucrats dictate to the politicians."

The late Jim Mitchell, the man who will long be remembered for his 'foggy, boggy' remark, said in the Dáil in January 1987 that Horan, by any standards, was an exceptional man. "To be truthful, when I first met him there was a certain antagonism but we quickly became very good friends. I came to respect him very much indeed. I often said to friends and to officials of my Department that I would have loved to have had him as chairman of one of my troublesome State companies because he would have been the man to sort them out."

Former Taoiseach Albert Reynolds said the State by its nature was not an enterprising unit; it relied on the input from sponsoring Ministers and business people agreeing to go ahead. "If there is a pro-enterprise view, rather than trying to protect it helps. There is a lot of risk in everything: I always remember Seán Lemass' response to a key project in Dublin, 'once you put it there they cannot take it away, once you put the facility there someone will use it'. That was Monsignor Horan's philosophy in relation to Knock Airport. He believed, he knew it would work. He was a visionary."

Sociologist Fr Harry Bohan of Clare says Horan was used to running against the tide. "But the only trend he bucked was the trend towards a few growth centres. Dublin is to Ireland what no other capital is in Europe . . . you have to go to Athens in Greece and to the Third World to find anything like the influence of a capital city on the rest of the nation that Dublin has on Ireland. It has all the policy makers, all the media and it has the bulk of the population as well. Horan had to confront all of that.

"He struck out at a time when the economy was poor, but he was a single-minded man. You have to believe deeply and listen to opinions but there is never a right time to do a thing like the airport . . . is there ever a right time to do anything, to be able to take up the challenge when the country seems to be bankrupt?" said Fr Bohan.

Former Government Minister in the Fine Gael/Labour coalition during the 1980s, Paddy O'Toole, says Monsignor Horan had many good points. "He was a determined man who, when he had decided on something, proceeded to tolerate no excuses, no obstacles and insisted on getting his way. He was very good at dealing with the media. His view of bureaucrats was tempered by the experience he had of the neglect of the West and he felt that bureaucrats were at fault as much as politicians. I don't think that civil servants set out to get him. The normal reaction of public servants is that once the Government has made its decision, their function is to implement the decision as best they can. They normally do not get involved with personalities."

O'Toole said the Airport was now a very important part of our infrastructure. It had great potential. It had been slow to adapt to 'Celtic Tiger' conditions but the current management were about to get it right. "In the next ten years Knock Airport should become a hub of economic activity and will become a major centre not only for travel but also for outside investment," he predicted.

Trade-unionist Michael Kilcoyne says it is a pity the region did not have another person like Horan. "It would have made such a difference. He should really have been a politician, and if he had been we would not be how we are in the West of Ireland today. His philosophy was: 'It is much better to ask for forgiveness than permission'. In other words do it. If it is wrong, ask for forgiveness. But if you ask for permission you won't get it. The Monsignor used to say he was an old man in a hurry and that is why he had to cut through the red tape."

Tom Neary, who knew him better than most, said he never wanted people to be looking up to him. "He wanted to be known as an ordinary simple countryman and he loved country people, and he studied them closely, even the guy at the back of the church down on one knee and the cap . . . he was a great man to study character . . . he got a great kick out of it, and that was why when he was singing in the concerts he'd feel he was with his own. He'd sit down in his room at night and put on a tape or a bit of music. He loved that. That was the real James Horan. He had no personal interest in money or accumulating it for anybody else either. He'd say if people gave money for doing things let's get on with it. That was his philosophy always. Then he'd say, 'Why didn't all of this happen to me when I was younger?'."

And Taoiseach Bertie Ahern sees Monsignor Horan's airport project as standing out from the mid-1980s as a bright symbol of hope rather than the white elephant scorned by the sceptics. "It represents all that is best about the West of Ireland, its resilience, determination and self-help approach to life. Monsignor Horan had the vision to see that things could and would get better."

There is no question but that the old parish priest of Knock has been proved right. There is a story told of a Mayo businessman who wrote to Archbishop Cunnane in the early 1980s complaining about Horan and his 'madbrained' airport scheme. When the letter was shown to Horan his reaction was defiant: "Let's put it in an envelope and leave it there for ten years and when it is opened we will see who was right."

Today Knock Airport, or Ireland West Airport Knock as it is now known, is a great success. It is expanding. It is making money. It is owned in trust for the people of Connaught. Passenger figures are heading towards 600,00 pa. By 2020 it will have served more than 20 million passengers. It will have sustained 2,000 jobs and contributed 25 million bed nights worth €2bn to the region. Profits made will be ploughed back into the operation, to the benefit of the region. Not bad going for a derided white elephant!

*   *   *

Finally, an insight not shared publicly before. We have seen and read about the confident, no-problem James Horan through the passages of this book. We have seen that he was ambitious, decisive, caring, humorous, even ruthless. But there was another side to him that the public did not see.

When Horan died, his sister Nancy used to visit Fr Colm Kilcoyne in the presbytery in Knock. One day she told him something he was unaware of, though he had known the clerical dynamo for many years and for the last of those had been his curate.

"She told me how very often he would cry in her presence, wondering if the whole thing would end in disaster, if he would be able to handle the aggro, if people would see him as a failure.

"It was a side of him rarely seen. That day I'd have seen and heard him full of laughter and optimism with journalists and others. Or heard him on the radio, full of bounce."

Bibliography

Byrne, Joe *Songs of the Past and People 2* (1995)

Cowley, Ultan *The Men who Built Britain*
(Wolfhound Press, 2001)

Coyne, Dame Judy *Providence My Guide* - Edited Ethna Kennedy
(Mercier Press, 2004)

Creaton, Siobhan *Ryanair: How a Small Irish Airline Conquered Europe*
(London: Aurum Press, 2004)

Horan, Monsignor James *Memoirs 1911-1986.* Edited Fr Micheál
Mac Gréil SJ. (Brandon, 1992)

Horner, A. A. *Population Distribution and the Location of Airports in
Ireland* (Royal Irish Academy Dublin, 1980)

Keogh, Dermot *Twentieth Century Ireland: Nation and State* (Dublin:
Gill and Macmillan, 1994)

Lee, J.J. *Ireland 1912-1985 Politics and Society*
(Cambridge: Cambridge University Press, 1989)

Meehan, Rosa *The Story of Mayo* (Mayo County Council, 2003)

Neary, Tom *I Saw Our Lady* (Custodians of Knock Shrine, 1983)

O'Flynn, Criostoir *Blind Raftery* (Clo Iar-Connachta, 1998)

O'Hara, Bernard *Mayo* (Galway: The Archaeological, Historical and
Folklore Society, 1982)

Varley, Tony; Boylan, Thomas; Cuddy, Michael D.
Perspectives on Irish rural development
(Galway: Centre for Development Studies, 1991)

www.irelandwestairport.com
www.worldaerodata.com
http://en.wikipedia.org

Other publications drawn on, mainly newspapers and magazines, are
mentioned at point of reference throughout text.

Appendix
Fact File
Owned in Trust

Ireland West Airport Knock is a private limited company, owned in trust for the people of Connaught but Mayo in particular. In accordance with its non-profit Trust status, all profits are invested back in the business.

Passenger Numbers

1986 = 9,208	1993 = 107,508	2000 = 173,312;
1987 = 54,665	1994 = 129,702	2001 = 202,832*
1988 = 116,784	1995 = 138,001	2002 = 195,785
1989 = 145,198	1996 = 161,449	2003 = 247,721;
1990 = 145,749	1997 = 171,347	2004 = 372,992
1991 = 101,281	1998 = 194,832	2005 = 530,000
1992 = 105,646	1999 = 207,994	2006 = 650,000 (est.)

* Foot-and-Mouth outbreak in UK,
and attack on Twin Towers in New York, Sept. 11, 2001.

Diversion Rates

In 2004 there were 7,589 total aircraft movements at Ireland West Airport; 4,391 of these were commercial passenger aircraft; 29 of these commercial flights (or 0.66%) were diverted.
In 2005 there were 8,636 total aircraft movements at Ireland West Airport; 5,335 of these were commercial passenger aircraft; 30 of these commercial flights (or 0.56%) were diverted.

Development Fee

A Development Fee of €10 is charged on departing passengers, with the exception of children under the age of 12 years.
The money collected is used to fund passenger and airline services and the ongoing maintenance and operation of the airport.

Turnover

2006: €13m (estimated)
Staff 2006: 125

Fire Safety
Full fire-fighting equipment Category 9.

Airport Technical Data

Country:	*Ireland*
ICAO ID	*EIKN*
Time	*UTC 0(+1DT)*
Latitude	*53.910297*
	53° 54' 37.07" N
Longitude	*-8.818492*
	008° 49' 06.57" W
Elevation	*665 feet*
	203 metres
Type	*Civil*
Magnetic Variation	*006° W(01/06)*
Beacon	*Yes*
Operating Agency	*Civil Government (Landing Fees and Diplomatic Clearance may be required)*
Alternate Name	*Knock*
Daylight Saving Time	*Last Sunday in March to last Sunday in October*

COMMUNICATIONS

TWR	130.7
GND	121.9

RUNWAYS

Dimensions	7,546 x 148 feet
	2,300 x 45 metres
Surface	Asphalt
PCN	057FAWT
ILS	YES

NAVAIDS

Type	VOR-DME, NDB
ID	CON, OK
Name	Connaught
Channel Freq.	121 x 117.4, 398
Distance from Field	4.3 NM
Bearing from Navaid	266.2

SUPPLIERS EQUIPMENT

Fuel — Jet A1-, Jet A1
with icing inhibitor
100/130 Mil Spec., low lead,
aviation gasoline (blue)

REMARKS

CSTMS/IMG — CSTMS avbl 24 hr. PN
Fuel — (NC-100 LL, A1)
LGT — ABn flg. w/green. PAPI
Rwy 09/27 MEHT 50'
Opr 0600-1830Z ++ Mon.-Fri
0700-1830Z
++ Sat, 0830-1830Z ++ Sun.

Sources: worldaerodata.com • worldaerodata.com
www.irelandwestairport.com

Business Park

All enquiries should be addressed to the
Airport's Commercial Manager, Kevin Corrigan on 00353 9493 68105
or email: kevincorrigan@irelandwestairport.com

Car Parking Facilities (as at 2006)

Set down (15 mins) Free.
Under 1 hour: €1.50 • Under 2 hours: €3.00
Daily Charge: €8.00 • 2 days: €16.00 • Weekly: €22.00
Fortnightly: €30.00 • Monthly: €40.00
Car Park opening hours: Monday - Sunday: 05.15 - 22.00.

Car Hire

The following car-hire providers service Ireland West Airport Knock:
Budget: www.budget.ie
Tel: 090 6624668/087 2695461. Fax 094 9367577
Hertz: www.hertz.com
Tel: 094 9367333/071 9160111. Fax: 094 9367333
Murrays/Europcar: www.europcar.ie
Tel: 094 9367221. Fax 094 9367221
Caseys: www.caseycar.com
Tel: 094 9021411. Fax 094 9023823
Diplomat/National/Alamo: www.carhire.ie
Tel: 094 9367252. Fax 094 9367374
Avis: www.avis.ie
Tel: 094 9367707

Rail

Irish Rail website: www.irishrail.ie • The nearest railway station from the Airport is Claremorris (31 km) or Ballyhaunis (22 km). Taxi/bus service connections.

Bus

Bus Éireann Website: www.buseireann.ie
Ireland West Airport Knock in conjunction with Bus Éireann offers a shuttle bus service between the Airport and Charlestown which links with the Bus Éireann network. Phone 096 71800 for timetables, etc.

Taxi

Specific taxi cabs are licensed by Ireland West Airport and are available outside the Terminal Building.
Rate estimate of €1.30 per mile/cash fares.
Ordering a taxi: Phone Airport at 094 9367222 and ask for the licensed taxi on rota duty for that day. For international dialling use the prefix 00 353, drop the 0 in the area code and continue with the remaining numbers.

Distances/Times to Local Destinations

Achill	101.2 km	1 hr 40mins
Athlone Town	99.3 km	1 hr 25mins
Ballina	50.7 km	40mins
Belmullet	113km	1hr 40mins
Belturbet	111.4 km	1hr 55mins
Carrick-on-Shannon	55.8km	50mins
Castlebar	48.9km	35mins
Clifden	132km	2hrs
Donegal Town	122km	1hr 40mins
Enniskillen	124km	Ihr 45mins
Galway City	85.8km	1hr 10mins
Leitrim Town	61.6km	1hr
Longford	81.3km	1hr 10mins
Roscommon Town	66.9km	55mins
Sligo Town	61.2km	50mins

Tourism Information Websites West & North West of Ireland

Ireland West Tourism- Galway, Mayo, Roscommon
www.irelandwest.ie

Ireland North West Tourism- Sligo, Donegal, Cavan, Leitrim, Monaghan
www.irelandnorthwest.ie

Galway East Tourism www.galwayeast.com

Irish Tourist Board www.ireland.ie

Ireland West Airport Knock contact details
Address: Charlestown, Co. Mayo, Ireland.
Website: www.irelandwestairport.com
Tel: LoCall (in Ireland) 1850 67 22 22
Tel: Outside Ireland: +353 94 936 8100

Index

A

Abbeyshrule Airport, 58
Abbott, 31
Aer Arann, 260
Aer Lingus, 11, 46, 50, 63, 65, 75,
    126, 163, 165, 175-176, 206-207,
    216, 229, 239, 243, 249, 251, 260
Aer Rianta, 27, 36, 46, 48, 50, 54, 57,
    59, 62, 98, 162, 176
Agca, Mehmet Ali, 66

Atlantic Road Corridor, 298
Ahern, Bertie, 186, 255, 268, 286, 304
Air rally, 254
Airport directors, 270
Alcock and Brown, 248
Alibrandi, Dr Gaetano, 195
Altamount, Lord, 106
Andrews, Niall, 89
Arnold, Bruce, 72, 99
Aspect magazine, 174
Auriesville, NY, 16

B

Balfe, John (Sean), 17-27, 36-37,
    48, 50, 61-62, 94, 100, 109,
    114, 194, 258
Bank of Ireland, Ballaghaderreen, 42
Ball, Kenny, 9-10
Ballina UDC, 85
Barnalyra Wood, 96
Barrett, Dr Sean, 73-74, 181
Barry, Peter, 168
Bartlett, Mary Ann, 252
Basta, 63
BBC, 6, 162, 166
Beaten Path, 32, 65
Bedford, Sean Patrick, 177, 197
Belamy, David, 248
Beiceadan, an 96
Beirne, Geraldine and Sean, 88
Beisty, Jim, 183
Beisty, Tom, 11, 183-184, 243
Birmingham Airport, 293
Black Triangle, 31, 279, 291
Blaney, Neal 67
Blessed Virgin, 14, 45
Blowick, Joe, 29
bmibaby, 260

Bohan, Fr Harry 303
Boles, Marian, 267
Bord Failte, 19, 27-28, 31, 46, 179
Bowler, Gillian, 236
Bowman, John X1
Boycott, Captain, 1
Boyd, William, 188
Brennan, Brian, 15
Brennan, Louis, 15
Brennan, Mattie, 91, 230, 245
Brennan, Seamus, 230, 232, 237, 239,
    243, 245-246, 285
Brezhnev, Lenoid, X111
British Airport International (BAI),
    173, 175-176, 178, 217-218
British Airways, 260
Brophy, Eanna, 46
Browne, Jimmy, 231
Bruton, John, 89, 202
Buckby, Maurice, 176, 182, 200, 202,
    205, 207, 219
Buick, Robin, 253
Burke, Ray 88
Busby, Sir Matt, 103
Business and Finance, 46-47, 77, 243,
    245, 255
Business Park, 253
Byrne, Dominick 2
Bryne, Frank 93
Byrne, Gay, 105
Byrne, Gerry, 126-127
Byrne, Henry, X1, 41
Byrne, John, 113
Byrne, Margaret, 2
Byrne, Mary, 2

C

Cairns Airport, 108-109
Calleary, Aidan, 80
Calleary, Sean, 26, 29, 48, 64, 86, 90,
    91, 238, 248
Calvi, 22
Carney, Tom 96
Car rentals row, 223, 230-231
Carrickfin Airport, 249
Carroll, Doc, 107
Carroll, John, 78-79
Carty, John, 119
Casey, Bishop Eamon, 21, 186
Casey, PJ, 60
Cassidy, Bishop Joseph, 186, 241, 245
Cassidy, Colman, 122

INDEX

STAMPA: CENTRO POLIGRAFICO MILANO S.p.A.